# Revolutionary lives of the Red and Black Atlantic since 1917

Manchester University Press

# Racism, Resistance and Social Change

### FORTHCOMING BOOKS IN THIS SERIES

*Citizenship and belonging*
Ben Gidley

*Transnational solidarity: Anticolonialism in the global sixties*
Zeina Maasri, Cathy Bergin and Francesca Burke (eds)

*Spaces of Black solidarity: Anti-black racism and urban activism in Paris*
Vanessa Eileen Thompson

### PREVIOUSLY PUBLISHED IN THIS SERIES

*A savage song: Racist violence and armed resistance in the early twentieth-century U.S.–Mexico Borderlands*
Margarita Aragon

*Race talk: Languages of racism and resistance in Neapolitan street markets*
Antonia Lucia Dawes

*Black resistance to British policing*
Adam Elliott-Cooper

*The Red and the Black: The Russian Revolution and the Black Atlantic*
David Featherstone and Christian Høgsbjerg (eds)

*Global white nationalism: From apartheid to Trump*
Daniel Geary, Camilla Schofield and Jennifer Sutton (eds)

*In the shadow of Enoch Powell*
Shirin Hirsch

*Black middle-class Britannia: Identities, repertoires, cultural consumption*
Ali Meghji

*Race and riots in Thatcher's Britain*
Simon Peplow

# Revolutionary lives of the Red and Black Atlantic since 1917

*Edited by*

David Featherstone, Christian Høgsbjerg
and Alan Rice

MANCHESTER UNIVERSITY PRESS

Copyright © Manchester University Press 2022

While copyright in the volume as a whole is vested in Manchester University Press, copyright in individual chapters belongs to their respective authors, and no chapter may be reproduced wholly or in part without the express permission in writing of both author and publisher.

Published by Manchester University Press
Oxford Road, Manchester M13 9PL

www.manchesteruniversitypress.co.uk

British Library Cataloguing-in-Publication Data
A catalogue record for this book is available from the British Library

ISBN 978 1 5261 4478 2 hardback
ISBN 978 1 5261 7674 5 paperback

First published 2022

The publisher has no responsibility for the persistence or accuracy of URLs for any external or third-party internet websites referred to in this book, and does not guarantee that any content on such websites is, or will remain, accurate or appropriate.

Typeset
by Cheshire Typesetting Ltd, Cuddington, Cheshire

# Contents

List of figures — vii
List of contributors — viii
Series editors' foreword — xiii
Acknowledgements — xiv

Introduction: a galaxy of stars to steer by – David Featherstone, Christian Høgsbjerg and Alan Rice — 1

## I – Black Bolshevism

1 Hubert Henry Harrison: Black radicalism and the Colored International – Brian Kwoba — 31
2 Wilfred Domingo under investigation: the 'Negro menace' of 1919 – Peter Hulme — 55
3 Cyril Briggs: guns, bombs, spooks and writing the revolution – Jak Peake — 72
4 Gendering the black radical tradition: Grace P. Campbell's role in the formation of a radical feminist tradition in African-American intellectual culture – Lydia Lindsey — 94

## II – Interwar intersections of Red and Black

5 Clements Kadalie, the ICU and the transformation of Communism in Southern Africa, 1917–31 – Henry Dee — 145
6 Pan-Africanism and Marxism in interwar France: the case of Lamine Senghor – David Murphy — 172
7 Black Americans in Russia: Ira Aldridge and Paul Robeson – Lisa Merrill and Theresa Saxon — 193

## III – Politics and poetics

8 Raya Dunayevskaya: the embodiment of the Red/Black Atlantic in theory and practice – Chris Gilligan and Nigel Niles — 217
9 European Marxist or Black intellectual? C.L.R. James and the advancement of Marxism beyond Russian-Leninism – Tennyson S.D. Joseph — 235
10 Poetry and Walter Rodney's unfinished revolution – David Austin — 255
11 'Hard Facts': Amiri Baraka and Marxism-Leninism in the 1970s – David Grundy — 275

Afterword – Hakim Adi — 304
Index — 313

# Figures

0.1 Captain Hugh Mulzac, Los Angeles, 1944. Credit: Uncredited/AP/Shutterstock. 3
1.1 Hubert Henry Harrison. Credit: Photographs and Prints Division, Schomburg Center for Research in Black Culture, The New York Public Library. 31
2.1 Wilfred A. Domingo in debate, 1940. Left to right: Wilfred A. Domingo, Joel Augustus Rogers, Richard B. Moore and George Weston. Credit: Photographs and Prints Division, Schomburg Center for Research in Black Culture, The New York Public Library. 65
3.1 'The Worm Turns', *The Crusader*, 2:3 (November 1919). 80
4.1 Grace P. Campbell, *The Messenger*, 2:10 (November 1920). 108
5.1 A linocut cartoon by CPSA leader Eddie Roux, depicting Clements Kadalie and AWG Champion of the ICU and Abdullah Abdurahman of the African People's Organisation, from the front cover of *Umsebenzi*, 16 January 1931. 163
7.1 Ira Aldridge by Taras Shevchenko, 1858. 197
7.2 Paul Robeson in front of Pushkin, 1949. 206

# Contributors

**Hakim Adi** is Professor of the History of Africa and the African Diaspora at the University of Chichester in the UK. Trained as an historian focusing on Africa and African history in the twentieth century, his publications have focused on the history of the African diaspora in Britain and the influence of Communism and Pan-Africanism on anti-colonial activism. He is the author of numerous works including *West Africans in Britain, 1900–1960: Nationalism, Pan-Africanism and Communism* (Lawrence and Wishart, 1998); *Pan-Africanism and Communism: The Communist International, Africa and the Diaspora, 1919–1939* (Africa World Press, 2013); *Pan-Africanism: A History* (2018) and is the editor of *Black British History: New Perspectives* (Zed Books, 2019).

**David Austin** is the author of *Dread Poetry and Freedom: Linton Kwesi Johnson and the Unfinished Revolution* (Pluto Press, 2018) and *Fear of a Black Nation: Race, Sex, and Security in Sixties Montreal* (Between the Lines, 2013), winner of the 2014 Casa de las Américas Prize; author/editor of *Moving Against the System: The 1968 Congress of Black Writers and the Making of Global Consciousness* (Pluto Press, 2018); and editor of *You Don't Play with Revolution: The Montreal Lectures of C.L.R. James* (AK Press, 2009). He currently teaches in the Humanities, Philosophy and Religion Department at John Abbott College and in the McGill Institute for the Study of Canada.

**Henry Dee** is a historian of empire, labour and migration in twentieth-century Southern Africa based at the University of the Free State's International Studies Group. His current research focuses on how the Industrial and Commercial Workers' Union of Africa and the All-India Trade Union Congress championed socialist internationalism and challenged heightening worker repression and anti-immigrant restrictions in the 1920s and 1930s.

List of contributors    ix

**David Featherstone** is Reader in Human Geography at the University of Glasgow. He is the author of *Resistance, Space and Political Identities: The Making of Counter-Global Networks* (Wiley-Blackwell, 2008) and *Solidarity: Hidden Histories and Geographies of Internationalism* (Zed Books, 2012). David is co-editor with Christian Høgsbjerg of *The Red and the Black: The Russian Revolution and the Black Atlantic* (Manchester University Press, 2021). He is currently working on a monograph with the provisional title of *Politicising Race and Labour: Seafarers' Struggles for Equality and the Anti-Colonial Left, 1919–1953*. He is a member of the editorial collectives of *Antipode: A Radical Journal of Geography* and *Soundings: A Journal of Politics and Culture*.

**Chris Gilligan** is the Administrator of the Raya Dunayevskaya Archive on the Marxist Internet Archive and a part-time lecturer at the University of the West of Scotland. He has been involved in pro-migrant rights activism for over a decade, including work with Scottish Detainee Visitors, Massive Outpouring of Love, Open Borders Scotland and One Day Without Us. Chris is the author of *Northern Ireland and the Crisis of Anti-racism* (Manchester University Press, 2017).

**David Grundy** is a British Academy Postdoctoral Fellow at the University of Warwick, and the author of *A Black Arts Poetry Machine: Amiri Baraka and the Umbra Poets* (Bloomsbury, 2019). A poet and publisher, he co-runs the small press Materials. He is currently working on a book concerning queer poetics in Boston and San Francisco, provisionally titled *Never By Itself Alone*, and co-editing the forthcoming *Selected Poems of Calvin C. Hernton* and, with Tonya Foster and Jean-Phillipe Marcoux, *The Umbra Galaxy* (both Wesleyan University Press).

**Christian Høgsbjerg** is Lecturer in Critical History and Politics in the School of Humanities and Social Science at the University of Brighton. He is the author of *C.L.R. James in Imperial Britain* (Duke University Press, 2014) and *Chris Braithwaite: Mariner, Renegade and Castaway* (Redwords, 2014). He is the co-editor with David Featherstone of *The Red and the Black: The Russian Revolution and the Black Atlantic* (Manchester University Press, 2021). He has also edited and co-edited several volumes for the C.L.R. James Archives series with Duke University Press, including a special edition of James's 1937 work *World Revolution, 1917–1936: The Rise and Fall of the Communist International* (2017).

**Peter Hulme** is Emeritus Professor at the University of Essex, where he taught for forty years. His books include *Colonial Encounters: Europe and the*

*Native Caribbean, 1492–1797* (Routledge, 1986); *Remnants of Conquest: The Island Caribs and Their Visitors, 1877–1998* (Oxford University Press, 2000); *Cuba's Wild East: A Literary Geography of Oriente* (Liverpool University Press, 2011); and *The Dinner at Gonfarone's: Salomón de la Selva and his Pan-American Project in Nueva York, 1915–1919* (Liverpool University Press, 2019). He is currently working on the political and cultural relationships between Harlem, the Caribbean and Mexico in the 1920s, as well as writing a biography of W.A. Domingo.

**Tennyson S.D. Joseph** is a Senior Lecturer in Political Science at the University of the West Indies. He attained his PhD from the University of Cambridge. His publications include *General Elections and Voting in the English-speaking Caribbean 1992–2005* (co-authored with Cynthia Barrow-Giles; Ian Randle, 2010), *Decolonisation in St Lucia: Politics and Global Neoliberalism 1945–2010* (University Press of Mississippi, 2011) and *Defending Caribbean Freedom* (Carib Research & Publication, 2019). Tennyson is also a regular columnist for the *Daily Nation* newspaper in Barbados. He served briefly as the Administrative Attaché to the Prime Minister of St Lucia (Kenny Anthony) between 2000 and 2005, and was an Opposition Senator in the Parliament of St Lucia for a brief period in 2007.

**Brian Kwoba** was born in the United States to a Black Kenyan father and white American mother. His story and journey have been shaped fundamentally by questions of racial and ethnic identity and belonging. As a graduate student he co-founded the Rhodes Must Fall movement in Oxford to decolonise education at one of Europe's oldest universities. He is currently an assistant professor at the University of Memphis and working on a book about the unsung 'father of Harlem radicalism', Hubert Henry Harrison.

**Lydia Lindsey** is an Associate Professor of European and British Empire and Commonwealth History and Women's & Gender Studies Program at North Carolina Central University. She teaches and writes about the African Presence in Europe, black immigration in the British Isles, and black radical women within the African diaspora. She received her BA and MA in European History from Howard University and her PhD in British Empire and Commonwealth History and Modern European History from the University of North Carolina at Chapel Hill. During her graduate studies, she was in residence at the Centre for Research in Ethnic Relations, University of Warwick. She has published several articles on twentieth-century British history with a special focus on the intersection of race, gender and class from a neo-Marxist perceptive. Lydia is presently working on biographies of Claudia Jones and Grace P. Campbell, as well as a study on black leftists' anti-colonial organising in the British Isles.

**Lisa Merrill** is Professor of Performance Studies, Rhetoric & Public Advocacy at Hofstra University, New York. Her research focuses on performance history, race and representation. Recent publications and awards include the Eccles Centre Visiting Professorship in North American Studies (2010–11) for 'Performing Race and Reading Antebellum American Bodies'; the Brockett Prize for 'Most Fitting Companions: Making Mixed-Race Bodies Visible in Antebellum Public Spaces', *Theatre Survey: Special Issue on Racial Hybridity*, May 2015; and 'Amalgamation, Moral Geography, and "Slum Tourism": Irish and African Americans Sharing Space', *Slavery and Abolition*, 37 (September 2016). And with Dr Theresa Saxon 'Replaying and Rediscovering *The Octoroon*', *Theatre Journal*, 69 (June 2017). Lisa was Visiting Scholar at the Institute for Black Atlantic Research, University of Central Lancashire, 2016 and Spring 2021, and delivered keynote lectures 'Spectacularising Black Bodies on 19th Century Stages', for the International Slavery Museum, Liverpool (June 2017), and 'Sounding Antislavery Voices in Antebellum Spaces', for the Revisiting the Black Atlantic conference, University of Liverpool (June 2019).

**David Murphy** is Professor of French and Postcolonial Studies at the University of Strathclyde. He has published widely on various aspects of modern and contemporary francophone West African culture, including the monographs *Sembene: Imagining Alternatives in Film and Fiction* (James Currey, 2000) and (with Patrick Williams) *Postcolonial African Cinema* (Manchester University Press, 2007). He has also published numerous edited volumes, including (with Charles Forsdick) *Postcolonial Thought in the French-Speaking World* (Liverpool University Press, 2009) and *The First World Festival of Negro Arts, Dakar 1966* (Liverpool University Press, 2016). He is currently preparing a biography of the interwar Senegalese anti-colonial militant, Lamine Senghor.

**Nigel Niles** is a science educator and retired activist from the heydays of the 1980s, still interested in the project of a Revolutionary Humanity.

**Jak Peake** is a Fulbright Scholar and Senior Lecturer in Literature in the Department of Literature, Film, and Theatre Studies at the University of Essex. His monograph, *Between the Bocas: A Literary Geography of Western Trinidad*, was published by Liverpool University Press (2017). His current research examines early twentieth-century Caribbean–New York literary networks. Recent publications include a book chapter, 'Island

Relations, Continental Visions, and Graphic Networks' in *The Cambridge History of Harlem Renaissance Literature* (Cambridge University Press, 2021) and a journal article, 'Watching the Waters': Tropic Flows in the Harlem Renaissance, Black Internationalism and Other Currents' in *Radical Americas* (2018). He also co-edited a double issue of *Comparative American Studies* (15:3–4) in 2019.

**Alan Rice** is Professor in English and American Studies at the University of Central Lancashire, co-director of the Institute for Black Atlantic Research and director of the Research Centre in Migration, Diaspora and Exile. His books include *Radical Narratives of the Black Atlantic* (Bloomsbury, 2003) and *Creating Memorials, Building Identities: The Politics of Memory in the Black Atlantic* (Liverpool University Press, 2010). He co-curated 'Trade and Empire: Remembering Slavery' at the Whitworth Gallery, Manchester in 2007, and has contributed to a variety of documentaries with the BBC and others. His latest co-written work, *Inside the Invisible: Memorialising Slavery and Freedom in the Life and Works of Lubaina Himid* (Liverpool University Press, 2019), is the first academic monograph on the 2017 Turner Prize Winner. In 2020–21 he is curating the exhibition 'Lubaina Himid: Memorial to Zong' for the Lancaster Maritime Museum.

**Theresa Saxon** is a founder member of the Institute for Black Atlantic Research at the University of Central Lancashire, and her research publications focus on transatlantic theatre histories in the late eighteenth and nineteenth centuries. Theresa's most recent publications include 'Ira Aldridge in the North of England: Provincial Theatre and the Politics of Abolition', in *Britain's Black Past* (ed. Gretchen Gerzina, Liverpool University Press, 2020), and with Lisa Merrill, 'Replaying and Rediscovering *The Octoroon*', *Theatre Journal*, 69 (June 2017). Research for her forthcoming book on transatlantic theatre (Edinburgh University Press) has been funded by the Eccles Centre for North American Studies at the British Library.

# Series editors' foreword

*Series editors: John Solomos, Satnam Virdee, Aaron Winter*

The study of race, racism and ethnicity has expanded greatly since the end of the twentieth century. This expansion has coincided with a growing awareness of the continuing role that these issues play in contemporary societies all over the globe. *Racism, Resistance and Social Change* is a new series of books that seeks to make a substantial contribution to this flourishing field of scholarship and research. We are committed to providing a forum for the publication of the highest quality scholarship on race, racism, anti-racism and ethnic relations. As editors of this series we would like to publish both theoretically driven books and texts with an empirical frame that seek to further develop our understanding of the origins, development and contemporary forms of racisms, racial inequalities and racial and ethnic relations. We welcome work from a range of theoretical and political perspectives, and as the series develops we ideally want to encourage a conversation that goes beyond specific national or geopolitical environments. While we are aware that there are important differences between national and regional research traditions, we hope that scholars from a variety of disciplines and multidisciplinary frames will take the opportunity to include their research work in the series.

As the title of the series highlights, we also welcome texts that can address issues about resistance and anti-racism as well as the role of political and policy interventions in this rapidly evolving discipline. The changing forms of racist mobilisation and expression that have come to the fore in recent years have highlighted the need for more reflection and research on the role of political and civil society mobilisations in this field.

We are committed to building on theoretical advances by providing an arena for new and challenging theoretical and empirical studies on the changing morphology of race and racism in contemporary societies.

# Acknowledgements

This volume, and the preceding linked edited collection, *The Red and the Black: The Russian Revolution and the Black Atlantic* (Manchester University Press, 2021), originated at an international conference held at the Institute for Black Atlantic Research (IBAR), University of Central Lancashire, in Preston in the United Kingdom in October 2017. Held to mark the centenary of the Russian Revolution, it was a remarkable event which was in many ways very different from a standard academic conference, featuring as it did special performances from Tayo Aluko, Linton Kwesi Johnson and David Rovics. We are grateful to these artists and performers, and also to the British Association for American Studies, the Lipman-Miliband Trust and the US Embassy in London for their generous support. We would like to thank all of those who attended, presented and in so many various ways contributed towards making it the memorable and successful event it was, often travelling from far and wide to do so. In particular we would like to give special thanks to those at IBAR who helped with the conference organisation, principally Izabella Penier with the support of Olga Tabachnikova, Yvonne Reddick and Raphael Hoermann.

We would also like to thank Jenny Webster at IBAR for her editorial assistance, and the editors of the series on 'Racism, Resistance and Social Change', particularly Satnam Virdee, and Tom Dark, Lucy Burns, Humairaa Dudhwala, Anthony Mercer and the wider editorial and production team at Manchester University Press for their work, support and patience. We would also like to acknowledge the Centre for Memory, Narrative and Histories Research Support Fund at the University of Brighton for helping make this publication possible. There are many others deserving of our thanks, including Talat Ahmed, Cathy Bergin, David Broder, Mo Hume and Jacob Zumoff. Finally, we would like to thank those who have contributed to this volume for their patience, assistance and support for this project, not least as its appearance has been a long time coming, and matters were inevitably further delayed in the final stages by the COVID-19 pandemic, a crisis with its roots in the wider multiple crises of racially structured capitalism which characterise our epoch.

# Introduction:
# a galaxy of stars to steer by

*David Featherstone, Christian Høgsbjerg and Alan Rice*

Few revolutionary life stories could be said to embody the Red and Black Atlantic in the twentieth century more than that of Hugh Nathaniel Mulzac. Of African and Scottish descent, Mulzac was born in 1886 on Union Island, near Saint Vincent in the Grenadines, then part of the British West Indies. He went to sea after high school in 1907, sailing on British vessels, joining every trade union open to him (including the National Sailors' and Firemen's Union in Liverpool in 1909), and attending Swansea Nautical College in South Wales, earning a second mate's licence in 1910. Mulzac moved to America in 1911 and with his new credentials was able to serve as a deck officer on various ships during the First World War, being awarded full US citizenship in 1918. The same year, Mulzac passed the examination to win a Master's licence, the first black seafarer in the United States to do so, giving him the rank of captain which qualified him to skipper an ocean-going cargo ship, though racism meant he could only find work in the stewards' department or as a ship's cook.[1]

Becoming politicised in response to the racism he had encountered throughout his life, in 1920 Mulzac joined the mass movement around the Jamaican Pan-Africanist Marcus Garvey who had founded the Universal Negro Improvement Association (UNIA) in 1914 and in 1919 launched the Black Star Line, its name a response to the Cunard dynasty's famous White Star Line. Mulzac served as a 'mate' – second in command – on the SS *Yarmouth*, one of the three (barely seaworthy) ships acquired by the Black Star Line. As he recalled, Garvey 'advocated increased trade between the United States, the West Indies, and Africa, under black men's control ... the appeal to race patriotism, the promise of an African renaissance under their own control, and the attraction of rapidly multiplying dollars drew colored folk to the Garvey movement as they had not been drawn by any other since the Civil War and Reconstruction'.[2] When the *Yarmouth* sailed into the Panama Canal Zone, Mulzac remembers 'literally thousands of Panamanians swarmed the docks with baskets of fruit, vegetables and gifts. I was amazed that the *Yarmouth* had become such a symbol for colored people of every land.'³ Nonetheless, as Mulzac witnessed first-hand, 'the use to which the worthless Black Star ships were put represented the triumph of propaganda over business'. In 1922 the Black Star Line collapsed into insolvency and so 'what had begun as a great adventure for me and hundreds of thousands of others ended in tragedy and disillusionment'.⁴ In late 1921, while still 'caught up with the vision of the "Black Fleet"' and 'looking ahead to the time when there would be a demand for colored officers on merchant ships' he founded Mulzac's Nautical Academy. Mulzac rented 'three large rooms at 442 St. Nicholas Avenue' in New York where he could 'teach navigation, engineering and wireless to young aspirants'. Initially, the initiative went well and he quickly 'enrolled fifty-two students most of them eager youngsters aflame with the spirit of the Garvey movement'. But the collapse of the Black Star Line had a devastating impact on the Academy as recruits no longer saw a realistic prospect of being employed as ship's officers given the entrenched racist hierarchies in merchant shipping.⁵

For most of the interwar period, Mulzac suffered poverty and unemployment, occasionally relieved by work in the stewards' department of various shipping lines. In 1937, life changed when Mulzac became a founding member of the National Maritime Union (NMU), and also then politically shifted towards Communism after 1938.⁶ As Mulzac recalls, he 'began to develop a political philosophy' and an 'international political outlook' beyond a basic detestation of 'British imperialism and its handiwork throughout the world' and seeing 'the terrible effects of exploitation in most of the countries of the world'. Before then 'I had but one goal: to sail as master of an oceangoing ship' and this personal ambition meant he 'never understood my struggle in its wider *social* context'.⁷ In 1942, following a shortage of trained seafarers during the Second World War and a change in employment legislation under Franklin D. Roosevelt after decades of struggle by organisations like the National Association for the Advancement of Colored People (NAACP) and the more recent fight by NMU militants in the 1930s, Mulzac finally realised his dream. After thirty-five years of rejection he became the first African-American merchant marine naval officer to command a mixed integrated crew on the SS *Booker T. Washington*, which successfully made twenty-two voyages across the Atlantic.⁸

One of those who sailed with Mulzac on the *Booker T. Washington* was Irwin Rosenhouse, who was interviewed by *The Village Voice* in 1964:

> 'The Booker T. was the only ship I've ever been on which had a sense of purpose from the top down', Rosenhouse told *The Voice*. He recalled the classes in seamanship, in art, and in international affairs, as well as the tongue-lashing he'd received when he chose to stand watch on a stormy night inside. 'On the bridge we called Mulzac "captain", but when he came to union

**Figure 0.1** Captain Hugh Mulzac, Los Angeles, 1944

meetings we called him "brother". Beefs between the officers and the men could be settled on that ship.'⁹

The political significance of Mulzac's role was also noted by black seafarers interviewed in 1948 by the anthropologist St Clair Drake in the multi-ethnic dockside community of Butetown, Cardiff. Noting that Mulzac 'had to be a cook in the Yank's merchant marine till the war broke out' they spoke of the reception they had given the *Booker T. Washington* when it had docked in the port during the Second World War in January 1943. One of these seafarers told Drake that 'We gave him a proper time when the

*Booker T. Washington* was in port here – and all the boys aboard too. It was like a homecoming. We were really glad to see a black skipper put his boat in here so that all these bloody Englishmen could see what a black man can do if you let him.'[10]

Back out of work due to institutional racism in 1947, Captain Mulzac remained politically active, winning over 15,000 votes as a candidate for President of the New York City borough of Queens on the American Labor Party ticket in 1950. This saw him blacklisted under McCarthyism and his Masters' licence was revoked until 1960, when he was able to return briefly to work as a seafarer. An artist who had begun painting maritime scenes during the Second World War, in the early 1960s some of his paintings were displayed. In 1963 his remarkable autobiography, *A Star to Steer By*, hailed by Gerald Horne as a 'classic work of proletarian literature', was published, a few years before his death in 1971.[11]

Mulzac's life speaks to themes that are significant across many of the lives discussed in this collection. There is the shift from Garveyism to Communism in the interwar period; the pervasive effects of racism and involvement in various forms of organising to challenge it. There is Mulzac's involvement in the NMU with its articulation of struggles at the intersections of race and class. There is the expansive geography of Mulzac's life with its Atlantic connections, trajectories and experiences. Further there is the importance of broader global and geographical contexts. Key here were the inspirational effect of the Russian Revolution of 1917 and the concerted repression of the Cold War with its disproportionate impact on the lives of radical black leftists. Even after the Cold War's end, the fact that Mulzac's life of struggle remains little known (and he still lacks a scholarly biography for example) also highlights how much work remains to be done to fully recover many twentieth-century 'revolutionary lives'.

Mulzac's life also signals the importance of thinking about how individual revolutionary lives were articulated through particular political trajectories. This extraordinary life brings a vivid and distinctive lens to bear on how racialised social and political worlds were negotiated and experienced. Moreover, it illuminates black engagements with left political movements and grassroots organising. This book brings together eleven essays which engage with the diverse experiences of a wide range of key figures who led revolutionary lives at the intersection of the Red and Black Atlantic. We use the Red and Black Atlantic to refer to exchanges, connections and relations forged through and in relation to various forms of black radical political activity.[12] There is a much longer pre-history to the Red and the Black Atlantic, stretching back to the birth of socialism amid the bourgeois revolutions of the late eighteenth century, including the intersections of solidarity between those engaged in the Haitian Revolution with those on the

Introduction 5

left of the French Revolution like Gracchus Babeuf.[13] The black actor and writer Ira Aldridge's Russian visit during the nineteenth century is discussed in this volume in the context of Paul Robeson's sojourn in the Soviet Union. However, this collection is primarily concerned with the twentieth century. Its focus is on radical individuals whose political activity was catalysed or profoundly shaped by the global impact and legacy of the Russian Revolution of 1917. The Russian Revolution represented a beacon of hope for a significant number of black colonial subjects and black Americans, and it led to a reconceptualisation of strategies and tactics relating to race and resistance through the powerful blows against racism and imperialism it had struck in 1917.[14] For those living under regimes of white supremacy, whether European colonialism or the Jim Crow United States, it came to be seen, in Mulzac's words, as 'a star to steer by'.[15]

The chapters that follow are written by scholars from a range of disciplinary and intellectual perspectives, who are concerned in various ways with foregrounding key figures and often neglected aspects of their political contribution in relation to the intersection of the Red and the Black Atlantic. In various ways their interventions situate the contributions and experiences of these individual figures as part of – or in relation to – broader black radical movements. The chapters engage with activists from across the African diaspora including the Caribbean, the United States, Southern and West Africa – as well as the Russian-born but US-based Raya Dunayevskaya, whose life and politics were shaped profoundly by the process of revolution and counter-revolution in the Russian Empire. The chapters in the book are largely, though not exclusively, informed by an engagement with Anglophone sources; this partly reflects how engagement with internationalist trajectories is always necessarily shaped by particular perspectives.

The opening section engages with a group of activists based in the United States who might productively be described in one sense as 'Black Bolsheviks' – to borrow from Harry Haywood's concept – figures who (like Haywood himself) were inspired to engage in revolutionary socialist politics in organisations like the African Blood Brotherhood (ABB) and then the Communist Party of the United States of America (CPUSA) in the period directly following the Russian Revolution.[16] Brian Kwoba examines the life of possibly the most important black revolutionary socialist in America when the Russian Revolution erupted in 1917, Hubert Henry Harrison, born in St Croix, in the Danish West Indies. Peter Hulme examines the Jamaican radical Wilfred A. Domingo who became alongside Nevis-born Cyril V. Briggs – the subject of Jak Peake's chapter – one of the leading figures in the ABB and under intense state scrutiny in the aftermath of the Russian Revolution. Lydia Lindsey contributes a biographical portrait of another much neglected ABB leader, the black American socialist Grace

P. Campbell, and through doing so develops an important set of reflections on the importance of gendering the black radical tradition.

The middle section of the book primarily engages with key figures who came to prominence a little later and articulated different intersections of Red and Black politics in the interwar period. Henry Dee examines the black South African trade union leader Clements Kadalie. David Murphy looks at another black African leader, the Senegalese Communist active in France, Lamine Senghor. Lisa Merrill and Theresa Saxon examine one of the great revolutionary lives whose connection to the Soviet Union perhaps most famously epitomises the connection of the Red and the Black, the black American singer and actor Paul Robeson, and his journey to Russia. The final section titled 'Politics and poetics' engages with the long legacies/articulations of Red and Black radical politics through exploring two critical revolutionary Marxist theoreticians. Chris Gilligan and Nigel Niles explore Raya Dunayevskaya's writings on black liberation in the United States, while Tennyson Joseph examines the political and intellectual thought of one the most famous twentieth-century black intellectuals to turn to Marxism, the Trinidadian C.L.R. James. The section ends with David Austin's chapter on the Jamaican dub poet Linton Kwesi Johnson's account of Walter Rodney's death, while David Grundy examines the African-American Amiri Baraka's revolutionary poetry. The volume concludes with an afterword by Hakim Adi which reflects on the importance of countering exclusion of black radicals from constructions of the left.

This introductory chapter sets out a framework for understanding the formation of revolutionary lives at the intersection of trajectories and linkages of the Red and Black Atlantic. Drawing on the important tradition of work adopting a politicised understanding of Black Atlantic worlds, the introduction sets out a sense of how diverse political lives were shaped both in relation to Russia but also in ways which traversed various maritime spaces associated with the African diaspora. Through doing so it outlines a dynamic framework for articulating some aspects of the racialised, gendered and classed articulations of revolutionary, political lives in the wake of the Russian Revolution.

## Atlantic trajectories, the Russian Revolution and resistance

The lives discussed here are engaged with to open up a set of perspectives and engagements on both the Black Atlantic but also more broadly black internationalisms in the wake of the Russian Revolution. Through doing so the collection seeks to foreground some of the different and contested articulations of black internationalism and the nuanced situated ways in which these relations were negotiated and lived. Recovering and foregrounding these revolutionary lives is an important political and intellectual project, as too often notions of the left have been shaped by a rather whitened imaginary of who or what counts as left politics. By developing the rich tradition of life writing and life histories that already exists in this field, this collection seeks to contribute to what is now a very significant body of work which challenges such restricted accounts of the left.[17]

Such restricted imaginaries of the left are also related to particular ways in which left politics has been configured and understood. Thus nation-centred accounts of the left have frequently erased or downplayed the contributions of figures from what Cedric Robinson termed the black radical tradition, whose political trajectories were shaped by exchange, circulation and movement between places, rather than being neatly confined within particular 'national' left political traditions.[18] This runs counter to some influential articulations about how ways of understanding left and revolutionary politics have been configured in ways which at best implicitly construct exclusionary notions of what counts as left politics.[19] Recent scholarship has, however, dramatised the significant relations between differently positioned activists in ways which challenge such exclusionary ways of envisioning the left. Thus with respect to the British Empire, in *Insurgent Empire*, Priyamvada Gopal argues that 'several politically inclined travellers' from Britain to different imperial contexts underwent a process of what she terms 'reverse tutelage' which involved such figures 'learning from what they witnessed, shifting their views, and even being radicalised in the process'. She argues that such 'reverse tutelage' was 'furthered by the presence of strong anticolonial black and Asian voices within the metropole, who took on the function of interpreters between British dissidents and the millions who were resisting being governed by Britain.'[20]

In line with such an approach the contributions to this collection retrieve and foreground diverse lives in ways which reconfigure existing understandings and histories of the left in significant ways. These interventions resonate with what Ali Raza has described, in the context of 'histories of leftist movements in India', as 'the importance of treating a multi-faceted portrayal of the Left'.[21] Raza argues that barring 'some notable exceptions' such histories have 'listened to the Left in only one or a few voices, never quite taking a fuller measure of the variety of voices through which the Left made itself known and heard'. To engage with the political trajectories of various figures involved in or linked to the black left necessarily involves opening up different ways of viewing the emergence and articulation of left politics. In this respect Carole Boyce Davis has written recently of Caribbean left traditions that 'since the Caribbean is the site of the first major black revolutions against oppressions, as typified by the Haitian Revolution, then there exists an unfulfilled or deferred promise, still articulated in the music, or art, in the popular practices and in the literature and political thought as well'. As a consequence Boyce Davies argues that '[t]races of this resistance' have created 'a left tradition with many nodal points, one that refuses to acquiesce to domination even in the face of imperialism and neo-colonial state practices'.[22] Boyce Davies's attention to 'a left tradition with many nodal points' usefully offers an important contrast to singular and nation-centred constructions of the left.

The contributions here seek to contribute to such a plural, diverse and contested reckoning with black left trajectories. In this respect engaging with the lives and struggles of Mulzac and other black radical seafarers offers a useful, generative alternative to ways of thinking about the left in the restricted ways bounded by the nation state. Further, they can open up different ways of thinking about the relation between life writing and the spaces of the 'global left'. Mulzac's hard-lived experience of maritime labour and struggle opens a portal onto a wider world of black radical seafarers in the twentieth century. These stand in a longer tradition of true 'mariners, renegades and castaways' – to follow the Trinidadian Marxist C.L.R. James and evoke a famous line from Herman Melville's *Moby-Dick*, hailing the multiracial working class who composed the crew of the doomed *Pequod*.[23] Black seafarers in earlier periods (particularly the eighteenth and nineteenth centuries) have begun to attain the scholarly attention they deserve.[24] Yet the likes of Mulzac and the wider work of black militants in the NMU illuminate wider often hidden subaltern networks of black radical seafarers who came together to organise in the aftermath of the Russian Revolution through organisations like the International Propaganda Committee of Transport Workers, the International of Seamen and Harbour Workers and the Colonial Seamen's Association, and so were central to the making of the twentieth-century Red and Black Atlantic.[25] In Britain, for example, figures like Chris Braithwaite from Barbados (who used the pseudonym 'Chris Jones') and Harry O'Connell from what was then British Guiana, engaged with the Communist Party of Great Britain (CPGB) in the interwar period and played important roles in organising black seafarers to fight for their rights and shaped subaltern articulations of anti-colonial politics.[26] Such seafarers and their radical networks were seen as a significant threat to racialised boundaries in this period.

Thus in the late 1930s, William McFee, a mainstream American journalist, feared the growth of Communist-led trade unions like the National Maritime Union, which he denounced as 'Seagoing Soviets' and the 'real Trojan Horse of America'. Alluding perhaps to the raising of the red flag during the famous mutiny on the battleship *Potemkin* during the 1905 Revolution, McFee reminded his readers that the 'Russian Revolution began in the navy'.[27] The Suriname-born Otto Huiswoud (1893–1961), who was one of the first black figures to join the Communist Party in the United States in 1919, had previously worked as a sailor in the United States and Caribbean. Claude McKay, Langston Hughes, Ralph Ellison and Kwame Nkrumah (who was a member of the NMU) all spent time at sea.[28] The co-founder of the National Maritime Union, the Jamaican-born Communist Ferdinand Smith (1893–1961), who became one of the most powerful black trade unionists in the United States, looms large in this story, not least thanks to the work recovering his remarkable life undertaken by Gerald Horne.[29] Like Mulzac his later life was to be blighted by the effects of McCarthyite repression – and he was deported to Jamaica in 1951.

The articulations between black seafarers and left politics were not always smooth and uncontested. These are themes which emerge in Claude McKay's recently published 1933 novel *Romance in Marseille* which dramatises the contested relations between black seafarers, imperial violence and left politics in the 1920s. The protagonist of the novel is Lafala, a stowaway from West Africa who loses his feet after being discovered on board and imprisoned. As Gary Holcomb and William J. Maxwell note, the novel engages with the 'the modern reunion of the peoples of the black diaspora, dispersed and wounded by the violence of slavery and imperialism' but also is 'plotted as a changeable passionate romance instead of a resolute political epic'.[30]

Further, they suggest that McKay's engagement with same-sex relationships in the novel offers ways of 'queering' black internationalism.[31] *Romance in Marseille* is also significant for its depiction of the fraught and uneven terms of engagement with Communism, which is developed most notably through the character Etienne St Domingue, whose very name evokes the Haitian Revolution. Holcomb and Maxwell note that McKay based this character on Lamine Senghor, the Senegalese radical who is the subject of David Murphy's chapter in this volume. McKay also signals the contested sites through which such exchanges and relations happened, such as the seamen's institute linked to the Communist-affiliated International of Seamen and Harbour Workers in Marseilles. As Brent Hayes Edwards has argued, such sites and organising were important for the production of black internationalism through 'boundary crossing', including across linguistic differences.[32] He stresses how such engagements could be productive. Thus he notes that through their encounters, the Trinidadian radical George Padmore and Tiemoko Garan Kouyaté, who was from what was then the French Sudan, were '"forced by the pressures of the times" to cross boundaries, to move through and beyond the "decided differences" of their Francophone and Anglophone colonial contexts'.[33]

The socialist, novelist and travel writer Ethel Mannin has described how other types of traveller – mainly tourists – set off to visit Soviet Russia from Britain in the mid-1930s on a Soviet ship, known jokingly as 'the Bolshy boat', which went from London to Leningrad. On her voyage in October 1935, Mannin describes how one fellow passenger was 'a young Negro going out to study music', while one of the ship's crew was also black. 'The *Daily Worker*, and a selection of Communist booklets are for sale on the covered hatch of the ship, in charge of a Negro.'[34] While some black seafarers clearly used the mobilities and connections afforded through their labour to circulate radical literature and ideas, then, the mobilities of seafarers did not always align neatly with leftist political projects. Erik McDuffie's account of the experiences of Audley Moore notes how seafarers' experiences could also reconfigure the terms on which they envisioned left politics. In 1946 Moore, a union organiser for the National Maritime Union 'crossed the Atlantic ten times aboard NMU affiliated merchant vessels while working as a steward for the US army's Civilian Army Department'.[35] Her commitment to Communism was, however, unsettled by travelling beyond the US to Europe as these experiences 'compounded her frustration with her outside-inside status in the Communist Left' and she began 'to see black people globally, not white workers, as the revolutionary vanguard'.[36]

These diverse experiences of black seafarers suggest the importance of tracing strong connections between black radical lives and seafaring trajectories. Such experiences and exchanges have been a significant theme in scholarship engaging with both the Red and Black Atlantic. Thus in *The Black Atlantic*, Paul Gilroy draws attention to the 'involvement of Marcus Garvey, George Padmore, Claude McKay and Langston Hughes with ships and sailors' noting that the intensity of these connections 'lends additional support' to Peter Linebaugh's prescient suggestion that 'the ship remained perhaps the most important conduit of Pan-African communication before the appearance of the long playing record'.[37] In this respect both Gilroy's *Black Atlantic* and Peter Linebaugh and Marcus Rediker's pioneering work of Atlantic working-class history 'from below' *The Many Headed Hydra* engage with and are animated by discussions of revolutionary lives in various ways.[38] The next section mobilises work which has engaged with and stretched the implications of Atlantic approaches for black internationalist life writing to create a set of key problematics which are engaged with in different ways by the chapters in this volume.

## Revolutionary life writing and the Red and Black Atlantic

In *Beyond the Color Line and the Iron Curtain* (2002), Kate Baldwin argues for extending Gilroy's analysis of the Black Atlantic to Russia, and that this 'demonstrates how the frame of the Soviet Union alters the black Atlantic model'. She contends that 'Because Russia's own position vis-à-vis Europe and the West was historically vexed, Russia cannot be easily appended onto Europe, and is own intellectual heritage cannot be uniformly traced to Western models without some difficulty.'[39] Baldwin's book engages with the encounters staged between four prominent black intellectuals and the Soviet Union. Through detailed discussion of the experiences of W.E.B. Du Bois, Langston Hughes, Claude McKay and Paul Robeson in the USSR, Baldwin demonstrates how engagement with particular lives can generate textured accounts of encounters and relations. Her approach allows a sense of comparative engagement with the different terms on which different black intellectuals and political activists engaged with the Russian Revolution and its aftermath.

Further, Baldwin eschews a tendency to see African Americans as 'dupes' of Soviets and Communists displacing a trend which had been dominant in some early historiography on the relations between Communism and African Americans.[40] While certainly not overlooking tensions and uneven power relations her account is significant in the ways in which it recovers forms of political agency in narrating encounters between 'the Black and the Red'. She argues that some of the ambiguities and political spaces opened up by 'Lenin's internationalism' were pivotal here. Moreover, that for 'McKay, Hughes, Robeson and Du Bois alike, the ambiguity between the support for black self-determination and the call to disband ethnic particularity through affiliated countercultures to combat imperialism and racism was an enabling one'.[41]

As this passage indicates, Baldwin seeks to open up the productive and generative engagements between the Red and the Black. Her fine-grained engagement with particular lives and experiences also demonstrates the potential of life-writing approaches to enrich understandings of left politics in various ways. In this respect through engaging with the particular political trajectories of Du Bois, McKay, Hughes and Robeson she also helps to draw attention to the differently placed dynamics through which racialised politics, solidarities and internationalist engagements were shaped. Thus rather than seeing such black internationalist politics as axiomatic and shaped by appeals to broad universals, Baldwin demonstrates sensitivity to particular placed dynamics, such as in her discussion of Langston Hughes's engagement with Central Asia.[42]

A similar focus on the differently placed character of racialised political identifications in enriching ways of understanding black internationalist politics is developed in Winston James's seminal book *Holding Aloft the Banner of Ethiopia*.[43] James's book foregrounds the Caribbean–US trajectories of many key black radicals in the United States in the early twentieth century. James argues that having been formed in less intensely racialised contexts in the Caribbean such figures were radicalised by the experience of living under Jim Crow conditions in the US and its associated and entrenched racialised violence. He demonstrates how Caribbean radicals such as Cyril V. Briggs, Richard B. Moore and Wilfred A. Domingo became leading figures in organisations such as the African Blood Brotherhood which developed a militant opposition to racial violence and racism, especially in the context of the horrific racist violence that marked the 'Red Summer' of 1919. Through tracing these connections James's work has also sought to reconfigure accounts of US black radicalism in important ways by demonstrating the extent to which it is forged out of rich connections with Caribbean contexts rather than just emerging from internal dynamics.

Many of the figures discussed by James are central to the first section of this book on Black Bolsheviks which engages with four figures who had significant connections to the Caribbean, but became prominent figures in the US. These are Cyril V. Briggs who was from Nevis, Grace P. Campbell who grew up in Georgia and whose father was Jamaican, Wilfred A. Domingo who was Jamaican and Hubert Harrison who was from St Croix in the Danish Virgin Islands. The contributions to this section signal the depth and importance of the articulation of Caribbean radicals in the US with the emergent impact of the Russian Revolution. These contributions also raise key issues in relation to the work that engaging with different revolutionary lives can do in historical and political terms. In this regard the rest of this section considers a set of key problematics around the terms on which revolutionary lives are discussed and engaged with. It is these problematics that we see as central to the contributions of the book.

Firstly, a key contribution of the chapters here is to foreground the dynamic political trajectories of figures involved in the black left. In different ways these engagements with revolutionary lives in the wake of the Russian Revolution are attentive to the active geographies of connection, solidarity and internationalism that they both shaped and were shaped by. In line with the promise of Black Atlantic perspectives to unsettle and disrupt nation-centred histories of political radicalism these contributions offer important ways of thinking about such trajectories as part of the circulations that made up 'global' left practices, ideas and political identities.

Through doing so the volume contributes to broader challenges to linear and nation-centred histories of the left and of anti-racist struggles.

Carole Boyce Davies's work has engaged with Claudia Jones's transnational trajectories and notes that 'the specifics of location raised by black women across various cultures became by the end of the twentieth century significant for reassessing various subject positions and redefinitions of black feminism'.[44] Barbara Ransby, in her biography *Eslanda: The Large and Unconventional Life of Mrs Paul Robeson*, underlines that Eslanda Goode Robeson was a transnational subject within a black internationalist tradition:

> Essie Robeson was a part of the Black Atlantic world. She traversed the rough waters of the Atlantic more than a dozen times by boat and many more times by air: from New York to Ghana to London to Cairo to Cape Town and back again. And in the process of talking, working, arguing, making friends, writing, and listening to other people's stories, she ultimately synthesised that amalgam of experiences, and local histories, into her own hybrid Black identity, which was at the same time a political identity. She became one of Robin Kelley's 'race rebels,' fighting simultaneously for 'the race' and the working class across many national borders.[45]

Ransby's focus on gender, race and class is one which reimagines the contours of the left. By tracing the political trajectories of the diverse figures brought together in this book an engagement with different articulations of black left politics emerges. In this vein, while the book engages with the Red and Black Atlantic in the wake of the Russian Revolution the contributions through their engagements with different figures are keenly alive to the different terms on which such figures engaged in black left and black internationalist politics. Thus as well as figures indelibly shaped by their engagements with Communism, such as Lamine Senghor and Paul Robeson, the volume engages with figures who were central to articulations between Trotskyism and the black left, notably C.L.R. James and Raya Dunayevskaya. There are also engagements with figures such as Grace P. Campbell, who would break with Communism and suffer significant vilification for doing so, as well as figures such as the South African trade unionist Clements Kadalie who, as Henry Dee notes, shaped a direct opposition to Communist articulations of trade unionism.

A key contribution that emerges in this regard both across and within individual chapters is an attentiveness to the multiple articulations through which radical figures envisioned black left politics. Through doing so the book contributes to historiographies of the left through refusing to neatly confine the figures discussed here within singular left traditions and positions. Rather, being alive to the shifting political identifications of the figures discussed and their diverse contributions to debates, organising and political trajectories offers an alternative to narrow readings of past left politics as operating within 'siloes' of sealed political traditions. Through such interventions the chapters make a contribution to Ali Raza's aim, referred to earlier in this introduction, to develop a 'multi-faceted portrayal of the Left'.

Secondly, and in related terms, through stressing the dynamic trajectories of the individuals discussed here and positioning them in relation to the multiple articulations of left politics in different ways the chapters practice a style of life writing which refuses to abstract individual lives from the broader movements and social relations that make up left politics. In this regard, Robin 'Bongo Jerry' Small's comments on Walter Rodney's approach to groundings, collaborations and politics are insightful. Small argues that Rodney 'knew that class could be dismantled; and he sensed that race could be consolidated, then transcended. Rodney had this sense from early in life and being equipped with a sense of time and timetable he achieved much in his record run. Of course none of this could have been attained without a team: great leaders are always part of a squad.'[46] Small's comments on leadership are significant here and signal the importance of thinking about the different forms of labour and engagement that shape movements and whose agency and roles are recognised. In this respect many of the contributions to this volume approach key leadership figures in ways that situate their work in relation to the dynamics of broader movements, rather than thinking about figures in narrow individualised ways. Thus Henry Dee's engagement with Clements Kadalie usefully locates Kadalie's interventions in relation to Communism as part of ongoing discussions and dialogues on the subject within the Industrial and Commercial Workers' Union (ICU). Through doing so Dee uses Kadalie's position as a way into understanding a set of diverse and contested positions on the South African left in the 1920s, rather than providing a narrow reading of Kadalie's contributions.

Thirdly, we seek to open up a sense of the gendered dynamics which were constituted through revolutionary lives and to dislocate the centrality of key male figures in relation to the black left. This is relatedly a question of power-knowledge and the archive. Thus in her chapter on Grace P. Campbell, Lydia Lindsey notes that understandings of 'Black women's theoretical perspectives within the communist movement remain underdeveloped'. Through her work on Campbell, Lindsey demonstrates how 'articulations of black women's perspectives on the Negro Question, self-determination, and the Black Belt thesis has increasingly become visible in the literature and have provided a radical analysis in black women's voices on gender, race, capitalism, and class.'

Discussions of the gendering of black left politics can also usefully challenge the terms on which key figures have been understood and memorialised. Thus writing of Paul Robeson in *In Search of the Black Fantastic* (2008), Richard Iton scrutinises the limited ways in which he was 'revived and recuperated' during the Cold War in terms that disarticulated 'race and class, black politics and internationalism, while treading the safer waters of manhood rights'. For Iton such a prioritising of Robeson's masculinity served 'as political infratext' which would 'in the decades after his death function as a race man containable within the borders of a postage stamp and of discourses that in many respects, avoided the political'.[47] Iton's remarks offer a powerful reminder of the ways in which restricted articulations of gender can co-produce narrow and limited understandings of the spaces of black left politics.

In her discussion of the relative absence of women's contributions to black left politics Lindsey draws attention to the relative scarcity of sources for reconstructing women's experiences of, and contributions to, organising. By doing so she highlights a key set of questions about the practices through which left politics is remembered and understood. The question of the terms on which sources are used for the reconstruction of revolutionary lives is a vexed one, as is discussed by a number of the contributors here. In this respect invariably a key and fraught source for such lives is the surveillance files held on militants by different government agencies. Thus Peter Hulme's chapter engages in depth with material about Wilfrid A. Domingo in police files relating to the surveillance of Domingo.

Hulme engages carefully with these examples of what Ranajit Guha of the Subaltern Studies collective described as 'counter-insurgent' prose.[48] Rather than straightforwardly use such sources as unproblematic repositories of information about militants like Domingo, Hulme positions such surveillance and knowledge as a fragmentary and incomplete archive of information, the construction of which was integral to political repression. This is most notable in his discussion of the raid on the Rand School of Social Sciences in New York on 21 June 1919, when agents acting for the Lusk Committee 'seized a large quantity of papers suspected of encouraging sedition'. Hulme notes that Archibald Stevenson, who coordinated the raid, collaborated with reporters to intensify the seditious character of the findings which, as he describes, were not targeted as 'basically they took away every piece of paper they could find and then proceeded to read through it all, looking for signs of subversion'.

While the use of such 'official' sources is necessarily fraught, given their collection was integral to repression of black left politics in different parts of the world, the engagement with the left's own archives and writings also raise significant challenges and issues. As Ali Raza has argued the writing of the left's own history has been constitutive of left political practice in various ways. He contends that in claiming to represent the downtrodden, an otherwise anodyne act of history-writing was transformed into an ethical practice with clear moral stakes attached to it. Whether published in memoirs and scholarly accounts, serialised in newspapers and pamphlets or invoked in public rallies, meetings and demonstrations revolutionary histories were ubiquitous in leftist practices.[49]

Such writings, as Raza notes, have their own silences, evasions and priorities. He notes, for example, the silencing of women's voices, which has also been a key critique of feminist writings on the left.[50] These questions are of particular importance in relation to questions relating to the memorialisation and remembering of revolutionary lives. Whose voices/lives are engaged with and in what terms are they envisioned through so doing?

Fourthly, in related terms, the contributions to the collection raise a set of questions about the terms on which different black left political movements/figures are remembered and articulated. This relates to a broader set of issues about memory, anti-colonial politics and Communism. In *Conscripts of Modernity* (2004), David Scott's powerful set of reflections on the relevance of C.L.R. James's *Black Jacobins* for the 'bleak ruins of our postcolonial present' argues that 'Our generation looks back so to put it through the remains of a present that James and his generation looked forward to (however contentiously) as the open horizon of a possible future.'[51] For Scott the implications of this disjuncture between the present and the hopes of anti-colonial militants such as James need to be subject to serious scrutiny in both political and theoretical terms.

Scott's arguments raise important questions and challenges for the terms on which anti-colonial black left histories are envisioned and written and the ways in which lives are engaged with whose horizons and political imaginaries were shaped by markedly different political circumstances to our own. In this respect the fine-grained engagements with the lives discussed here offer perhaps some different potential answers to the problematics posed by Scott. Engaging with the long-term if at times shifting commitments of these subjects potentially offers more hopeful narratives of the ongoing importance and relevance of black left politics than the rather remorseless pessimism that informs Scott's work. The contributions also speak to an important set of issues that bear on the terms on which different figures are remembered and engaged with.[52]

These issues are raised most explicitly in this volume in David Austin's detailed reflections on Linton Kwesi Johnson's elegy for Walter Rodney, 'Reggae fi Radni'. Through engaging with the elegy form Austin raises a set of questions about the terms on which political activists are remembered, issues which are particularly significant in Rodney's case given the circumstances of his assassination in 1980, by figures linked to Forbes Burnham's People's National Congress government, and assessments of Rodney's political trajectory. Austin reads 'Reggae fi Radni' as part of a transnational set of dialogues about, and elegies on, Rodney, arguing that central to Johnson's poem is a dialogue with the statement *Walter Rodney and the Question of Power* written by Rodney's friend and mentor C.L.R. James after Rodney's death. Through drawing attention to these dialogues Austin argues that 'Reggae fi Radni'

> combines respect, admiration, and even celebration of Rodney's life with critical questions about his praxis and the circumstances surrounding his assassination. In the process we encounter Rodney, not simply as a martyr or heroic figure, but a human being, someone who is vulnerable, forlorn, and even prone to doubt which, rather than diminishing him in our eyes, brings his struggle closer to us while at the same time elevating his humanity.

In doing so he emphasises how such an elegy can do active work in considering the terms on which lives are remembered and articulated politically and has significant relevance for how engagements with revolutionary lives might be approached and understood.

Finally, assessing the state of the literature on life writing and life histories in relation to the Red and Black Atlantic, many of the most famous figures have of course long become objects of academic study in their own right, as for example in the case of W.E.B. Du Bois, Langston Hughes, Aimé Césaire, Frantz Fanon or C.L.R. James, while a steady stream of scholarly literature now proliferates on the likes of Claude McKay, George Padmore, Paul Robeson, Claudia Jones and Walter Rodney.[53] This is now being rightly followed up – as is evident in this very volume – with further studies underway of those figures who have tended to be less well recognised, such as Hubert Harrison, Wilfred A Domingo, Cyril V. Briggs, Lamine Senghor and Harry Haywood.[54] Black women who, like Claudia Jones, played a key role in the black left struggle, such as Grace P. Campbell, Louise Thompson Patterson and Williana 'Liana' Burroughs in the United States, or Elma François, founder of the National Unemployed Movement (NUM) and Negro Welfare Cultural and Social Association (NWCSA) in 1930s colonial Trinidad, remain often overlooked, but are beginning to attract the scholarly attention that in general they have often lacked.[55]

One scholar whose dedication to writing biographical portraits of lives lived in the intersection of the Red and Black Atlantic, particularly those in or around the Communist Part of the United States of America, is Gerald Horne, who as well as his work on Ferdinand Smith has written on figures including W.E.B. Du Bois, Shirley Graham Du Bois, Ben Davis, William Patterson and Paul Robeson.[56] Yet with respect to the CPUSA there is arguably further work to be done with respect to life writing, even for some of those who were emblematic figures in the interwar period. Important activists like the organiser and political prisoner Angelo Herndon, author of *Let Me Live* (1937), and James W. Ford, who became the first black American to run for a presidential ticket during the twentieth century when he was three times the CPUSA candidate for US Vice-President between 1932 and 1940, have yet to receive the detailed biographical treatment one might have expected, perhaps because both later severed ties with the party. Within the American Trotskyist movement, while C.L.R. James's critical role has long received attention, as recently has that of one of James's one-time collaborators, James Boggs, other black Trotskyists such as Ernest Rice McKinney and Simon P. Owens remain almost unknown figures.[57]

There remains much work still to be done on recovering the lives of more rank-and-file activists of the Red and Black Atlantic, especially those black trade union or party organisers who didn't necessarily deliver eloquent speeches or write theoretical essays on socialism and black liberation – and who were never deemed noteworthy enough, like say Hugh Mulzac, to have an opportunity for an autobiographical memoir to be published. Here the apparent lack of archival sources present challenges, though this has of course been a longstanding issue facing researchers of 'the black Atlantic'.[58] However, as more sources come to light (including the digitisation of newspapers) and knowledge of black internationalism increases, so do the possibilities to begin to recover more 'revolutionary lives'.[59]

As Hakim Adi's afterword indicates, a key way in which these engagements with the Red and Black Atlantic can be developed is through engagement with non-Anglophone figures and sources. Thus Robin D.G. Kelley and Franklin Rosemont have highlighted the significance of circuits of surrealism and Negritude in shaping forms of anti-imperialist internationalism. They draw attention to the importance of relatively well-known figures such as Aimé and Suzanne Césaire, but also to a range of others, suggesting that from the early 1930s onwards 'well over fifty individuals of African descent [...] participated actively' in the Surrealist International.[60] Recent historiographical work in a range of contexts has engaged with the importance of articulations of black internationalism in different locations and in ways which move beyond Anglophone contexts and sources. This work has drawn attention to a range of individuals, organisations, political events and sources which are now beginning to attract their much-warranted scholarly attention. Thus Anne Garland Mahler has usefully traced some of the trajectories of Sandalio Junco, the black Cuban Trotskyist who was assassinated in 1942 by members of the Cuban Communist Party, and his distinctive articulations of the 'Negro Question' from an 'Afro-Latin' perspective.⁶¹ Such engagement has also drawn attention to significant ways of configuring the relations between black internationalism and anti-fascism. Ariel Lambe has traced some of the engagements of black Cuban anti-fascists in the Spanish Civil War.⁶² Bernhard H. Bayerlein and João Fábio Bertonha have drawn attention to diverse forms of anti-fascist internationalism in Brazil, including the Comintern-backed 'military uprising against the government of Getúlio Vargas' in 1935.⁶³

Writing from the perspective of our location in different parts of the UK we would contend that just in terms of black revolutionary socialist activists in interwar Britain, though some – like the Manchester-based Communist boxer Len Johnson (1902–74), the son of a West African sailor and engineer – have received some attention, there are still many fascinating and critical figures who remain somewhat occluded.⁶⁴ What for example of Reuben Gilmore, a black seafarer and friend and comrade of Claude McKay in Sylvia Pankhurst's Workers' Socialist Federation? Gilmore was an important organiser in the East End and North London in the aftermath of the First World War and by 1920 was the Secretary of the Poplar Unemployed Workers' Committee.⁶⁵ What of Neil Johnston, a black socialist from Barbados based in Scotland in the early 1920s, who described the legendary Scottish revolutionary socialist John Maclean as 'the truest and best friend I had in Europe'? As Maclean once wrote about Johnston in a letter to his family:

> Neil Johnston comes from the Barbados Is[land], away in the West Indies, and he was telling me all about life there and in other islands in that warm region – Haiti, San Domingo, St Thomas, Jamaica, Cuba, etc. He learnt English, Spanish, Portuguese, French and German out there, and he can speak Dutch, Danish and Flemish too.⁶⁶

Or take Jim Headley, a seafarer from colonial Trinidad who had been a ship's cook in the United States where he became a member of the Young Communist League and came to know George Padmore, before moving to London to continue his activism which included setting up an International Seamen's Club in Poplar around 1930. Headley then returned to Trinidad to work alongside Elma François in helping found the NUM in 1934 and the NWCSA in 1935.⁶⁷ What of Arnold Ward, born in Barbados in 1886, who had been interned in Germany at the outbreak of the Great War, and then became (in the words of a 1938 Special Branch report) 'one of the principal negro agitators in the UK'? As a CPGB member, Ward had helped found the Negro Welfare Association in 1931, and his fiery speech at one public meeting Paul Robeson later noted was a critical inspiration behind his first visit to the Soviet Union.⁶⁸ Another unjustly neglected black Barbadian in Britain deserving of closer scholarly attention is Peter

Blackman, a Communist writer and poet.[69] In terms of other little-known black Communists in interwar Britain, one memoir refers to a John Douglas – known as 'Black Douggie' – who during the 1930s was a well-known and liked black activist in Leeds Communist Party, and who on a local May Day demonstration in 1934 helped knock a policeman's helmet off with the Communist Party banner pole – but about whom little else is known.[70] It is only in recent years that the remarkable life of the mixed heritage Communist Charlie Hutchinson (1918–93), whose father was from Ghana and who fought fascism during the Spanish Civil War as 'Britain's only black International Brigadier', has begun to receive the attention and recognition he deserves.[71] There is then still much work to be done.[72]

## Conclusion

If then for many black radicals during the twentieth century the Russian Revolution represented what Mulzac called 'a star to steer by', it might be suggested that all of the 'revolutionary lives of the Red and Black Atlantic' discussed in this volume – including that of Mulzac himself – in their own way represent part of 'a galaxy of stars to steer by', some inevitably shining brighter than others. Mulzac himself remained a 'red' to the end, and his radicalism lived on through his remarkable daughter, Una Mulzac (1923–2012), who after working for the People's Progressive Party's bookstore in British Guiana, in 1967 moved to New York City and founded the Liberation Bookstore in Harlem on behalf of the Marxist-Leninist organisation she had joined, the Progressive Labor Party (PLP). In the PLP's newspaper, *Challenge*, Liberation was praised for answering 'a crying need for the revolutionary works from China, Asia, Africa, Latin America and on the Black Liberation struggle here in the U.S.'. After breaking with the PLP, Una Mulzac would re-establish Liberation in the 1970s as the leading Pan-Africanist bookstore in Harlem, a title it retained until its closure in 2007.[73] Reflecting on his life in the early 1960s, in his mid-seventies, Hugh Mulzac, in words which can still speak to us today amid the Black Lives Matter movement, stressed how he came to see that 'only in common, co-operative action can all of our individual dreams come true'.

> And if, therefore, there is any sense I can impart to the younger generation it would be this: *commit yourself*! Fight through the early private illusions as speedily as possible, admit, as quickly as you discover it, that separate, individual actions will get you nowhere, and join the common struggle. Fight for the liberation of oppressed people everywhere, fight for an honest, moral political system, fight for the fullest appreciation of every human need, for fighting for the good life for all people is the only way to live and win it for yourself.[74]

## Notes

1. Hugh Mulzac, *A Star to Steer By* (Berlin: Seven Seas Publishers, 1965), 55, 70–74. On Mulzac's family history, see also Joan Anim-Addo, 'A Brief History of Juliana "Lily" Mulzac of Union Island, Carriacou and Grenada', in Giovanni Covi, Joan Anim-Addo, Velma Pollard and Carla Sassi (eds), *Caribbean–Scottish Relations* (London: Mango, 2007), 46–92. On the racism Mulzac encountered on arriving in the United States, see Winston James, *Holding Aloft the Banner of Ethiopia: Caribbean Radicalism in Early Twentieth-Century America* (London: Verso, 1998), 92–93. With thanks to Cathy Bergin for reading and commenting on our introduction in draft.
2. Mulzac, *A Star to Steer By*, 80. The Cunard shipping fleet refused to allow black seafarers anywhere near the decks of their passenger liners until the 1950s.
3. Mulzac, *A Star to Steer By*, 85, 89. In Black Star Line publicity, the *Yarmouth* was renamed the SS *Frederick Douglass*; other ships were to be named after Booker T. Washington, Phyllis Wheatley and the Haitian revolutionary leader Toussaint Louverture.
4. Mulzac, *A Star to Steer By*, 90–91. See also the material relating to Mulzac's time with the Black Star Line in Robert A. Hill (ed.), *The Marcus Garvey and Universal Negro Association Improvement Papers* (Berkeley, CA: University of California Press, 1983–2006), esp. Vol. 3, 48–49, n.1, 69, Vol. V, 317, 342, 401, 403, 472–478, Vol. 9, 326–327, n. 7.
5. Mulzac, *A Star to Steer By*, 91–93.
6. For more on the NMU, see Gerald Horne, *Red Seas: Ferdinand Smith and Radical Black Sailors in the United States and Jamaica* (New York: New York University Press, 2005).
7. Mulzac, *A Star to Steer By*, 128.
8. *Ibid.*, 155–235.
9. Susan Goodman, 'Trailblazing Captain Opens Art Show Here', *The Village Voice*, 9:13, 16 January 1964, www.villagevoice.com/2009/06/17/hugh-mulzac-at-78/ (accessed 3 August 2021).
10. St Clair Drake, 'Value Systems, Social Structure and Race Relations', PhD dissertation, University of Chicago, 1954, 191; Mulzac, *A Star to Steer By*, 177–179. Also see *The Pilot*, 18 September 1942 and 23 October 1942; George Padmore, 'Negro Sea Captain', *Tribune*, 26 February 1943.
11. Horne, *Red Seas*, 61. See also 'Biography of Hugh Mulzac, *c.*1944', Box 9, Nelson Frank Papers, New York University Library; obituary, *New York Times*, 1 February 1971.
12. For more discussion of the Red and the Black Atlantic, see Paul Gilroy, *The Black Atlantic: Modernity and Double Consciousness* (London: Verso, 1993); Alan Rice, *Radical Narratives of the Black Atlantic* (London: Continuum, 2003); David Armitage, 'The Red Atlantic', *Reviews in American History*, 29:4 (2001), 479–486, a review of Peter Linebaugh and Marcus Rediker, *The Many-Headed Hydra: Sailors, Slaves, Commoners and the Hidden History of the Revolutionary Atlantic* (Boston, MA: Beacon Press, 2000). For more on how the

Red and the Black Atlantic can be seen as 'co-constituted and overlapping, rather than as neatly separate political and theoretical projects', see David Featherstone and Christian Høgsbjerg, 'Introduction: Red October and the Black Atlantic' in David Featherstone and Christian Høgsbjerg (eds), *The Red and the Black: The Russian Revolution and the Black Atlantic* (Manchester: Manchester University Press, 2021), 1–38, at 14–15.

13 Babeuf hailed the Jacobins' decision to abolish slavery across the French Empire on 4 February 1794 as 'this benevolent decree which has broken the odious chains of our brothers the blacks'. See Charles Forsdick and Christian Høgsbjerg, *Toussaint Louverture: A Black Jacobin in the Age of Revolutions* (London: Pluto, 2017), 137.

14 For an overview of the historic relationship between 'Red October and the Black Atlantic', see David Featherstone and Christian Høgsbjerg (eds), *The Red and the Black: The Russian Revolution and the Black Atlantic* (Manchester: Manchester University Press, 2021), particularly the introduction. See also Anne Garland Mahler and Paolo Capuzzo (eds), *The Comintern and the Global South: Global Designs/Local Encounters* (London and New York: Routledge, forthcoming).

15 See also the evocative title of a recent work on the impact of the Russian Revolution, Vijay Prashad, *Red Star over the Third World* (New Delhi: LeftWord Books, 2017). The lived realities of such connections, however, proved in some cases to be extremely difficult, as for example with figures such as the black American Lovett Fort-Whiteman dying in a Soviet gulag in 1939 amid the concerted repression of dissent under Stalin. See Dick J. Reavis, 'The Life and Death of Lovett Fort-Whiteman, the Communist Party's First African American Member', *Jacobin*, 7 April 2020, www.jacobinmag.com/2020/04/lovett-fort-whiteman-black-communist-party (accessed 3 August 2021).

16 Harry Haywood, *Black Bolshevik: Autobiography of an Afro-American Communist* (Chicago, IL: Liberator Press, 1978). For more on the idea and concept of 'Black Bolshevism', see Christian Høgsbjerg, 'Communism and the Colour Line: Reflections on Black Bolshevism' in Anne Garland Mahler and Paolo Capuzzo (eds), *The Comintern and the Global South: Global Designs/Local Encounters* (London and New York: Routledge, forthcoming).

17 With respect to labour history, the rise of the 'New Imperial History', post-colonial studies, and then the rise of global labour history have been identified by Yann Béliard as important trends which have led to the rise of a more transnational approach in recent decades. See Yann Béliard, 'Introduction: Labour, Empire and Decolonisation: Historiographical Landmarks' in Yann Béliard and Neville Kirk (eds), *Workers of the Empire, Unite: Radical and Popular Challenges to British Imperialism, 1910s–1960s* (Liverpool: Liverpool University Press, 2021), 1–22.

18 Cedric Robinson, *Black Marxism: The Making of the Black Radical Tradition* (London: Zed Books, 1983).

19 Thus Gilroy critiques the forms of nation-centred imaginaries of dissent which structured the work of key intellectuals associated with the New Left such as

E.P. Thompson and Raymond Williams. See Gilroy, *The Black Atlantic*, 11. Exclusionary imaginaries of the left also shaped the work of other figures associated with the New Left, notably Perry Anderson's formulation of 'Western Marxism', which tends to constitute *such a project* in isolation from the many articulations with anti-colonial and anti-racist politics which have impacted on, challenged and reconfigured left politics and practices in Western Europe and the US; Perry Anderson, *Considerations on Western Marxism* (London: New Left Books, 1976).

20 Priyamvada Gopal, *Insurgent Empire: Anticolonial Resistance and British Dissent* (London: Verso, 2019), 8.
21 Ali Raza, *Revolutionary Pasts: Communist Internationalism in Colonial India* (Cambridge: Cambridge University Press, 2020), 13.
22 Carol Boyce Davies, 'Introduction: Re-Grounding the Intellectual-Activist Model of Walter Rodney' in Walter Rodney, *Groundings With My Brothers*, ed. Asha T. Rodney and Jesse J. Benjamin (London: Verso, 2019), xi–xxii, at xxii.
23 See C.L.R. James, *Mariners, Renegades and Castaways: Herman Melville and the World We Live In* (London: University Press of New England, 2001), 17. The passage can be found in *Moby Dick*, Chapter 26, 'Knights and Squires'.
24 For earlier periods, see for example W. Jeffrey Bolster, *Black Jacks: African-American Seamen in the Age of Sail* (Cambridge, MA: Harvard University Press, 1998), which focuses on the period 1740–1865. For recent works on black seafarers in Britain that discuss their experience in the twentieth century, see for example Ray Costello, *Black Salt: Seafarers of African Descent on British Ships* (Liverpool: Liverpool University Press, 2012) and Laura Tabili, *'We Ask for British Justice': Workers and Racial Difference in Late Imperial Britain* (Ithaca, NY: Cornell University Press, 1994).
25 See Holger Weiss, *Framing a Radical African Atlantic: African American Agency, West African Intellectuals and the International Trade Union of Negro Workers* (Leiden: Brill, 2014) and Holger Weiss, *A Global Waterfront: The International Propaganda Committee of Transport Workers and the International of Seamen and Harbour Workers, 1921–1937* (Leiden: Brill, 2021).
26 David Featherstone, 'Harry O'Connell, Maritime Labour and the Racialised Politics of Place', *Race & Class*, 57:3 (2016), 71–87; Christian Høgsbjerg, *Mariner, Renegade and Castaway: Chris Braithwaite; Seamen's Organiser, Socialist and Militant Pan-Africanist* (London: Redwords, 2014).
27 Horne, *Red Seas*, x.
28 Ibid., 7–8.
29 Ibid.
30 Gary Holcomb and William J. Maxwell, 'Introduction' in Claude McKay, *Romance in Marseille* (London: Penguin, 2020), vi–li, at xiii.
31 Ibid.
32 Brent Hayes Edwards, *The Practice of Diaspora: Literature, Translation and the Rise of Black Internationalism* (Cambridge, MA: Harvard University Press, 2003), 243.
33 Ibid., 243.

34 Ethel Mannin, *South to Samarkland* (London: Beacon, 1938), 27–28, 35. Mannin noted however that 'the Negro confesses, with a far-away look in his mournful eye, that he is lonely in the ship'.
35 Erik McDuffie, *Sojourning for Freedom: Black Women, American Communism and the Making of Black Left Feminism* (Durham, NC: Duke University Press, 2011), 152.
36 Ibid., 153.
37 Gilroy, *The Black Atlantic*, 13.
38 Linebaugh and Rediker, *The Many Headed Hydra*.
39 Kate A. Baldwin, *Beyond the Color Line and the Iron Curtain: Reading Encounters Between Black and Red, 1922–1963* (Durham, NC: Duke University Press, 2002), 9.
40 E.g. Harold Cruse, *The Crisis of the Negro Intellectual* (New York: New York Review of Books, 2005 [1967]). For a detailed critical engagement with Cruse, see 'Harold Cruse and the West Indians: Critical Remarks on *The Crisis of the Negro Intellectual*' in Winston James's *Holding Aloft the Banner of Ethiopia: Caribbean Radicalism in Early Twentieth-Century America* (London: Verso, 1998), 262–291. For a useful overview of the wider historiography of US Communism, see the introduction to Jacob A. Zumoff, *The Communist International and US Communism, 1919–1929* (Chicago, IL: Haymarket, 2015), 1–23.
41 Baldwin, *Beyond the Color Line and the Iron Curtain*, 10.
42 Ibid., esp. 108–118. See also Matthieu Renault, 'From Russian Colonies to Black America … and Back: Lenin and Langston Hughes' in David Featherstone and Christian Høgsbjerg (eds), *The Red and the Black: The Russian Revolution and the Black Atlantic* (Manchester: Manchester University Press, 2021), 81–96, at 89–93.
43 James, *Holding Aloft the Banner of Ethiopia*.
44 Carol Boyce Davies, *Left of Karl Marx: The Political Life of Black Communist Claudia Jones* (Durham, NC: Duke University Press, 2008), 11.
45 Barbara Ransby, *Eslanda: The Large and Unconventional Life of Mrs Paul Robeson* (New Haven, CT: Yale University Press, 2014), 278.
46 Robin 'Bongo Jerry' Small, 'The Conscious Youth' in Walter Rodney, *Groundings With My Brothers*, ed. Asha T. Rodney and Jesse J. Benjamin (London: Verso, 2019), 87–92, quote on 92. See also Kimani S.K. Nehusi's critical reflections on the dominance of engagement with the key leadership figures of Forbes Burnham and Cheddi Jagan on work on the Guyanese left. See Kimani S.K. Nehusi, *A People's Political History of Guyana, 1838–1964* (Hertford: Hansib, 2018), esp. 64–65.
47 Richard Iton, *In Search of the Black Fantastic: Politics and Popular Culture in the Post-Civil Rights Era* (Oxford: Oxford University Press, 2008), 80.
48 Ranajit Guha, 'The Prose of Counter Insurgency' in *The Small Voice of History: Collected Essays*, ed. Partha Chatterjee (New Delhi: Permanent Black, 2008), 194–238.
49 Raza, *Revolutionary Pasts*, 18–19.
50 See the essays in Sheila Rowbotham, *Dreams and Dilemmas: Collected Writings* (London: Virago, 1983); Boyce Davies, *Left of Karl Marx*.

51 David Scott, *Conscripts of Modernity: The Tragedy of Colonial Enlightenment* (Durham, NC: Duke University Press, 2004), 45.

52 See also Jake Hodder, 'Toward a Geography of Black Internationalism: Bayard Rustin, Nonviolence and the Promise of Africa', *Annals of the American Association of Geographers*, 106:6 (2016), 1360–1377; Mark Rhodes II, 'The Absent Presence of Paul Robeson in Wales: Appropriation and Philosophical Disconnects in the Memorial Landscape', *Transactions of the Institute of British Geographers*, 46:3 (2021), 763–779.

53 In addition to other work cited on these figures in this volume, and much else that could be cited, see for example David Levering Lewis, *W.E.B. Du Bois: A Biography 1868–1963* (New York: Henry Holt, 2008); Bill V. Mullen, *W.E.B. Du Bois: Revolutionary Across the Color Line* (London: Pluto, 2016); Arnold Rampersad, *The Life of Langston Hughes, Volume I: 1902–1941, I, Too, Sing America* (New York: Oxford University Press, 1986) and Arnold Rampersad, *The Life of Langston Hughes, Volume II: 1914–1967, I Dream a World* (New York: Oxford University Press, 1988); David Macey, *Frantz Fanon: A Biography* (London: Verso, 2012); Leo Zeilig, *Frantz Fanon: A Political Biography* (London: I.B. Tauris, 2021); Gregson Davis, *Aimé Césaire* (Cambridge: Cambridge University Press, 2008); Paul Buhle, *C.L.R. James: The Artist as Revolutionary* (London: Verso, 2017); Winston James, *Claude McKay: The Making of a Black Bolshevik* (New York: Columbia University Press, 2022); Leslie James, *George Padmore and Decolonisation from Below: Pan-Africanism, the Cold War, and the End of Empire* (New York: Palgrave Macmillan, 2015); Lindsey R. Swindall, *Paul Robeson: A Life of Activism and Art* (Lanham, MD: Rowman & Littlefield, 2013); Marika Sherwood, *Claudia Jones: A Life in Exile* (London: Lawrence and Wishart, 2000); 'Claudia Jones: Foremother of World Revolution', *Journal of Intersectionality*, 3:1 (2019), whole issue; Leo Zeilig, *A Revolutionary for Our Time: The Walter Rodney Story* (Chicago, IL: Haymarket, 2022).

54 On Harrison, as well as Brian Kwoba's work in this volume, see for example Jeffrey B. Perry, *Hubert Harrison: The Voice of Harlem Radicalism, 1883–1918* (New York: Columbia University Press, 2008) and Jeffrey B. Perry, *Hubert Harrison: The Struggle for Equality, 1918–1927* (New York: Columbia University Press, 2020). Harry Haywood's famous 1978 autobiography *Black Bolshevik* has been complemented now by Gwendolyn Midlo Hall (ed.), *Black Communist in the Freedom Struggle: The Life of Harry Haywood* (Minneapolis, MN: University of Minnesota Press, 2012).

55 For a classic pioneering study of François see Rhoda Reddock, *Elma Francois: The NWCSA and the Worker's Struggle for Change in the Caribbean* (London: New Beacon Books, 1988). For a recent biography of Louise Thompson Patterson, see Keith Gilyard, *Louise Thompson Patterson: A Life of Struggle for Justice* (Durham, NC: Duke University Press, 2017).

56 See Gerald Horne, *Black and Red: W.E.B. Du Bois and the Afro-American Response to the Cold War* (Albany, NY: SUNY Press, 1986) and Gerald Horne, *W.E.B. Du Bois: A Biography* (Santa Barbara, CA: Greenwood Press, 2009);

Gerald Horne, *Black Liberation/Red Scare: Ben Davis and the Communist Party* (Newark, DE: University of Delaware Press, 1994); Gerald Horne, *Race Woman: The Lives of Shirley Graham Du Bois* (New York: New York University Press, 2002); Gerald Horne, *Black Revolutionary: William Patterson and the Globalization of the African American Freedom Struggle* (Champaign, IL: University of Illinois Press, 2013); Gerald Horne, *Paul Robeson: The Artist as Revolutionary* (London: Pluto Press, 2016).

57 On James's writings on black liberation in the United States while part of the American Trotskyist movement, see Scott McLemee (ed.), *C.L.R. James on the 'Negro Question'* (Jackson, MS: University Press of Mississippi, 1996). On James Boggs, see Stephen M. Ward (ed.), *Pages from a Black Radical's Notebook: A James Boggs Reader* (Detroit, MI: Wayne State University Press, 2011) and Stephen M. Ward, *In Love and Struggle: The Revolutionary Lives of James and Grace Lee Boggs* (Chapel Hill, NC: University of North Carolina Press, 2016). Ernest Rice McKinney wrote under the pseudonym 'David Coolidge', while Sy Owens, who wrote under the names Charles Denby and Matthew Ward, did successfully pen a 1952 memoir. See Charles Denby [Sy Owens], *Indignant Heart: Testimony of a Black American Worker* (London: Pluto, 1979).

58 For a valuable set of essays exploring the challenges and possibilities for life writing when it comes to enslaved Africans in the Atlantic world, see Lisa A. Lindsay and John Wood Sweet (eds), *Biography and the Black Atlantic* (Philadelphia, PA: University of Pennsylvania Press, 2014).

59 With respect to post-war Caribbean radicalism, see for example the interviews conducted by David Scott in *Small Axe* journal; Khafra Kambon, *For Bread, Justice and Freedom: A Political Biography of George Weekes* (London and Port of Spain: New Beacon Books, 1988); Paul Buhle, *Tim Hector: A Caribbean Radical's Story* (Jackson, MS: University Press of Mississippi, 2006); David Austin (ed.), *Alfie Roberts Speaks* (Montreal: Alfie Roberts Institute, 2005); Matthew Quest (ed.), *Workers' Self-Management in the Caribbean: The Writings of Joseph Edwards* (Atlanta, GA: On Our Own Authority!, 2014); Alissa Trotz (ed.), *The Point is to Change the World: Selected Writings of Andaiye* (London: Pluto, 2020).

60 Franklin Rosemont and Robin D.G Kelley (ed.), *Black, Brown and Beige: Surrealist Writings from Africa and the Diaspora* (Austin, TX: University of Texas, 2009), quote from introduction 'Invisible Surrealists', 2.

61 Anne Garland Mahler, 'The Red and the Black in Latin America: Sandalio Junco and the "Negro Question" from an Afro-Latin Perspective', *American Communist History*, 17:1 (2018), 16–32. For more on this region, see for example Sandra Pujals, 'Racialising the Caribbean Basin: The Communist Racial Agenda for the American Hemisphere, 1931–35' in David Featherstone and Christian Høgsbjerg (eds), *The Red and the Black: The Russian Revolution and the Black Atlantic* (Manchester: Manchester University Press, 2021), 174–197 and Margaret Stevens, *Red International and Black Caribbean: Communists in New York City, Mexico and the West Indies, 1919–1939* (London: Pluto, 2017).

62 Ariel Lambe, *No Barrier Can Contain It: Cuban Antifascism and the Spanish Civil War* (Chapel Hill, NC: University of North Carolina Press, 2019), 141–147.
63 João Fábio Bertonha, 'Anti-Fascism in Brazil during the Interwar Period: International Repercussions, National Expressions and Transnational Networks between Europe and the Americas' in Kasper Braskén, Nigel Copsey and David Featherstone (eds), *Anti-Fascism in a Global Perspective: Transnational Networks, Exile Communities and Radical Internationalism* (London: Routledge, 2020), 43–57, and Bernhard H. Bayerlein, 'Addis Ababa, Rio de Janeiro and Moscow 1935: The Double Failure of Comintern Antifascism and Anticolonialism' in Kasper Braskén, Nigel Copsey and David Featherstone (eds), *Anti-Fascism in a Global Perspective: Transnational Networks, Exile Communities and Radical Internationalism* (London: Routledge, 2020), 218–233, quote on 218.
64 On Len Johnson, see Michael Herbert, *Never Counted Out!: The Story of Len Johnson, Manchester's Black Boxing Hero and Communist* (Manchester: Dropped Aitches Press, 1992), and also Alan Rice, 'Tracing Roots and Routes: African Atlantic Residents and Sojourners Make their Mark in the Cottonopolis 1789–1956' in Koyo Kouoh, Christine Eyene and Lubiana Himid (eds), *We Face Forward: Art from West Africa Today* (Manchester: Manchester City Galleries and Whitworth Art Gallery, 2012), 16–21. Len Johnson once described how meeting Paul Robeson proved an inspiration for his own struggles. 'Paul Robeson put new life in me with a few words. He drew me a picture of his fight for recognition. He pointed out that my job was fighting, and that if I could fight in the ring I ought to be able to fight outside it. I took his words to heart and made every effort to show that the British colour bar is just so much nonsense … So I must thank Paul Robeson for helping me over a tough case of the blues.' See Herbert, *Never Counted Out!*, 71.
65 On Gilmore, see Winston James, 'Claude McKay's Bolshevisation in London' in David Featherstone and Christian Høgsbjerg (eds), *The Red and the Black: The Russian Revolution and the Black Atlantic* (Manchester: Manchester University Press, 2021), 41–80.
66 Nan Milton, *John Maclean* (London: Pluto, 1973), 292, 303. Maclean had been appointed Soviet Consul to Scotland by Lenin in 1918. For a more recent biography of Maclean, albeit one that sadly does not mention Johnston, see Henry Bell, *John Maclean: Hero of Red Clydeside* (London: Pluto, 2018).
67 Reddock, *Elma Francois*, 12–13. See also David Featherstone, *Solidarity: Hidden Histories and Geographies of Internationalism* (London: Zed, 2012), 90–91; Adam Elliott-Cooper, *Black Resistance to British Policing* (Manchester: Manchester University Press, 2021), 24–29.
68 On Arnold Ward see the numerous references in Hakim Adi, *Pan-Africanism and Communism: The Communist International, Africa and the Diaspora, 1919–1939* (Trenton, NJ: Africa World Press, 2013), and also Susan D. Pennybacker, *From Scottsboro to Munich: Race and Political Culture in 1930s Britain* (Princeton, NJ: Princeton University Press, 2009). See also Martin Duberman, *Paul Robeson* (New York: New Press, 1989), 627n.59.

69 On Blackman, see Marika Sherwood's entry on him for the *Oxford Dictionary of National Biography* and his recently published poems, Peter Blackman, *Footprints* (Middlesborough: Smokestack Books, 2013), which also contains an introduction by editor Chris Searle.
70 Ernie Benson, *To Struggle is to Live: A Working Class Autobiography, Volume 2: Starve or Rebel* (Newcastle upon Tyne: People's Publications, 1980), 132–133.
71 Marcus Bennett, 'Britain's Black International Brigadier', *Tribune*, 31 October 2020, https://tribunemag.co.uk/2020/10/britains-black-international-brigadier (accessed 3 August 2021).
72 More work is also needed on exploring the relationship of revolutionary socialist figures who are not racialised as black to questions of black and colonial liberation, as well as their personal relationships to people from Africa or of African descent. Chris Gilligan and Nigel Niles's chapter on Raya Dunayevskaya in this volume may be seen to be exemplary in this respect, examining a lesser-known aspect of her political and intellectual thought.
73 Joshua Clark Davis, 'Una Mulzac, Black Women Booksellers, and Pan-Africanism', *Black Perspectives*, 19 September 2016, www.aaihs.org/una-mulzac-black-women-booksellers-and-pan-africanism/ (accessed 3 August 2021).
74 Mulzac, *A Star to Steer By*, 263.

# I

# Black Bolshevism

# 1

# Hubert Henry Harrison: Black radicalism and the Colored International

*Brian Kwoba*

Hubert Henry Harrison (1883–1927) ranks among the most scandalously neglected voices within the Black radical tradition. Because he was such a deeply influential journalist, activist, educator, and community organiser in his own time, restoring Harrison to history and memory requires us to rethink the Black–Red encounter in the early twentieth century. Harrison was the first Black leader of the Socialist Party of America to devote special attention towards actively organising Black workers for socialism. He helped cultivate the First World War-era 'New Negro' movement by spearheading its first organisation, newspaper, nationwide congress, and political

**Figure 1.1** Hubert Henry Harrison

party. Harrison exerted a decisive influence on the rise of Marcus Garvey and the Garvey movement. He spearheaded the socio-cultural tradition of street corner speaking in Harlem, which established an eclectic, working-class, and African-centred intellectual culture that endures to this day. As the Black trade union organiser A. Philip Randolph put it, Hubert Harrison was 'the father of Harlem radicalism'.[1]

Despite his wide-ranging influence on the Black awakening of his generation, Harrison has been marginalised in historiography. For example, Henry Louis Gates Jr's survey of African-American history from 1513 to 2008 (*Life Upon These Shores*) makes *no mention* of Hubert Harrison. Similarly, the University of Oxford's five-volume *Encyclopedia of African American History* mentions Harrison's name only four times, always in passing. In recent years, a small but growing interest in Harrison's life and legacy has begun to emerge thanks to the tireless efforts of independent scholar Jeffrey B. Perry.[2] Perry has published the only book-length treatments of Harrison's life and writings in existence, and has dedicated the better part of his life's work to restoring Harrison to his proper place in both popular memory and scholarly historiography.[3] A few scholars from past generations wrote about Harrison, and the more recent studies are indebted to their work.[4] Yet despite their work, Harrison remains an underappreciated figure.

As a result of his near erasure from popular memory and marginalisation in historiography, restoring Harrison to the history of the Black–Red encounter throws new light on a set of old political questions about the relationship between socialism and Black people. Harrison's experience, particularly during and after his time as a prominent Black organiser in the Socialist Party in its 1911–12 heyday, in many ways set a tone for many of the debates that would continue for the rest of the twentieth century about the relationship between the dynamics of race and class, white supremacy and capitalism, Black nationalism and socialism. And because these debates remain alive today, the questions raised by Harrison's ideological and political engagement with the Marxist left remain painfully relevant in the twenty-first century.

Hubert Harrison was born in 1883 to labouring-class parents of black African ancestry on the Caribbean island of St Croix. Harrison obtained a ninth grade education in the Danish colony as well as some religious training in the Anglican Church.[5] After his mother died, he sought out better life prospects in the United States, joining a wave of tens of thousands of Caribbean immigrants who moved to the United States in the early twentieth century as a result of adverse economic conditions on their islands of origin. Thanks to the assistance of his sister Mary, he managed to relocate to New York City as a bright 17-year-old in 1900.

In the early twentieth century, people racialised as Black in the United States lived under the pervasive terror of racial oppression. Lynching, segregation, and political disfranchisement reigned supreme in the south, while anti-Black pogroms and other mechanisms of white supremacist racial cleansing gave rise to an epidemic of all-white 'sundown towns', largely in the north.[6] While Black life in the Caribbean emerged from a similar history of European transatlantic enslavement, Hubert Harrison's native St Croix (like most of the Caribbean islands) lacked the presence of lynching, Ku Klux Klan-style terrorism, and violent white supremacy that characterised the United States.[7] As a result, scholars of early twentieth-century Harlem have shown how the encounter of Caribbean migrants like Harrison with the virulent racial oppression of the US comprised a major factor in their political radicalisation.[8]

Upon his arrival in New York, Harrison followed a path trod by most West Indian migrants to the city: working various service jobs to eke out a living. At different times, he earned a living as a messenger, bellhop, elevator operator, and as a stock clerk in a Japanese-fan company.[9] In 1907, Harrison moved to Harlem, which would become the largest and most concentrated Black neighbourhood in New York City between 1900 and 1930.[10] Thanks to *de facto* segregation and the influx of African-American migrants from the south and Afro-Caribbean migrants from the Antilles, Harlem became its own hub of economic, cultural, and international exchange with numerous benevolent associations, churches, fraternal orders, and other voluntary associations combining to form a rich tapestry of social and community institutions.[11] In the chambers of Black church lyceums at St Mark's and St Benedict's, Harrison received a rigorous training in critical intellectual debate, eventually breaking with Christianity and joining the anti-religious Freethought movement.[12]

After some years of struggling to find steady work and pay the bills, Harrison eventually secured salaried and consistent employment as a clerk at the Post Office in 1907. As a postal worker, Harrison chafed under the twelve-hour days, six- to seven-day working weeks, poor ventilation, and abusive managers. He also witnessed the tense labour organising competition between the pro-management United National Association of Post Office Clerks (Local no. 1) and the pro-worker National Federation of Post Office Clerks (Local no. 10), which was affiliated with the American Federation of Labor (AFL).[13] Despite the oppressive working conditions, postal work was one of the better-paying jobs that a Black immigrant could hope for as the first decade of the twentieth century drew to a close, and he was promoted for his diligent work ethic each year for the next four years.[14]

Although the growth of the Black industrial working class offered new opportunities for multiracial union organising along industrial lines, in the first two decades of the twentieth century it often prompted white workers to cling ever more tightly to their racially based economic privileges. For example, as the largest federation of organised labour, the AFL generally abided by the exclusion of Black workers from its affiliates.[15] In terms of housing and geographical space, white workers in small towns across the country engaged in hysterical mob attacks and countless massacres against Black communities, culminating in the formation of thousands of all-white 'sundown towns'.[16] Meanwhile, Jim Crow laws affected political disenfranchisement, social segregation, and the coercive mechanism of the lynch rope that terrorised the African-American psyche, particularly in Southern Black communities.

In this context, Harrison wrote a pair of op-ed pieces in the *New York Sun* in December 1910, which defended progressive Black critics of Booker T. Washington, the powerful president of the Tuskegee Institute, and a nationwide 'Tuskegee Machine' of ideological repression inside the Black community which had achieved nearly full-spectrum dominance by 1900.[17] Washington had recently claimed, while travelling in London, that the South offered better opportunities for Blacks 'than almost any other country in the world'.[18] Harrison's response used numerous facts and simple logic to argue that insisting on the real grievances of the race and fighting against them was a better course of action than the denial-based approach that Washington articulated.[19] In retaliation, the Black Tuskegee-aligned Republican party official Charles Anderson arranged for Harrison to be fired from his job at the Post Office. Given Harrison's exemplary workplace performance record, this was an unequivocally underhanded and vindictive act of the Tuskegee Machine.[20] But far from silencing Harrison, the termination in 1911 fuelled his growing interest in radical politics, leading him to join the Socialist Party as a full-time speaker and organiser.

### The so-called 'Negro Question' in the Socialist Party

Formed in 1901 from a merger of the Social Democratic Party and Socialist Labour Party, the Socialist Party of America steadily grew in the first decade of the twentieth century to become perhaps the largest class struggle-based political party in US history.[21] By 1912, it boasted over 100,000 members, with over a thousand of them holding elected offices throughout the country. It had 323 newspapers, including the *Appeal to Reason* with a circulation of 761,000.[22] Ethno-linguistic associations of Italians, Hungarians, Jews, Germans, Poles, and Finns made up nearly a sixth of total party membership. With moderate reformists and radical revolutionaries, northerners and southerners, immigrant and native-born workers, the party Harrison joined was a 'seething complex of diverse, often antipathetic, groups, persons, and political tendencies', as historian Albert Fried put it.[23]

The most distinguishing line of difference that shaped Harrison's experience in the party was the colour line, and the Socialist Party he joined was marked by variations of the white political position on the race question. For example, the state secretary of the Mississippi state party lamented the Reconstruction period of multiracial democracy and praised the Ku Klux Klan. With racist attitudes like this featuring so prominently, it is not surprising that there is no record that the party as a whole (or as a matter of party policy) ever actively opposed discrimination against Black people in the first decade of its existence. However, the most popular party leader and perennial Socialist Party candidate for president, Eugene V. Debs, did personally oppose discrimination and called on Black workers 'to reject the false doctrines of meekness and humility'. To his credit, Debs refused to speak to segregated party branches in the South and welcomed African Americans into the labour and socialist movement. Yet even this prominent left-winger insisted that the Socialist Party had 'nothing special to offer the Negro' because 'the class struggle is colorless'.[24] Consequently, Debs did little to mobilise the party to fight against lynching, segregation, disfranchisement, and other specific manifestations of racial oppression faced by Black workers.[25]

Given this context, Hubert Harrison found himself uniquely positioned to advance a different approach to the so-called 'Negro question'. In 1911–12, he wrote a five-part series of articles on 'The Negro and Socialism' for local New York newspaper the *New York Call* and a three-part series for the nationally distributed and Chicago-based *International Socialist Review*, which articulated the key elements of his case for building the socialist movement in Black communities.[26] Overall, the series represented two of Harrison's signal contributions to the socialist movement: the first systematic and historical materialist analysis of race and class by a Black socialist and the first public challenge to the party on its racial politics.

Harrison's argument emphasised the class position of African Americans. As he put it, 'the ten million Negroes of America form a group that is more essentially proletarian than any other American group'. Not only that, but Black workers were generally paid less than other workers for their labour and worked longer hours under worse conditions. Therefore, 'the exploitation of the Negro worker is keener than that of any group of white workers in America'.[27] He argued that race prejudice was a product of economic subjection, a problem with 'roots in slavery past and present'.[28] Race prejudice harmed Black workers because they could get no protection from the courts, the ballot, or public opinion. Meanwhile, even white workers who enjoyed these protections could not demand higher wages, better conditions, or strike action without the employers threatening to replace them with Black workers. In short, white workers were also harmed by race prejudice, which the capitalist class actively perpetuated in order to keep wages low, strikes infrequent, and workers divided.[29]

From this, Harrison concluded that because the mission of the Socialist Party was to free the working class from exploitation and since Blacks were the 'most ruthlessly exploited working class group in America', then the duty of the party to champion their cause was clear. The party needed to organise African Americans, teach them the tenets of socialism, and stimulate them with the hope of a new republic founded on the 'brotherhood of man'. Harrison then bolstered his argument by appealing to the authority of Karl Marx, pointing out that Marx advocated the economic organisation of workers because a working class that was united and conscious of its proletarian interests and objectives could achieve anything.[30]

Harrison was not the first Black socialist in the United States, but he was among the first to maintain that Black socialists had a special role to play in recruiting African Americans to the party and that white comrades would need to adopt a posture of respect and humility if they wanted to recruit Blacks.[31] For a brief and local moment, Harrison's arguments bore fruit. In October 1911, the secretary of the party's Harlem branch wrote to local New York headquarters that because Harrison understood Black life and history and was a good public speaker, the branch proposed that he be made a paid speaker and organiser for special work in Black communities.[32] Harrison had found a receptive ear in the New York party leadership and the Harlem branch moved to make him the local's first full-time Black organiser to help the party reach Black workers.

In practical terms, support from the New York leadership opened the door to a new organisational formation, the Colored Socialist Club (CSC). The CSC represented the first Black-led and multiracial party formation, which held meetings and distributed socialist literature specifically oriented towards Black people. Under Harrison's leadership, it held weekly meetings in Harlem, and educated participants about the specific role of Black workers in the class struggle as well as what socialism could do for African Americans.

In late February 1912, less than three months after it got off the ground, the Executive Committee (EC) abandoned the project, supposedly due to lack of available funds, poor attendance, and concerns about a party structure based on 'segregation'. Given that the club was funded by donations from local branches and ethno-linguistic associations, the excuse of a depleted party treasury did not hold water. As for attendance, Harrison acknowledged that it had recently been uneven, but argued that attendance was spotty at other party meetings, and in those cases did not necessarily indicate lack of interest. He claimed that the party had not 'done its full duties yet' to support the club.[33] Given Harrison's race politics, and his own clear and public repudiation of the notion that a separate Black-only branch was intended, the charge of a formation based on segregation also remained dubious, especially given how racially exclusive towards Blacks the party had been up to that point.[34] Nevertheless, the EC terminated the project.

While rejected locally, Harrison was keen to see what the party's response to his arguments would be at a national level. In May 1912, the party's national convention did not even address the 'Negro Question' directly, but the majority report of the committee on immigration passed a resolution declaring that

> Race feeling is not so much a result of social as of biological evolution. It does not change essentially with changes of economic systems. It is deeper than any class feeling and will outlast the capitalist system. It persists even after race prejudice has been outgrown. It exists ... as a product of biology ... Class consciousness must be learned, but race-consciousness is inborn and cannot be wholly unlearned.[35]

In other words, race prejudice was biologically rather than socially determined, timeless and inborn rather than contingent and extinguishable. In taking this position, the party unequivocally and at a national level effectively rejected Harrison's pre-convention arguments about the political, historical, and socio-economic roots of racism.

Meanwhile, Harrison was moving further to the left of the local and national party moderates. He spoke in Elizabeth, New Jersey in November 1912 advocating industrial unionism, syndicalism, and direct action in the workplace, tendencies which emerged from the reaction among rank-and-file workers to the older exclusionary and craft-based unionism. Harrison spoke favourably of the racially inclusive and industry-wide organising strategy of the Industrial Workers of the World (IWW). He supported industrial sabotage, direct action, and the general strike.[36] In practical terms, he supported the massive 25,000-strong Paterson, New Jersey silk strike of 1913, sharing speaking platforms with such national left-wing labour leaders and strikes supporters as 'Big' Bill Haywood and Elizabeth Gurley Flynn.[37] In one speech, Harrison thundered:

> We consider, whether right or wrong, every blow struck by labour against capital is a blow for labour ... As for the Socialist party, no one asked the Socialist party to come into this strike. Let it stay out – if it dares! In season and out of season, we Socialists must go to the workers to hear what we must do. The revolution is not coming from above, remember, but from below, working its way up from the depths ... We are not here because they invaded

our rights. We have none. We never had any. We are working not to get rights, but to get might, and when we have *that*, we will have right![38]

This speech not only highlighted Harrison's militancy ('might begets rights'), but also his radical humility ('we must go to the workers to hear what we must do'). It also reveals his conception of revolution coming 'from below' and his criticism of (and growing distance from) the Socialist Party.

Though eyewitness accounts from these speeches are sparse, evidence emerged in the press reports of the strike regarding the electrifying effect that Harrison's forceful Black oratory had on the scores of European-descended workers who filled the strikers' meeting halls and rallies. The Paterson *Evening News* found Harrison's statements 'unfit to print', to which Flynn replied 'he tells plain facts and the bosses don't like them'.[39] Even the Socialist Party's *New York Call*, which he had criticised for refusing to print a letter from a prominent speaker at the IWW's Paterson Defense Conference, praised one of Harrison's speeches, reporting that 'he filled in the remarks of the [other] speakers as the ocean does a chain of islands'.[40] Harrison embodied a major asset to the socialist movement, but his passion for industrial unions, direct action, sabotage, mass strikes, and industry-wide organising at the point of production would soon place him in the crosshairs of the moderate Socialist Party leaders.

In response to Harrison's outspoken independence and radical left-wing positions, the local New York executive committee began to discipline him. First, they reduced his pay to one third of that offered to white speakers. Then they removed him from the party's speakers list and forbade all branches from scheduling their own speakers. They declined a request to have him speak in favour of 'industrial action' for other branches. They cast suspicion upon him by smearing his name in the party press for his public support for other outspoken left-wingers who had been arrested for pro-sabotage speeches. They attempted to prohibit him from speaking and from publicly debating the anti-socialist lecturer Frank Urban, despite the fact that Harrison earned his living as a lecturer. Eventually, they suspended him for disobeying their order. For its failure to state what party laws or policies he had violated, Harrison suggested the EC's behaviour represented 'a most contemptible form of persecution'.[41] A few months later, Harrison resigned from the party.

Hubert Harrison's break from the Socialist Party proved a decisive moment because it forced him to drastically rethink his racial politics. Initially, he had taken the socialists at their word, trusting that they stood for the emancipation of the whole working class. Its racial ignorance and white supremacist behaviour showed how the party, in Harrison's words, was putting the '[white] race first and class after'. Harrison's call for special attention towards the 'most essentially proletarian group' was unequivocally rejected by the same white radicals who claimed to stand for proletarian emancipation. As historian John Henrik Clarke put it, Harrison 'was a socialist until he discovered that most socialists are not true to the teachings of socialism'.[42] By 1915, Harrison had concluded that in order for Harlem to get 'more schools and playgrounds, lower rents, higher wages, [and] better treatment at the hands of policemen', African Americans would have to unite to demand these things for themselves. 'For the money, the organisation, the push, we must depend upon ourselves and not upon white people.'[43]

## The Liberty League of Negro-Americans

After leaving the Socialist Party, Hubert Harrison devoted himself to agitating and organising Black workers in his home neighbourhood of Harlem. By 1917, he and his 'New Negro Manhood movement' were on the rise.[44] Though the 'manhood' was later dropped for the more gender-neutral sounding 'New Negro movement' which would come to define the era, the initial manhood-oriented discourse within the movement spoke to the centrality of Black men and their gender politics in articulating counter-hegemonic claims to dignity, respect, and honour. As Michelle Stephens has shown, the masculine global imaginary of Black Caribbean-born intellectual men in the early twentieth century also 'contributed to a particular kind of discourse on Black masculinity and political subjectivity as part of a construction of the race as a *global* formation and political unit and consciousness'.[45] Black men living, migrating, and moving between different spaces ruled by white colonisers in this period embarked on a quest for political agency that had an inherently complex and contradictory relationship to the Eurocentric standards of masculinity, respect, and authority that oppressed them. Marcus Garvey, for example, sought to fashion a Black empire equal in stature to that of the European empires. Harrison, as an anti-imperialist, naturally had a very different approach.

In April 1917, President Woodrow Wilson made the fateful decision to take the US into the carnage of the inter-European war, in order to 'make the world safe for democracy'. In response, Hubert Harrison put out a call to 'make the South safe for democracy'. On 12 June 1917, some two thousand people packed the Bethel AME (African Methodist Episcopal) Church in Harlem to inaugurate the formation of the Liberty League of Negro-Americans, whose purpose would be to protest against lynching, disfranchisement, and racial oppression. The Liberty League passed resolutions calling on all true friends of democracy to help Black people secure their democratic rights, demanding that the government uphold the 13th, 14th, and 15th amendments to the Constitution. The League also declared it would fight lynching, segregation, Jim Crowism, and peonage, with every means available, including armed self-defence.[46]

Thanks to Harrison's internationalism, the Liberty League resolutions declared solidarity with the struggles of oppressed peoples across the world, mentioning explicitly the Irish (who waged the Easter Rising fourteen months prior), the Russian people (who had overthrown the Tsar three months prior), and the anti-colonial struggle on the Indian subcontinent (which witnessed the start of Mahatma Gandhi's first Satyagraha movement in India two months prior). The League also articulated a 'special sympathy' for the '250 millions of our brethren in Africa', which was undergoing a whole range of post-war anti-colonial resistance movements.[47] The meeting took up subscriptions for a new newspaper called *The Voice* in order to give militant journalistic expression to the movement.

Notably, as against the talented tenth's compromising deference to white liberals, the League maintained an all-Black membership and distinctive emphasis on racial self-determination. In that regard it followed in the tradition of organisations like William Monroe and Geraldine Trotter's National Equal Rights League and the Afro-American Council of T. Thomas Fortune and Ida B. Wells. As Harrison put it, the League emerged from 'the need for a more radical policy than that of the NAACP'.[48] In 1918, William Monroe Trotter, Adam Clayton Powell Jr, and Hubert Harrison organised the Liberty Congress of Negro Americans in Washington, DC, the only organisationally independent gathering of Black dissidents during the war. The Liberty Congress elected Hubert Harrison as its chairman and presented a petition to the US Congress against lynching, disfranchisement, and segregation, demonstrating Harrison's emergence as a leader of the wartime 'New Negro' movement at a national level.

In addition to founding the Liberty League, Harrison also influenced the intellectual and print culture of Harlem political life through the inspiring example of his newspaper *The Voice*. While Black newspapers like the *Chicago Defender* or the *Pittsburgh Courier* emerged in the early 1900s, the Harrison-edited *Voice* in July 1917 crystallised a new genre of First World War-era New Negro journalism that subsequently expanded with publications like A. Philip Randolph and Chandler Owen's socialist *Messenger* in the fall of 1917, Garvey's *Negro World* in 1918, Cyril Briggs's *The Crusader* in 1919, and W.A. Domingo's short-lived *Emancipator* in 1920. Each of these products of the First World War-era Black political awakening in Harlem can be traced to the pioneering example of Harrison's *Voice*, which set a concrete local example for a cutting-edge and politically radical

Black paper. As W.A. Domingo put it, 'Garvey like the rest of us all followed Hubert Harrison.'[49]

## The 'White World War' and the Russian Revolution

Beyond sparking the formation of the Liberty League, the entry of the United States into the European war invited a whole generation of Black people to awaken, both politically and racially. Harrison's speeches, for example, began to dissect the racial and economic politics of the 'white world war'.[50] Because he maintained an oppositional course despite the extreme pressures from government repression, the pro-war mainstream media, and the patriotic Black press, Harrison's leadership during the war marks him as a leader who consistently maintained anti-imperialist politics. Having no high-paying job or elite celebrity status to defend, Hubert Harrison maintained a distinctive clarity of vision during the war, noting how the rhetoric of 'democracy' was used 'mainly as a convenient camouflage behind which competing imperialists masked their sordid aims'.[51]

Though he had been speaking about the subject since 1915, Harrison seems to have penned his first analysis of the First World War in a piece for *The Voice* in August 1917 entitled 'The White War and the Colored World'. He argued that twelve out of seventeen hundred million people in the world were 'colored – black brown and yellow', and at relative peace until the eruption of a European conflagration. Therefore, he argued, it was 'a war of the white race wherein the stakes of the conflict are the titles to possession of the lands and destinies of [the] colored majority in Asia, Africa, and the islands of the sea'. The white race was superior 'not because it has better morals[,] more religion, or higher culture', but because it had the guns, soldiers, and economic resources to dominate other peoples.

With this framework, Harrison contested the official justification for the war: it was not about the democracy of the Allies versus the tyranny of Germany, but a war of clashing European empires. More specifically, the struggle represented a conflict of interests that would determine 'whose will shall be accepted as the collective will of the white race'. Although he lamented the loss of life that the war entailed, he found consolation in the hope that the white world's blood-soaked bout of fratricidal slaughter would inevitably weaken its ability to oppress and dominate the non-white people of the world. Harrison looked forward, quite prophetically, to the darker peoples of the world getting independence, because the 'majority races' would not be coerced into accepting white domination forever.[52]

Harrison's racial analysis of the war offered a lens that the leading Marxist and white radical theoreticians lacked. While some of the most prominent European Marxists, including V.I. Lenin, supported the self-determination of oppressed ethnic nationalities, they did not theorise anti-imperialist politics in *racial* terms.[53] Harrison himself noted this, remarking in 1919 how although some minimal signs of racial awareness could be seen in a recent Bolshevik declaration, nevertheless 'eyes which for centuries have been behind the blinders of Race Prejudice cannot but blink and water when compelled to face the full sunlight'.[54] In other words, white leftists had a long way to go in terms of developing race consciousness. By contrast, Harrison's racial analysis was not of mere secondary or incidental relevance to the class question, as the well-meaning and 'colorblind' socialists like Eugene Debs had treated it. As early as 1915, Harrison began pointing out that 'the racial aspect of the war in Europe was easily the most important' because of the earth-shattering implications of the adoption of democracy and self-determination for the colonised and coloured peoples, who comprised the majority of the world's population.[55]

To be clear, Harrison supported and took great inspiration from the Russian Revolution. He saw it as a model Blacks could learn from, given that when the Russian masses moved, 'they swept not only the Czar's regime but the whole exploiting system upon which it stood into utter oblivion'.[56] The implication here, of course, is that if the masses in the US would do likewise, they could sweep away their own 'whole exploiting system' too. We saw how Harrison's Liberty League declared itself in solidarity with the Russian people following the February Revolution, and after the October Revolution US government surveillance noted Harrison's warm appraisals of Lenin's government. A military intelligence report from 1919 compiled a list of Black figures who were actively giving speeches in Black communities, including figures like Marcus Garvey, Hubert Harrison, William Monroe Trotter, A. Philip Randolph, and Chandler Owen. According to the report, 'All of the speakers named on [the enclosed] list are radicals and ... this is especially true of Mr. Hubert Harrison, who claims that "Bolshevism is the salvation of America".'[57] His experience with the white ignorance, denial, and arrogance of the Socialist Party kept him from ever joining the Communist Party. Yet his anti-capitalist radicalism led him into coalition work with Black Communists, as we will see momentarily.

In this connection, Harrison made arguments to the Marxist left about the dialectical relationship between race and class consciousness. For example, Harrison pointed out that when white British workers insist that 'no one will maintain that the Africans are fit for self-government', it represented the same elitist attitude whereby the British ruling class told those same workers, 'no one maintains that the laboring classes of Britain are fit for self-government'. Both positions sprang from a superiority complex, one racial and the other class-based. The 'selfish and ignorant' white worker with such a superiority complex thus failed to realise that his destiny was inseparably bound up with 'the hundreds of millions of those whom he calls "niggers"'.[58] Working-class 'self-government' – i.e. workers' control of the means of production – formed the cornerstone of revolutionary socialism. So if white workers maintained such elitist attitudes towards African workers, they clearly lacked the respect and humility towards racially oppressed people necessary for a truly 'proletarian internationalism' of the kind that a working-class revolution would require – especially in the US context, where African Americans were the most thoroughly proletarian demographic of all racial groups in the country, yet also woefully underrepresented in the ranks of the Socialist and Communist Parties of Harrison's day.

## Hubert Harrison and the rise of Garveyism

Marcus Garvey was born in the rural peasant community of Saint Ann's Bay, Jamaica in 1887. He trained as a printer's apprentice and led a strike of print workers in 1907. He travelled extensively in Latin America, observing the poor working conditions and treatment of Afro-Caribbean migrants, which provided stimulus for his emerging global Black racial consciousness. He made his way to London in 1912, where he would work for Duse Mohammed Ali's *African Times and Orient Review*. Reading Booker T. Washington's autobiography *Up From Slavery* inspired Garvey to join with his future first wife Amy Ashwood to create an organisation that would establish an industrial school modelled on Washington's Tuskegee Institute. Founded in 1914, the Universal Negro Improvement Association and African Communities League (UNIA-ACL) struggled to gain much traction initially, prompting Garvey to attempt to raise money in the US and visit Washington's Tuskegee Institute in particular for support.[59]

Booker T. Washington died in 1915, so when Garvey arrived in the US in 1916 he was not able to meet him. Garvey's subsequent speaking tour of the country placed him in touch with other West Indians and African Americans who discouraged him from the idea of building an industrial school in Jamaica.[60] Yet he did not have a clear alternative in mind. By the time he returned to New York in the spring of 1917, he had run out of money and strained his relationship with his partner Amy Ashwood such that he seriously considered returning to his home country.[61] As summer approached, Garvey found his UNIA industrial school-building project in a desperate situation. Thanks to Harrison's Liberty League, Garvey would soon opt for Harlem as the headquarters of his reimagined UNIA as he built it into one of the largest international organisations of African-descended people in history, with tens of thousands of members and countless supporters spread across hundreds of Black communities along both sides of the Atlantic Ocean.[62]

Radical Harlem activist Wilfred Adolphus Domingo knew Marcus Garvey from their boyhood days in Jamaica. When Garvey got to New York, Domingo showed him around, introducing him to various Harlem activists like Hubert Harrison, whose Liberty League they both joined in 1917. It would prove a decisive moment in the meteoric rise of both Garvey and Garvey*ism*. Perhaps most crucially, Harrison's Liberty League *catalysed the strategic transition in Garvey's vision for the UNIA*, from a vehicle for building industrial education in Jamaica to an international movement for Black nationality. In addition, the Liberty League modelled many of the key strategic, ideological, and cultural components that Garvey would adopt for his own organisation: the United States and Harlem in particular as a headquarters, cultivating African consciousness and a 'race first' ideology, support for nationalist struggles of other oppressed peoples, and a tricolour flag to symbolise Black liberation, to name a few. Garvey had the brilliance and marketing savvy to combine these ideas with the fraternal, separatist, African emigrationist, religious, and entrepreneurial elements of the Black nationalist tradition of the nineteenth century, and develop them into a global Black nation-building project.[63] But the practical model and racial ideology for cohering a mass organisation that combined (for the first time in US history) African Americans and Afro-Caribbeans of various national origins on a large scale with a programme of collective Black self-help – this came from Harrison's Liberty League.[64]

Harrison's importance to the Garvey movement continued to grow when at the end of 1919 he accepted Marcus Garvey's invitation to edit the *Negro World*. During Harrison's editorship, the paper saw a conceptual redesign, expansion from six to ten pages per issue, and a five-fold increase in circulation.[65] In addition, Harrison's tenure as editor of Garvey's paper afforded a unique service for the Garvey movement by defending it from attacks by Black socialists. For example, in the spring of 1920, Randolph and Owen's *Messenger* and W.A. Domingo's *Emancipator* attacked the political doctrine of 'race first'. They argued that 'class first' formed a sounder policy for Black workers since capitalism produced race prejudice as a divide-and-rule mechanism for keeping wages low and all workers exploited.

Harrison forcefully defended the 'race first' principle on the grounds that the Socialist Party itself practiced a 'race first' doctrine for white workers with its biological conception of racial difference, that it tokenised its Black exponents in the tradition of 'white man's Negroes', and that Randolph and Owen's financial subsidy from a white organisation fundamentally threatened to 'betray the race into alien hands just as surely as "the old crowd"'.

With his past experience as the Socialist Party's first Black historical materialist theoretician, very few other people in the country (much less the UNIA) knew the party and its racial politics better than Hubert Harrison. Marcus Garvey could not have hoped for a better polemicist for this battle. Though space does not permit a full account of all the exchanges, according to Jeff Perry, Harrison's defence of 'race first' temporarily silenced criticism from the Black socialists.[66]

Although Harrison helped catalyse the rise of the Garvey movement and became the editor of its far-reaching and influential newspaper, Harrison's first-hand observations of Garvey's leadership and behaviour did not endear him to the Jamaican. As a result of working full time in the UNIA headquarters editing the *Negro World*, attending the first international UNIA convention, and observing Garvey up close in other settings, Harrison came to conclude that Garvey was egomaniacal, corrupt, dictatorial, imperialistic, and a liar. As a result, Harrison tried to reform the UNIA from within. One of the efforts he undertook in this regard was to push the Garvey movement in a socialist, rather than capitalist, direction.

In the spring of 1921, Harrison explored the possibility strengthening the anti-capitalist wing of the official Garvey movement leadership. Claude McKay, the queer Jamaican-born Marxist who wrote the poetic anthem of the post-war New Negro movement ('If We Must Die'), represented a key collaborator in this endeavour.[67] In his autobiography, McKay recounted how when his good friend Hubert Harrison came downtown to congratulate him on getting the job of assistant editor of *The Liberator*, Harrison suggested having a meeting that would include the 'black Reds'.[68] The meeting took place at the *Liberator* office, and in addition to Harrison and McKay, Grace Campbell (a leading organiser of the African Blood Brotherhood), Richard B. Moore, W.A. Domingo, Cyril Briggs, Joseph Fanning (a Brotherhood member who owned the only Black cigar store in Harlem), and Otto Huiswoud (first Black member of the Communist Party) were present. These were all members of the African Blood Brotherhood, which had recently tethered itself to the Communist Party USA. According to McKay, the objective of the meeting was 'to discuss the possibility of making the Garvey Back-to-Africa Movement more class-conscious'.[69]

There are various notable things about McKay's account. First, that Harrison instigated the meeting. As biographer Jeff Perry so aptly put it, Harrison was not only 'the most race-conscious of the class radicals' in the Socialist Party, but subsequently 'the most class-conscious of the race radicals' in the Garvey movement. As noted earlier, Harrison vociferously defended the 'race first' position from attacks by his 'class first' Black socialist proteges, and in 1921 he refused a funding offer from Rose Pastor Stokes, on behalf of the Communist Party, to become the party's 'stalking horse' against Garvey. After his experience in the Socialist Party, Harrison was loathe to become beholden, politically or otherwise, to any white financial sponsor. Yet Harrison clearly concurred enough with their Marxist critique – of Garveyism as a petty-bourgeois movement for Black capitalism and Black empire – to initiate a discussion with the key Black Communists in Harlem about building class consciousness inside the Garvey movement. Harrison's discussions with 'Black Reds' undoubtedly helped stimulate the unsuccessful attempt by Cyril Briggs and the African Blood Brotherhood to push Garvey's second international UNIA convention in a left-wing direction later that same year.[70]

As a result of his experiences building the Socialist Party, the Liberty League, and now the Garvey movement, Harrison advanced a race-conscious and radical global political theory that built upon previous examples, yet broke fundamentally with them to produce a historically new – 'colored' – internationalism. This theoretical framework received its most sweeping, comprehensive, and politically advanced expression in a call to action Harrison wrote in 1921 for Garvey's *Negro World* entitled 'Wanted – A Colored International'.[71]

As we saw in his analysis of the 'white world war', Harrison located the global problems of imperialism and white domination in capitalism. Because white domination and imperialism were an international problem, it would require an international solution. In particular, 'a call should be issued for a congress of the darker races which should be frankly anti-imperialistic and should serve as an international centre of co-operation from which strength may be drawn for the several sections of the world of colour'. Harrison argued that this congress should include the voices of oppressed people from places like India, Egypt, China, West and South Africa, the West Indies, Hawaii, the Philippines, Afghanistan, Algeria, and Morocco. The congress 'should be made up of those who realise that capitalist imperialism which mercilessly exploits the darker races for its own financial purposes is the enemy which we must combine to fight with arms as varied as those by which it is fighting to destroy our manhood, independence and self-respect'. By his inclusion of armed struggle in the vision, Harrison here made clear that his was no half-hearted vision of revolution.

Despite his negative experience with white liberals and radicals in the Socialist Party, Harrison did not rule out working with white people who were genuine in their commitment to overturning systems of domination. As he put it, 'the international of the darker races must avail itself of whatever help it can get from those groups within the white race which are seeking to destroy the capitalist international of race prejudice and exploitation which is known as bourgeois "democracy" at home and colonial imperialism abroad'. Implicitly speaking to the Communist Party, Harrison allowed that if there were white workers who wanted to fight the system, they could be allies. However, whatever alliances were possible with white political forces had to be on Black-emancipatory terms. African Americans could not allow white leftists to break down Black racial solidarity, and 'until we can co-operate with them on our own terms we choose not to co-operate at all, but to pursue our own way of salvation'.

Harrison was unequivocal about the need for radical humility on the part of the white leftists: 'Sauce for the black goose ought to be sauce for the white gander, and the temporary revolutionists of today should show their sincerity by first breaking down the exclusion walls of white workingmen before they ask us to demolish our own defensive structures of racial self-protection.' In other words, African Americans had every right to put 'race first' – and white progressive voices had no business complaining about it – as long as the root problem of structural white supremacy remained intact. White radicals seeking collaboration across the colour line could demonstrate sincerity by first breaking down the racial superiority complex of white workers: 'Those who will meet us on our own ground will find that we recognise a common enemy in the present world order and are willing to advance to attack it in our joint behalf.' In other words, white radicals who demonstrated in practice their opposition to white supremacy could join forces with the Colored International for a common purpose.

Failing to transform the UNIA from within, Harrison eventually parted ways with the Garvey movement in 1922. By giving voice to its most politically engaged, anti-imperialist, and anti-capitalist elements, Harrison symbolised the Black radical wing of the Garvey movement officialdom, within its home base of Harlem. Harrison's commitment to Black people lay not with a particular leader or organisation, but as he put it retrospectively, with 'the principles of the New Negro Manhood Movement, a portion of which had been incorporated by [Garvey] and his followers of the UNIA and ACL'.[72] 'Incorporation' here referred to the chartering of Garvey's Black Star Line corporation (among other UNIA business enterprises) and an internal power structure and hierarchy that in modern parlance might be called 'corporatist'. In other words, if the UNIA represented the 'corporate sector' of the militant, First World War-era New Negro movement, then Garvey was its CEO. As an anti-capitalist and radical internationalist, Harrison naturally had a very different aspiration for New Negro politics, as compared with Garvey's dreams of a Black empire based on capital accumulation.

## Harrison's memory ... and erasure

Following his departure from the Garvey movement, Harrison's subsequent and final political project was the International Colored Unity League (ICUL), an organisation which he founded in 1924. The ICUL launched a campaign to establish branches across the country, raise money, and publish a magazine, the *Voice of the Negro*. By the end of 1925, the ICUL had some 550–600 members.[73] Despite Harrison's secular and agnostic world view, the ICUL programme demonstrated an explicit respect for (and desire to work with) churches, on account of their role in fostering cohesion in Black communities. Most notably, a distinguishing feature of the ICUL programme was the call for a separate Black state. This idea echoed the one raised by Cyril Briggs in 1919 and prefigured a similar demand in the 1960s by organisations like the Republic of New Africa, which called for a territorial resolution of the land question for African Americans.[74] On the grounds that 'America is ours and we are hers', Harrison conceived of the Black state as another one of the United States of America, rather than a separate country.[75]

Harrison died in December 1927, a mere eight months after the ICUL published its first issue of the *Voice of the Negro*. According to his biographer Jeff Perry, Harrison's family was always suspicious of Hubert's death, which ostensibly occurred from a routine appendicitis operation. Perhaps even more suspicious was his erasure over time from popular memory and history. Harlem activist Hodge Kirnon, writing two months after Harrison's death, noted how the prominent race magazines – *The Messenger*, *The Crisis*, and *Opportunity* – all failed to run obituaries and how the absence of any mention of him had become a subject of popular discussion in Harlem. 'This concerted silence is ominous', wrote Kirnon, 'it does appear that there is something wrong somewhere.'[76] Harlem resident and Harrison collaborator Edgar Gray offered an explanation of that something: 'Your big Negro newspapers and business houses, schools and other organisations who had positions allowed themselves to be so hateful that they would not hire [Harrison]. He died, yes, died for his convictions, but he died at 44, starved, underpaid, abused, hated by jealous men who feared the force of his mind and the immensity of his information.'[77] Harrison did not maintain any long-standing ties to any single organisation and his outspoken criticisms of prominent individuals and institutions and figures seems to have stung those who otherwise might have kept his memory alive.[78]

Inevitably, rediscovering Harrison's life and work raises questions about how and why he has been so thoroughly marginalised in history, given his importance during his lifetime. Some of the contributing factors include: his humility and visceral aversion to lavish praise, his economic poverty and lack of university degrees, the general lack of interest in Black radicalism among mainstream academic historians, his position as a Caribbean-born immigrant to the United States, and the failure of Harrison-conscious individual scholars and Harlem community members to overcome all of the preceding factors.[79]

A more complex reason for Harrison's historical erasure concerns the political genealogy of the so-called 'Harlem Renaissance'. Many of Harrison's achievements could be described, like they were at the time of his passing, as contributions to the 'New Negro movement'. However, Alain Locke's 1925 *New Negro* anthology effectively appropriated and rewrote the meaning of the 'New Negro movement' in terms of a 'Negro Renaissance' (later rebranded the '*Harlem* Renaissance') of Black artistic production. White liberal publishers like Paul Kellogg and Albert Boni contracted, financed, and ideologically vetted Locke's work. Locke and his sponsors deliberately removed Harrison and various other Black Marxist, Garveyist, and Black feminist voices from their 'Negro Renaissance' narrative in order to market a narrow and commercialised portrayal of 'the Negro' to white audiences. The 'Renaissance' peddlers thereby converted the common conception of the 'New Negro' from a race-radical, internationalist, working-class movement into a nonthreatening, patriotic, and elitist cultural fad for 'high art'. Harrison's own explicit and categorical rejection of the 'Renaissance' trope – combined with his deliberate exclusion by its architects – raises fundamental questions about the nature and meaning of the 'Harlem Renaissance', which remains the dominant conceptual framework for appraising the meaning and significance of the Black 'Mecca' of the early twentieth century.

Restoring Harrison to the history of the Black and Red Atlantic demonstrates his unique role as a spearhead of various political and intellectual transformations during the Black political awakening of his age. Speaking at Harrison's funeral, Black archivist and bibliophile Arturo Schomburg spoke of Harrison as being ahead of his time. In many ways, he remains ahead of ours too. For that reason, anyone seeking to better understand the emergence of Black Marxist, Pan-African, and Black (inter)nationalist radicalism in the twentieth century would do well to study the life and writings of Hubert Henry Harrison, whose hard-won political lessons and insights can only grow in importance as more insurgent uprisings of Black consciousness throughout the African diaspora continue in new forms today.

## Notes

1. Jarvis Anderson, *A. Philip Randolph: A Biographical Portrait* (New York: Harcourt Brace Jovanovich, 1973), 80.
2. Scholars here include people like Irma Watkins-Owens, John Henrik Clarke, Winston James, Joyce Moore Turner, Hakim Adi, Minkah Makalani, and Shelly Streeby.
3. Jeffrey B. Perry, *Hubert Harrison: The Voice of Harlem Radicalism, 1883–1918* (New York: Columbia University Press, 2009) and Jeffrey B. Perry (ed.), *A Hubert Harrison Reader* (Middletown, CT: Wesleyan University Press, 2001).
4. Here I think of scholars like J.A. Rogers, Richard B. Moore, Harold Cruse, Wilfred D. Samuels, Portia James, John G. Jackson, Philip Foner, Earnest Allen Jr, and Kevin K. Gaines.
5. Perry, *Hubert Harrison*, 39–46.
6. James W. Loewen, *Sundown Towns: A Hidden Dimension of American Racism* (New York: New Press, 2005); Elliot Jaspin, *Buried in the Bitter Waters: The Hidden History of Racial Cleansing in America* (New York: Basic Books, 2007); Cameron McWhirter, *Red Summer: The Summer of 1919 and the Awakening of Black America* (New York: Henry Holt, 2011); David F. Krugler, *1919, The Year of Racial Violence* (Cambridge: Cambridge University Press, 2015); Desmond King and Stephen Tuck, 'De-Centring the South: America's Nationwide White Supremacist Order After Reconstruction', *Past and Present*, 194:1 (2007), 213–253.
7. In the United States, poor and working-class whites formed a social control buffer between Black labour and white capital. In the Anglophone Caribbean, by contrast, a middle-class Black or Brown social layer performed this function. There, whites were a tiny minority and therefore relied upon socio-economic promotion of non-whites into positions of social management and administrative control. For this reason, the construction and function of race, though based on white superiority in both cases, remained fundamentally different. For more see Theodore W. Allen, *The Invention of the White Race*, Vol. 2 (London: Verso, 2012).
8. Winston James, *Holding Aloft the Banner of Ethiopia: Caribbean Radicalism in America, 1900–1932* (London: Verso, 1997), esp. chapters 1–3; Irma Watkins-Owens, *Blood Relations: Caribbean Immigrants and the Harlem Community, 1900–1930* (Bloomington, IN: Indiana University Press, 1996); Minkah Makalani, *In the Cause of Freedom: Radical Black Internationalism From Harlem to London, 1919–1939* (Chapel Hill, NC: University of North Carolina Press, 2011); Shannon King, *Whose Harlem is This, Anyway?: Community Politics and Grassroots Activism during the New Negro Era* (New York: New York Press, 2015).
9. Hubert Harrison, diary entry, 28 September 1914, Hubert Harrison Papers, 1893–1927, Rare Book and Manuscript Library, Columbia University Libraries (hereafter HHP), Box 9, diary 1; Perry, *Hubert Harrison*, 56.
10. Perry, *Hubert Harrison*, 87.

11 Irma Watkins-Owens, *Blood Relations*, 44, 49, 57. Joe W. Trotter, 'African American Fraternal Associations in American History: An Introduction', *Social Science History*, 28:3 (2004), 355–366.
12 Perry, *Hubert Harrison*, 70–78.
13 *Ibid.*, 83, 86.
14 *Ibid.*
15 In the first two decades of the twentieth century, labour organisations open to Black workers were few and far between. They included the Industrial Workers of the World, the United Mine Workers, the Brotherhood of Timber Workers in Louisiana, and the International Longshoremen's Association in New Orleans. But most of these 'integrated' unions failed to challenge the racially discriminatory divisions of labour within their industries. Eric Arnesen (ed.), *Encyclopedia of US Labor and Working-Class History*, Vol. 1 (New York: Routledge, 2007), 248.
16 Loewen, *Sundown Towns*.
17 Louis Harlan, *Booker T. Washington: The Making of a Black Leader, 1856–1901* (New York: Oxford University Press, 1972), 254.
18 Perry, *A Hubert Harrison Reader*, 164.
19 Hubert Harrison, 'Insistence upon Its Real Grievances the Only Course for the Race', *New York Sun*, 8 December 1910, 8.
20 See Perry, *Hubert Harrison*, 132–134.
21 Albert Fried (ed.), *Socialism in America: From the Shakers to the Third International: A Documentary History* (Garden City, NY: Doubleday, 1970), 12–15.
22 *Ibid.*, 382.
23 *Ibid.*, 387.
24 Eugene V. Debs, 'The Negro in the Class Struggle', *International Socialist Review*, November 1903, reprinted in *Writings and Speeches of Eugene V. Debs* (New York: Hermitage Press, 1948), 66–69.
25 *Ibid.*, 133–134.
26 Perry, *A Hubert Harrison Reader*, 51–52.
27 Hubert Harrison, 'Socialism and the Negro', *International Socialist Review*, 13 (July 1912).
28 Harrison, 'Socialism and the Negro', 65–68.
29 Hubert Harrison, 'Race Prejudice – II', *New York Call*, 4 December 1911, 6.
30 Perry, *Hubert Harrison*, 193.
31 Philip S. Foner, *American Socialism and Black Americans: From the Age of Jackson to World War II* (Westport, CT: Greenwood Press, 1977); Nikki M. Taylor, *America's First Black Socialist: The Radical Life of Peter H. Clark* (Lexington, KY: University Press of Kentucky, 2013).
32 Romansky to Gerber, 12 October 1911. The Socialist Party Papers of Local New York, Reel 6. New York University.
33 Foner, *American Socialism and Black Americans*, 207–215. Perry, *Hubert Harrison*, 166–172, 175–176.
34 Perry, *Hubert Harrison*, 170.

35 W.E. McDermut, assisted by C.W. Phillips, ed. J. Spargo, *National Convention of the Socialist Party Held at Indianapolis, Ind., May 12 to May 18, 1912* (Chicago, IL, 1912), 209–210, quoted in Hubert Harrison, *When Africa Awakes: The 'Inside Story' of the Stirrings and Strivings of the New Negro in the Western World* (New York: Porro Press, 1920), 81–82.
36 'Harrison Lecture', Elizabeth, NJ, 7 December 1912. HHP, flat box 740.
37 Steve Golin, *The Fragile Bridge: Paterson Silk Strike, 1913* (Philadelphia, PA: Temple University Press, 1988).
38 'Sabotage Coming in Silk Mills if Boyd Is Jailed: Negro Agitator Shouts That if Paterson Owners Want to Lose $200,000, Let Them Go Ahead', *New York World*, 1 December 1913, HHP, flat box 740.
39 Golin, *The Fragile Bridge*, 145–146.
40 *New York Call*, circa 29 January 1914, HHP, flat box 740.
41 Perry, *Hubert Harrison*, 190, 209, 212, 216–218.
42 John Henrik Clarke, 'Introduction' to Hubert Harrison, *When Africa Awakes* (Baltimore, MD: Black Classic Press, 1997), vi.
43 Hubert Harrison, 'Our Civic Corner', *New York News*, 9 February 1915, HHP, box 13, folder 2.
44 Perry, *Hubert Harrison*, 272 and 406n.27.
45 Michelle Ann Stephens, *Black Empire: The Masculine Global Imaginary of Caribbean Intellectuals in the United States, 1914–1962* (Durham, NC: Duke University Press, 2005), 8.
46 Hubert Harrison, 'Resolutions Passed at the Liberty League Meeting' in *The Negro and the Nation* (New York: Cosmo Advocate Publishing Company, 1917), 11–12.
47 Hubert Harrison, 'Resolutions', *The Voice* (New York, 19 Sept 1917), reprinted as 'Resolutions Passed at the Liberty League Meeting' in *When Africa Awakes* (New York: Porro Press, 1920), 9–13, at 11–12.
48 Harrison, *When Africa Awakes*, 58.
49 Perry, *Hubert Harrison*, 2.
50 H. Harrison, 'Some Reasons Why Such a Collection is Necessary', [undated c.1925], HHP, box 6, folder 28.
51 Harrison, *When Africa Awakes*, 5.
52 Hubert Harrison, 'The White War and the Colored World', *The Voice*, 14 August 1917, in Perry, *A Hubert Harrison Reader*, 202.
53 V.I. Lenin, 'The Socialist Revolution and the Right of Nations to Self-Determination', *Collected Works*, Vol. 22 (Moscow: Progress Publishers, 1960), 143–156.
54 Hubert Harrison, 'The White War and the Colored Races', *New Negro*, 4 (October 1919), 8–10. Harrison, *When Africa Awakes*, 116.
55 Harrison, *When Africa Awakes*, 113–114.
56 Hubert Harrison, 'Education and the Race' in *When Africa Awakes* (New York, Porro Press, 1920), 123–134, at 126–127.
57 W.H. Loving to the Director of Military Intelligence, 'Report of mass meeting during January 1919', 17 February 1919, reprinted in Robert A. Hill (ed.), *The*

*Marcus Garvey and Universal Negro Improvement Association Papers*, Vol. 1 (Berkeley, CA: University of California Press, 1983), 363.
58  Harrison, *When Africa Awakes*, 119, 121.
59  W.A. Edwards, 'Garveyism: Organizing the Masses or Mass Organization?' in Rupert Lewis and Patrick E. Bryan (eds), *Garvey: His Work and Impact* (Trenton, NJ: Africa World Press, 1991), 218.
60  (Author unknown), 'Garvey's Speech', Collegiate Hall, 25 March 1921, John Henrik Clarke Papers, folder: correspondence with Robert Hill, and 'Reception Given Marcus Garvey', *Gleaner*, 24 March 1921; Robert A. Hill (ed.), *The Marcus Garvey and Universal Negro Improvement Association Papers*, Vol. 3 (Berkeley, CA: University of California Press, 1984), 275.
61  'Reporter Sues Garvey', *Chicago Defender*, 28 September 1918, reprinted in Hill, *The Marcus Garvey and Universal Negro Improvement Association Papers*, Vol. 1, 282. Anselmo R. Jackson, 'Analysis of the Black Star Line', *Emancipator*, 27 March 1920; Colin Grant, *Negro with a Hat: The Rise and Fall of Marcus Garvey* (Oxford: Oxford University Press, 2008), 95.
62  Following the pioneering work of Garvey movement scholars like Amy Jacques Garvey, Tony Martin, Robert Hill, Rupert Lewis, E.D. Cronon, John Henrik Clarke, Theodore Vincent, and Judith Stein, more recent studies have expanded our sense of the vast breadth of the movement. For recent studies on Garveyism in the south, see Mary Rolinson, *Grassroots Garveyism: The Universal Negro Improvement Association in the Rural South* (Chapel Hill, NC: University of North Carolina Press, 2007); Claudrena N. Harold, *The Rise and Fall of the Garvey Movement in the Urban South, 1918–1942* (New York: Routledge, 2007). For women in the Garvey movement, see Ula Y. Taylor, *The Veiled Garvey: The Life and Times of Amy Jacques Garvey* (Chapel Hill, NC: University of North Carolina Press, 2002); Tony Martin, *Amy Ashwood Garvey: Pan-Africanist, Feminist, and Mrs Marcus Garvey no. 1, or A Tale of Two Amies* (Dover, MA: Majority Press, 2007); Nzingha Assata, *Women in the Garvey Movement* (Mitcham: N. Assata, 2008). For recent studies on the impact of Garveyism abroad, see Adam Ewing and Ronald J. Stephens (eds), *Global Garveyism* (Gainesville, FL: University Press of Florida, 2019); Adam Ewing, *Age of Garvey: How a Jamaican Activist Created a Mass Movement and Changed Global Black Politics* (Princeton, NJ: Princeton University Press, 2014); Frank A. Guridy, *Forging Diaspora: Afro-Cubans and African Americans in a World of Empire and Jim Crow* (Chapel Hill, NC: University of North Carolina Press, 2010); Robert T. Vinson, *The Americans Are Coming!: Dreams of African American Liberation in Segregationist South Africa* (Athens, OH: Ohio University Press, 2012); Grant, *Negro With A Hat*.
63  Wilson Jeremiah Moses, *The Golden Age of Black Nationalism, 1850–1925* (Hamden, CT: Archon Books, 1978), 197–198.
64  For more on Harrison's seminal role in stimulating the rise of the Garvey movement, see Brian Kwoba, 'Pebbles and Ripples: Hubert Harrison and the Rise of the Garvey Movement', *Journal of African American History*, 105:3 (2020), 1–28.

65　Hubert Harrison, 'Wednesday March 17, 1920' (diary entry), reprinted in Perry, *A Hubert Harrison Reader*, 183.
66　For the socialists' case, see 'Opinion of Owen & Randolph Editors of the "Messenger"', *Emancipator*, 3 April 1920; W.A. Domingo, 'Race First Versus Class First', *Emancipator*, 3 April 1920. For Harrison's case, see Harrison, *When Africa Awakes*, 55; Hubert Harrison, 'Race First Versus Class First', *Negro World*, 27 March 1920; Hubert Harrison, 'Just Crabs', *Negro World*, April 1920; and Hubert Harrison, 'An Open Letter to the Socialist Party of New York City', *Negro World*, 8 May 1920. Harrison's articles are reprinted in Perry, *A Hubert Harrison Reader*, 107, 109–110, 113.
67　Here, I use 'queer' in the same sense that the academic discipline of Queer Studies does. E. Patrick Johnson and Mae G. Henderson (eds), *Black Queer Studies: A Critical Anthology* (Durham, NC: Duke University Press, 2005).
68　'Claude M'Kay, African Poet, Made Co-Editor', *Chicago Defender*, 2 April 1921, 1.
69　Claude McKay, *A Long Way From Home* (New Brunswick, NJ: Rutgers University Press, 2007), 89.
70　Robert A. Hill (ed.), *The Marcus Garvey and Universal Negro Improvement Association Papers*, Vol. 2. (Berkeley, CA: University of California Press, 1983), 681–682n.1; Robert A. Hill (ed.), *The Crusader*, Vol. 1 (New York: Garland Publishing, 1987), xli. For Briggs's account of the ABB experience at the 1921 UNIA convention, see Cyril V. Briggs, 'The Negro Convention', *The Toiler*, 4 (New York, 1 October 1921), 13–14, www.marxisthistory.org/history/usa/groups/abb/1921/1001-briggs-negroconv.pdf (accessed 3 August 2021).
71　Hubert Harrison, 'Wanted – A Colored International', *Negro World*, 28 May 1921, reprinted in Perry, *A Hubert Harrison Reader*, 223–228. All the quotes in this section are taken from this source, unless otherwise noted.
72　Harrison, *When Africa Awakes*, 55.
73　Harrison to A. Hillard, 27 December 1925, HHP, box 2, folder 2.
74　Hill, *The Crusader*; Christian Davenport, *How Social Movements Die: Repression and Demobilization of the Republic of New Africa* (New York: Cambridge University Press, 2015).
75　'Program and Principles of the International Colored Unity League', *Voice of the Negro*, 1:1 (April 1927), reprinted in Perry, *A Hubert Harrison Reader*, 399.
76　Hodge Kirnon, 'Kirnon Flays Monthly Magazines', *New York News*, 28 February 1928. HHP, box 18, folder 8.
77　Edgar M. Gray, 'Why Great Negroes Die Young', *New York News*, 31 December 1927.
78　Perry, *Hubert Harrison*, 13–14.
79　Here I must honour and give thanks to those who have worked to preserve Harrison's memory, including people like Rev. Ethelred Brown, J.A. Rogers, Richard B. Moore, Harold Cruse, Philip Foner, Wilfred D. Samuels, Portia James, John G. Jackson, Jeff Perry, Ernest Allen Jr, Irma Watkins-Owens, John Henrik Clarke, Winston James, Joyce Moore Turner, and Thabiti Asukile.

# 2

# Wilfred Domingo under investigation: the 'Negro menace' of 1919

*Peter Hulme*

At 2.30 on the afternoon of Saturday 21 June 1919, agents acting for the Lusk Committee raided the Rand School of Social Science in New York City and seized a large quantity of papers suspected of encouraging sedition. A week later the committee announced that the greatest menace disclosed by the evidence bore the signature of a black Jamaican called W.A. Domingo. Domingo had a growing reputation in the black community in Harlem, based on his association first with the pre-eminent black radical of the time, Hubert Harrison, then with the flamboyant Marcus Garvey, and most recently with the socialists Chandler Owen and A. Philip Randolph; but he had not previously been on the radar either of the groups hunting subversives or of the mainstream New York press. By the end of the year, however, Wilfred Adolphus Domingo was a name being conjured by the New York State Senate, the United States Bureau of Investigation, and British Secret Service. He was soon editing his own newspaper, writing articles and editorials that were shaping black opinion in New York; and he would eventually become one of the most influential figures in the movement for Jamaican independence. While offering a brief sketch of Domingo's life and career, this chapter focuses on New York in 1919, when, as matters of race forced their way onto the socialist agenda in the aftermath of the Russian Revolution, Wilfred Domingo was very definitely under investigation.[1]

Wilfred Domingo belonged to that extraordinary generation of black Jamaicans born in the 1880s who had such an influence on New York and the Caribbean – and indeed beyond – in the first half of the twentieth century. He was just two months younger than Claude McKay and two years younger than Marcus Garvey, who he knew in Kingston when they were teenagers. In New York these three were joined by many others, including Joel A. Rogers, a prodigious researcher and writer, and James S. Watson, who became the city's first black judge.[2]

Born illegitimate in Kingston on 26 November 1889 to the second family of Francisco Domingo, reputedly Spanish but possibly Cuban, Wilfred never knew his mother, Alice Grant, who died when he was three, and he was brought up, initially in St Ann's Bay on the north coast, then in Kingston, by his mother's brother, Adolphus E. Grant, a master butcher.[3] While working as a bookkeeper in Kingston, Domingo was drawn into S.A.G. Cox's National Club, a political movement which shook up the colonial status quo for a couple of years. He and Garvey both served as secretaries for the group and together – it seems – wrote a pamphlet called *The Struggling Mass*, no copy of which has survived.[4] In August 1910 Domingo moved to Boston where one of his sisters ran a boarding house for Jamaicans. He attended night school there before moving to New York in 1912, where he worked in a variety of menial jobs while trying to establish an import business, and then during the war he worked for the Post Office. He may already have known fellow West Indians, Richard B. Moore (Barbados) and Cyril Briggs (Nevis): he certainly worked with them as part of Hubert Harrison's Liberty League, and Domingo's first piece of writing was for the opening issue in September 1917 of *The Clarion*, which published the 'Declaration of Principles of Liberty League of Negro Americans'.[5] By this time, however, Garvey had settled on New York as the new home for his organisation, the Universal Negro Improvement Association, and was beginning to compete with Harrison for followers: in August 1918 *Negro World* launched, with Domingo as its editor. Increasingly drawn by reports of the Russian Revolution, Domingo also worked with Chandler Owen and A. Philip Randolph in 1918 on the short-lived newspaper, *Negro Worker*. Soon, Domingo's socialist-leaning editorials in *Negro World* started upsetting Garvey and, refusing to boost the Black Star Line, Domingo resigned in July 1919 from *Negro World*, becoming associate editor on *The Messenger*, run by Owen and Randolph.[6]

The first half of 1919 had been a fraught time in New York which, with the war now in some sense over, was – at least for the moment – a very inward-looking city. Things had started to come to a boil on May Day with vigilante attacks on socialist and radical targets in New York, led by returning soldiers, the press whipping up anti-foreigner hysteria. The Rand School of Social Science (7 East 15th Street) was one of the targets, the fourth time it had been attacked since the Armistice. F. Scott Fitzgerald used the events of that night for his early short story, 'May Day'.[7] The Rand School belonged to the American Socialist Society, running adult education and training classes as well as housing various organisations and individuals associated with the Socialist Party of America – which was having its own fraught time in the summer of 1919. Elsewhere in the country racial violence flared, with several hundred black people killed in Chicago and Washington, DC and in rural Arkansas, leading James Weldon Johnson to call it the 'Red Summer'.[8]

After the Armistice, private vigilante bodies such as the American Protective League, originally set up to counter German espionage in New York, started to look for new targets: the anarchists, labour agitators, and radical socialists usually referred to in the round as Reds or Bolsheviki. The war was only *in some sense* over because in 1919 the USA was still formally in a state of war with Germany (as it in fact remained until the summer of 1921), which meant that wartime legislation was still in force throughout 1919. It was also the case that many official and unofficial agents of the US state saw the Bolsheviki as German-inspired revolutionists, so that for them the campaigns of 1919 were just a continuation of the war with Germany.

That was certainly the case with Archibald Stevenson, a lawyer who during the war had been the Director of the Military Information Division's Bureau of Propaganda. He had wanted to continue his work at federal level but the US Senate refused him authorisation, so he held his own investigation of radicalism in New York City under the auspices of the private Union League Club, still today one of the most exclusive of New York clubs. The Union League Club then petitioned the State of New York, which set up a Joint Legislative Committee Investigating Seditious Activities in the State of New York, chaired by junior State Senator Clayton R. Lusk – hence the Lusk Committee – with these terms of reference:

> Whereas, it is a matter of public knowledge that there is a large number of persons within the State of New York engaged in circulating propaganda calculated to set in motion forces to overthrow the Government of this State and the United States ...
>
> Now, Therefore, Be It Resolved, That a joint committee of the Senate and Assembly be, and hereby is, created to consist of four members of the Senate to be appointed by the Temporary President of the Senate, and five members of the Assembly, to be appointed by the Speaker of the Assembly, of which joint committee the Temporary President of the Senate and the Speaker of the Assembly shall be members ex-officio, to investigate the scope, tendencies, and ramifications of such seditious activities and to report the result of its investigation to the Legislature.[9]

Stevenson offered himself as unpaid special counsel: he was basically an unelected zealot who was prepared to do the hard work and so allowed to drive the agenda. He also knew the importance of publicity for influencing public opinion, so before the raid on the Rand School he made sure to acquire credentials for twenty-four reporters, along with the three furniture removal vans used to carry away the confiscated documents. Most of the raiders were members of the private American Protection League. This was no targeted raid: basically they took away every piece of paper they could find and then proceeded to read through it all, looking for signs of subversion. The front-page report in the *New York Times* on 22 June included the subheads: 'Revolution Openly Urged' and 'Bloodshed is Predicted in Change of Government'.[10] Just a week later Stevenson was ready to make public what he called the 'worst' of the evidence, which he did at a public hearing. This 'worst' turned out to be, in Stevenson's words, a 'startling plan for the organisation of the negroes into radical units' written by W.A. Domingo. The quite lengthy document was read out and, according to the *New York Times*, members of the committee 'expressed amazement'. As well they might, since this time the *New York Times* subheads included 'Planned Negro Uprising'.[11] Close reading was apparently not part of the skillset of the members of the Lusk Committee since nowhere in the piece in question did Domingo refer to anything that might be construed as a 'planned negro uprising'.

So just what was this piece of writing seized by the Lusk Committee that led to Wilfred Domingo being named as such a dangerous subversive? 'Socialism Imperilled, or the Negro – A Potential Menace to American Radicalism' – a piece of writing which, ironically, only survives at all because it was read into the evidence of the Lusk Committee and published in its findings – seems to have been intended as a policy document, written with some sophistication, both stylistic and political.[12] The idea of the black American as a potential menace to socialism had been raised by Hubert Harrison as early as 1912; and it was no accident that, just as Domingo was finishing his piece, the editors of *The Messenger* published an editorial in May 1919 called 'The Negro – A Menace to Radicalism'.[13] Randolph, Owen, and Domingo were – one can safely assume – on the same page because they'd already been in the same rooms discussing how to get the Socialist Party of America (SPA) to take matters of race seriously.[14]

This, then, was very much a strategy document, aimed at getting policymakers in the SPA to think about the threat that the absence of black members might ultimately pose to the socialist project. Showing an awareness of the importance of ideology, Domingo began with the statement that no reliance should be placed on the dogmatic assumption that oppressed groups would arrive at an instinctive understanding of how best to act in their own interests: 'Tactics based upon such a fallacious premise must, and will, result in a catastrophe to those who so calculate, for at the bottom it rests upon no firmer basis than that the wish is the father of the thought' (1490). What perhaps is most striking about the document was Domingo's authorial stance. He *observed* the current struggle between left and right within the SPA and analysed their respective positions with regard to the question of race, but you couldn't easily gauge his own position, except perhaps through an obvious admiration for what he called the 'statesmanlike farsightedness' (1492) manifest in the colour-blind perspective offered by the Industrial Workers of the World, and for a suggestion that the left wing of the party didn't understand the existence of group psychology. More surprisingly perhaps, you couldn't tell Domingo's colour from his syntax: in talking about 'negroes', he never used the pronoun 'we'. He situated himself, from a narrative point of view, in an almost ethnographic position, which gave his piece some of its rhetorical power: he never seemed to be arguing a special and personal case. This may have had something to do with his West Indian origins: he could analyse the US situation from the outside.

Domingo was critical of the SPA's focus on industrial centres and its neglect of the South. He explained Southern black distrust of white socialists by the sway of black churches presided over by the graduates of schools endowed by Northern white philanthropists who ensured that their curricula were dominated by capitalist values.[15] He explained how white workers and black were turned against each other, partly by the press, partly by entrenched racial attitudes. If this was to be transformed, Domingo wrote, then the SPA should begin by taking cognisance of the ingredients of 'negro' ideology, however contradictory and illogical they seemed to be.

The potential 'menace' of Domingo's title came from the danger that because black people tended to be better disposed to the white *upper* classes, they could be used as – and here Domingo deployed a very contemporary reference – 'black White Guards': reactionary troops used to defend the status quo against radical change, and against their own best interests.[16] At this point he sketched a possible scenario ('Let it be supposed ...' [1492]) in which a socialist president won the election, but in the four months before the socialist government took power the bourgeoisie organised a coup, for which it would turn to the South, to both whites and blacks, with the result that a Southern black militia could end up shooting Northern white workers. The detail provided is impressive:

> The scene for the general strike is set. Enthusiastic leaders fondly believe that this mass action will be transformed into mass movement and lay their plans accordingly. The strike is declared, but the plutocracy already anticipating every move on the part of the proletariat declares martial law, quickly mobilises thousands of negroes and uses them as slave drivers to compel unwilling white working men to return to the shops, mines and farms. (1503)

A left-wing attempt to establish a dictatorship of the proletariat would, wrote Domingo, have the same outcome. To avoid such 'imaginative pictures' (1504) becoming reality, he suggested, the SPA needed to make black Americans class conscious, and that could only happen as a result of an ambitious programme, which Domingo laid out, including making more of an effort to attract black activists into SPA membership, giving financial support to radical black publications, working to repeal racially discriminatory practices in labour organisations, and paying competent black speakers to tour the country (1504–5).

The need for this kind of tactical thinking, Domingo suggested, was validated by 'the willingness of Lenin to adjust his tactics to existing conditions provided there is no sacrifice of principle involved' (1501). Lenin 'uses realities, not theories to cope with the facts of a given situation' (1501), a lesson, Domingo implied, which the warring factions of the SPA needed to learn. That it would be in their interests to do so constituted his final argument, which came close to an open critique of the people who would be reading his document and deciding whether to publish it. 'It is clear', Domingo wrote, 'that the national leaders and the rank and file of the party do not comprehend their peril' (1509). Instead, 'they sentimentally flirt with the far distant problems of India and China in blissful disregard of the material fact that they will never be in a position to render tangible aid to these oppressed peoples until they succeed in making allies out of American negroes' (1509). Perhaps, Domingo suggested, white American radicals share the typical white American psychology towards blacks: 'If this is so, then their radicalism is not genuine and is deservedly doomed to failure' (1509).

Although it suited Stevenson to treat Domingo's piece as Rand School policy, it turns out that it wasn't. The *New York Times* had reported on the Lusk Committee's public hearing. The following day, the Rand School's secretary, Bertha Mailly, wrote to the *Times* to point out how misleading Stevenson's presentation had been, since it neglected to say that Domingo's essay had been taken from the desk of the editor of the Rand School publication committee, David Berenberg, along with a self-addressed stamped envelope and a letter of rejection. Far from being indicative of the American Socialist Society's views, Mailly pointed out, Domingo's essay had been rejected. It turns out that this wasn't quite true either. As Winston James noted, also among the seized documentation was a letter from Berenberg to a correspondent in Pittsburgh happily quoting Domingo's views:

> We have here a very active group of comrades – among them Comrades Chandler Owen and Domingo – who warn us that unless we make headway with the negroes, the capitalists may use them in time of a social revolution much as the Czecho-Slovaks are being used in Russia.[17]

In fact, Berenberg had written to Domingo suggesting that he come into the Rand School to talk about how to proceed, but at the time of the raid hadn't got round to sending the letter – which the Lusk Committee seized, but didn't publish.[18] So Domingo's pamphlet hadn't been accepted, but it hadn't been rejected.

In these precise months the SPA was in the process of tearing itself apart, and Berenberg – along with most of the other key players at the Rand School – belonged to its right wing: those who would remain after John Reed led the left-wing exodus into competing Communist organisations later that year. At this time Berenberg was editing the newspaper he'd just founded, called the *New York Socialist*, which was a response to the *New York Communist*, which John Reed had started in April.[19] This internecine struggle was undoubtedly absorbing most of Berenberg's attention. He probably didn't read Domingo's essay very carefully: questions of race would have seemed irrelevant to him in May and June 1919.

Also among the Lusk Committee papers, and also *not* reproduced in its four-volume report, is the letter Domingo had sent to Berenberg along with his essay. Perhaps one key as to why the essay did not find immediate favour lies in Domingo's suggestion that if the pamphlet were to be produced, it might carry endorsements from some important figures. 'For the pamphlet to be a success in rousing radicals to their danger', he wrote, 'it is necessary that it reach Anarchists, Lefts, Centres, Rights, and even Liberals.'[20] At the moment of the radicals' greatest fissiparousness, Domingo saw the larger picture, and the danger that could result from a lack of attention to questions of race. But the Socialist Party was just not listening.[21]

Seven other pieces from the frantic summer of 1919, all written by Domingo but two not carrying his name, give a sense of his interests and priorities at this crucial juncture, providing a context for the Rand document. A leader in the *Negro World* of 14 June, no copy of which has survived, is reported to have 'openly counselled negroes' to turn to Lenin and the Bolsheviks for assistance against their real oppressors, such as David Lloyd George, Woodrow Wilson, and Georges Clemenceau.[22] This piece may, Robert Hill surmises, have contributed to Garvey's attempt to sack Domingo as editor of *Negro World*.[23] However, matters of race were also clearly on Domingo's mind in these months as the first piece he published in *The Messenger* offered his well-informed argument in favour of the use of the term 'Negro' rather than 'colored'.[24] This dual focus continued. A piece in *The Messenger* in July 1919 called 'Socialism the Negroes' Hope' was a shorter companion piece to 'Socialism Imperilled', addressed to his black readership. There he decried the tendency of US blacks to 'cling to past and present economic ideals with the desperation of a dying man' and urged them to look at examples from around the world of the broadness of the socialist vision towards all oppressed humanity.[25] And yet a week later, on 26 July, in perhaps his last editorial for *Negro World*, Domingo – clearly responding to the terrible events of those summer months – concluded: 'In a world of wolves one should go armed, and one of the most powerful defensive weapons within the reach of negroes is the practice of race first in all parts of the world.'[26]

This editorial was reprinted the following year in the same newspaper by Hubert Harrison, who had taken over the editorship.[27] Colin Grant argues – probably correctly – that Harrison republished the editorial in order to embarrass Domingo, who by 1920 was attacking Garvey; but Domingo always claimed that in many respects he agreed with Garvey's *ideas*, and certainly his constant quotation of Claude McKay's poem, 'If We Must Die', suggested a similar sentiment: a piece with that title, and quoting McKay's poem, appeared in *The Messenger* in September, Domingo paraphrasing the poem: 'If death is to be their portion, New Negroes are determined to make their dying a costly investment for all concerned. If they must die they are determined that they shall not travel through the valley of the shadow of death alone, but that some of their oppressors shall be their companions.' But then he followed up in the very same number with an essay asking 'Did Bolshevism Stop Race Riots in Russia?'[28] The Red and Black threads were being wound tightly together in Domingo's writing. In September 1919, *The Crusader* announced the formation of a new group called the African Blood Brotherhood, to serve as a self-defence organisation for blacks threatened by race riots and lynchings: Domingo became a member.[29]

There was, however, a third strand to Domingo's thought running through 1919. A March editorial in *Negro World* showed that part of his attention was still on the West Indies:

> It is the duty of West Indians of light and leading who are domiciled in foreign countries to lead in the demand for a West Indian renaissance. They should not be satisfied with mere assertions of loyalty to any particular country, for they owe a higher loyalty to the islands where they were born. Therefore we suggest that these men and women get together now, even as the Irish, Czecho-Slovaks, Alsatians, Poles and Hindoos have done, and begin to formulate plans for the betterment of the respective islands. This is not the time to be laggards; it is the time to be up and doing. WEST INDIANS, WAKE UP![30]

The opportunity here lay in the notion of 'self-determination', initially outlined by Lenin in October 1916 and articulated by the new provisional government in Moscow – under the influence of the Bolshevik-controlled Petrograd soviet – in April 1917.[31] Trotsky had then prominently denounced the hypocrisy of Western countries – including the USA – in claiming to fight for the rights of small nations in Europe while oppressing other national groups within their empires.[32] On the back foot, the Allies had started to adopt the same terminology. In January 1918 Lloyd George spoke about the need for the post-war settlement to respect 'the right of self-determination or the consent of the governed'.³³ Wilson's address to Congress on 11 February 1918 (the 'Four Points' speech) was crystal clear: 'In the coming settlement', he said, 'national aspirations must be respected; people may be dominated and governed only by their own consent ... "Self-determination" is not a mere phrase. It is an imperative principle of actions which statesmen will henceforth ignore at their peril.'³⁴ However, when the crunch came, at the Paris Peace Conference in the winter of 1918–19, Wilson made it very clear that self-determination was going to be ignored when it came to colonies. Domingo's response was a forensic Leninist analysis of why colonies are essential to the maintenance of capitalism: 'With the death of capitalism in the Mother or central country, will come the collapse of imperialism and its train [of] murder, high taxes, poverty, oppression and exploitation in the Colonies.'³⁵

Domingo's writing about colonialism did not go unnoticed. Given that a significant number of the black Reds in New York were West Indians, and therefore British citizens, the British Secret Intelligence Service (SIS) took a lively interest in their activities. An SIS office had been operative in New York since late 1915, originally concerned with German activity but latterly with Irish and Indian revolutionaries in the city. Just before the raid on the Rand School, one of the Lusk Committee's Russian translators jumped ship and gave an interview in which he said that the driving force behind the Lusk Committee was actually an Englishman called Robert Nathan. Nathan was an SIS agent who previously had been the police commissioner in Dhaka, suppressing Bengali revolutionaries. *His* contact, it turns out, was Raymond Finch, an American who had recently resigned from the Bureau of Investigation and was now both employed by Nathan – and so a British agent – *and* working as a special investigator for the Lusk Committee.³⁶ It's probably not therefore surprising that the British were interested in a Bureau of Investigation report by the African-American Walter Loving, a copy of which was sent by the SIS to London – where it was helpfully edited and sent back to the US State Department in October 1919.³⁷ Major Loving, a talented cornetist, had had a distinguished career in military music, leading the Philippine Constabulary Band and playing at the inauguration parade of President Taft in 1909. Charged with investigating subversive activities by African-American leaders, he attended rallies in plain clothes and developed a network of agents, but was clearly known to – and to a degree respected by – at least some of those leaders. He certainly assisted Hubert Harrison in upsetting W.E.B. Du Bois's plans to get an army commission, and his reports are usually respectful and insightful.³⁸ In this 'Final Report' he wrote that Domingo was 'a very able young man of West Indian birth. It was Mr Domingo who drafted the plan of campaign of the Socialist Party among Negroes.' It is perhaps telling that the British version, while keeping the substance, left out the 'very', left out the 'Mr', and lowered the uppercase initial letter in 'Negroes'.[39]

In the spring of 1920 Domingo started his own newspaper, the *Emancipator*, which only survived for seven issues. For a while he continued writing for *The Messenger* but fell out with Randolph and Owen over their anti-West Indian remarks made in the course of their campaign against Garvey – which Domingo had supported. Domingo had had to put his import business on hold during the war, but he now seemed to have limited his journalistic activities in order to concentrate on making a living: he had married in 1919, shortly before the birth of his son, and a daughter would follow in 1926.[40] However, during the mid-1920s he did write two long and authoritative essays about West Indians in New York, the first of which appeared in the *Survey Graphic* 'Harlem' issue and then in the landmark anthology, *The New Negro*; the second in *Opportunity*.[41] Unlike many of the other prominent members of the African Blood Brotherhood, Domingo did not join the Communist Party of America (CPA), but his Bolshevik sympathies remained strong. He was, for example, chair of the New York committee raising funds to send black actors to the Soviet Union for the ill-fated film *Black and White*: there is a photograph of him alongside the departing actors.[42]

From the mid-1930s, however, Domingo focused his energies on the movement for Jamaican independence, initially founding the Harlem-based organisation, the Jamaica Progressive League, alongside Walter Adolphe Roberts, and then playing an important role in Jamaica in the formation of the People's National Party (PNP).[43] Invited to Jamaica in 1941 by Norman Manley to work for the PNP, Domingo was locked up by the British authorities in a concentration camp in Kingston for twenty months and, after his release, the FBI ensured that he had to wait four years to get a visa to return to New York, describing him as having 'an unsavory record of radical activities and active agitation' and as being 'one of the chief trouble-makers among the negroes'.[44] Then, while many black leftists such as C.L.R. James, Claudia Jones, and Domingo's old friend Richard B. Moore supported the West Indies Federation, Domingo campaigned against it: along with Roberts, he kept up a barrage of letters and pamphlets and broadcasts arguing that Jamaica should first become a sovereign independent nation, which eventually happened, on 6 August 1962, not long before Domingo suffered the stroke which incapacitated him.[45]

It has never proved easy to get a handle on W.A. Domingo. He joined the Socialist Party, probably in 1918, and remained a staunch leftist but didn't follow his friends, Cyril Briggs and Richard B. Moore, into the CPA. He fell out with Marcus Garvey and then with Chandler and Owen, leading Harold Cruse to accuse him of being an 'Afro-Britisher', a

Figure 2.1 Wilfred A. Domingo in debate, 1940. Left to right: Wilfred A. Domingo, Joel Augustus Rogers, Richard B. Moore and George Weston

charge laid waste by Winston James.[46] Nonetheless, Domingo's career as a businessman, which obviously at times took a considerable effort, and his failure to explain himself in an autobiography or memoir, has left him a rather shadowy figure. The most recent assessment, by Margaret Stevens, sees him as a 'political chameleon', a term that arguably captures something of Domingo's ability to move relatively unscathed, apart from that detention in Kingston, through some turbulent decades, consistently active and yet rarely committed to a single clearly identifiable position.[47] But the term 'chameleon' is undoubtedly an accusation. Its established metaphorical usage is to refer to assimilated Jews who take on the characteristics of the culture they inhabit so successfully that they forget to be Jewish: Woody Allen's film *Zelig* is the classic exploration of that phenomenon. And to refer to somebody as an animal whose main feature is an ability to change their skin colour does seem particularly charged in the context of racial politics. The comparison has a long history in the English language and its moral implications are almost always negative: chameleons adapt their views in changing circumstances, often as a way of toadying to authority – toadying being an analogous reptilian metaphor.

The implication is of a lack of sincerity: we admire somebody who sticks to their true colours. The animal metaphor overlaps with the naval one. Pirates sail under false colours; every other ship carries true colours. But what are a chameleon's true colours? All of its many hues are in one sense true. But we don't trust 'many truths'; we need one. Ultimately, the description does less than justice to Domingo's activities and writings and ignores the kinds of political agency he shaped during his negotiation of a variety of very different historical situations.

Of his contemporaries, Domingo is perhaps closest to the slightly older Hubert Harrison, both in background – Harrison came to the USA as an impoverished 17-year-old orphan in 1900 – and in politics: socialist, but highly race conscious; aware of the attraction of Garvey's ideas, but impatient with the man's vanity and incompetence. Domingo was radicalised by Harrison in the Liberty League days and always admired him. Like Harrison 'he had no long-term, sustaining and identifying relationship with any organisation or institution, and so lacked the recognition and support that would have come with such a tie'.[48] But unlike with Harrison, there is no trove of papers and diaries and scrapbooks of the kind that have enabled Jeffrey Perry to write a more than 1,500-page biography. And, unlike Harrison, Domingo seems to have shunned the limelight: there are very few photographs of him, even though he was active on public platforms.

Nationalism is perhaps the key vector for understanding Wilfred Domingo, although that might not have been so apparent in 1919. In those early years in Harlem there were three kinds of nationalism that Domingo had no time for. He was – as he remained all his life – a British citizen, but a British West Indian who never visited the UK and took no particular interest in the country. Yet at the same time he never took out US citizenship – as he could have done – and so never seriously engaged with the issues of African-American identity in the USA that so preoccupied his contemporaries. The third kind of nationalism that Domingo rejected was Marcus Garvey's so-called black nationalism: he never had any sympathy for the fantasy of an African return. For Domingo, however, by 1919 it was clear that Lenin's espousal of 'self-determination' sutured issues of socialism and race, the Red and the Black, with that of anti-colonialism nationalism. For that reason Jamaica stayed on his mind and, as a mature thinker and activist in the 1930s, that is where he was finally able to make his greatest contribution – towards Jamaican independence – even if post-colonial Jamaican historiography has paid little heed to his achievements.

## Notes

1. An earlier version of this chapter was presented at the conference 'The Red and the Black – The Russian Revolution and the Black Atlantic' in October 2017, with thanks to the organisers, Christian Høgsbjerg, David Featherstone, and Alan Rice. For generously sharing materials and for discussions about Domingo, warm thanks also to Winston James, Jacob Zumoff, Cathy Bergin, Leslie James, Saje Mathieu, Susan Gillman, and Jak Peake. This chapter was completed while I was a Stuart Hall Fellow at the W.E.B. Du Bois Institute for African and African American Research in the Hutchins Center at Harvard: thanks to the Center and to the other visiting fellows for their collegial support.
2. Joel A. Rogers, b. Negril (1880–1966); James S. Watson, b. Spanish Town (1882–1952); Marcus Garvey, b. St Ann's Bay (1887–1940); Claude McKay, b. Nairne Castle (1889–1948); Wilfred A. Domingo, b. Kingston (1889–1968).
3. Reliable biographical information on Domingo is sparse. He sent Alain Locke some brief notes about his early life in September 1925, and was interviewed in 1958 by Theodore Draper. After Domingo's death, Robert A. Hill interviewed some family members, who obviously provided a rose-tinted version of the family background: the illegitimacy was not part of the story. See Letter from W.A. Domingo to Alain Locke (21 September 1925), Alain Locke Papers, Coll. 164, Moorland-Spingarn Research Center, Howard University, Box 25, Folder 28; Theodore Draper, Interview with W.A. Domingo (18 January 1958), Theodore Draper research files, 1919–1990, Stuart A. Rose Manuscript, Archives, and Rare Book Library, Emory University, Atlanta, MS coll. 579; Robert A. Hill (ed.), *The Marcus Garvey and Universal Negro Improvement Association Papers* (Berkeley, CA: University of California Press, 1983–2011), vol. 1, 527–531.
4. The pamphlet was published in Jamaica under Marcus Garvey's name, but Domingo later said that he had co-written it: see 'Report of a Pamphlet by Marcus Garvey' in Robert A. Hill (ed.), *The Marcus Garvey and Universal Negro Improvement Association Papers* (Berkeley, CA: University of California Press, 1983–2011), vol. 11, 3.
5. W.A. Domingo, 'The Press and the Negro', *The Clarion*, 1:1 (1 September 1917), 7. The Declaration is on the opening two pages. On the Liberty League, see Jeffrey B. Perry, *Hubert Harrison: The Voice of Harlem Radicalism, 1883–1918* (New York: Columbia University Press, 2009), 281–327.
6. On *The Messenger*, see Theodore Kornweibel, Jr, *No Crystal Stair: Black Life and the 'Messenger', 1917–1928* (New York: Greenwood Press, 1976).
7. F. Scott Fitzgerald, 'May Day', *The Smart Set*, 62:3 (July 1920), 3–32. See 'Rand School and Other Nests of Anarchy Are Wrecked by Mobs', *The Sun*, 2 May 1919, 1.
8. See Chad L. Williams, 'The War at Home: African American Veterans and Violence in the Long "Red Summer"' in his *Torchbearers of Democracy: African American Soldiers in the World War I Era* (Chapel Hill, NC: University of North Carolina Press, 2010), 223–260.

9 *Revolutionary Radicalism: Its History, Purpose and Tactics, with an Exposition and Discussion of the Steps being Taken and Required to Curb it, being the Report of the Joint Legislative Committee Investigating Seditious Activities, Filed April 24, 1920, in the Senate of the State of New York*, 4 vols (Albany, NY: J.B. Lyon Company, 1920), 1. See *The Truth About the Lusk Committee: A Report Prepared by The Legislative Committee of the People's Freedom Union* (New York: Nation Press, 1920); Julian F. Jaffe, *Crusade Against Radicalism: New York During the Red Scare, 1914–1924* (Port Washington, NY: Kennikat Press, 1972); Regin Schmidt, *Red Scare: FBI and the Origins of Anticommunism in the United States, 1919–1943* (Copenhagen: Museum Tusculanum Press, 2000); Todd J. Pfannestiel, *Rethinking the Red Scare: The Lusk Committee and New York's Crusade against Radicalism, 1919–1923* (New York: Routledge, 2003); and William J. Maxwell, *F.B. Eyes: How J. Edgar Hoover's Ghostreaders Framed African American Literature* (Princeton, NJ: Princeton University Press, 2015).
10 'Raid Rand School, "Left Wing," and I.W.W. Offices', *New York Times*, 22 June 1919, 1.
11 'Moves to Close the Rand School', *New York Times*, 28 June 1919, 1, 3.
12 Wilfred A. Domingo, 'Socialism Imperilled, or the Negro – A Potential Menace to American Radicalism' [1919] in *Revolutionary Radicalism*, 1489–1510. Page references are included parenthetically in the text. See the account in Winston James, *Holding Aloft the Banner of Ethiopia: Caribbean Radicalism in Early Twentieth-Century America* (London: Verso, 1998), 274–282.
13 Hubert Harrison, 'Socialism and the Negro', *International Socialist Review*, 13 (July 1912), 65–68, reprinted in Jeffrey B. Perry (ed.), *A Hubert Harrison Reader* (Middletown, CT: Wesleyan University Press, 2001), 72–76, at 73; 'The Negro – A Menace to Radicalism', *The Messenger*, May–June 1919, 20.
14 See Sally M. Miller, 'The Socialist Party and the Negro, 1901–1920', *Journal of Negro History*, 56:3 (1971), 220–229.
15 A phenomenon later discussed by E. Franklin Frazier, *Black Bourgeoisie: The Rise of a New Middle Class in the United States* (New York: Collier Books, 1962), 56–76.
16 He gave the examples of the White Guards in Finland and the Czechoslovak troops being used in Russia (1496).
17 Letter from David P. Berenberg to Francis J. Peregrino, Pittsburgh, 16 May 1919, reproduced in *Revolutionary Radicalism*, 1511. See James, *Holding Aloft the Banner of Ethiopia*, 280.
18 Letter from David P. Berenberg to W.A. Domingo, 12 June 1919, The Lusk Committee Papers, L0028, Box 1, Folder 14, New York State Archives, Albany.
19 See Theodore Draper, *The Roots of American Communism* (New York: Viking Press, 1957).
20 Letter from W.A. Domingo to David P. Berenberg, 6 June 1919, The Lusk Committee Papers, L0028, Box 1, Folder 14, New York State Archives, Albany.
21 For general background, see Barbara Foley, *Spectres of 1919: Class and Nation in the Making of the New Negro* (Urbana, IL: University of Illinois Press, 2003);

Theodore Kornweibel, Jr, *Seeing Red: Federal Campaigns Against Black Militancy, 1919–1925* (Bloomington, IN: Indiana University Press, 1998); and Mark I. Solomon, *The Cry Was Unity: Communists and African Americans, 1917–36* (Jackson, MS: University Press of Mississippi, 1998).
22 As reported in a letter from Reginald Popham Lobb, Administrator of St Vincent, to George Basil Haddon-Smith, Governor of the Windward Islands, dated 6 August 1919, in Hill, *The Marcus Garvey and Universal Negro Improvement Association Papers*, vol. 11, 268–269.
23 Hill, *The Marcus Garvey and Universal Negro Improvement Association Papers*, vol. 11, 270 n.5.
24 W.A. Domingo, 'What Are We, Negroes Or Colored People?', *The Messenger*, May–June 1919, 23–25.
25 W.A. Domingo, 'Socialism the Negroes' Hope', *The Messenger*, 2:7 (July 1919), 22.
26 Hill, *The Marcus Garvey and Universal Negro Improvement Association Papers*, vol. 1, 402.
27 *Negro World*, 10 April 1920. Hill, *The Marcus Garvey and Universal Negro Improvement Association Papers*, vol. 1, 468–470, at 469. Not surprisingly, this comment caught the attention of J. Edgar Hoover and was quoted in *Investigation Activities of the Department of Justice. Letter from the Attorney General transmitting in response to a Senate resolution of October 17, 1919, a report on the activities of the Bureau of Investigation of the Department of Justice against persons advising anarchy, sedition, and the forcible overthrow of the government* (Washington, DC: Government Printing Office, 1919), 163. The words are often mistakenly quoted as if written by Marcus Garvey.
28 Colin Grant, *Negro with a Hat: The Rise and Fall of Marcus Garvey* (New York: Oxford University Press, 2008), 489 n.39; W.A. Domingo, '"If We Must Die"', *The Messenger*, 2:9 (September 1919), 4; W.A. Domingo, 'Did Bolshevism Stop Race Riots in Russia?', *The Messenger*, 2:9 (September 1919), 26–27. McKay's poem had appeared that summer: 'If We Must Die', *The Liberator*, 2:7 (July 1919), 21.
29 See Jak Peake's chapter in this volume.
30 Hill, *The Marcus Garvey and Universal Negro Improvement Association Papers*, vol. 11, 188–189, at 189.
31 V.I. Lenin, 'The Socialist Revolution and the Right of Nations to Self-Determination' (1916), www.marxists.org/archive/lenin/works/1916/jan/x01.htm [20.vi.2017] (accessed 2 November 2021); and see Erez Manela, *The Wilsonian Moment: Self-Determination and the International Origins of Anticolonial Nationalism* (New York: Oxford University Press, 2007), 37. Domingo quoted Lenin on self-determination in 'Socialism Imperilled' (1501).
32 Manela, *The Wilsonian Moment*, 38.
33 *Ibid.*, 39.
34 As 'Only One Peace Possible', in Oliver Marble Gale (ed.), *Americanism: Woodrow Wilson's Speeches on the War – Why He Made Them – And – What They Have Done* (Chicago, IL: Baldwin Syndicate, 1918), 103–109, at 106. Cf.

Mark T. Gilderhus, *Pan American Visions: Woodrow Wilson in the Western Hemisphere 1913–1921* (Tucson, AZ: University of Arizona Press, 1986).

35 W.A. Domingo, 'Capitalism the Basis of Colonialism', *The Messenger*, 2:8 (August 1919), 26–27, at 27.

36 See 'British Provost Marshall Aided Lusk Probers with Documents', *New York Call*, 25 June 1919, 1–2; J.W. Pawa, 'The Search for Black Radicals: American and British Documents Relative to the 1919 Red Scare', *Labor History*, 16:2 (1975), 272–284; and Richard Spence, 'Englishmen in New York: The SIS American Station, 1915–1921', *Intelligence and National Security*, 19:3 (2004), 511–537.

37 W.H. Loving, 'Final Report on Negro Subversion', New York, 6 August 1919, Military Intelligence Division File 10218–361, Records Group 165, US National Archives (USNA); and 'Unrest Among the Negroes', British Special Report no. 10 to the US State Department (7 October 1919), Records of the Post Office Department, Office of the Solicitor, Reports and Exhibits Relating to Transmittal of Mail Violating 1917 Espionage Act, 1917–1921. Unarranged Box no. 53, file no. 398, Record Group 28, USNA. The latter is reproduced in W.F. Elkins, '"Unrest Among the Negroes": A British Document of 1919', *Science & Society*, 32:1 (1968), 66–79. Kornweibel (*Seeing Red*, 72) says that Special Report no. 10 was 'actually penned by' Loving, but the cover note to the USNA copy only states that the report was 'based entirely upon a statement made by' Loving. The British report itself says that 'it is especially interesting to hear the views' of Loving and, although clearly *based* on Loving's report, the two are not identical.

38 See Perry, *Hubert Harrison*, 386 and 513n.15.

39 Loving, 'Final Report on Negro Subversion', 3.

40 Domingo married Eulalie A.F. Manhertz (1898–1988), a Jamaican classical pianist, on 3 April 1919: they had two children, Karl Nikolai (1919–92) and Yolanda (1926–2002), and were divorced in 1943. In 1957 Domingo married Mabel Hunte (1907–99) and had a third child, Wilfred B. Domingo (b. 1958).

41 'The Tropics in New York', *Survey Graphic*, 'Harlem: Mecca of the New Negro', 53:11 (1 March 1925), 648–650, reprinted with new title and introduction (probably by Alain Locke) as 'Gift of the Black Tropics' in Alain Locke (ed.), *The New Negro: An Interpretation* (New York: Albert & Charles Boni, 1925), 341–349; 'The West Indies', *Opportunity*, 4:47 (November 1926), 339–342.

42 'Goes to USSR to Work on Soviet Film', *Afro-American* [Baltimore], 2 July 1932, 19. On the film project, see Steven S. Lee, 'From Avant-Garde to Authentic: Revisiting Langston Hughes's "Moscow Movie"' in his *The Ethnic Avant-Garde: Minority Cultures and World Revolution* (New York: Columbia University Press, 2015), 119–148.

43 See Birte Timm, *Nationalists Abroad: The Jamaica Progressive League and the Foundations of Jamaican Independence* (Kingston: Ian Randle, 2016).

44 'Memorandum for Mr Ladd Re. W.A. Domingo, Visa Applicant', Federal Bureau of Investigation, United States Department of Justice, Washington, DC, 8 July 1943.

45 W.A. Domingo, *British West Indian Federation: A Critique* (Kingston: Gleaner Co., 1956), with a preface by W. Adolphe Roberts; and *Federation – Jamaica's Folly* (Kingston: Gleaner Co., 1958), with a foreword by Yolanda Domingo. For background, see Eric D. Duke, *Building a Nation: Caribbean Federation in the Black Diaspora* (Gainesville, FL: University Press of Florida, 2016).
46 James, *Holding Aloft the Banner of Ethiopia*, 268–269, and 274–284 commenting on Harold Cruse, *The Crisis of the Negro Intellectual: From Its Origins to the Present* (New York: William Morrow, 1967).
47 Margaret Stevens, 'The Early Political History of Wilfred A. Domingo, 1919–39' in Rupert Lewis (ed.), *Caribbean Political Activism: Essays in Honour of Richard Hart* (Kingston: Ian Randle Publishers, 2012), 118–143.
48 These are Jeffrey Perry's words about Harrison: Perry, *Hubert Harrison*, 13.

# 3

# Cyril Briggs: guns, bombs, spooks and writing the revolution

*Jak Peake*

Against a backdrop of violent race riots, lynching, and the rise of the Ku Klux Klan, Cyril Briggs and his black radical associates in New York dared to imagine not only a world of racial equality, but also a world in which black people were empowered and militant. What Cyril Briggs shared with his black radical associate turned nemesis, Marcus Garvey, was a commitment to black sovereignty and international recognition. Both men believed that black nationalism was key to the deliverance of black people in Africa and the Caribbean from colonialism. In their roles as race leaders, with shared ambitions for black nationalism, and statehood – and in Briggs's case black federation – both emerged on a young J. Edgar Hoover's watch list of New Negro subversives.

If New Negro radicals like Garvey and Briggs contributed to and drew on imaginaries of black sovereignty, then US and British Intelligence agencies responded to them as threats to their national and imperial sovereignties. Garvey and Briggs as heads of the Universal Negro Improvement Association (UNIA) and African Blood Brotherhood (ABB) respectively propagated the view of their organisations' threats to the status quo; in turn, such propaganda fed intelligence agencies' interests in the UNIA, ABB and their members, creating something of a circular feedback loop in which black empowerment served as fuel to both black radical organisations and the intelligence networks which shadowed them.

Hoover's entry into the Bureau of Investigation (BOI) in August 1919, amid the 'Red Summer', coincided with Briggs's near one-year mark as editor of the radical black newspaper *The Crusader* and the designation of *The Crusader*'s office as the eastern office of the Hamitic League of the World, an Afrocentric organisation committed to fostering black pride.[1] It is unsurprising perhaps that Briggs would end up on Hoover's watch list given the former's pioneering role within black radical circles and the latter's interest in black radical literature from the outset of his tenure at the Bureau.

Cyril Briggs is primarily remembered for his journalism, but he also wrote two short stories published in early 1920 and mid-1921 respectively.[2] Both serialised over two issues, Briggs's short stories resemble his journalism in that they laud black revolutionary action and black sovereignty. In both his fiction and non-fiction writing, Briggs paid heed to the lived reality of black oppression while simultaneously championing black states and federations that might challenge white supremacy and hegemony. Briggs was somewhat ahead of his time, writing of a free black state as early as 1917 when working as a journalist for the *New York Amsterdam News* amid US engagement in the First World War. This may have contributed to his earning a reputation in intelligence circles as 'one of the extreme radical leaders among the Negroes'.[3] However, Briggs's founding and stewarding of the African Blood Brotherhood, alongside his editorials in *The Crusader*, the ABB's organ from June 1921, brought things to a tipping point, drawing the sustained attention of the BOI, US Military Intelligence Division (MID) and British Secret Intelligence Service (SIS).

Born on 28 May 1888, on the Caribbean island of Nevis, Cyril Briggs was the son of Mary M. Huggins, a mixed-race light-skinned woman of part African heritage, and Louis E. Briggs, a white Trinidadian who was a bookkeeper and an overseer of a sugar plantation in Nevis.[4] Mary and Louis did not marry and it appears likely that Briggs had little contact with his father. Fair-skinned and phenotypically white, Briggs would be described by George W. Harris, an editor and publisher of the *Amsterdam News*, as an 'angry blond negro' in later life – a phrase that captures something of his juxtaposing characteristics: his militant black nationalist and internationalist politics, his white appearance, and his identification as black.[5] He also had a speech impediment, which made public speaking difficult and ruled him out of the kind of 'stepladder' speaking from which Afro-Caribbeans like Hubert Harrison and Garvey built their careers.

Briggs had a fairly typical colonial education, attending Christian-affiliated schools in Nevis before completing his schooling in St Kitts in 1904. Ensconced in this religious-colonial environment, Briggs had an early political dawning on reading Robert Ingersoll, an American radical and freethinker, who championed agnosticism and, while not opposed to US expansionism, disagreed with US annexation through military force.[6]

In his mid-to-late teens Briggs worked in a variety of jobs, becoming a sub-reporter for the *St Kitts Daily Express* and the *St Christopher Advertiser* in 1905, and joined his mother in New York a year later, arriving in New York City on 3 July 1906.[7] Briggs joined a growing Caribbean diaspora in the metropolis. Succeeding Hubert Harrison by six years and preceding Claude McKay, W.A. Domingo, Marcus Garvey, Amy Ashwood and Amy Jacques Garvey, and Otto and Hermina Huiswoud,

Briggs was one of the first emigres of this coterie to seek residence in New York City.

While we do not know much about Briggs's early years in New York, SS *Trinidad*'s ship's manifest gives his intended place of residence as 318 W. 145th Street, placing Briggs in the Sugar Hill area. Interestingly, the manifest reveals some familial anxieties, as his mother is noted as a 'friend' – her surname of Huggins perhaps an embarrassing reminder of his parents' unmarried status. Under a column labelled 'Race or people', the manifest also lists Briggs in ink as 'White', with 'W[est] Indi[an]' scrawled over the top in pencil, an archival palimpsest that highlights the ambiguities concerning Briggs's categorisation. Perhaps the purser was confused about Briggs's identity, or noted down a preference by Briggs to be identified as Caribbean rather than white.[8]

In 1912, Briggs got his first break into US journalism, working for the *New York Amsterdam News*, a small independent black weekly newspaper founded in 1909. Briggs married Virginian-born Bertha Florence Johnson on 7 January 1914 and resigned from the *Amsterdam News* a year later to assume the role of editor of the *Colored American Review*, a business magazine billed as 'A Magazine of Inspiration'. Briggs's praise of black enterprise and condemnation of white exploitation in the magazine caught the attention of fellow Caribbean journalist, Hubert Harrison. Writing of the new periodical in the *New York News* in glowing terms, Harrison was briefly taken on as a contributing editor. Mysteriously, however, Briggs resigned after the magazine's second issue, probably on account of a difference of opinion between himself and its owner, Ernest Touissant Welcome, a black property developer.[9]

Briggs became a naturalised US citizen on 24 February 1916 and returned to the staff of the *Amsterdam News* four months later. On 22 January 1917, three months prior to the US's formal entry into the First World War, President Woodrow Wilson delivered his 'Peace without Victory' address to Senate, which was the first of many speeches defending the right of nations to self-determination. Despite later claims that he had 'refused to fight for a democracy denied my people', Briggs registered for the draft on 5 June 1917 without any notable resistance.[10] By September 1918, he had made a volte-face and was a fierce critic of Du Bois, who advocated black soldiers to join in the war effort in an article entitled 'Close Ranks'.[11]

The eruption of race riots in East St Louis in May and July 1917 and Houston in August 1917, combined with the secret execution of thirteen black soldiers of the Third Battalion by the state in December for their role in the Houston riots, galvanised black radicals. Following Wilson's response to Pope Benedict XV's peace appeal in late August 1917, Briggs called for the creation an independent black nation within the United States in a two-part editorial '"Security of Life" for Poles and Serbs – Why Not for Colored Americans?' Briggs's innovative notion of black self-determination within the US predated the official position adopted by the Workers' (Communist) Party in 1928 by eleven years. Comprising 'one-tenth of the population', blacks in the US, in Briggs's view, could justifiably 'demand' 10 per cent of US territory. Briggs contended that 'a colored autonomous State' be established in the states of Washington, Oregon and Idaho combined, or better still, California and Nevada – preferable on account of the warmer weather and its location between a reimagined US and Mexico. While the article does not advocate violence to achieve such ends, it nevertheless suggests self-sacrifice might be necessary: '[t]he race is more in need of martyrs than of leaders'.[12]

In January 1918 Wilson delivered his Fourteen Points, which proposed an 'impartial adjustment of all colonial claims' and the creation of a League of Nations.[13] In that same year Briggs became increasingly critical of US double standards abroad and particularly in the Caribbean.[14] In a letter to the *Globe* published in January 1918 and entitled significantly 'Africa for the Africans', Briggs argues for self-determination in Africa.[15] Briggs's *Globe* letter led indirectly to the creation of *The Crusader* magazine, as a West Indian merchant, Anthony Crawford, wrote to Briggs on 24 January 1918 offering to finance 'an organ – especially suited to your propaganda of "Africa for the Africans" – to educate the Caucasian in African history'.[16]

With $200 donated by Crawford and another $200 loaned, *The Crusader* was launched in September 1918. Alongside an avowed petition for African sovereignty, *The Crusader*'s first issue lists among its aims an awakening of 'the American Negro to the splendid strategic position of the Race in the South American and West Indian Republics'.[17] In this opening issue, Briggs also declares his support for the socialist candidates A. Philip Randolph and Chandler Owen on a 'Pro-Negro', rather than a 'pro-Socialist' stance – the capitalisation of the 'p' in the former clear emphasis of where Briggs's priorities lay.[18]

In December 1918, *The Crusader* was named the 'Publicity Organ of the Hamitic League of the World'. Leading with an article which publicised the League, it lists Briggs as the organisation's vice-president.[19] Briggs had formed an alliance with the organisation's creator, George Wells Parker, a businessman from Omaha who had founded the League in 1917. While one advertisement states that Briggs was one of the original founders of the League, there is no evidence of Parker and Briggs's association prior to 1918, when the League was revived after a period of dormancy.[20] The League undoubtedly served as a template for the African Blood Brotherhood that Briggs later founded in 1919. Briggs and Parker shared an ideological outlook that combined Pan-African liberation, race pride and something like the 'race first' principles espoused by Hubert Harrison from the mid-1910s onwards.

Unlike Briggs's journalism in *The Crusader* in early to mid-1919, the *Amsterdam News* had come under increasing pressure from the Translation Bureau of the Post Office. On 12 March 1919, Briggs's 'League of Thieves' *Amsterdam News* editorial explicitly denounced Wilson's proposals for a League of Nations. The issue was detained by the postal authorities, and, by April, according to Briggs, he was facing the second of two interviews with federal employees over the content of an April article concerning the ill-treatment of black officers serving in France.

While it's difficult to date Briggs's draw to international Communism precisely, the timing of his 'League of Thieves' article – published six days after the close of the founding congress of the Communist International (Comintern) in Moscow, 2–6 March 1919 – appears more than merely fortuitous. In contrast to the Second International, Lenin's International was unapologetically anti-colonial, its manifesto a revolutionary call to arms for non-European colonials: 'Colonial slaves of Africa and Asia! The hour of triumph of the Proletarian Dictatorship of Europe will also be the hour of your liberation.' Briggs's 1958 claim that his 'interest' in Communism was inspired by the 'national policy of the Russian Bolsheviks and the anti-imperialist orientation of the Soviet State', suggests that he was initially attracted to the international Communist movement which was kick-started by the 1917 October Revolution, and refired by the emergence of Comintern in March 1919.[21] Briggs's review of a play, *Darkest Russia*, featured in the March 1919 *Crusader* – denouncing Tsarist Russia and praising Bolshevik rule – followed by the publication of an anonymous poem, 'The Bolsheviki', in the May 1919 *Crusader*, hint at Briggs's admiration of the achievements of Lenin's Bolshevik Party.[22]

While Briggs found an outlet for Bolshevik sentiment in *The Crusader*, the screws began to tighten at the *Amsterdam News*, as the 29 May and 12 June issues were held up by the Post Office on account of their being judged by Post Office Solicitor, W.H. Lamar, as 'nonmailable'. Refusing to capitulate to pressure from the authorities, Briggs resigned in July 1919.[23]

In April 1919, the MID, disregarding orders not to spy on civilians, produced a report on 'Negro Agitation'. It was apparently based on British intelligence and information prepared by Rev. R.D. Jonas, a Welshman who shared information with US intelligence services while working as a British undercover agent. The report exposes Anglo-American anxieties about the spread of 'Pan-Negroism' globally and the contact of this movement with Bolshevism and other oppressed national groups, namely the Irish, Jews and Hindus. In it, *The Crusader* is defined alongside another black periodical, the *Challenge*, as a 'very extreme magazine', with 'much abuse of Great

Britain'.²⁴ Perhaps reading this as a British imperial affair, the MID took no immediate action against the magazine.

On 2 July 1919, three weeks before the biggest of the Red Summer riots, Robert A. Bowen, Director of the Post Office's Bureau of Translations and Radical Publications in New York, produced a report on 'Radicalism and Sedition Among the Negroes as Reflected in Their Publications'. Bowen expressed concerns that the 'radical movement in the negro press' had 'become remarkably accelerated during the past six months'. Bowen also grouped *The Crusader* bizarrely among the more conservative publications, such as the *Amsterdam News* and *The Crisis*, against which the *Negro World* was seen as a necessary remedial by black radicals.

In October, an advert for the 'African Blood Brotherhood for African Liberation and Redemption' featured in *The Crusader*. It caught the attention of MID Director, Brigadier General Marlborough Churchill, who, thinking the advert 'revolutionary in nature', ordered an investigation into the organisation.²⁵ This, and subsequent adverts for or statements about the ABB would keep federal authorities exercised for the next four years. The advert's open-ended call for applicants only 'willing to go to the limit!' undoubtedly unnerved intelligence operatives.²⁶ Both the MID and BOI filed a serialised short fiction piece, '"Punta" Revolutionist', by St Thomas-born Romeo L. Dougherty from the October *Crusader* – Dougherty's last instalment, despite expressed intentions to continue the serial.²⁷ This final episode expands on the plans of Punta Hernandez, the eponymous Caribbean revolutionary hero, to initiate a 'Black Revolution' delivering 'freedom to black men'.²⁸ Specifically, this instalment details how Punta intends to realise his vision: through the construction of a 'deadly aerial bomb' that will be shipped to Africa and guided by 'wireless station' on an uninhabited island off Miami.²⁹

The MID's and BOI's cataloguing of '"Punta" Revolutionist' raises several questions. Were these US intelligence agencies specifically interested in such fiction? Or did they not discriminate between different genres of writing in radical magazines? A report by an unidentified MID agent on 20 October 1919 contains some clues. In the agent's view, the 'story by Mr Dougherty' was 'directly connected' with the October ABB advert and functioned 'purely and simply [as] propaganda to arouse interest in the plan of the young Negroes of this country'.³⁰

While we do not know about the precise origins of the ABB, the placement of the October advert and Briggs's recollection that the organisation was founded some months after *The Crusader* was inaugurated, point towards its foundation in early to mid-1919. Founded by Briggs as a protective black organisation, the ABB contained features of a secret society, fraternal order and paramilitary organisation. Divided into posts located throughout the US and Caribbean and headed by commanders, the ABB probably had no more than 3,000 members at its peak, with perhaps no more than 50 members in its headquarters, Harlem's 'Menelik Post'.[31]

In a June 1920 *Crusader* article, the ABB's 'sole purpose' was defined as 'the liberation of Africa and the redemption of the Negro race'.[32] No original document of the ABB's 1920 programme exists, but post-1920 and undated sources attribute a nine- and eight-point agenda with broadly anti-colonial, socially progressive and black emancipatory aspirations to a 1920 convention.[33] Membership of the ABB was restricted to those of 'African blood', but, unlike Garvey's UNIA, co-operation between the races was encouraged.[34] Like the UNIA, the ABB had a significant number of members hailing from the Caribbean. Early and founding members included Theophilus Burrell, Benjamin E. Burrell, Richard B. Moore, W.A. Domingo, Claude McKay, Arthur Reid, Grace P. Campbell and Joseph P. Fanning.[35] The overlap between Harrison's Liberty League, Garvey's UNIA and the ABB cannot be overstated; Reid joined Harrison's league, drifted into Garvey's UNIA, and left the UNIA to become an ABB member; Domingo (Liberty League and ABB member) and Harrison were close to all three organisations at different stages, if not strictly members.

Among the range of Black and Red groups with heartlands in New York, the ABB occupied a position which overlapped with the 'race first' policies of the Liberty League and UNIA and the socialist and Communist orientation of a range of black radicals, including socialists A. Philip Randolph, Chandler Owen, W.A. Domingo, and Communists Otto Huiswoud and Harry Haywood. While initially race-conscious and broadly socialist in orientation, the ABB shifted to the left roughly two years after its inception, becoming a Communist cell in mid-1921.[36]

Taking *The Crusader* as a barometer of Briggs's mindset, and by extension the political leaning of the ABB, its October 1919 issue illustrates the magazine's non-doctrinaire position on the spectrum of Black–Red politics. Officially affiliated to the Hamitic League (an association that lasted until December 1920), the issue contains the editorials 'Bolshevist!!!' and 'Negro First!' While the latter advocated a race first policy, the former was not strictly an endorsement of the Bolshevik Revolution, but rather a criticism of its application to all suspected 'bad agitators'. Published roughly a month on from the formation of both the Communist Party of America (CPA) and the Communist Labor Party of America, amid the splintering of the Socialist Party of America (SPA), the October *Crusader* issue significantly came out in support of the SPA and declared that there was 'no finer man' in the US than the SPA leader, Eugene Debs.[37] Hence whatever Briggs's admiration for Lenin's successes abroad and international Communism at this stage, he was evidently not closely allied to any of the actors involved in the formation of the US Communist parties.

MID correspondence concerning the October ABB advert cast doubts on the ABB's threat to the US government specifically, seeing it as 'aimed solely at the European governments' with colonies in Africa; nevertheless it confirmed a 'definite movement on foot [sic] between intelligent Negroes of the United States, the West Indies and Africa'.[38] A flurry of activity in that month raised *The Crusader*'s and Briggs's profiles in intelligence circles transnationally. A British SIS report, 'Unrest Among the Negroes', of 7 October 1919, was passed on to the MID. The British report borrowed heavily from an August report by Major Walter H. Loving, a distinguished black MID officer who had served in the Philippine Constabulary. Mirroring Loving's report, the British report describes *The Crusader* as 'radical', but lacking the influence of *The Messenger* or *The Crisis*.[39]

The passing of Poindexter's resolution on 17 October – a Republican manoeuvre to pressure Wilson's government to take action against 'Reds' – led to Palmer's report a month later, 'Investigation Activities of the Department of Justice', and undoubtedly induced Palmer to begin his raids in November. 'Investigation Activities' made public the work of the BOI and the Post Office Department, raising the profile of *The Crusader* considerably as a seditious magazine. The report included a section entitled, 'Radicalism and Sedition Among the Negroes as Reflected in Their Publications', which was a much expanded version of Robert Bowen's 2 July report of the same name. Palmer's report stated that 'the Negro' identified 'with such radical organisations as the I. W. W.', noting 'outspoken advocacy of the Bolsheviki or Soviet doctrines'. Distinct from Bowen's 2 July report, the Palmer report describes *The Crusader* as 'full of significant material' and offers something approaching a close ghostreading.[40]

'Investigation Activities' is critical of *The Crusader*'s attacks on the conservative negro press and singles out an article in the September 1919 issue, 'Why Lynching Persists' which lambasted the *Amsterdam News* – Briggs's old employer – for an unctuous editorial which praised the government and condemned radical journalists. Such a 'lick-spittle' attitude, Briggs stressed, explained why white superiority and, by extension, lynching continued.[41] Palmer's report presents *The Crusader* as typical of radical black publications in its critique of the conservative black press and old guard representatives like Booker T. Washington. As such, it purveys considerable animosity to the most politicised wings of the New Negro. According to Justice Department officials, *The Crusader*'s publishing of McKay's 'If We Must Die' – which was ubiquitous within black radical periodicals – served as shorthand for the magazine's dangerous radicalism. To make its point, the report quotes *The Crusader*'s use of the sonnet in full alongside Andy Razafkeriefo's poem 'Don't Tread on Me'.[42]

What was most offensive about *The Crusader* according to Palmer's report was its use of an 'obnoxious' cartoon in its November issue which illustrates a white lyncher from the US South being chased by a gun-wielding black man all the way to the Capitol Building, the seat of the US Congress (Figure 3.1). The cartoon registers a new militancy among New Negroes, depicted by the lyncher's caption which reads, 'Hey! Help! Help!

Figure 3.1 'The Worm Turns', *The Crusader*, 2:3 (November 1919)

This nigger problem has changed'. Beneath the cartoon is an editorial by Briggs critical of the repressive powers of the Lusk Committee – established in 1919 by the New York State Legislature to investigate sedition in the state – and the US government's approach to race relations in the wake of the race riots. Briggs's editorial notes the 'strange' irony that a 'call for a Congressional investigation' came from the South that 'squealed at the first taste of Negro steel'.[43] In addition, Briggs outlined how the editors of *The Crusader* and *The Messenger* were questioned, threatened with fines or imprisonment and denied legal counsel by the Lusk Committee on 17 October. Notably, Briggs did not name the editors, who were principally A. Philip Randolph, Chandler Owen and himself; as a contributing editor of *The Messenger*, and an implicated figure in the Rand School raid, Domingo may well have been among the interviewees. This 'antifile' is barely mentioned in Palmer's report which papers over the inconvenient truths raised by the editorial, and instead casts it as 'boasting of the success the negro has attained … in bringing the negro problem before Congress'.[44]

By late 1919, Briggs, *The Crusader* and the ABB were now firmly on the radar of several intelligence outfits: the British Secret Intelligence Service (SIS), the Lusk Committee of the New York State Legislature, and three US organisations: the MID, Post Office and Justice Department's BOI. Although the MID reported concerns about the worldwide spread of 'negro propaganda' in early 1920, it faced sharp cuts.[45] The BOI filled this apparent intelligence gap. In August 1919 during his first month as Director of the newly established Radical Division, J. Edgar Hoover targeted black radicals specifically and had hoped to indict *The Messenger* editors under the Espionage Act. That month, a Bureau agent interviewed Robert Bowen, who described *The Crusader* as 'entirely radical, pro-Negro and pan-African' as well as 'entirely sympathetic with Bolshevism, Sinn Fein, Jewish agitation'.[46]

In January 1920, the BOI made a small breakthrough: infiltration of Briggs's circle by a black Bureau operative, William A. Bailey ('W.W.'). From January through to March, Bailey divided his time between gathering information on Briggs, Garvey, W.A. Domingo and the National Association for the Advancement of Colored People. Volunteering in the *Crusader* office, which was just a block away from the *Messenger* office, Bailey enticed Briggs with an offer to increase *The Crusader*'s circulation.[47] Talking to Domingo in late January, Bailey also got wind of the short-lived weekly that Domingo would edit, the *Emancipator*.[48] Two months later, Bailey stated that 'Briggs is a Socialist as also is Domingo' and made reference to the *Emancipator* being supported by the SPA.[49]

Bailey's observations about Briggs's socialist orientation in 1920 are more or less corroborated by *The Crusader*'s output. The February 1920

*Crusader* published the first instalment of Briggs's short fiction, 'The Ray of Fear' – filed along with the October 1919 instalment of '"Punta" Revolutionist' by the BOI – which presents a revealing insight into Briggs's black nationalist and class politics.[50] The story opens with the decision made by the Congress of the 'Black Republic' to go to war against 'Central, Western and Southern Europe' and European forces in Africa. Paul, a close friend of the President and suitor of his daughter Mazima/Nazima, relates how the Republic intends to deploy a secret weapon, the Ray of Fear, alongside 'super-airships' equipped with 'aerial torpedoes, machine guns and bomb-throwers' and '50,000 bombing-planes'. Notably, the Republic aims to form allegiances with 'Soviet Russia, Japan, Siam, Turkey, China … India, Persia and Ireland' and produce a manifesto 'for presentation to the Socialists and Liberals of Europe and America'.[51] Briggs's choice to have the black President negotiate with Soviet Russia and yet liaise with socialists and liberals is telling. It mirrors Briggs's early journalism in *The Crusader* in its pro-Bolshevist sentiment, but generally socialist, rather than Communist, leaning.

Similar in many respects to Dougherty's '"Punta" Revolutionist' with its detailing of advanced weaponry of a black army, Briggs's 'The Ray of Fear' could be read as propaganda. Briggs's and Dougherty's fiction reflects a genre of black war and romance fiction which combine details of scientific innovation and aspects of speculative and science fiction. With events often poised on the brink of a race or revolutionary war, the stories pivot on the roles of secret societies or plans. Borrowing from thriller fiction, Briggs's and Dougherty's serials' most obvious forerunner is Martin Delany's *Blake; or, The Huts of America*. Serialised in 1859 and 1861–62, *Blake* is the story of Henry Blake, a free-born, Afro-Cuban who, with a mixture of rationalism, sharp intellect and astronomical knowledge, liberates slaves and plans a large-scale slave rebellion in the United States and Cuba.[52]

In '"Punta" Revolutionist' and 'The Ray of Fear', revolutionary war is initiated by black and mixed-race armies in response to a legacy of white imperialism. However, in Briggs's 1921 serialised short story, 'Secret Service', a 'colored' chambermaid, Nada, uncovers the plot of 'a secret Cracker organisation' – a thinly veiled Ku Klux Klan (KKK) – to initiate a race war. To achieve this end, the organisation's 'Wizard' and Nada's employer, Mr Graham, scheme on getting white mobs to black up and attack white women throughout the US. The attacks are thwarted, however, as Nada aids in the photographing of the white supremacists' plans which are sent to 'a secret Negro organisation' who take appropriate counter measures.[53]

Briggs's emphasis on the role that secret Negro societies had to play in protecting black people obviously had parallels in his formation of the

Brotherhood, which was modelled on a secret society. In June 1920, Briggs claimed that the ABB was 'probably the first Negro *secret* organisation' to be founded in the Western world, and often publicised the organisation's protective capabilities and secrecy – however contradictory the latter gesture.[54] Briggs's fiction indicated the hypothetical role that the ABB might play, foiling organisations like the KKK, as well as readying black people for armed resistance when racially motivated violence broke out. As authors of fictional propaganda, Dougherty and Briggs could clearly sidestep official censure and avoid criminal charges. Briggs's use of his middle name and adoption of the pseudonym, 'C. Valentine', for his short fiction, suggests that he pre-empted the interest of intelligence agencies in this material, and wanted to place distance between himself and his revolutionary fiction.

*The Crusader*'s fiction can also be read as a counter to Anglo-Saxonism, which had romanticised and propagated the superiority of the Anglo-Saxon, Nordic or Teutonic people over all other ethnic groups. In 'The Ray of Fear', Mazima/Nazima is a beauty known as the 'Rose of Africa', which bears its obvious parallel in an 'English Rose' – used to describe an unadorned, rare English beauty. Briggs's adoption of the rose, a plant native to north Africa, Asia and Europe, to portray the African-born Mazima/Nazima, raises doubts about the entrenched geography associated with this signifier of English beauty. The President also rhapsodises about Ethiopia – the name derived from the ancient Greeks to refer to the lands of black Africans – in ways which echo Thomas Carlyle's encomiums about Britain and the Teutonic world: 'Ethiopia of old, "the most just of nations"'.[55] In promoting fiction about black heroes, heroines, soldiers and revolutionaries, Briggs appears to have been rebalancing the books in terms of racial representation, endowing black people with noble and attractive qualities hitherto seen as the preserve of white characters. While US intelligence agencies may have perceived a racial ideology at work in such fiction, they would have been unlikely to examine the reasons – however compelling – for such pro-Negro sentiment, preferring indubitably to brand this material as straightforwardly anti-white and, therefore, seditious.

In late March 1920, tensions between Garvey, and Domingo and Briggs arose, as the latter pair headed a campaign in the *Emancipator* to expose Garvey over misleading claims about the Black Star Line's ownership of the SS *Yarmouth*. A month later, Bailey was replaced by BOI operative, William E. Lucas ('P-135'), who became a contributor to *The Crusader*, his name featuring on the magazine's masthead until June 1920 when his undercover operations at the magazine ceased.[56]

On 31 May 1921 a bloody race riot erupted in Tulsa after a small band of armed blacks arrived at a jail to protect a potential black victim from a lynch mob. On 4 June 1921, the *New York Times*, led with a front-page article which implicated the ABB as fomenting the riot.[57] In his press statement for the *Times* on 5 June, Briggs denied the ABB's involvement, but used the opportunity to promote the Brotherhood. The *Times* articles gave the ABB a national prominence it had never had, and Briggs wasted no time in touting the size of the Brotherhood which he claimed comprised 150 branches and 50,000 members. Furthermore, Briggs asserted the ABB's support for black armed self-defence, asking, a generation before Malcolm X: 'Haven't negroes the right to defend their lives and property when these are menaced[?]'[58]

While Briggs denied that members of the Brotherhood's Tulsa branch were 'aggressors' in the riots, he later traded on its association with the riots in *The Crusader* and elsewhere.[59] In a letter intended to woo Garvey to the ABB, Briggs wrote that while claims that the Brotherhood 'fomented and directed the Tulsa riot' were 'not literally true', they did provide 'an idea of the nature of our organisation'.[60] Briggs understood that notoriety – however misinformed – had propagandistic value. This was not Hoover's view, however, who took seriously Briggs's 'pernicious activities' when forwarded Briggs's letter by an African-American attorney, William C. Matthews.[61]

Perhaps to capitalise on the ABB's sudden fame, Briggs chose the June 1921 issue of *The Crusader* to announce its status as the 'Organ of the African Blood Brotherhood'. In jettisoning the latter's secret status, the ABB paralleled the US Communist Party's move from an underground to an aboveground legal party. These developments led inevitably to re-energising the BOI's interest in the ABB. In June 1921, an undercover operative, Jamaican-born Herbert S. Boulin ('P-138'), succeeded in infiltrating the ABB and turned Hubert Harrison's friend, Edgar Grey, into an informant. Through Grey, secretary of Harrison's Liberty League, Boulin also got wind of what is likely to have been Briggs's first contact with the CPA wing seeking aboveground status. According to Grey, Rose Pastor Stokes, a CPA founding member, invited Briggs, Harrison, W.A. Domingo, Claude McKay and Grey to supper at her home in Greenwich Village in either late May or early June. The aim of the meal was to see whether either the League or the ABB would assist with 'spreading communism among negroes' – an offer apparently refused by Harrison, but accepted by Briggs. Grey further claimed that the ABB was 'financed by' and a 'mouthpiece of the Communist Party'.[62]

As Briggs's association with US Communists became closer, the content in *The Crusader* rapidly evolved. In an April 1921 editorial, Briggs discussed the merits of an independent black 'Socialist Co-operative Commonwealth' in Africa, South America or the Caribbean with reference to Soviet Russia and Communist states in Africa.[63] By August 1921, his editorials took a sharp turn. The SPA was rebuked as betraying revolutionary socialism, just as US Communism was embraced.[64] Hence, Briggs's and the ABB's association with the US Communist Party was consolidated in the summer of 1921.

As the ABB moved closer to the US Communist movement, so the BOI's surveillance of its members increased. In August 1921, the ABB was shadowed by four BOI operatives: Boulin, P-134, P-137 and, crucially, James Wormley Jones (aka 'Agent 800'). Jones was the first black, full-time BOI agent and had served as a captain in the US Army in the First World War. Using his military background, he maintained a public persona as 'Captain Jones' and, after infiltrating the UNIA, became head of its African Legion by June 1920. On becoming a full-fledged member of the ABB in August he effectively became a double agent between the two rival black organisations, while remaining a loyal agent of the US Justice Department.[65]

In mid-August 1921, ABB members attended the UNIA convention with the aim of influencing its delegates. In his letter to Garvey, Briggs held out an olive branch, asking the UNIA leader to consider an ABB-UNIA coalition: 'think of what we might be able to do for the race through conscious co-operation'.[66] Yet, in spite of this conciliatory gesture, ABB members' criticisms of Garvey and his management of the Black Star Line increased. Relations reached their nadir as ABB delegates were publicly expelled from the convention.

What followed was a war of words between Briggs and Garvey that turned litigious. In early September 1921 Briggs sent an open letter to *Negro World* editor William Ferris, critical of Garvey's and the *Negro World*'s conservatism and Ferris's insinuations that *The Crusader*'s editorials were anti-American.[67] By October, BOI agent Jones was stirring the pot: 'I have been telling Briggs that the article in the *Negro World* about Briggs being a white man was libel, Briggs went to the district attorney and he issued a summons for Garvey.'[68] With Jones's encouragement, Briggs sued Garvey for libel, taking his mother to court as proof of his 'colored' (mixed-race) status.[69]

On 4 September 1921, Jones turned in a curious report concerning Briggs's apparent paramilitary ambitions for the ABB. Jones claimed that Briggs was considering ordering two Thomson sub-machine (Tommy) guns and organising rifle clubs in the US South and West. Jones was to teach members the guns' 'nomenclature' and serve as a field agent. Up until this point, Jones's report resembles Boulin's from a month before; Boulin had claimed that Briggs had showed him a Tommy gun from a catalogue and ordered 300 for ABB members.[70] Jones's report becomes more spectacular, however, as a near-bomb plot is unveiled: 'he [Briggs] said had it not been for the famine in Russia there would have been a bomb set off in this country that would have opened the eyes of the world'.[71]

Jones's report is a conundrum. On the one hand, it could be entirely fabricated – driven by the fear of submitting nothing substantial to the Bureau. On the other hand, Jones's account may be accurate. Briggs, however, knowing full well or suspecting Jones of being an agent, may have been stringing him along. Another and arguably more plausible hypothesis is that Briggs did have some paramilitary ambitions for the ABB, and was exaggerating for effect to keep Jones, the ex-captain and a useful agent against Garvey, on board. Briggs was prone to magnifying the size and the threat posed by the ABB and had employed the same tactic when making overtures to Garvey.

In a certain light, Jones's report has some parallels with Briggs's fictional story, 'The Ray of Fear'. Where the Black Republic aims to start a global race war and petition socialists and liberals in Briggs's serial, Jones's report hints at a Communist-ABB attack designed to initiate a race war in the US South. In both accounts, Soviet Russia forms an alliance (albeit one that it can't follow through with in Jones's narrative) with black-led forces. While clearly different genres, both draw on an imaginary of black power, with Briggs's fiction celebrating what Jones presents as a national menace.

From September through to November 1921, Briggs and Garvey's feud escalated. In late September Briggs asked Jones for insider information, requesting the names of UNIA division presidents. Briggs aimed to send them copies of *The Crusader* so as to smear Garvey. Jones sought some guidance from his headquarters in Washington, DC before doing as Briggs requested, torn on account of his equal aversion to both.[72] Briggs learned of Garvey's offering up of Briggs's August 1921 letter to the authorities – most probably through Jones – and accused the UNIA leader of being an informer and a traitor to his race in the November *Crusader*.[73] Attempting to settle the score, Garvey took Briggs to court for libel over an October article in *The Crusader* which implied that Garvey abandoned his wife and raped a white woman in London.[74] Briggs might have occupied the moral high ground were it not for his own provision of evidence that the government eventually used to convict Garvey of mail fraud in June 1923. The hostility appeared to work against both men; while Garvey would be deported in 1927 after serving a two-year jail sentence, Briggs had turned *The Crusader* into a repository of anti-Garvey sentiment, a move which did not help its languishing sales. A few months before *The Crusader*'s last issue of January–February 1922, Briggs had tried and failed to drum up funding for a weekly newspaper, *The Liberator*.[75]

By April 1922, Jones's reports on the ABB ceased. *The Crusader* was no more, and in the void BOI attention shifted to Garvey. A few months before, in December 1921, Briggs had apparently admitted to Jones that he aspired to draw Garvey's followers to the ABB and therefore continue his propaganda against Garvey. That month, writing under the pseudonym C. Lorenzo in the Communist magazine *The Toiler*, Briggs asserted that the ABB was 'the only Negro organisation that the capitalists view with any degree of alarm' in stark contrast with Garvey's apparently moribund UNIA.[76] Hinting that the organisation's reputation in the wake of the Tulsa riots had played its part, Briggs still flirted with the image of the ABB's potential menace.

In the wake of *The Crusader*, Briggs continued to run the Crusader News Service bulletin, which circulated news to more than one hundred black newspapers. By September–October 1923, the entire ABB's Supreme Executive Council – with the exception of Domingo and McKay – had joined the Workers' (Communist) Party.[77] In 1924, Briggs attempted to organise the Negro Sanhedrin conference in Chicago with the aim of creating a federation of black organisations. As secretary, Briggs had a very different political orientation to the conference head, Kelly Miller, who managed to circumvent the most left-wing and Communist black radicals' plans.[78] By 1924 the ABB was virtually dissolved, and would be replaced in 1925 by the American Negro Labor Congress (ANLC), a Communist Party organisation intended to recruit black members and propagandise Communist causes. Briggs became editor of the ANLC organ, *Negro Champion*, and realised his goal in 1929, when the *Negro Champion* was succeeded by a weekly founded by the ANLC, *The Liberator*. Briggs was editor of the newspaper until 1933 and, while not an official Communist Party newspaper, the periodical was clearly aligned with Communist Party USA (CPUSA) politics.[79]

In the 1930s, Briggs's race-conscious politics clashed with that of his Communist colleagues. In 1930, Earl Browder named him as a comrade susceptible to 'the propaganda of the Negro bourgeoisie' in his direction of 'race hatred ... against all whites without distinction'.[80] In 1939, he was expelled from the Party, along with ex-ABB members Richard Moore and Otto Hall, after quarrels with the leading black CPUSA member, James W. Ford, over black nationalist matters. In 1944, Briggs moved west to Los Angeles and worked for *Now* magazine, followed by the *California Eagle*. In 1948, he rejoined the CPUSA, and became an active member of the Ella May Wiggins Club of the LA County Communist Party. By December 1950, as a second Red Scare set in, Briggs began operating in the Communist Party underground.[81] As a result of this and his Communist past, Briggs earned himself an interview with the House of Un-American Activities on 3 September 1958. In response to the Chairman's claim that Communists were insincere in their 'efforts to improve' the lot of black people, Briggs answered accordingly:

> I don't know what Communists or communism have to do with my position because this has been my position since 1912 before there was, as I understand it, a Communist Party in the United States. It will continue to be my position despite any attempt by this committee to intimidate me ... it is said that the Communist Party is exploiting the Negro people.
>
> I think, gentlemen, that the Negroes would be very glad to accept such exploitation at the hands of the Republicans.[82]

Spoken eight years before his death, this speech conveys something of Briggs's independent spirit. While he had obviously come to believe that the 'Negro's' lot would be best improved through Communism, it was his loyalty to black people that remained paramount. His ironic play on exploitation, while intended to highlight Republican neglect of black causes, also contains the seeds of his openness to other political pathways. In many senses, the statement is consistent with Briggs's outlook from the 1910s onwards: that he would serve whatever cause he believed best served black folk.

## Notes

1 Robert A. Hill (ed.), *The Marcus Garvey and Universal Negro Improvement Association Papers*, Vol. I (Berkeley, CA: University of California Press, 1983), 523.
2 See notes 51 and 53.
3 Col. Parker Hitt to Brig. Gen. Churchill, 23 June 1920, 10218–424, Records Group 165, Military Intelligence Division, National Archives, Washington, DC [hereafter RG165, MID, NA].
4 There is some uncertainty as to Briggs's place of birth. Most scholars state that Briggs was born in Nevis. However, some claim that he was born in St Kitts, a statement which is itself ambiguous as this may be a shorthand reference for the country's full title, St Kitts and Nevis. I have not been able to locate a copy of Briggs's birth certificate, but believe Richard B. Moore's ascription of him as Nevisian to be persuasive given his close association with Briggs in New York. Richard B. Moore, *The Name 'Negro': Its Origin and Evil Use* (Baltimore, MD: Black Classic Press, 1992), 15. James, for example, refers to Briggs as born in St Kitts – see Winston James, *Holding Aloft the Banner of Ethiopia: Caribbean Radicalism in America, 1900–1932* (London: Verso, 1998), 17.
5 Mark Solomon, *The Cry Was Unity: Communists and African Americans, 1917–1936* (Jackson, MS: University Press of Mississippi, 1998), 316.
6 Robert A. Hill, 'Racial and Radical: Cyril V. Briggs, the Crusader Magazine, and the African Blood Brotherhood, 1918–1922' in Robert A. Hill (ed.), *The Crusader: A Facsimile of the Periodical* (New York: Garland, 1987), v–lxx, at vii–viii.

7 Minkah Makalani, *In the Cause of Freedom: Radical Black Internationalism from Harlem to London, 1917–1939* (Chapel Hill, NC: University of North Carolina Press, 2011), 31. The date of Briggs's arrival in New York City is generally believed to be 4 July 1905. However, this date seems questionable, given that no record of Briggs's arrival is noted in the New York passenger arrival lists for Ellis Island until the following year. The SS *Trinidad* ship's manifest records his arrival as 3 July 1906. In a letter to Theodore Draper, Briggs stated 'I came to the United States in 1905 (4 July)'; Cyril Briggs to Theodore Draper, Theodore Draper papers, 4 June 1958, Box 31, Hoover Institution Archives. In a 1910 census, Briggs's arrival date in the US is recorded as 1906, however on both the 1920 and 1930 censuses his US arrival date is noted as 1905. This suggests that from 1920 onwards, Briggs misremembered his true arrival date. It's possible that this was a second visit, but at present I have been unable to locate any evidence to prove this. 1910 United States Census, New York, Population, Commerce and Labor, Digital image, 17 April 2019, http://ancestry.com. 1920 United States Census, New York, Population, Commerce, Digital image, 16 April 2019, http://ancestry.com. 1930 United States Census, New York, Population, Commerce, Digital image, 16 April 2019, http://ancestry.com

8 The manifest has '318 145 W NY' penned on it, which I interpret as 318 West 145th Street. Passenger record for Cyril Briggs, arr. 3 July 1906, manifest of SS *Trinidad*, from West Indies to New York, 16 April 2019, http://ancestry.com.

9 Hill, 'Racial and Radical', x.

10 *Ibid*., xi.

11 'Digest of Views', *The Crusader*, 1:1 (September 1918), 13–14.

12 '"Security of Life" for Poles and Serbs – Why Not for Colored Americans?', *New York Amsterdam News*, 1917: transcribed copies, Theodore Draper papers, Box 31, Hoover Institution Archives.

13 Woodrow Wilson, *Address of the President of the United States, Delivered at a Joint Session of the Two Houses of Congress, January 8, 1918* (Washington, DC: Government Printing Office, 1918), 6.

14 'Liberty for all', *New York Amsterdam News*, 1918: transcribed copies, Theodore Draper Collection, Box 31, folder Briggs.

15 Cyril Briggs, 'Africa for the Africans', *New York Globe*, 23 January 1918. Quoted in Hill, 'Racial and Radical', xiii–xiv, liii.

16 Hill, 'Racial and Radical', xvii.

17 'Aims of the Crusador [sic]', *The Crusader*, 1:1 (September 1918), 4.

18 'The Negro Candidates', *The Crusader*, 1:1 (September 1918), 8.

19 'Negroes of the World Unite in Demanding a Free Africa', *The Crusader*, 1:4 (December 1918), 3.

20 Hill, 'Racial and Radical', xxi.

21 Cyril Briggs to Theodore Draper, Theodore Draper papers, 17 March 1958, Box 31, Hoover Institution Archives. Hill, 'Racial and Radical', xxv.

22 Cyril Briggs, 'Darkest Russia', *The Crusader*, 1:7 (March 1919), 24–25. 'The Bolsheviki', *The Crusader*, 1:9 (May 1919), 6.

23 Hill, 'Racial and Radical', xxiii.

24 Capt. John B. Trevor to Brig. Gen. Churchill, 5 April 1919, 10218–324, RG165, MID, NA. Hill, *The Marcus Garvey and Universal Negro Improvement Association Papers*, vol. 1, 405. Theodore Kornweibel, *Seeing Red: Federal Campaigns Against Black Militancy, 1919–1925* (Bloomington, IN: Indiana University Press, 1998), 133.
25 Brig. Gen. Churchill to Maj. H.A. Strauss, 13 October 1919, 10218–349, RG165, MID, NA.
26 'Mr Cyril V. Briggs, Editor of The Crusader Announces the Organisation of the African Blood Brotherhood for African Liberation and Redemption', advertisement in *The Crusader* (October 1919), 27.
27 Romeo L. Dougherty, '"Punta" Revolutionist', *The Crusader*, 2:2 (October 1919), 15–16. *The Crusader*, 1919, 10218–349, RG165, MID, NA. *The Crusader*, 1919–1920, OG387162, RG65, BOI, NA.
28 Romeo L. Dougherty, '"Punta," Revolutionist', *The Crusader*, 2:1 (September 1919), 16. The punctuation of the serial title slightly alters on each instalment – note the inclusion of a comma after 'Punta' in the September issue.
29 Dougherty, '"Punta" Revolutionist', 15.
30 Unidentified MID operative to ?, 20 October 1919, 10218–349, RG165, MID, NA.
31 Makalani has speculated that the ABB might have had up to 8,000 members, but 3,000 is generally deemed the upper limit. Hill, 'Racial and Radical', xlvi. Makalani, *In the Cause of Freedom*, 45.
32 'The African Blood Brotherhood', *The Crusader*, 2:10 (June 1920), 7.
33 Two slightly divergent ABB programmes were published in 1924: Preuss cites a letter by Briggs attributing nine aims to a 1920 convention; Whitney cites an eight-point programme seized in a 1922 raid on a Communist Party convention. McDuffie has located a nine-point programme in CPUSA records, Library of Congress, Washington, DC. See Arthur Preuss, *A Dictionary of Secret and Other Societies* (St Louis: B. Herder Book Co., 1924), 4–7; R.M. Whitney, *Reds in America* (New York: Berkwith Press, 1924), 190–192; Erik S. McDuffie, '"[She] devoted twenty minutes condemning all other forms of government but the Soviet": Black Women Radicals in the Garvey Movement and in the Left during the 1920s' in Michael E. Gomez (ed.), *Diasporic Africa: A Reader* (New York: New York University Press, 2006), 219–250, at 240.
34 Joyce Moore Turner with the assistance of W. Burghardt Turner, *Caribbean Crusaders and the Harlem Renaissance* (Urbana, IL: University of Illinois Press, 2005), 56.
35 Hill, *The Marcus Garvey and Universal Negro Improvement Association Papers*, vol. 1, 523.
36 A contention exists concerning the ABB's affiliation to the US Communist Party, with most historians agreeing with Theodore Draper's observation that the ABB joined with the US Communist Party in 1921. Contesting Draper's thesis, Robert Hill argued that the ABB was closely tied to the US Communist Party in late 1919, an argument most convincingly rebutted by Winston James.

Theodore Draper, *American Communism and Soviet Russia* (New York: Viking Press, 1960), 326; Hill, 'Racial and Radical', xxiv–xxvii; James, *Holding Aloft the Banner of Ethiopia*, 161–163.
37  'Martyrdom', *The Crusader*, 2:2 (October 1919), 10. 'What Your Vote for the Socialist Party Would Do', *The Crusader*, 2:2 (October 1919), 11.
38  Unidentified MID operative to ?, 20 October 1919, 10218-349, RG165.
39  This document borrows heavily from Loving's 'Negro Subversion' report of 6 August 1919. See Peter Hulme's chapter in this volume. Directorate of Intelligence, 'Unrest Among the Negroes', 7 October 1919, Special Report No. 10, Public Records Office, Cabinet Papers 24/89/89. Maj. W.H. Loving to Brig. Gen. Churchill, 6 August 1919, 10218-361, RG165, MID, NA.
40  US Department of Justice, *Investigation Activities of the Department of Justice* (Washington, DC: Government Printing Office, 1919), 162, 166. Maxwell defines ghostreading as 'a duplicitous interpretative enterprise' and has argued that the Bureau is one of 'the most dedicated and influential forgotten' critics of African-American literature. William J. Maxwell, *F.B. Eyes: How J. Edgar Hoover's Ghostreaders Framed African American Literature* (Princeton, NJ: Princeton University Press, 2015), 5, 127.
41  C. Valentine [Briggs], 'Why Lynching Persists', *The Crusader*, 2:1 (September 1919), 6.
42  US Department of Justice, *Investigation Activities*, 166–167.
43  'Congress, the Lusk Committee and the Radical Leaders', *The Crusader*, 2:3 (November 1919), 5–6.
44  US Department of Justice, *Investigation Activities*: 168. I am borrowing the term 'antifile' – a form of writing back to intelligence agencies – from Maxwell. Maxwell, *F.B. Eyes*, 7, 23.
45  Kornweibel, *Seeing Red*, 135.
46  Agent M.J. Davis to Bureau, 29 August 1919, OG387162, RG65, BOI, NA. Kornweibel, *Seeing Red*, 134; Regin Schmidt, *Red Scare: FBI and the Origins of Anticommunism in the United States* (Copenhagen: Museum Tusculanum Press, 2004), 201.
47  WW to Bureau, 6 February 1920, OG258421, RG65, BOI, NA.
48  WW to Bureau, 30 January 1920, OG258421, RG65, BOI, NA.
49  WW to Bureau, 20 March 1920, OG258421, RG65, BOI, NA. Kornweibel, *Seeing Red*, 136–137.
50  *The Crusader*, 1919–1920, OG387162, RG65.
51  C. Valentine [Briggs], 'The Ray of Fear', *The Crusader*, 2:6 (February 1920), 18–20. The President's daughter's name is inconsistently spelt as Mazima and Nazima. See also C. Valentine [Briggs], 'The Ray of Fear', *The Crusader*, 2:8 (April 1920), 11–12. For further discussion of 'The Ray of Fear', see Michelle Ann Stephens, *Black Empire: The Masculine Global Imaginary of Caribbean Intellectuals in the United States, 1914–1962* (Durham, NC: Duke University Press, 2006), 35–38.
52  Martin Robison Delany, *Blake; or, The Huts of America: A Corrected Edition*, ed. Jerome J. McGann (Cambridge, MA: Harvard University Press, 2017).

53 C. Valentine [Briggs], 'Secret Service', *The Crusader*, 4:3 (May 1921), 14–15. See also C. Valentine [Briggs], 'Secret Service', *The Crusader*, 4:4 (June 1921), 11–12.
54 'The African Blood Brotherhood'.
55 Valentine [Briggs], 'The Ray of Fear', *The Crusader*, 2:6 (February 1920), 19. Thomas Carlyle, *The Works of Thomas Carlyle (Complete)* (New York: P.F. Collier, 1897), 281, 564.
56 Kornweibel, *Seeing Red*, 137–138.
57 'Military Control is Ended at Tulsa', *New York Times*, 4 June 1921, 1, 14.
58 'Denies Negroes Started Tulsa Riot', *New York Times*, 5 June 1921, 21.
59 *Ibid.* Andrea [Andy] Razafkeriefo, 'Black Tulsa's Answer', *The Crusader*, 4:6 (August 1921), 6. 'Communists Champion Negro', *The Crusader*, 4:6 (August 1921), 12.
60 Briggs's 15 August letter is replicated in 'Garvey Turns Informer', *The Crusader*, 5:3 (November 1921), 5.
61 Robert A. Hill (ed.), *The Marcus Garvey and Universal Negro Improvement Association Papers*, Vol. 4 (Berkeley, CA: University of California Press, 1985), 196.
62 P-138 to Bureau, 13 July 1921, Bureau Section case file [hereafter BS] 202600–2031, RG65, BOI, NA. Kornweibel, *Seeing Red*, 141–143.
63 'The Salvation of the Negro', *The Crusader*, 4:2 (April 1921), 8–9.
64 'The Socialist Surrender', *The Crusader*, 4:6 (August 1921), 8–9. 'Communists Champion Negro'; 'Congress of the Communist International', *The Crusader*, 4:6 (August 1921), 12–13.
65 Colin Grant, *Negro with a Hat: The Rise and Fall of Marcus Garvey and his Dream of Mother Africa* (London: Jonathan Cape, 2008), 220–221. Kornweibel, *Seeing Red*, 145–147.
66 'Garvey Turns Informer'; Makalani, *In the Cause of Freedom*, 67.
67 When the *Negro World* failed to publish Briggs's letter, Briggs published it in *The Crusader*: Cyril Briggs, 'An Open Letter to Marcus Garvey and His Man "Friday"', *The Crusader*, 5:2 (October 1921), 30–31.
68 800 to George F. Ruch, 18 October 1921, 61–826, Freedom of Information Act request, Federal Bureau of Investigation (hereafter FOIA, FBI). Hill, *The Marcus Garvey and Universal Negro Improvement Association Papers*, Vol. 4, 125.
69 Hill, *The Marcus Garvey and Universal Negro Improvement Association Papers*, Vol. 4, 139–141.
70 P-138 to Bureau, 26 August 1921, BS202600–2031, RG65, BOI, NA.
71 800 to George F. Ruch, 4 September 1921, 61–826, FOIA, FBI.
72 800 to George F. Ruch, 23 September, 1921, 61–826, FOIA, FBI. 800 to George F. Ruch, 29 September 1921, 61–826, FOIA, FBI.
73 'Garvey Turns Informer'.
74 Hill, *The Marcus Garvey and Universal Negro Improvement Association Papers*, Vol. 4, 232.
75 Robert A. Hill (ed.), *The Marcus Garvey and Universal Negro Improvement Association Papers*, Vol. 11 (Durham, NC: Duke University Press, 2011), 202.

76 C. Lorenzo [Briggs], 'The Negro Liberation Movement', *The Toiler*, 4:200 (10 December 1921), 7.
77 Hill, *The Marcus Garvey and Universal Negro Improvement Association Papers*, Vol. 1, 525.
78 Robert A. Hill (ed.), *The Marcus Garvey and Universal Negro Improvement Association Papers*, Vol. 5 (Berkeley, CA: University of California Press, 1987), 558.
79 Hill, *The Marcus Garvey and Universal Negro Improvement Association Papers*, Vol. 1, 525–526.
80 Solomon, *The Cry Was Unity*, 165.
81 Hill, *The Marcus Garvey and Universal Negro Improvement Association Papers*, Vol. 1, 526.
82 House of Representatives, *Investigation of Communist Infiltration and Propaganda Activities in Basic Industry (Gary, Ind., Area)* (Washington, DC: Government Printing Office, 1958), 78.

# 4

# Gendering the black radical tradition: Grace P. Campbell's role in the formation of a radical feminist tradition in African-American intellectual culture

*Lydia Lindsey*

There is a growing body of scholarship and literature that explores the impact of the revolutionary events across the African diaspora and the subsequent critical intellectual influence of Marxism and Bolshevism on the stream of revolutionary 'black internationalism' in its aftermath, in particular the pre-eminent work of Cedric J. Robinson, *Black Marxism: The Making of the Black Radical Tradition* (1983).[1] In his work, Robinson identifies three intellectuals as illustrative of the black radical intellectual tradition – W.E.B. Du Bois, C.L.R. James, and Richard Wright.[2] In this framing, one does not get a sense that black women were activists and theoreticians who carved out intellectual spaces to define and contextualise leftist revolutionary theory. Black women's theoretical perspectives within the Communist movement remain underdeveloped. In contrast, articulations of black women's perspectives on the Negro Question, self-determination, and the Black Belt thesis have increasingly become visible in the literature and have provided a radical analysis in black women's voices on gender, race, capitalism, and class.

There has been a neglect of black women as intellectual contributors because there is a preoccupation with text as the source of intellectual history, and less attention is paid to the spoken word. Grace P. Campbell was a founding member of the African Blood Brotherhood (ABB) that holds the distinction of being the precursor to black national radical organisations in the twentieth century, and was also a chartered member of the Communist Party.[3] She was a formidable public speaker, gave lectures around the city, sponsored lyceum [public lectures], and even held a position on the New York City school board, which allowed her to sponsor lectures by various radicals throughout the city. She had considerable administrative skills in organising and maintaining key institutions that fostered New Negro radical thought. Campbell taught the Principles of Communism at the Harlem Workers School as well as courses in the Current Negro Liberation

Movement. When the Central Control Committee expelled her, she was identified as an intellectual.[4] The primary purpose of this chapter is to give voice to Campbell's gendering of intellectual thought and activism within the radical left New Negro movement. Her voice on the left has often been muted because she did not leave a plethora of writings. But the finding of her analysis of the Negro Question among the papers of the Russian State Archive of Socio-Political History (RGASPI), writings within the *Daily Worker*, *Negro Champion*, and the *Working Woman*, as well as excerpts from her speeches, allows us to hear her voice while helping to secure her place within the ranks of black leftist feminist intellectuals.[5] A subsidiary intent is not to isolate Campbell from other black women who were also engaged in carving paths of black feminist thought and activism. For this reason, the chapter situates Campbell in the context of other black women from the Progressive Era and on the left as they intersect with her life and work.

I approach this inquiry by interrogating Campbell's lived experiences and writings, as well as situating them in relation to black and Marxist feminist theory. Campbell's role in experiencing and understanding the radical feminist tradition in black intellectual culture shifts from dissembling to the politics of respectability as a strategy to mitigate intense racial, gender, and class oppression, as a way of gaining equal rights within the context of the existing political economy. It then shifts, in a deviation from traditional Marxist theorists, to where she saw the intersectionality of race, class, gender, and value in wage and non-wage domestic or reproductive work for black women which suggested that waged industrial workers were not the only participants in the battle for human emancipation. This helped to inform her evolving criticism of industrial capitalism in terms of 'domestic production' among black women in a critical way that shifted her from 'racial uplift' to leaning left and then to Red. Some of the tactics that she used were educating, voting, running for political office, organising communities, and workers.

Grace Campbell's activism and writings exemplify historian Brittany C. Cooper's definition of a 'race woman'. Cooper defines a 'race woman' as a black woman who held leadership positions between the 1890s and 1970s, and who attempted to theorise and 'transform intellectual and physical spaces' for uplifting and empowering the black community from race, class, and gender tyranny.[6] Campbell's activities and writings provide a unique insight into the ways in which race women pieced together fragmented histories of black people and their struggle for full equality and human dignity. Campbell's life and writings illustrate the primary strength of the black radical tradition in its ability to change and shift and merge, to disappear and then reappear again in new spaces and new forms as it reacts to the cycles of capitalism and nationalism. Before joining the Workers Party (WP) in 1921, Campbell had been active in the Niagara Movement, racial uplift charity work in Washington, DC and New York City, as well as a member of the Socialist Party of America (SPA). Campbell's work was in the black community, gendered, and left-leaning, but not yet Red.

## Family ties and early life

Campbell wrote her analysis of the 'Negro Question in the U.S.A' and other writings under her pseudonym Grace Lamb or Belle Lamb. In 1930, when George Schuyler, a socialist turned conservative columnist, refers to Campbell as one of the pioneer Red leaders, he used her pseudonym, Grace Lamb.[7] Her pseudonym is further confirmed by the minutes of the First Re-organisation National Negro Committee, for the Communist Party, on 14 August 1928, where there was a proposal for additional members to the Committee. One of the people recommended was 'Mrs Lamb (Court attendant)'.[8] Grace Campbell was a court attendant at the Court of General Sessions in New York.[9] In 1928, a black female court attendant was a rarity. Before 1924 there were three black people employed in such a court position in the nation.[10] In her *Daily Worker's* obituary, her name is given as 'Grace Campbell (Lamb)'.[11] The surname Lamb was taken from her father, who was named William Alexander Lamb Campbell. The appropriation of the name Lamb reinforced her West Indian identity. The pseudonym Bell Lamb also included her father's name as well as the name Bell taken from the first school established for blacks in the District of Columbia, and the school where her maternal aunt, Laura F. Dyson, had been principal for many years.

Campbell was a product of a strong family tradition that prepared and encouraged her to resist the constraints of class, race, and gender antagonism. The process for resisting societal constrictions resonated in the legacy of her West Indian and African-American parentage and was manifested throughout her life. For Campbell, the personal was political, because her personal and professional decisions informed her shift to the left. Campbell's mother, Emma Virginia Dyson, and her father were early graduates of Howard University. In 1871, Campbell's mother was in the second class to graduate from the Normal Preparatory Department. She had the distinction of being among five or six women in her class. Campbell's mother became a teacher in the District of Columbia public schools, along with her sisters Laura F. Dyson and Grace A. Dyson.[12]

In 1874, Campbell's father, a Jamaican, was in the first graduating class of Howard University's Theology Department and was ordained as a Congregational minister. He was married to her mother on 7 August 1874, at her residence in Washington, DC, by Reverend Father Boyle of St Augustine's Catholic Church. The church is one of the oldest black Catholic churches in the United States, and Campbell's mother's family was among the founding members of the church. After the wedding, the newlyweds moved to Macon, Georgia, where he had been assigned to minister Norwich Chapel under the auspices of the American Missionary Association.[13]

On a Monday morning, about six o'clock, on 11 October 1875, Grace Philomena Campbell was born.[14] Campbell's mother died on 10 November 1876. Grace was the only child of that union. She and her father returned to Washington, DC, where they resided in her grandparent's home.[15] In August 1882, her father remarried and later moved to Galveston, Texas, with his new wife and son.[16] He left Grace Campbell in the care of her mother's family, the Dysons, in the District of Columbia. Campbell's mother's family emerged from slavery, sharing many of the characteristics that were possessed by Washington's aristocracy of colour. Her grandparents had purchased their freedom before slavery was abolished, owned property, educated their children, and were Republicans. They operated within the orbit of elite families of colour.[17]

From her father's second marriage, six children were born. One son, Henry (1880), was born before the couple left for Texas, and Mary V. Campbell (1891) and Ralph E. Campbell (1888) were born in Galveston. So far, only three of the couple's living children have been identified.[18] Grace Campbell had a relationship with Mary and Ralph in her adult life because both of them lived with her for a while, and she would babysit for her sister.[19] Neither Campbell's sister nor brother embraced her leftist political activism. Her brother was a conservative, and her sister joined the Father Divine movement. However, her cousin, Zita Emma Dyson, who was the daughter of her mother's brother, Frederick A. Dyson, who had been a delegate to the Republican National Convention, worked with Campbell's endeavours in the ABB, such as organising the 1924 All-Race Conference or Negro Sanhedrin.[20] Before moving left, Campbell and Zita Dyson had worked together in racial uplift work such as improving conditions on playgrounds, participating in benefits to raise money for the Willow Tree Alley Mission, and participating in Associate Charities endeavours.[21]

Campbell's schooldays in the District of Columbia public schools shared some spaces with Nannie Burroughs, who became a leading educator, civil rights activist, feminist, and religious leader. They did not attend the same schools, but they were engaged in some of the same extracurricular activities. Campbell was a grade ahead of Burroughs. Campbell attended Lincoln School, and Burroughs was a student at the Sumner School.[22] In 1891 Campbell was promoted to the Colored High School.[23] Between 1893 and 1896, Campbell was enrolled in Howard University's Preparatory

Department. In her third year, she was in the Scientific Program, along with eight other students, where the 'curriculum was rigorous'.[24]

## Professional uplifting and culture of dissemblance: District of Columbia

In 1897, Campbell graduated from the Colored Woman's League Kindergarten Training School. In Washington, DC, the creation of kindergarten classes was among the earliest projects of the Colored Women's League (CWL). Campbell's commencement from the CWL Kindergarten Training School was held in the People's Congregation Church on M Street between Sixth and Seventh Streets NW. Anna J. Cooper, Chairperson of the CWL Kindergarten Committee, spoke at the commencement. She gave the graduates sound advice on the way to overcome the difficulties which they would find in their chosen profession. Cooper had recently published her book *A Voice From the South by a Black Woman of the South* (1892), which was an African-American feminist text.[25] In *A Voice From the South*, Cooper placed black women and their work squarely at the centre of the struggle for racial justice when she wrote: 'Only the BLACK WOMAN can say when and where I enter, in the quiet, undisputed dignity of my womanhood, without violence and without suing or special patronage, then and there the whole Negro race enters with me.'[26] Here Cooper problematised intragroup race and gender politics by insisting on the significance of the black women at the core of racial progress. As a young woman, Cooper exposed Campbell to the reality that black women faced a unique struggle due to overlapping racism and sexism while trying to create a better world.

In 1898, the District of Columbia public schools incorporated kindergartens for white and black children. To assure herself a position in the public schools, Campbell went back to school for additional training. In 1899, she graduated from the Park Temple kindergarten training that certified her for teaching kindergarten work in public schools.[27] For further preparation for teaching kindergarten lecture courses, Campbell attended the Normal Teachers College at Howard University. In 1902, she was one of thirteen students awarded a Kindergarten Course Diploma of Teaching.[28] Then, in 1908, Campbell graduated from the Chicago School of Advanced Kindergarten Work.[29]

In 1901, in the first edition of *National Capital Searchlight* that is seen as a precursor to the *Journal of Negro Education*, Grace Campbell wrote an article on 'Kindergarten Ideal'. The journal was published in Washington by 'colored people' and devoted exclusively to the educational welfare of black people.³⁰ The *Washington Post* reported that it 'presents a splendid display of practical intelligence and [in] good taste'. Some of the other articles that accompanied Grace Campbell's in the first issue included 'The Negro Exhibit: At the Paris Exposition' by Anna J. Cooper, 'Historical Sketch of Colored Schools in the District of Columbia' by George F.T. Cook, ex-superintend of schools, 'Timely Suggestions' by John W. Cromwell, principal, and 'Drizzle', a poem by Paul Lawrence Dunbar. Among those on the advisory staff were the principals of the high and normal schools, Robert H. Terrell and Lucy E. Moten, respectively. Terrell was an attorney and the second black person to serve as a justice of the peace in Washington, DC. In 1911, he was appointed as a judge to the District of Columbia Municipal Court.³¹ Moten was a black educator and doctor. She was the first African-American principal of the Miner Normal School. Moten was responsible for training many of the teachers in Washington, DC, including Zita E. Dyson, Campbell's cousin.³²

In July 1903, Campbell established a model kindergarten at the Magruder School.³³ The intent of kindergarten was always to form rather than reform.³⁴ In 1906, Campbell was appointed assistant to the kindergarten to supervise the work of coloured kindergarten classes and teachers. Her appointment was a tribute to her 'good work as she was selected from among a corps of kindergartens' who had been in service longer than her. Campbell kept in close touch with the teachers and occasionally visited the kindergarteners in their regular class setting.³⁵ These were significant changes 'that marked the progress of work in the kindergarten department'. Campbell made reports to the United States Congress.³⁶ In September 1907, she held the title 'principal model kindergarten' in the Tenth Division, a black division. Her career appeared to have been on the fast track.³⁷ Campbell received professional recognition for her outstanding kindergarten work that rivalled the work of Anna Evans Murray, the wife of the well-known bibliophile Daniel Murray of the Library of Congress. Murray was known as being primarily responsible for establishing the kindergarten programme in the District's Colored Schools.³⁸

But in 1908, because of the guile of Anna E. Murray, a member of Washington's black elite, Campbell was forced to move to New York, where she took a position at the Lincoln Kindergarten in Brooklyn.³⁹ Campbell's troubles stemmed from the inability of a black woman to accept her for her talents and abilities, just as she was becoming a leader in kindergarten work. Restrictions on gender, racial, and class norms influenced Campbell's treatment. She was seen as not toeing the line of the economic, racial, and social hierarchy. Anna E. Murray could not control her. She could not accept her as competent to supervise others because she had spoken up on her behalf against a member of the coloured elite. Campbell had broken the protocol of the culture of dissemblance that had been constructed to protect the inner, private lives of the women of the coloured aristocracy that was played out behind the enduring walls of Jim Crow.[40]

For aristocrats of colour, such as Murray, genteel performance in both private and public were to be modelled as a significant factor in advancing the 'progress of the race' within the paradigmatic frames of the culture of dissemblance and the politics of respectability.[41] Murray could only imagine Campbell as in need of supervision herself. Murray had insinuated that Campbell was a sexual degenerate and in need of supervision herself. Murray characterised Campbell as dangerous to the success of the educational system and someone who needed to be driven out. The CWL had propagated the culture of dissemblance as they sought to destroy what was perceived as harmful or malicious depictions of black women's sexuality embedded in the legacy of slavery. The CWL did not see where black women had the social, political, or economic power to change these tropes. For this reason, the CWL thought it imperative to collectively create alternative self-images to 'protect the sanctity of inner aspects of their lives'.[42]

Campbell could not readily divest herself of the dynamics of the culture of dissemblance because she was part of a group of black women who were less than a generation away from slavery that had been victims of systematic sexual exploitation. She was subjugated by a racist, patriarchal society, and third-class citizenship. For black women, like Campbell, the politics of respectability tended to reinforce status distinctions by linking worthiness for respect to sexual propriety and behavioural decorum. It helped them to navigate the hostility of the public sphere within the frame of black patriarchy that minimises situations where they might encounter sexual improprieties. Respectability served as 'a gatekeeping function, establishing a behavioural "entrance fee" to the right of respect, to full citizenship'.[43]

The scandal penetrated the walls of the culture of dissemblance and adversely impacted Campbell and her family. In 1908, Laura Dyson was demoted, and Grace Anne Dyson lost her longevity pay. The local black newspaper, the *Washington Bee*, spoke out on the family's behalf. It reaffirmed that their demotions were without just cause and that they were two of the best teachers in the system.[44] There were no external institutions designed to protect women of the middling sort within the orbit of the black elite. Black middling-class women were supposed to find refuge in their families or marriages under the guise of the black patriarchy. But Campbell's family was under assault, and neither she nor any of her aunts were married. There was no patriarchal figure to protect her. Campbell's middling-class priority, under the paradigmatic frames of the culture of dissemblance and the politics of respectability, was under assault.

Campbell was vulnerable and unprotected. In this instance, a black woman spawned Campbell's vulnerability. Campbell was a victim of misogyny and anti-feminism.

Mary Church Terrell and Fannie Barrier Williams, two black clubwomen who were activists in a variety of capacities and had spent their lives intellectualising the problematics of race and gender discrimination as well as fighting against it, came to Campbell's aid. Terrell was an influential educator and activist who championed racial equality and women's suffrage. She was on the school board and investigated the accusation of mismanagement of the kindergarten. Terrell learned that Campbell had been falsely accused. Her accuser was trying to advance her interests.[45] Williams was an educator, political and women's rights activist, as well as a journalist. Her sister, Ella D. Barrier, had long worked with Campbell's aunts in the District public schools. Williams helped to find Campbell a lucrative position in New York at Lincoln Settlement in Brooklyn as Director of Kindergarten.[46] Despite how this scandal played out against her and her family, Campbell did not reject the substance of the culture of dissemblance as a source of protection, nor abandon the politics of respectability as a strategy for uplifting.

## Professional uplifting and the politics of respectability: New York

Once in New York, Campbell became affiliated with the newly formed Empire State Federation of Women's Clubs (ESFWC), a gateway organisation of the National Association of Colored Women (NACW), and a sister organisation of the Colored Women's League (CWL). Campbell was a dutiful worker, and the members congratulated themselves on having a representative such as her who was a woman 'of intelligence and broad sympathy'.[47] Through the ESFWC, Campbell was exposed to new ideas and black feminist intellectuals who were moving beyond the politics of respectability. These progressive black women, such as Ida B. Wells and Marie C. Lawton, were not only fighting against the idea of 'respectability' as a prerequisite for being heard and accepted but against the tendency of white women and black men not to hear them and erase their contributions.[48] They heighten her awareness of the interlocking structures of subjugation that characterised black lives. Campbell had met the well-known anti-lynching crusader Ida B. Wells-Barnett when she was in Chicago and was in the audience when Wells delivered speeches on 'Woman Suffrage' and on 'Higher Ideals'.[49] Campbell's affiliation with the ESFWC brought her under the mentorship of Marie C. Lawton, the third president of the ESFWC. Lawton had been characterised by military intelligence as a dangerous woman. The goal of the ESFWC was to promote the welfare of people wherein needed, and to assist in civic affairs.[50] These race women were public intellectuals committed to race, gender, and class uplift and the liberation of black people.[51]

By October 1911, in New York City, it was publicly acknowledged that Campbell had 'done yeoman service for the betterment of conditions among women'.[52] Her career as a social reformer took a turn in 1911 when she left the Lincoln Kindergarten, took a position with the National League for the Protection of Colored Women (NLPCW) and became a probation officer. Campbell was known as one of the most successful probation officers in the Court of General Sessions. She was 'the first and only one of her race', and had attracted a great deal of attention by her work at the Tombs. There was not anyone who did not respond to her sympathy.[53] She was more intelligent and a deeper thinker than others in this line of work. She knew the conditions and gave the facts. Campbell aroused public awareness of the need for a home for delinquent girls.[54]

In her role as a probation officer with the NLPCW, she embraced the politics of respectability. Historian Evelyn Brooks Higginbotham explains that the politics of respectability was a strategy for social reform employed by many black church women, black club women, and political activists during the nineteenth and early twentieth centuries. The politics of respectability emphasised reforming 'individual behavior and attitudes both as a goal in itself and as a strategy for reform of the entire structural system of American race relations'.[55] Campbell and other black female reformers 'hoped to create a set of guidelines and behavioural patterns that portrayed a moral, well-mannered, and culturally advanced group'. The politics of respectability was a strategy to mitigate or dissemble away intense racial, gender, and class oppression, as a way of gaining equal rights within the context of the existing political economy.[56]

Campbell said that she had been drawn to her work with NLPCW through her kindergarten work in Washington, Chicago, and New York. The NLPCW came under the auspices of the National League on Urban Conditions, commonly called the Urban League. Recognising the shortcomings of the politics of respectability to engage racism and class inequities, Campbell shifted to using her voice in public spaces to inform the people of the problems facing black women while taking steps towards amelioration of these situations in and outside the parameters of the NLPCW.[57] Since 1912, Campbell had been making a plea before club women's groups for a detention house for coloured girls and women. She had identified a need for a home for girls and women who came before the courts and either were sent to jail or returned to their surroundings because there was no home to send them. All of the detention homes were for white women. The home intended to offer a helping hand and another chance, rather than pushing the women further down with a prison term.[58] Mary B. Talbert, President of the ESFWC, heard Campbell's appeal for a home for delinquent girls; she thought it was 'forcibly put and clearly outlined'. Talbert applauded Campbell's intelligence and work.[59]

Yet Campbell was dismissed from the NLPCW because a white woman and black men could not accept Campbell's contributions. She was dismissed from the NLPCW not because there were any problems with the quality of her work, but because she made Elizabeth Walton, a white reformer, and two black men, Eugene Kinckle Jones, first Executive Secretary of the National Urban League, and George Haynes, co-founder and first Executive Director of the National Urban League, feel uncomfortable. Once again, Campbell upset the racial and gender protocol.[60] The chairperson of the Committee for Women was Walton, a white reformer; in a letter, she acknowledged that she felt threatened by Campbell. Walton questioned the direction of Campbell's 'work and argued that the organisation was established for preventive reform, not criminal justice'.[61] Walton opposed Campbell's shift in focus. Jones insisted that Campbell had overstepped her bounds, thought too highly of herself, and 'subordinates the work of the entire Committee, to her fractional part of the movement'. As a man, he reduced the conflict between Campbell and Walton to the bickering between women 'rather than identifying it as a legitimate struggle over ideological and methodological differences'. George Haynes, another black man, thought that he could personally manage her.[62]

Campbell's dismissal was rooted in the inability of white men and women and black men to see black women as their equals. The dilemma inherent in interracial-racialism, historian Nell Irvin Painter said, stems from 'No matter how patient the Negroes or well-meaning the whites, cooperating interracially in a segregated world that assumed black inferiority imposed strains on both sides.'[63] Just like in the Anna E. Murray scandal, assumptions about race and gender influenced how the Urban League treated Campbell. Her colleagues failed to accept her as an equal just as she was becoming a leader in criminal justice. They could only imagine a black woman as in need of supervision, not as competent to supervise others. Campbell, a college-educated, well-respected professional, was characterised in the same terms as the black female migrants she was helping.

In the same way that society labelled the recent migrant black women as immoral and in need of policing, reformers' references to Campbell as 'not able to fall into line', an 'insubordinate' who 'lacks respect for authority', and a problematic employee who disrupted the 'order and discipline of the office' defined her as a problem that needed to be excised from the Urban League. While they never claimed that Campbell was sexually degenerate, she was characterised as dangerous to the success of the organisation. Within NLPCW, once again, the culture of dissemblance did not protect her, nor did the politics of respectability advance her acceptability.[64]

The Harlem community and the ESFWC expressed surprise at her dismissal. When the ESFWC met that week, they protested Campbell's 'summary dismissal', expressing 'indignation' at 'the manner' in which Campbell was discharged. On 12 June 1913, *New York Age* printed on page one that Marie J. Stuart, Secretary of the Federation, spoke to the gathering on 'the value and importance of a united effort on the part of women'. She then connected it to the dismissal of Campbell. The anger of those present was most pronounced, and 'by a rising vote, the clubs decided to protest against the manner of Miss Campbell's discharge'.[65] Then, within a few days of Campbell's dismissal from the NLPCW on 24 June 1913, it was announced that she would become the supervisor of the Union Rescue Mission; this was later reorganised and became the Empire Shelter for Friendless Women.[66] Once again, the club women came to Campbell's aid to help in her uplift work that was centred on the politics of respectability.

## Moving left: embracing socialism

In 1914, Campbell began to abandon the Republican Party with her affiliation with the Independent and Political Council (IPC) in Harlem. Left-leaning activist Asa Philip Randolph and Chandler Owens organised the IPC, a debate group that folded after the First World War. The socialist newspaper, *The Call*, reported that the IPC was 'composed of 400 colored men and women and 200 white men and women', and that it was 'the most important organisation of colored residents of Harlem'. Marie C. Lawton was associate with the IPC. The 'primary, sole and immediate aim' of the IPC was 'to fight for progressive, clean and honest government' and to use the ballot, the mightiest weapon of the ages, to obtain 'a just political status for the colored people' in particular.[67] The group addressed critical social and political issues that confronted African Americans.

The IPC social engagement is credited with making socialist ideas appealable to Campbell and her influence and intellectual circle. The debates laid out syllogisms whereby its membership reached the intellectual point from which they could 'discern the worthlessness of the Republican party to the Negro as a medium for bettering conditions for that race', and that many of them, such as Campbell, went even further, and 'recognise that the well-being of the Negro is ultimately bound up with Socialism'. Randolph thought this was no small accomplishment because popular history had recorded that the Republican Party had 'emancipated the Negro'. It had never permitted 'the Negro to forget the alleged fact'. For this reason, Randolph said, 'the Republican Party is a religion to the colored man', but the 'Awakening of the Negro' had begun.[68]

Between 1911 and 1914, Hubert Harrison was the leading black activist, orator, and theoretician in the Socialist Party of New York, and he also inspired many IPC members to embrace socialism. At a testimonial dinner, Campbell and others praised Harrison for 'his breadth of learning, his intellectual honesty, and the splendid work' he had done in the educational field.[69] His lectures were considered the preparatory classes for radical thought in that they 'prepared the minds of conservative Negroes to receive and accept socialism'.[70] As Campbell began to develop a stronger class consciousness in the years after the First World War, one can look back on her early association with Harrison and her involvement with IPC as important markers in her radicalisation.

Around 1916, when Campbell was embracing socialism, Otto Huiswoud's mother, Jacqueline Bernard Huiswoud, moved in with her. Campbell joined the Socialist Party of America, and this membership marked a leftward shift in her radical and gender activism. In 1901, the SPA was founded in Indianapolis, Indiana. In its membership, the SPA had some of the most ardent suffrage activists, such as Helen E. Holman. Holman was one of the ablest and most eloquent advocates of socialism and women's suffrage in Harlem.[71]

In 1917, socialist Randolph and Owens established the 21st District Socialist Club. Campbell served as secretary for the Socialist Party's 21st Assembly District in Harlem. Socialist Richard Moore described the 1917 Twenty-First District as a unique branch of the Party, in that it was made up of 'militant, vocal, young men and one woman', Grace P. Campbell. The socialist headquarters had little control over the curriculum. There was no centralised democracy or official party line. They were allowed to develop their own study group and educational forum. They met on Sunday morning, gathered together out of the benefit of interest, and read, studied, and commented on pertinent theories.[72] The New Negro in Harlem was known as the 'Socialist Negro'. They were 'waging an earnest campaign' by using the spoken and the written word from their headquarters at 2305 Seventh Avenue. Other black women became members of the 21st District Socialist Branch, such as Emily Jones, Anna Jones, and Lucille G. Randolph. They sought to acquaint 'their brothers and sisters with the treachery of the Republican and Democratic Parties'. The Socialist banner replaced the Republican banner that once waved on the avenue between 135th and 136th Streets.[73]

In 1917, the socialists were committed to the passage of the women's suffrage amendment and racial equality. Campbell agreed with the socialist position on voting. Female suffrage was one of the most pressing issues and one in which black women wanted to demonstrate their political clout.[74] Campbell and other black suffragists were not naïve; they did not trust white suffragists. They knew that they had been excluded from suffragist activity because of their race. Black suffragists knew that white national suffrage leaders, while courting black support, endorsed equal suffrage; then, in their public actions and statements to the white rank and file, often contradicted their assertions of equalitarianism.[75] White women's conception of suffrage had not envisioned the needs and interests of black men and women. The suffrage movement was largely segregated, and black women rarely acquired leadership within interracial women's organisations. America's women's suffrage movement was only committed to the interests of white middle- and upper-class women. Traditional enfranchisement was white male to the core: to be a man was to have the right to vote. Enfranchisement was, therefore, a statement about the system of gender that established and monitored boundaries between masculinity and femininity, as well as how race informed the political critique of the democratic will.

As the Woman's Suffrage referendum was pending in the New York state legislature, black women complained of discrimination by white suffragists.[76] Then in 1917, the Woman Suffrage Party refused to record a protest against the East St Louis murders, where white people murdered between 40 and 250 black people and left about 6,000 blacks homeless. Eslanda Cardozo Goode, a member of the IPC and mother of anthropologist and author Essie Robeson (the wife of actor and activist Paul Robeson), expressed significant reservations about aligning with white suffragists. Goode said that with white women in the majority, 'we cannot but fear that when given the ballot, they will use it to our detriment'.[77] Goode saw white women enfranchisement as a way to ensure white supremacy. She wanted black suffragists to maintain independent organisations from white women, and she wanted black men to withhold their vote on the amendment until the Women's Suffragist Party declared its position on the status of black women. As a member of the IPC, Campbell was well aware of Goode's position and strategies. Goode formed the Negro Women's Campaign Committee and spoke on 'Liberty Corner' 134th and Lenox Avenue to an immense gathering on the 'New Negro Woman'.[78]

On 6 November 1917, women received the right to vote in the State of New York. About 75,000 black women were enfranchised, and the first black representative to the New York State Assembly, Edward A. Johnson, and first black Alderman of New York City, James C. Thomas Jr elected. The political landscape of the city was changing.[79] In Harlem, black women had shown an unusual interest in politics and, within three months, had held numerous meetings. Organisations were actively engaged in getting the women out to vote. It had been argued that if women received the vote that they would not use it, but this allegation was refuted by the political activities of the black women in Harlem. They had formed two leagues: the Woman's Non-Partisan League and the Women's Political League. It was argued that the election of Campbell, or any other black woman, would stimulate and electrify black people throughout the country.[80] In 1919, the Republican Club of Jamaica held a convention and invited Campbell to speak. The object of the convention was to bring about a feeling of unity between the various political clubs among women.[81]

Campbell's socialist partisanship affiliation was a statement on race and gender that established and monitored boundaries between race and femininity as well as an informed critique of how political parties thwarted the democratic will. Traditional partisanship complemented and reinforced white male supremacy in a variety of ways. Campbell's socialist partisanship was an antithesis to white male dependency.[82] Her candidacy was significant in that she was more than a radical suffragette, but she was a black woman espousing a militant platform that characterised a working-class movement.[83] Campbell's 1919 run opened the door for other black women to run on third-party tickets.[84]

Throughout the Harlem community, Campbell was a well-known socialist, but tacitly received support from long-time Republicans Nannie Burroughs and Ida B. Wells-Barnett when they encouraged black people to vote for the socialist ticket in 1919. In response to a question posed in the *Afro-American*: 'Should we Vote Socialist?', the response of Burroughs, of the National Training School, was that 'Unless the two great political parties – Republican and Democratic – declare themselves on the Suffrage, Labor and Lynching questions, the Negro should go to the Socialist Party that has already declared itself for exact justice and equal opportunity for all, regardless of race.'[85] *The Crusader*, the official organ of the ABB, reprinted segments of Burroughs comments.[86]

As President of the Negro Fellowship League, Ida B. Wells-Barnett wrote, 'You ask what stand we ought to take toward the Socialist Party. I am very much of the opinion that as a matter of self-protection that the Negro should divide their vote.' She explained that, for the past forty years, the Republican Party has felt as though the black vote belongs to them, and have stood by and watched black people stoned to death, and 'when they have not actually participated in the stoning, they have stood by and watched and held the clothes of those who' were stoning – while the Democratic Party had been uncompromising in its prosecution of black people. So, if blacks were to 'turn to some party that gives promise of practicing what it preaches without prejudice, there seems only the Socialist Party left'. Indeed, Campbell's shift to the Socialist Party was indicative

Figure 4.1 Grace P. Campbell, *The Messenger*, 2:10 (November 1920)

of the indifference displayed 'toward race, in general by both parties'. The socialists were committed to racial equality, including recommending a federal law against lynching and the passage of the women's suffrage amendment.[87]

In succeeding years, there were continuous calls for Campbell to run for national office. She twice ran, in 1919 and 1920, for State Assembly on the Socialist Party electoral ticket, and in 1922 for the United States Congress on the Workers Party ticket. It was believed that she would make a worthy representative in Washington.[88] In 1920, *The Crusader* ran an ad encouraging its readers to vote for the Socialist Party, identifying Campbell as an Assembly Candidate from the 19th District. The advertisement stated that because of their readers' 'dual interests as workers and Negroes' they 'all must make their vote count to the very limit of its possibilities'. They 'should use it to protest against present economic exploitation of the Many in the interests of the Few!' They should 'use it to rebuke the Republican and Democratic Parties because both were jointly responsible for the wrongs of the last fifty years!'[89] Then, in an editorial, *The Crusader* doubled down on its appeal. It wrote that 'On the grounds of race, the Socialist Party is alone among American parties in its unequivocal stand for equality of opportunities and rights for the Negro.' It pointed out that 'The Socialist

Party not only states in clearest terms, free from the slightest trace of ambiguity, its promises to the Negro, but has time and again to the fullest extent of its power translated those promises into action, as in its nomination of Negroes for the highest offices.'[90]

Although handicapped by a lack of sufficient funds to make her campaigns as intense and complete as possible, in 1920, Campbell made a fair showing in the election. She compelled the attention of her opponents. The campaign waged by Grace Campbell moved along with significant features. She issued a letter to voters, which was the subject of lively commentary. The purpose of the letter was to inject some life into the political battle and force the Democrats and Republicans to discuss things more than a candidate's birthplace, professional records, or philanthropies. She invited representation of the two old parties to a roundtable discussion of issues at the People's Educational Forum. She said that since all the candidates were black, the campaign was 'robbed of a racial issue'. She thought this fact was right and 'served to center the entire attention of the voters on the three-party platforms'. Campbell opened the discussion and set the tone for her opponents, who were deluged with questions about the merits of capitalism.[91]

In 1928, Campbell urged black women to vote. She told them that voting served as a function to allow them to protect their rights. Campbell suggested that they vote for the Workers Party candidates. She maintained that its platform was the only one 'that can serve the interests of the black women voter as a worker; which expresses her struggle to win for her posterity an equal opportunity for life, liberty and normal human development'. She pointed out that since the close of the First World War, black women had voted for Democratic and Republican candidates, and a stamp of inferiority had been placed on all black people because both capitalist parties had supported 'Jim Crowism, segregation southern disfranchisement, general terrorism; lack of opportunity of making a living and educational facilities'. She argued that not voting was not an option because someone was going to win the election, and black women would have relinquished their rights.[92]

In 1920, with A. Philip Randolph, Richard Moore, Otto Huiswoud, and Cyril Briggs, Campbell founded the People's Educational Forum, an organisation that hosted radical political events in Harlem. The Forum was established as a means of orientating themselves and the public with issues, and Campbell became the chairperson. And although Washington, DC Bethel Literary and Historical Association had a different constituency from the People's Educational Forum, both shared the same intent. The respective organisations were used as intellectual forums to attract blacks and whites from across the nation to discuss and debate issues of importance to the race. As an educator, Campbell realised the importance of education to racial uplift and her responsibility as an educator to take the lead in that direction.[93] 'The Forum is the center of all.'[94] As chairperson of the Forum she brought speakers such as Ida Crouch-Hazlett, noted socialist, lecturer, and newspaper writer to speak on 'The Economic Aspects of Lynching', and Franz Boas, who taught anthropology at Columbia University, on 'Supposed Race Inferiority'. When Walter White of the National Association for the Advancement of Colored People (NAACP) spoke, he agreed with the black radicals and Bolshevism, but thought that black people should establish 'co-operative societies and organise themselves pending the grand arrival of the social revolution'.[95]

## Gendering left: Campbell's understanding of Black women's proletarianization

Campbell's writings, speeches, and activism connected the interplay of gender with race and class in the context of her evolving Marxism. She sought to expose every kind of discrimination and domination. She resisted the notion that any form of oppression was more 'fundamental' or 'important' than others, or that any single form was reducible to another. Her analysis showed the ways that varying types of discrimination could operate – within the same social spaces and in complex connections – to shape the complicated unequal outcomes that result when many principles of domination and privilege operate simultaneously in the lives of groups and individuals 'othered' and marginalised in American society. In this way, Campbell's writings, speeches, and activities expand on Anna J. Cooper's paradigm that black women face a unique struggle due to overlapping racism and sexism while embracing an intersectionality approach. Intersectionality is a relatively recent term used by numerous feminists since the 1990s that was developed mainly by women of colour to understand, explain, resist, and transform the unequal outcomes of principles and systems of oppression they have experienced.[96]

Campbell's writings and activism in sundry ways addressed women's issues most aggressively in terms of the intersectionality of race, gender, and class from the spectrum of the politics of respectability by using her body and voice in public domains to stage racial dramas and to create situations that informed the public of problems facing black women, while taking steps towards improving those situations in and outside the labour movement as well as within the Workers Party.[97] Hermie Huiswoud, the wife of Otto, recalled that Campbell extensively did women's work. She worked among the unemployed and homeless in Harlem 'with an ear for everybody woes.' When asked, she would share the contents of her purse with every needy case, and Claude McKay, the poet, appeared to have been a regular needy case.[98]

Campbell worked to organised black women workers and knew that they were the most exploited part of the workforce. She understood that within the proletarian struggle, there was also a gender struggle. The dirty deals that fall to all working women in capitalist society fell heaviest on black women workers. Yet she did not distinctly address the plight of women in her 'Analysis of the Negro Question'.[99] As historian Robin D.G. Kelley has pointed out, the language of the Black Belt thesis was masculine, and even in Campbell's analysis she uses masculine language. Masculine language prioritised black liberation over the women's struggle and ignored a profound framework that might combine the 'Negro' and 'Woman' questions.[100] However, the Black Belt thesis did break new ground in that the resolution specifically discussed black women workers. The resolution acknowledged that 'Negro women in industry and on the farms constitute a powerful potential force in the struggle for Negro emancipation', and because they were 'unorganised to an even greater extent than male Negro workers, they ... [were] the most exploited section'.[101] In addressing this condition, Campbell wrote an article titled 'Negro Working Women Must Take Place in the Class War'.[102]

Campbell made the first sustained effort to think about black women's centrality to the proletarian struggle because, in the voice of Anna J. Cooper, Campbell understood that where and when black women enter the proletarian struggle, the 'Negro race' would enter with them. So Campbell took up this task by raising class consciousness among black women workers and organising them. She was mainly focused on bringing black women workers to a consciousness of their position in the working class and drawing them into the class struggle. She wrote that a 'persistent effort must be made to develop in the Negro Woman worker a real working-class ideology'. She understood that 'Negro women workers must broaden their outlook on the labor movement and must gain a conception of the class struggle as a whole and the international struggle against capitalist imperialism.'[103] She recognised that there was an 'unintelligent attitude' of black women workers as well as a feeling of alienation towards trade unions, but the root of the problem did not lay merely with them – it was a shared problem among black women workers and trade unions who delayed in trying to organise black women until a strike came.[104]

Campbell believed that it was the duty of the class-conscious workers 'to teach the oppressed Negro women workers the true nature of capitalism and imperialism' and to show them that theirs is a struggle of class and not only race. She pointed out that the working class in America is composed of black and white together, and 'that imperialism is the common enemy of all workers'. For this reason, Campbell maintained that black and white working women 'must stand together firmly organised and united to the end of strangling imperialist power'. At the same time, black women 'with their white sisters, must give resistance to the capitalist oppressors everywhere, in the shop, in the homes, in political campaigns, and must fight together'.[105] She was critical of the trade unionist tactics that were 'short-sighted' and did not offer a long-term strategy for organising black working women.[106]

Campbell paced with picketers and explained to them 'at meetings the wisdom underlying union principles'.[107] She spoke on 'the extreme exploitation of Negro women workers and the necessity for them to join with the white workers in the building' of a trade union movement.[108] Within the ranks she was characterised as a 'Negro woman militant'. In 1928, her dedication to the cause earned her an enthusiastic greeting by a spontaneous singing of 'The International' from over 1,000 women workers when she rose to the platform to speak on the anti-labour role of the Democratic, Republican, and Socialist parties, and to urge all women workers and working-class housewives to support the class struggle programme of the Workers Party. She outlined the struggles and working conditions among black women in the needle trades and other industries. She emphasised the necessity of these workers to join the unions in their respective plants. She opened the eyes of the workers to the necessity of carrying on a bitter class struggle against the capitalist system.[109]

Campbell deviates from traditional Marxist theorists in that she saw the intersectionality of race, class, gender, and value in wage and non-wage domestic or reproductive work as well as the family. In her writings, like historian Joan Wallach Scott, she does not remove black women workers from their family contexts; instead, she saw it as an essential aspect of their lives. She discussed it as an institution within which women defined their relationships around race, economic, and domestic issues, with the latter as an aspect of the former. For Campbell, black women's families reflected and embodied a racial cast, and economic order and politics dramatically affected it.[110]

Domestic labour was not a part of Engels's analysis of *The Condition of the Working Class in England*. Nothing was said about women, domestic labour, sexuality, procreation, or family. As historian Jane Humphries pointed out, 'The theoretical perspective of Marx and Engels denied that the kinship ties of the working class had any material basis and led them to postulate the imminent decay of the traditional working-class family.'[111] Some later Marxist authors have attempted to remedy this deficiency by explaining that the continuation of the existence of the working-class family remained because of its role in the reproduction of labour power. These writers emphasised that capital derives certain benefits from the existence of family structures in the form of additional surplus value and political stability. From this they deduce that the family survives because it is in the interests of capital that it should do so.[112] This is not incorrect because, under capitalism, women play a key role in reproducing the 'labour power' necessary for the reproduction of the capitalist system as a whole. But Campbell understood that explanations of this sort did not adequately explain the survival of black working-class kinship structures under capitalism.

Marx believed that waged industrial work was the stage on which the battle for humanity's emancipation would be played. 'Housework, as a specific branch of capitalist production, was below Marx's historical and political horizon.' Marx failed to recognise the importance of reproductive work because he accepted the capitalist criteria for what constituted work.[113] But Campbell saw domestic work as the critical engine for the reproduction of the industrial workforce, creation of community, and survival of the family. It was the breeding ground for the intersectionality of tripartite oppression. She saw black women's position in their families as a source of resistance against capitalism, which affected her standard of living, class cohesion, and ability to wage the class struggle. Marx and Engels failed to see this, and their analysis of the family failed to see the interrelationship of so-called 'domestic' life and labour and the workplace as points of production. Marxist analysis of capitalism tends almost exclusively to focus on commodity production and is blind to the significance of women's unpaid reproductive work.

Reproductive labour involved a far broader range of activities since food had to be prepared, clothes had to be washed, bodies had to be stroked and cared for. Because black women's domestic work for whites was paid labour, Campbell came to an advanced analysis of the fundamental role of household labour in reproducing the capitalist system: their wages literally produced and reproduced the black labouring classes that were their own families. She did not see black women revolting against paid and non-paid reproductive work; instead, she saw them as having a value in their lives because of the connection between the material conditions and familial relationships. Black women were driven by life needs and not just commodity production. Of course, this led to heightened misery and oppression, as well as the tripartite oppression of women. Still, Campbell also saw it as creating situations that would provoke circumstances that could be used as sources of organising for resistance. For example, an advertisement in *The Crusader* encouraged every woman to join a bank club because the 'Future Of The Race, Of Your Children, Is At Stake!'[114]

In another instance, Campbell used these conditions to help organise the Harlem Tenants League, a group whose focus on black women around housing, health care, and consumption provided the template for the Communist Party's Unemployed Councils. Campbell used a feature article in *Women Today* on exorbitant Harlem rents to highlight their effects on black women in the domestic sphere as a consciousness organising tool. She wrote that 'This strain falls heavily upon the Negro mothers and wives who must of necessity supplement their husbands' small pay by their hard earnings. These women of the working class have borne the hardship of unsanitary housing conditions' and broken facilities.[115] Dumbwaiter service, mostly a small elevator inside a home that transports goods between floors, that could have saved some steps, had often been bad for years. Black women 'had to live in apartments that were fire traps with wooden stairways, and often lacking fire escapes'. They had 'suffered all manner of housing injustice, such as a lack of repairs, poor heat, and no hot water'. Then 'they added to the burdens of the hardship of higher rents and the landlord insolence without protection'.[116]

Campbell saw housing as a women's issue that affected their quality of life and directly attributed to their tripartite oppression. She followed up her article with a call to action. As vice president of the Harlem Tenants League she said that it was time for tenants to create a more comprehensive organisation. Campbell said that many of the dire conditions in Harlem were due to 'social pressures which segregated negroes in a comparatively limited section of the city'.[117] On another occasion, at a meeting chaired by Campbell, in a speech, she connected the housing conditions to Negro Children Suffering. She spurred on the passage of a resolution that pointed 'out the evils of child labour and the sufferings which the children of Negro workers must endure because of segregation and discrimination both in industry and in housing', and called on 'Negro children to form a united front with their parents and with the white working-class children'. The resolution was unanimously passed.[118]

Campbell spoke and wrote about the conditions of black women, both as reproductive workers and wageworkers. For example, when she wrote about the drudgery of black women as industrial workers, she connected it to reproductive and domestic work as well as family ties. She explained that besides unsanitary workspace and 'the long hours of factory work, the working day of the majority of Negro working women' is lengthened by home duties. 'A woman with five small children told her that she rises at 5 o'clock in the morning, dresses; and feeding her children, and is on the job by 6, returns from work, does laundry, cleaning and cooking at night and retires past midnight, frequently too weary to sleep.'[119]

Campbell would agree with sociologist and grassroots organiser David Staples's assessment that 'women's work and women's labor are buried deeply in the heart of the capitalist social and economic structure'.[120] It was not unusual for Campbell to incorporate black feminist themes in her speeches. On 2 June 1920, at the first meeting of the Friends of Negro Freedom, Campbell was elected Vice-Chairman of the Executive Council and Chair of the Committee of Propaganda and Finance. She delivered a speech that embraced a black feminist theme. The title of her speech was 'What Women Can Do to Help the Cause of Negro Freedom'.[121] On 12 November 1922, at Harlem Community Church, Campbell spoke on 'New Women in a New Age'.[122] Within the Party, Campbell continued to build shop committees and awareness among black working women that led to the establishment of the Trade Union Committee for Organizing Negro Workers.[123] In 1929, the Harlem Section of the Communist Party at the Harlem Labor Center called a mass meeting to denounce 'the open shop exploitation of Negro working women in Harlem factories and laundries'.[124] For the most part, black women were employed as laundresses and servants; but even in this capacity, there was fierce competition with women of other races.[125] Campbell continued to stress that the average wages of women of colour were less than those of white women. This capitalist tripartite exploitation contributed to coloured women becoming prostitutes to survive and provide for their children.[126]

At times Campbell's position on prostitution was counterintuitive because of the lingering vestiges of the politics of respectability juxtaposition in her work in the criminal justice system. Her qualms were couched on the understanding that in the aftermath of slavery, black women's status as slaves changed. Yet there remained the belief permeating the American psyche that black women were sexually promiscuous and prone to prostitution. Yet, as an employee of the criminal justice system, Campbell spoke and wrote about how racial bigotry, class bias, gender chauvinism, cultural prejudice, and legal double standards operated to render unjust prosecutions and exploitation that led black women to be charged with prostitution, and then incarceration.[127]

In a 1911 interview Campbell explained that, as a probation officer, she went to the docks where she met young black women lured from the rural South by 'spurious employment agents' with the promise of plenty of work. She said that many women who found their way to the night courts were 'often victims of these spurious employment agents'. Campbell explained that the girls were flattered by these assurances and left their 'homes with little or no money, few clothes and destitute of experience'. When they 'reach the big city penniless and with no place to go', and the lack of a decent lodging house, this situation became one source of these women's downfall from 'respectability' and deconstruction of any semblance of cultural dissemblance. Campbell said their downfall was not merely a moral issue, but often it created legal problems. The women were then arrested for vagrancy, prostitution, theft, and incorrigibility.[128]

Then, in a 1925 article written after she joined the Workers Party, Campbell continued to echo the sentiments about employers that she voiced in her 1911 interview. But she rejected any notion of moral downfall. She had moved away from the paradigm of the politics of respectability that would have said to her it was just merely a matter of getting to young black women with a few words that would 'put them on the right road'; instead, she ascertains that there was an interplay between race, class, gender, and state power that explained the incarceration rate of black women for prostitution.[129]

## Transforming the political economy: The African Blood Brotherhood, American Negro Labor Congress and League of Struggle for Negro Rights

When the Harlem-based African Blood Brotherhood (ABB) was established, Campbell was probably the most widely known of its founders because of her previous civic engagements. The ABB began as a small black cadre of radical activist-intellectuals whose members would later become some of the first black Communists in the world. Even though the Constitution of the African Blood Brotherhood, Section 2, Article 1 read: 'The purpose and aims of this organisation shall be the mobilisation of Negro thoughts and the organisation of Negro manhood and womanhood toward meeting intelligently and fearlessly our problems and Conquering the enemies of the Negro race wherever they are found', the radicals primarily understood black liberation in terms of race manhood and routinely structured their organisation to privilege black men as movement leaders and thinkers.[130] Campbell's attempt to link race, class, gender, and colonialism was an intellectual endeavour that often brought the ABB to the edges of gender concerns. Still, for the most part, the ABB never adopted anything resembling a feminist platform. Campbell worked within the confines of a male-dominated radical organisation but often played a central role in not only raising questions, but also in sustaining the organisation through which such concerns could be addressed.[131]

During the existence of the ABB, Campbell, a woman in her mid-forties, played an essential role in facilitating the organisation. She was somewhat older than her male comrades. Her professional and personal life had laid the foundation for her to assume a leadership role. She had a solid formal education. By the time the organisation was established, she had experience working with a variety of women's organisations and charity associations in two cities, the NAACP and the Urban League. Campbell had been the director of kindergartens, a probation and parole officer, and superintendent of a shelter. She was a member of the Socialist Party. Her life's path had crisscrossed many of the black male and female radical and reformist leaders of her day, from historians W.E.B. Du Bois, Joel Augustus Rogers, and John E. Bruce, orators Hubert Harrison and Helen Holman, educators Nannie Burroughs and Mary Church Terrell, to poets Alice Dunbar Nelson and Claude McKay. She turned her home into an intellectual salon for weekly debate: a social space for social and political engagement. Much of what is known about Campbell's demeanour during this period comes from the recollections of Hermie Dumont, who married Otto Huiswoud. She recalled visiting Grace Campbell's home regularly in the company of Huiswoud.[132]

Campbell's open house was a hotbed of radical discourse. Even though she had been forced out of two jobs and her fiancé had run off with her inheritance, she was financially secure. Even though her voice was soft and well-modulated, she was persuasive.[133] She was no shrinking violet. She was prepared and ready to facilitate the African Blood Brotherhood. Her jet-black glistening eyes were on the future.[134] Campbell held various positions within the ABB – secretary, treasurer, director of the Consumers Co-operative, and member of the Committee of Finance and Executive Council.[135] The young men accepted Grace Campbell as their mentor. She contributed militant opinions in her quiet way and possessed an 'unwavering dedication to the socialist cause'.[136]

Campbell's contributions to the workings of the ABB were immeasurable. She recruited, attended to secretarial details, collected dues, arranged meetings, and offered her home as a venue for meetings. Campbell went into the field to recruit new members, but most were recruited through *The Crusader*.[137] She conducted active campaigns among 'colored women' but was not always successful. According to government accounts, black women were not interested in socialism and did not want to learn about it;[138] while, in 1923, Cyril Briggs claimed that there were about 2,000 women in the organisation who were all good members,[139] Campbell contributed resources to meetings and campaigns.[140] Even when attendance was low, Campbell still went to most of the business meetings and mass gatherings. Sometimes she was the only person in attendance at meetings, and when she was ill, sometimes the meetings had to be postponed. She was a key figure in organising meetings, and thereby mobilising Harlem's rank and file.[141]

Campbell also shared responsibility for organising the educational forums that were usually held on Sunday. She held the chairpersonship of the Forum. Like the People's Forum, the ABB forums were established as a means of orientating members and the public with issues. As an educator, she realised the importance of education to racial uplift, resistance, and revolution, and felt it was her responsibility to take the lead in that direction. In these settings, activist Richard B. Moore emerged as the young star orator. Campbell helped to organise a series of meetings at Lafayette Lodge Room and the Harlem Community Church, as well as street meetings.[142] She also delivered speeches outside the Forum, such as when she spoke on 'Present Day Economics' at the Young Women's Christian Association (YWCA).[143] In 1921, following the race riots in Tulsa, Oklahoma, Campbell delivered several anti-lynching messages. The mainstream press had blamed the African Blood Brotherhood for the riots. The Committee of Propaganda convened mass meetings and delivered speeches on lynching, peonage, Jim Crowism, disenfranchisement, and a plan of action for removing these injustices as well as other injustices blacks suffered, with others, as workers.[144] In 1923, a radical journalist, L.F. Coles, invited Grace Campbell to speak at a Philadelphia church. He said that she did not think like most Communists.[145]

There was widespread misunderstanding propagated by the press 'that the A. B. B. is a bolshevist organisation with all the bolshevist trappings and propaganda'.[146] The *New York Herald* reported that immediately following the race riots throughout the country in 1919, Moscow seized on the opportunity to agitate racial unrest and rushed secret agents to the US to organise the ABB. In 1922, the Supreme Executive Council of the African Blood Brotherhood declared in a statement printed in the *New York Herald* that the charges were false that the organisation was connected with 'the Soviets at Moscow or with being the agent of the Third International or the Communists'.[147]

As a founder of the ABB, Cyril Briggs said that 'the Communist Party had no part in initiating the organisation of the Brotherhood'. The ABB did not 'owe its inspiration to the Communist movement', nor was the ABB programme Communist inspired. The ABB's programme recognised the economic nature of the struggle, but pointed out that it was 'not wholly economic but nearly so', because it also recognised the racial aspects of the struggle. The ABB was already in existence when Briggs joined the Communist Party.[148] In a special report, 'Work Among the Negro Toilers: The Northern Part of the United States', prepared by K. Karatov for the Communist Party of the United States of America, he wrote that the ABB was organised in 1918 by Briggs.[149] In 1958, Briggs was unable to recall 'the exact date that the organisation of the Brotherhood was begun'. He was positive, however, that it was a few months after the publication of the first issue of *The Crusader* magazine in the fall of 1918, and before he joined the Communist Party of America in 1919.[150] The CPA was established in 1919 as an illegal political party after a split in the Socialist Party of America following the Russian Revolution.

In June 1921, *The Crusader* became the official organ of the ABB, but ceased publication in February 1922.[151] Campbell was indispensable to the publication of *The Crusader* and later became the co-founder and editor of the Crusader News Service.[152] It 'was the first black national news service to be organised in this country. It preceded by several months the Associated Negro Press (ANP).' The intent was to target the broadest possible audience for the ABB's polemics. Press releases were sent 'to some 200 Negro papers throughout the country, and in the West Indies and Africa'. Since there was 'no charge for the service, it found immediate acceptance, particularly among the smaller' black newspapers. Its motto was 'The News Through Negro Eyes'.[153]

Although Campbell was not the editor of *The Crusader*, in May 1921 her home was raided by the authorities along with three other homes of black editors. The three black editors were men. They were J. Finley Wilson, editor of the *Washington Eagle*, Wesley Porter, editor of the *East Tennessee News*, and W.E.B. Du Bois, editor of *The Crisis* magazine. Campbell was the only woman and not an official editor of any publication. Cyril Briggs was editor of *The Crusader*, but Campbell was the target because her role was central in the publication of the magazine. In the *New York Times* she reminded the public that, in the last election, she had been defeated as a Socialist candidate for a seat on the New York State Assembly. She underscored that 'the communist party was a secret organisation'. Moreover, she added that 'if it had intended to proselyte among negroes it would do them little good'.[154]

There were women on the staff of *The Crusader* including Bertha F. Briggs, Bertha De Basco, and Gertrude E. Hall. Bertha F. Briggs was the wife of Cyril Briggs. She was the business manager. Briggs's wife left him a year after he joined the CPA because of her hostility to his political involvement. Bertha De Basco edited the Women's Department, and Gertrude Hall wrote a column.[155] An editorial in *The Crusader* acknowledged the value in women's work in and outside of the cause, and captured Campbell's role within the ABB. It stated that 'Our women have never yet failed us. We have always expected great things of them, and never yet have they disappointed us. Often when the men would limp and hesitate, it is the women – our women – who have taken up the standard of the race and borne it to the immortal heights.' It pointed out that 'The female of the species is deadlier than the male', and 'ours have been among the most uncompromising of the battlers for equal rights'. It underscored that 'our women have never known the meaning of the idiotic phrase that "woman's place is in the home"'. Yet, 'they have raised a race of men without learning that phrase'. Furthermore, they have taken 'up the task when disheartened men would lay it down in abject surrender'. It has been women who 'have shown the way in many a fine endeavor'.[156] At least 50 per cent of the early subscribers to *The Crusader* were women, and many of the advertisements were from female businesses, particularly hairdressers.[157] An outcome of this view of black women as nurturers of racial manhood, albeit entirely unintentional, was that it forced ABB radicals to take seriously black women's daily lives and experiences, not only as workers but also in terms of their reproductive work as domestics, mothers, and wives, who bore the responsibility of caring for their families on meagre budgets while supporting radical activity.[158]

Campbell sought to mitigate some of the tripartite exploitation in black women's reproductive work by advocating for the establishment of co-operatives. She understood that black people must have food, clothes, and shelter, and that if people spent their money collectively, rather than as individuals, they could get these necessities cheaper. She recognised the need to include programmes that addressed the immediate suffering of black people so that they could improve their quality of life, while always connecting their day-to-day struggles to a broader vision because struggles against all of the ways in which oppression and exploitation express themselves in black women's lives were critical to their lives and their families' basic survival. In the African Blood Brotherhood, Campbell was the Director of the Consumers' Co-operative. The ABB had plans to establish a co-operative store. This movement began in the Supreme Council in July 1923.[159]

Over the years, Campbell favoured the establishment of co-operative stores run by working-class Harlemites as a solution to unemployment and community control over commercial life. She argued that co-operative ventures were potent weapons that would help 'oppressed people throughout the world'. George Schuyler and Ella Baker shared Campbell's faith in co-operatives. There was close contact between Campbell, Schuyler, and Baker's co-operative activities through the Pure Food Co-operative. Campbell was responsible for the educational bureau that taught co-operative workers in the dress and waistmakers' industry.[160] The idea of co-operatives was also put forward by the Friends of Negro Freedom. It advocated that co-operatives 'be organised by city blocks, apartment houses, church congregations, fraternal societies, and, in rural districts, by counties or convenient sections'. The intent was that co-operatives would eliminate the middleman and enable producers, whether farmers or industrial workers, 'to secure more for his goods, and at the same time, to reduce the price to the consumer'.[161]

Campbell had done a study of English and Scandinavian co-ops, and throughout the 1930s she continued to believe that co-operative enterprise would help the black masses if they were educated to appreciate them. She opened a co-operative store with the help of some competent professional blacks, but the store received little support from fellow Communists. As a pioneer in the Party she expected more support from her fellow 'comrades in the initial phase of her enterprise'. She delivered many speeches to explain the co-operative idea. On one occasion, when she spoke at a meeting, Claude McKay accompanied his long-time friend. The meeting was well attended and presided over by James W. Ford, former candidate for vice president of the United States on the CPUSA ticket. McKay recalled that Campbell appealed to Ford 'for Communist support and new members to join the first store opened'. She felt the Communists should do something other than just agitating. She thought the people's grievances were just. White merchants made their profits in the Harlem community and spent it all in other communities. She wanted them to help the community. McKay said that she had 'made a simple, earnest speech, and the audience was moved. But when she had finished speaking, Ford took the floor and declared that real communists could not support their own comrade's scheme because it was not communist.'[162]

In 1921, Campbell spoke on May Day praising Communism.[163] In July 1921, before the Workers Party was formally established, she participated in a 'round table'. The topic of discussion was what benefits black people derive from the Russian Revolution. The group advocated for the use of force as it had been used in the revolution and agreed that the 'Russian people were the only free people in the world'. There was also a general opposition to the conservative methods and teachings of W.E.B. Du Bois.[164]

In August 1921, the ABB was urging their audience in meetings to join the Bolsheviks, but according to federal surveillance in July there were only two fully pledged Communists in Harlem – probably Cyril Briggs and Otto Huiswoud, both members of the CPA.[165] On 21 December 1921, the Workers Party of America was established as a 'legal' means of carrying on public activity and of reaching broader sections of the working class. Campbell was a charter member of the Workers Party. The Workers Party changed its name to the Workers (Communist) Party in 1925 and to the Communist Party of the United States of America in 1930.[166] By 22 March 1922, Campbell was the secretary of the Yorkville Section of the Workers Party. In August 1922, the Harlem West Side Branch was organised and was preparing to grapple with the problems faced in work among black workers in Harlem. Campbell was elected to serve on the Propaganda and Educational Committee along with Claude McKay and Richard Moore.[167]

At its November 1923 meeting, the Supreme Council of the ABB agreed that the best policy for the ABB was to align with the WP because they had no office, and the Workers Party would help them in this matter, while the

ABB could also help the WP.[168] The WP wanted to use the ABB to build a party presence within the black community. The ABB decided to affiliate with the WP because it needed funds, but the WP withheld financial support to the ABB. The Party would not and did not stop the ABB's financial haemorrhaging.[169] A close reading of the Military Intelligence Files and Federal Bureau of Investigation reports shows tensions about pocketbook issues between the Party and the ABB.[170]

As a member of the ABB's leadership, Campbell shared in the decision for moving to affiliate with the WP, but at the same time expressed concern about the solvency of the ABB and reservations about the WP,[171] even though, in September, she had expressed a concern that the WP did not consider black people very much because there were so many people coming up from the South. She said that the WP considered the ABB a race party more than anything else, and black people had other ideas outside of the Party, such as those expressed by black nationalist Marcus Garvey. For this reason, the WP was 'taking more interest in the White people'.[172] Campbell was correct in her assessment that the WP did see the ABB as a potential black political party, but she did not realise how this conflicted with Soviet policy.[173]

After the ABB came under the wing of the WP, it recognised the potential of the ABB to become a 'Negro political party'. The ABB came closest to developing a political line that was appropriate for building a revolutionary black working-class movement. This then would make the ABB a future competitor, and as such, it would be another cadre; the WP would have to work within a united front. As a black political party, the ABB could clearly move the black masses forward as agents of their liberation with or without the WP, and this would not enhance Soviet interests. On the basis of this understanding, the WP decided to liquidate the organisation. The liquidation of the ABB was a betrayal of black interests.

Although white women were not members of the ABB, gender tensions and antagonisms reverberated between Campbell and white women on the left, as they had in bourgeois reformist organisations – particularly with Rose Pastor Stokes, a white member of the WP. McKay recalled Stokes's obsession with spies in Harlem. He wrote that one night, when she came to Campbell's house for a meeting, she arrived 'breathless, and sank into a chair, exhausted'. Stokes asked for a glass of water, and 'Campbell hurried to get a glass'. Stokes then proceeded to explain 'that a colored man had been watching her suspiciously while he had attempted to follow her'. To evade him 'she hurried and dodged through the insouciant Harlem crowd' and went around many blocks to elude the spy. Campbell responded to Stokes's assertion by saying that 'there aren't any Negroes spying on radicals in Harlem. That colored man maybe he was attempting – kind of – to get friendly with you.'[174] Campbell saw where Stokes was making assumptions about race and gender. Hence, no matter how well-meaning Stokes was in pursuing interracial co-operation, she assumed something devious and ominous about the black community, and Campbell picked up on it. Campbell had come to see the dilemma inherent in interracialism as the inability of white men and women and to see black people as equals.

Despite her exhaustion, Stokes jumped right up and told Campbell that she was shocked by her response. McKay described the tenor and tone of Stokes's voice and her manner as a perfect bourgeois expression of the superior person. Campbell explained to Stokes that she did not 'mean to insinuate anything, but any person is likely to be mistaken for something else'.[175] The internal security reports clearly showed that spies had infiltrated the ABB, but they were not cloak and dagger spooks. The agents assigned were not on the outside looking in; they were at the table. They shared chit-chat conversations with Campbell and were initiated into the inner circles. Stokes was correct in her contention that there were spies, but she was incorrect in saying that a spy was following her that evening. More significantly, the nature of her tale and her decorum were symptomatic of the endemic race and class chauvinism within the Communist movement.

On the one hand, Campbell's response to Stokes addressed the stereotypical sexual fear white women have around black men. On the other, Stokes's bourgeois tone rung out as condescending to Campbell and embodied nuances of paternalism, pseudoscientific racism, and elitism. And though white women had less power than white men due to their gender, they had greater power than black women. White women contributed to the tripartite oppression of black women. Stokes's demur was symptomatic of the gender antagonism between white and black women that would placate the Party.

In 1925, the American Negro Labor Congress (ANLC) was the first mass organisation of the American Communist Party dedicated to advancing issues of importance to American blacks. It was conceived as a forum for addressing racism in labour unions and the workplace.[176] As a member of the ANLC, this was Campbell's most active period within the Party, and she was adamant that black women must take their place in the class war. She held leadership roles in the Harlem Tenants League and the Negro Relief Committee.[177] She worked alongside George Padmore in a proposal to expand the Committee of Ethiopian Mutual Aid League for the South.[178] During this period her writings appeared in the *Daily Worker*, the *Negro Champion*, and the *Working Woman*. These writings provide a juxtaposition of Marxist and feminist theory to capture Campbell's understanding of the proletarianisation of black women.

While Campbell was affiliated with the ANLC she wrote an analysis of the 'Negro Question'. Since her affiliation with the ABB, Campbell had supported black self-determination led by working-class activism that would fit into women's gender experiences and objectives. Yet she did not address the Black Belt slogan as an idiomatic expression for self-determination, as reflected in her 'Analysis of the Negro Question' which she wrote for the Negro Committee of the Workers Party of America in response to the Communist Sixth World Congress' Black Belt thesis. Campbell argued that the solution to the Negro Question lay in winning equality and economic opportunity, which was an inherently revolutionary strategy in itself. In her 'Analysis of the Negro Question', Campbell described the circumstances that had spawned the web that deprived black people of full social and political inequality.[179]

As Campbell's voice on black women within the Party was becoming more robust, it was stifled with the unfolding of Lovestoneite factionalism.[180] She challenged the patriarchy within the Party and met with other black women comrades to change structural and political-cultural [word missing] that would centre their lives and work within the Communist Party that was spearheaded by her male comrades.[181] In 1929, 'The Central Control Committee expelled Grace [Lamb] Campbell, an intellectual from the C. P. of U.S.A.' for her 'active support of the Lovestone group of splitters, for participating and speaking in their group meetings and otherwise promoting their disruptive activities'.

Some fences were mended between Campbell and the Party, but her allegiance waned to the Party though not the cause. She had a less visible role in the League of Struggle for Negro Rights (LSNR) that was established in 1930 after the ANLC was disbanded. In the 1930s she taught at the Harlem Workers' School under the name of Grace Lamb. She spoke at large gatherings such as the Second Harlem Legislative Council conference attended by some 500 people that was devoted to the economic, political, and social problems confronting the people of Harlem.[182] Campbell was on the National Executive Committee of the National Scottsboro Committee of Action and the Emergency Harlem Provisional Scottsboro Defense with Audley Moore and Claudia Cumberbatch.[183] The campaign to free the Scottsboro boys, more than any other single event, gave the Party international recognition. While the Scottsboro case was a rape trial and elicited gender and sexuality rhetoric, the Communist movement was able to create sympathy for racial justice in Latin America, Asia, Africa, across Europe, and throughout the United States. It became one of the great defining moments in the struggle against injustice in the twentieth century.[184]

Audley Moore epitomises the fusion between socialism and nationalist traditions within the Party's ranks. She had been a member of Marcus

Garvey's Universal Negro Improvement Association before she became a Communist. She was one of the Party's most visible speakers. Her working-class background and 'down-home' eloquence resonated with the less educated black women.[185] Cumberbatch became better known as Claudia Jones. In 1936, she joined the Young Communist League. Cumberbatch would later serve on the Communist Party's National Committee. She would become a well-known activist and theoretician on the Black Belt thesis and super-exploitation and triple oppression of black women. In the press releases and flyers, Cumberbatch was identified as representing the Harlem Federation of Youth Clubs, and Campbell was representing the Harlem branch of the Progressive Women's Council.[186] In 1940, Campbell was the 'chairlady' of the mass meeting for the lower Harlem delegation report of the National Negro Congress.[187]

Grace Campbell continued to be held in high esteem by black women in the Party until her death. By 1938, several black women were active in the CPUSA and had risen to a degree of prominence within the Party; yet, it was Campbell's home they gathered at to discuss matters that specifically target gender and racial chauvinism that had been expressed by Maude White in a meeting of the Central Committee on Negro Work and Louise Patterson in the *Party Organizer*. Party leaders never came up with any systematic plan to organise or recruit black women into the Party.[188]

## Conclusion

Campbell's gendering of the black radical tradition began in Washington, DC under the guidance of her aunts. Her aunt, Laura Dyson, who was a member of the Colored Women's League, reared her within the paradigmatic frames of the culture of dissemblance and the politics of respectability while exposing her to a highly organised network of black clubwomen who emphasised uplift and the responsibilities incumbent upon the 'better class' of black folk.[189] Campbell's charity work, as well as those individuals who were personally connected with them, provided her with role models such as Anna J. Cooper. It allowed her to acquire social work experience and organisational skills that would later be used in her various endeavours in New York City. Of course, her skills were amply modified to fit the particular needs of the New York community from her charity work in Washington, DC. Still, she had been exposed to racial uplift programmes, organisational models, and a systemic way of getting things done.

Campbell's gender analysis deviated from traditional Marxist theorists in that she saw the intersectionality of race, class, gender, and value in wage and non-wage domestic or reproductive work as well as the family.

She saw domestic work as the critical engine for the reproduction of the industrial workforce, creation of community, and survival of the family. It was the breeding ground for the intersectionality of tripartite exploitation. She saw black women's positions in their families as a driver of resistance against capitalism, which affected their standard of living, class cohesion, and ability to wage the class struggle. For this and related reasons, it was incumbent on revolutionary forces to organise black women.

Campbell's relationship with other black female and male radicals, the fight for women's suffrage, the criminalisation of black women's labours, the struggle for organising women workers, and the demand for better quality housing and education, were vital to her intellectual development because of their substantial impact on her awakening class consciousness and the rejection of the politics of respectability. In addition to forming a unique backdrop for the development of her nascent radicalism, it also nurtured a significantly more militant racial attitude associated with the growing ghetto and the cultural outpouring of the Harlem Renaissance, while at the same time undergirding her evolving critique of industrial capitalism juxtaposed with 'domestic production' among black women in a critical way that shifted her thinking and activism from 'racial uplift' to leaning left, then to Red.

Campbell was able to think seriously about the intersectionality of race, class, and gender in black women's oppression because of her involvement in building organisations in which her theoretical work was applied. Later, fellow comrade Williana Burroughs, as director of the Harlem Workers School and contributing editor of the *Harlem Liberator*, broadened the work Campbell began in Harlem, which helped to reshape the WP into an entity that could facilitate, to some degree, the work of future black radical feminists.

Grace Campbell was an elegant and sophisticated first lady of Harlem's Communist community. She was educated and erudite. In the 1930s she was puzzled about what the Party was doing, but not about Communism. She began her career as a radical activist when she joined the Socialist Party. During the early 1920s, Campbell was convinced that the Communist Party would deliver on its promise of equal rights, and she shifted her allegiance. She cultivated a remarkable ability to remain involved in a myriad of groups that used different strategies for black freedom.

Campbell operated on both sides of the left–right polarity among the black radical left. She was involved in a network of activities in and outside of the Communist community, such as in 1920 the Friends of Negro Freedom, and in 1925 the Trade Union Committee for Organising Negro Workers. Both organisations were broad-based groups that included diverse elements from socialist unions to the NAACP. Her role as a superintendent of the Empire Friendly Shelter coincided with her position as a parole officer for the New York State Prison for Women at Auburn. Unlike many of Grace Campbell's male counterparts, she always held a job, provided for herself as well as others, and remained highly active. Hermie Huiswoud recalled that Campbell 'was as active as her job and age permitted'.[190] In 1935, in a letter to Claude McKay, she gave a broad outline of her weekly schedule. She wrote, 'I am at home every evening at about 6 o'clock and rarely leave home for meetings before 8 o'clock. I am at home on Sundays until 3 p.m. and most always on Saturday until 1 or 2 p.m.'[191]

Classism, chauvinism, sexism, and factionalism brought Campbell into conflict in the District public schools, the Urban League, and the Communist Party with the black elite, white women, and the patriarchy. She had to fight to be heard and not to have her contributions erased. Her affiliation with the Socialist Party, the ABB, the ANLC, and the LSNR did not derail her career as a municipal and state worker, nor did it disentangle her from various prominent black female leaders in Harlem. She continued to demand justice within the justice system for women, and social justice for all.

On 19 December 1942, Campbell retired from the General Sessions Court as a court attendant earning $3,000 a year.[192] She died on Tuesday 8 June 1943, after a long heart illness, in Harlem Hospital. When she died, she was a member of the Communist Cub, 11 Assembly District, formerly Abraham Lincoln Branch of the Communist Party, 17 Assembly District.[193] In 1927, Ruth Dennis of the *Pittsburgh Courier* recognised Grace P. Campbell as one of fifty black women who had made racial progress possible in the nation.[194]

## Notes

1 Cedric J. Robinson, *Black Marxism: The Making of the Black Radical Tradition Black Marxism* (Chapel Hill, NC: University of North Carolina Press, 2000 [1983]).
2 Carole Boyce Davies, 'A Black Left Feminist View on Cedric Robinson's Black Marxism', *Black Perspectives*, 10 November 2016, www.aaihs.org/a-black-left-feminist-view-on-cedric-robinsons-black-marxism/ (accessed 6 December 2016).
3 'Grace Campbell: Dead Old CP Member', *Daily Worker*, 10 June 1943, 3.
4 'Party Life', *Daily Worker*, 18 October 1929, 4; 'What's Doing in the Workers' Schools of the U.S', *Daily Worker*, 11 April 1934, 5; 'Conference Called On Workers' School', *Amsterdam News*, 27 December 1933, 1.
5 Viola Justin, 'Making a Success', *Washington Bee*, 5 August 1911, 1.
6 Brittney C. Cooper, *Beyond Respectability: The Intellectual Thought of Race Women* (Chicago, IL: University of Illinois Press, 2017), 12.

7 George Schuyler, 'Ex-Communists says "Red" as bad as GOP Party: Williams Says Shelves Black Pioneers', *Pittsburgh Courier*, 18 June 1930, 5.
8 Other proposed additions to the Re-organised Negro Committee were Briggs and Golden Ford. Other members of the Committee were Huiswoud, Rosemond, Moore, Padmore, Miller, King, and Minor; Russian State Archive of Socio-Political History (RGASPI) 534/3/104: 1366, Minutes of the First Re-organisation Negro Committee (Nat'l), Friday, 14 August 1928.
9 'Women's real in Current Topics', *New York Age*, 25 April 1925, 3; 'Miss Grace Campbell Wins High Rating in Court Attend't Exam', *New York Age*, 6 September 1924, 2.
10 Arnold de Mille, 'The Appointment of Negroes to the Courts in New York City', Federal Writers Project, NY, 21 April 1936, Reel 5.
11 'Grace Campbell: Dead Old CP Member', 3.
12 The Howard University Alumni Directory listed a Mrs Emma Campbell as a graduate of the class of 1871. *Alumni Directory 1867–2005: University* (Chesapeake, VA: Harris Connect, 2005), 547. Emma Dyson's graduation was confirmed by the university archivist on 7 January 2007; 'Teacher's Roll Honor', *Washington Bee*, 24 October 1903, 1.
13 Letter to Rev. E.M. Cravath, Field Secretary American Missionary Association (AMA), from Frank Haley, Macon Georgia, 26 August 1874; Letter to Rev. E.M. Cravath, Field Secretary AMA, from W.A.L. Campbell, Howard University, Washington, DC, 26 December 1874; Letter to Rev. E.M. Cravath, Field Secretary AMA, from W.A.L. Campbell, Beaufort, NC, 18 September 1874, AMA, American Missionary Association Archive (AMAA), Amistad Research Center, Tulane University, New Orleans.
14 Letter to M.E. Strieby, Cor. Secy., from W.A.L. Campbell, Macon, GA, 15 October 1875, AMAA; 'Married: Campbell-Dyson', *Washington Evening Star*, 7 August 1874, n.p.; Marriage License, Marriage Bureau, Superior Court of the District of Columbia, Washington, DC, 7 August 1874; Morris J. MacGregor, *The Emergence of a Black Catholic Community: St Augustine's in Washington* (Washington, DC: Catholic University of America Press, 1999), 31, 41, 520.
15 Emma V. Campbell's death notice on 20 November 1876 in the *Washington Evening Times* states that she died in Green Cove Springs, Florida. In 1877, William Campbell was ministering as Presbyterian pastor in Jacksonville, Florida. In 1879 when the *Washington Post* reported that he had married Francis V. Bank, the notice stated that he was from Magnolia Springs, Florida, which was a short distance from Green Cove Springs. See Presbyterian Church in the US General Assembly, *Minutes of the General Assembly of the Presbyterian Church in the United States* (New York: Presbyterian Board of Publications, 1877), 719.
16 Letter to Rev. G.P. Stuart from W.A. Lamb Campbell, 10 July 1879, Academy of the New Church Archives, Bryn Athyn, Pennsylvania, File 802.
17 Letitia Woods Brown, *Free Negroes in the District of Columbia, 1790–1846* (New York: Oxford University Press, 1972), 106; Manumission Record [District of Washington County], II, Record Group 21, US National Archives,

419 (1835); Bureau of the Census, *Negro Population, 1790–1915* (Washington, DC, 1918), 57, in Dorothy Provine, 'The Economic Position of the Free Blacks in the District of Columbia, 1800–1860', *Journal of Negro History*, 58:1 (1973), 61–72, at 61. 1860 United States Federal Census [database online], Ancestry.com. Provo, UT, USA: MyFamily.com, 2004. Original data: United States of America, Bureau of the Census, Eighth Census of the United States, 1860, Washington, DC: National Archives and Records Administration, 1860. M653, 1,438 rolls; 1860 United States Federal Census, Roll M653–102, 417. Willard B. Gatewood, *Aristocrats of Color: The Black Elite, 1880–1920* (Bloomington, IN: Indiana University Press, 1990).

18 Year 1880; Census Place: Washington, District of Columbia; Roll: 124; Family History Film: 1254124; Page: 92B; Enumeration District: 074; Image: 0188. Year: 1900; Census Place: Washington, District of Columbia; Roll: 164; Page: 22B; Enumeration District: 0126; FHL microfilm: 1240164. All Census references were taken from the Ancestry.com and the Church of Jesus Christ of Latter-day Saints. 1880 United States Federal Census [database online], Provo, UT, USA: Ancestry.com Operations Inc.

19 Year: 1920; Census Place: Manhattan Assembly District 19, New York, New York; Roll: T625_1221; Page: 1A; Enumeration District: 1350; Image: 1049. Year: 1930; Census Place: Manhattan, New York, New York; Roll: 1560; Page: 13A; Enumeration District: 0520; Image: 816.0; FHL microfilm: 2341295.

20 Winston James, *Holding Aloft the Banner of Ethiopia: Caribbean Radicalism in Early Twentieth-Century America* (London: Verso, 1998), 260; 'Early Years and Political Parties', n.d., Box 1, Folder 21, Otto Edward Huiswoud Papers, Tamiment Library and Robert F. Wagner Labor Archive, New York University; Casefile #61–50: African Blood Brotherhood, Department of Justice–Bureau of Investigation Surveillance of Black Americans, Freedom of Information Act Retrievals, 1923, Accession #: 001360–003–0168, 24 September1923–23 September 1923. Department of Justice–Bureau of Investigation files have been take from Surveillance of Black Americans, Freedom of Information Act Retrievals, 1923, Federal Bureau of Investigation (FBI) Marcus Garvey and the African Blood Brotherhood files on microfilm, and Fold3, a database that provides access to Federal Bureau of Investigation files. The sources have overlapping files, but the information is cited according to the source it was retrieved from.

21 James Borchert, *Alley Life in Washing: Family, Community, Religion, and Folklife in the City, 1850–1970* (Chicago, IL: University of Illinois Press, 1982), 8, 47, 116–117, 138; Mary Cromwell, Associate Charities Manuscript, 15; J.L. Love, 'Washington Poor People', *New York Age*, 18 July 1907; FBI Marcus Garvey and the African Blood Brotherhood, 31 August 1923, Reel 1.

22 'The Amateur Authors', *Washington Post*, 9 June 1889, 16.

23 'Forth into the World', *Washington Post*, 19 June 1891; 'The Colored High School', *Evening Star*, 24 June 1892, 3.

24 *Catalogue of Howard University of Officers and Students for March 1893 to March 1894* (Washington, DC: Howard University Press, 1894), 23; *Catalogue*

of *Howard University of Officers and Students for March 1894 to March 1895* (Washington, DC: Howard University Press, 1895), 20; *Catalogue of Howard University of Officers and Students for March 1895 to March 1896* (Washington, DC: Howard University Press, 1896), 25, 66.
25 'Trained to Teach Tots: Eighteen Young Colored Ladies Graduate from a Kindergarten Normal School', *Washington Post*, 8 June 1897, 7.
26 Anna J. Cooper, *The Voice of Anna Julia Cooper*, ed. Charles Lemert and Esme Bhan (Lanham, MD: Rowman & Littlefield, 1998), 63.
27 'Kindergarten Training Class', *Washington Post*, 7 September 1899, 7: 'Kindergarten Training Class', *Washington Bee*, 9 September 1899, n.p.
28 Grace P. Campbell's graduation was confirmed by Dr Clifford L. Muse, Jr, Howard University Archivist, Washington, DC, 7 January 2008; Rayford W. Logan, *Howard University: The First Hundred Years, 1867–1967* (New York: New York University Press, 1969), 111.
29 *New York Age*, 8 October 1908, n.p.
30 'Searchlight', *Washington Bee*, 16 February 1901, n.p.
31 The motto of the journal was: 'If our schools inculcate intellectual training, love of country, cordial submission to lawful authority, moral rectitude, and: some knowledge of the theory and organic structure of our government, then shall our citizens-be truly men.' 'The Searchlight; A New Local Journal Devoted to Education Among the Colored People', *Washington Post*, 4 February 1901, 10. In the second edition of *Searchlight*, Zita E. Dyson, Campbell's cousin, wrote an article entitled 'Fire at Normal School'. She reported that the fire did very little damage, but she also stressed the benefits of having a fire drill system. See *The National Capital Searchlight*, 1 (March 1901), 45. Anna J. Cooper's papers and the Cook family's papers at the Moorland-Spingarn Research Center (MSRC) have been reviewed for this journal.
32 'Back to Schoolroom; The Summer Vacation Season Draws Near its End. Board Prepares for Opening: Changes in the Teaching Force and Other Necessary Preliminaries Given Attention at Last Night's Meeting – Opening of the New Dent and Webb Schools – Superintendent Stuart Says Enrollment Will Not Be Very Much Larger Than Last Year', *Washington Post*, 21 September 1901, 4.
33 Letter to Mrs Benjamin Swan [Anna Day] from Lavinia Lofton, 3 July 1903, Washington, DC, The Haynes-Lofton Family Papers, Catholic University Washington, DC, Box 2, Folder 7.
34 House of Representatives, 'Report of the Director of Kindergartens', *Report of the Commissioners of the District of Columbia for the year ended June 30, 1903, IV, 58th Congress, 2nd Session, Doc. No. 7* (Washington, DC: Government Printing Office, 1903), 171.
35 House of Representatives, 'Report of the Director of Kindergartens', *Report of the Commissioners of the District of Columbia for the year ended June 30, 1906, IV, 59th Congress, 2nd Session, Doc. No. 8* (Washington, DC: Government Printing Office, 1907), 116–119; 'Home Talents Wins', *Washington Post*, 5 September 1906, 2; 'School Board Approves Mr Chancellor's Nominees', *Washington Bee*, 8 September 1906, n.p.

36 *Ibid.*
37 'Row over School Job', *Washington Post*, 22 September 1907, 2.
38 Anna Evans Murray graduated from Oberlin College in 1876. She was the daughter of Henry Evans, who in 1858 defied fugitive slave laws in Oberlin, Ohio and was arrested and imprisoned with eighteen others in Cleveland. Her great-grandfather and Jewel Murray's great-great-grandfather Lewis Leary befriended abolitionist John Brown. Before her marriage, she taught music at Howard University and at the Mott School. She dedicated her life to establishing free kindergartens and training kindergarten teachers throughout the District of Columbia. She chaired the Education Committee of the National League of Colored Women (NLCW) in Washington. In 1898, she successfully lobbied for a $12,000 federal appropriation to establish kindergarten classes. She was an early advocate for child welfare and for children getting an early start with their education. With her vast contacts, she helped to secure a second appropriation from Congress in 1906 for the inclusion of a kindergarten teacher training course at Miner Teachers College in Washington; seemingly Grace Campbell taught these courses. 'Nathaniel Allison Murray', Alpha Phi Alpha Fraternity, Inc. – Omicron Delta Lambda Chapter, www.odlchapter.com/wordpress/?page_id=340 (accessed 10 November 2011).
39 'Letter Turned Down: Board of Education Declines to Hear Mrs Murray', *Washington Post*, 5 April 1906, 2.
40 Darlene Clark Hine, 'Rape and the Inner Lives of Black Women in the Middle West: Preliminary Thoughts on the Culture of Dissemblance', *Signs: Journal of Women in Culture and Society*, 14:4 (1989), 912–920, at 915.
41 Gatewood, *Aristocrats of Color*, 35.
42 Clark Hine, 'Rape and the Inner Lives of Black Women in the Middle West'.
43 Evelyn Brooks Higginbotham, *Righteous Discontent: The Women's Movement in the Black Baptist Church, 1880–1920* (Cambridge, MA: Harvard University Press, 1997), 185–230.
44 'President Oyster', *Washington Bee*, 11 January 1905, 4.
45 Letter to Mary C. Terrell from Eva F. Ross, 23 September 1906, Mary Church Terrell Papers, Reel 3, frame 501.
46 'Two Chosen in Primaries', *New York Age*, 20 August 1908, 1; *New York Age*, 8 October 1908, n.p.; 'Lincoln Settlement', [Brooklyn] *NY Daily Eagle*, 20 November 1908, 12.
47 The Empire State Federation of Women's Clubs (ESFWC) was founded in Brooklyn in August 1908 as an apparatus to promote womanhood. M.C. Lawton, 'New Federation of Women's Clubs', *The Bystander* [Des Moines, Iowa], 3 September 1909, 5; May Martel, 'Of Interest to Women: Impressions from the Session of the Empire State Federation', *New York Age*, 11 July 1912, 5.
48 Cooper, *Beyond Respectability*, 4–11.
49 'The massive Clubwomen Hear Mrs Barnett', *Indianapolis Recorder*, 27 March 1909, n.p.; 'A notable social event', *New York Age*, 25 March 1909, 7.
50 Case 364 – IO-NYC to MID. Re: Maj. H.A. Strauss forwards copy of report gathered by one of Military Intelligence Allies regarding 'Negro Agitation',

25 August 1919, 8. Correspondence of Military Intelligence Surveillance related to Negro Surveillance, 1917–1914, www.fold3.com/image/183968580/ (accessed 5 January 2013); May Martel, 'Of Interest to Women: Some Impressions from the Sessions of the Empire State Federation', *New York Age*, 12 July 1912, n.p. The ESFWC, founded in Brooklyn in 1908 by Alice Wiley Seay, was an umbrella organisation of New York State black women's groups. The women who started the ESFWC had two main goals: to do 'uplift work among girls and young women' and to care for the aged Harriet Tubman and her Auburn, Cayuga County home. See Empire State Federation of Women's Clubs, Inc. Records, 1938–1991, Series 2: Annual Convention Materials, 1944–91, M.E. Grenander Department of Special Collections & Archives University Libraries/University at Albany/State University of New York, Box 1; M.C. Lawton Civic and Cultural Club Records, 1921–2004 (APAP-027), M.E. Grenander Department of Special Collections & Archives University Libraries/University at Albany/State University of New York.
51 Cooper, *Beyond Respectability*, 11, 15.
52 'For Benefit of the Colored Race', [Brooklyn] *NY Standard Union*, 11 October 1911, 14.
53 Justin, 'Making a Success'.
54 'Mrs Talbert Defends Club Women', *New York Age*, 11 July 1912, 1.
55 Higginbotham, *Righteous Discontent*, 187.
56 Lashawn Harris, 'Running with the Reds: African American Women and the Communist Party during the Great Depression', *Journal of African American History*, 94:1 (2009), 21–43, at 33.
57 Justin, 'Making a Success'; G. Elise Johnson McDougald, 'The Double Task: The Struggle of Negro Women for Sex and Race Emancipation', *Survey*, 53 (1 March 1925), 689–691; http://historymatters.gmu.edu/d/5126/ (accessed 25 May 2006).
58 'Club Women Meet: State Federation Held Annual Session', *New York Age*, 4 July 1912, n.p.
59 'Mrs. Talbert Defends Club Women', *New York Age*, 11 July 1912, 1.
60 Minutes of a Special Meeting of the Executive Board of the National League on Urban Conditions Among Negroes, Inc., 11 June 1913, Manuscript Collection Library of Congress, Washington, DC, Box 1; Letter from Eugene Kinckle Jones to George Haynes, 20 May 1913, National Urban League, Correspondence, 1175 Box 55, The Quaker Collection, Haverford College, Haverford, PA; Cheryl Hicks, *Talk with You like a Woman: African American Women, Justice, and Reform in New York, 1890–1935* (Chapel Hill, NC: University of North Carolina Press, 2010), 167.
61 Letter from Elizabeth Walton to George E. Haynes, 6 August 1911, Box 3, George Haynes Collection (GHC), Fisk University, Special Collections, Nashville, TN; Letter from George Haynes to Elizabeth Walton, 14 August 1911, Box 3, GHC, in Hicks, *Talk with You like a Woman*, 163.
62 Letter from Eugene Kinckle Jones to George Haynes, 20 May 1913, National Urban League, Correspondence, 1175 Box 55, The National Urban

League on Urban Conditions Among Negroes Papers (LHWC), Manuscript Collection, Library of Congress, Washington, DC; Hicks, *Talk with You like a Woman*, 167.
63 Nell Painter, *The Narrative of Hosea Hudson: The Life and Times of a Black Radical* (New York: W.W. Norton, 1994), 20.
64 Minutes of a Special Meeting of the Executive Board of the National League on Urban Conditions Among Negroes, Inc., 11 June 1913; Hicks, *Talk with You like a Woman*, 168.
65 'Protest against Removal', *New York Age*, 12 June 1913, 1.
66 'Home Reorganised', *New York Age*, 24 July 1913, 1; 'The Empire Friendly Gets Charter', *New York Age*, 22 April 1915, 8.
67 'Harlem Colored Residents are for Benson', *The Call*, 29 October 1916, 2; Jeffery B. Perry, *Hubert Harrison: The Voice of Harlem Radicalism, 1883–1918* (New York: Columbia University Press), 268, 343–344, 508f51; Joyce Moore Turner with the assistance of W. Burghardt Turner, *Caribbean Crusaders and the Harlem Renaissance* (Urbana: University of Illinois Press, 2005), 25; Minutes of Joint Conference of National Executive Committee and State Secretaries, Chicago, IL, 10, 11, 12 August 1918, Socialist Party Papers, Reel 7; 'Donation to the Socialist Party', *The Call*, 4 December 1914, 6; 'Socialist Suffrage Campaign', *Evening Call*, 19 February 1915, 4; 'Socialist-Suffrage Meeting', *The Call*, 11 June 1915, n.p., 27 June 1915, 4, 28 June 1915, 4, 29 June 1915, 4, 4 July 1915, 4, 30 June 1915, 4, 10 July 1915, 4, 16 July 1915, 4, 11 August 1915, 4; 'Campaign for Women Nearing its End', *New York Age*, 1 November 1917, 1; Oakley C. Johnson, *Marxism in United States History before the Russian Revolution 1876–1917* (New York: Published for A.I.M.S. by Humanities Press, 1973), 81, 196.
68 'The Awakening of the Negro', editorial page, *New York Call*, 2 November 1916, n.p.
69 Perry, *Hubert Harrison*, 456f11; W. Burghardt Turner and Joyce Moore Turner (eds), *Richard B. Moore, Caribbean Militant in Harlem: Collected Writings, 1920–1972* (Bloomington, IN: Indiana University Press, 1988), 29; 'Hubert Harrison tendered Dinner', *Amsterdam News*, 26 May 1926, 9.
70 Case 361 Maj. W.H. Loving to MID. Re: Final report on Negro Subversion 6 August 1919, Correspondence of Military Intelligence Surveillance related to Negro Surveillance, 1917–1914, 11, www.fold3.com/image/183197372/ (accessed 20 January 2015).
71 'Donation to the Socialist Party', *The Call*, 4 December 1914, 6; 'Socialist Suffrage Campaign', *Evening Call*, 19 February 1915, 4; 'Socialist-Suffrage Meeting', *The Call*, 11 June 1915, n.p., 27 June 1915, 4, 28 June 1915, 4, 29 June 1915, 4, 4 July 1915, 4, 30 June 1915, 4, 10 July 1915, 4, 16 July 1915, 4, 11 August 1915, 4; 'Campaign for Women Nearing its End', *New York Age*, 1 November 1917, 1; Johnson, *Marxism in United States History before the Russian*, 81, 196.
72 Turner and Turner, *Richard B. Moore*, 30.

73 'Negro Socialists are Helping to Solve Race Problem in New Way', *Evening Call*, 4 November 1918, n.p.
74 Rosalyn Terborg Penn, *African American Women in the Struggle for the Vote, 1850–1920* (Bloomington, IN: Indiana University Press, 1998), 127.
75 Terborg Penn, *African American Women in the Struggle for the Vote*, 122–123.
76 *Ibid.*, 127.
77 'Negroes to Hold Rally The Independent Political Council', *New York Tribune*, 17 October 1917, 14.
78 Perry, *Hubert Harrison*, 350–351.
79 Terborg-Penn, *African American Women in the Struggle for the Vote*, 142.
80 'Wants Woman Name', clipping, Gertrude Elsie McDougald-Ayer Scrapbook, Gertrude Ayer Papers (GAP), Schromburg Center for Research in Black Culture (SCRBC), New York Public Library, New York.
81 'Voters Hold Convention', *Chicago Defender*, 2 August 1919, 3.
82 'Wants Woman Name', clipping, Gertrude Elsie McDougald-Ayer Scrapbook, GAP; 'Workers Party Pick List of Candidates At the New York Convention', *Daily Worker* [Chicago], 5 August 1922, n.p.; Turner, *Caribbean Crusaders and the Harlem Renaissance*, 86.
83 Ellen Carol Du Bois, *Harriot Stanton Blatch and the Winning of Woman Suffrage* (New Haven, CT: Yale University Press, 1997), 102.
84 'Wants Woman Name', clipping, Gertrude Elsie McDougald-Ayer Scrapbook, GAP.
85 Nannie Burroughs, 'Divide Vote or Go To Socialists', *Afro-American*, 22 August 1919, 4; Case 364 – IO-NYC to MID. Re: Maj. H.A. Strauss forwards copy of report gathered by one of Military Intelligence Allies regarding 'Negro Agitation', 17 September 1919, 1, Correspondence of Military Intelligence Surveillance related to Negro Surveillance, 1917–1914, www.fold3.com/image/183968672/ (accessed 5 January 2013).
86 'Should We Vote the Socialist Ticket', *The Crusader*, 2:2 (October 1919), 29–30.
87 'Negro Calls Upon His Race to Vote Straight Socialism', *The Call*, 4 November 1919, 5.
88 'Wants Woman Name', clipping, Gertrude Elsie McDougald-Ayer Scrapbook, GAP.
89 'Upon you Devolves a Sacred Duty', *The Crusader*, 3:2 (October 1920), 3.
90 'Editorials: A Double Appeal', *The Crusader*, 3:3 (November 1920), 8.
91 'Socialist in 21st Waging Brisk Battle', *New York Call*, 30 October 1919, 6.
92 Grace Lamb [Campbell], 'How shall the Negro Woman Worker Vote? Just one Party Favors Racial Equality', *Daily Worker*, 29 October 1928, 5.
93 Turner and Turner, *Richard B. Moore*, 29–30.
94 African Blood Brotherhood: Negro Activities, 6/10/1923–9/10/1923, Casefile #61 -50: African Blood Brotherhood, Department of Justice–Bureau of Investigation Surveillance of Black Americans, Freedom of Information Act Retrievals, 1923.

95 'New York News Brief', *Chicago Defender*, 11 December 1920; Negro Activities, 4 March 1921; 'New York News Brief', *Chicago Defender*, 2 April 1921, 9; Negro Activities, 27 March 1921–29 March 1921.

96 Kimberlé Crenshaw, 'Demarginalizing the Intersection of Race and Sex: A Black Feminist Critique of Antidiscrimination Doctrine, Feminist Theory and Antiracist Politics', *University of Chicago Legal Forum*, 1:8 (1989), 139–167, at 139, 154; Dana Bisignani, 'Understanding Intersectionality: Navigating Racism and Sexism', *Gender Press*, 2 March 2015, https://genderpressing.wordpress.com/2015/03/02/the-crooked-room-race-gender-and-advertisings-beauty-ideal/ (accessed 7 March 2016); Patricia Hill Collins, *Black Feminist Thought: Knowledge, Consciousness, and the Politics of Empowerment* (New York: Routledge, 2000), 299.

97 Grace Campbell [Grace Lamb], 'Negro Working Women Must Take Place in the Class War', *Daily Worker*, 8 March 1929, 1.

98 'Early Years and Political Parties', n.d., Box 1, Folder 21, Otto Edward Huiswoud Papers, Tamiment Library and Robert F. Wagner Labor Archive, New York University.

99 RGASPI, 515/1/1130/1687, Grace Lamb [P. Campbell], 'An analysis of the Negro Question in the USA'.

100 Robin D.G. Kelley, *Race Rebels: Culture, Politics and the Black Working Class* (New York: Free Press, 1994), 114.

101 'The Resolution of the Communist International', 26 October 1928 [online], Revolutionary Review Press, Washington, DC: 1975, www.marx2mao.com/Other/CR75.html#s1 (accessed 12 September 2013).

102 Campbell, 'Negro Working Women Must Take Place in the Class War'.

103 *Ibid.*

104 McDougald, 'The Double Task'.

105 Grace [Lamb] Campbell, 'Negro Working Women Must be Class Fighters', *Daily Worker*, 9 March 1929, 3.

106 McDougald, 'The Double Task'.

107 *Ibid.*

108 'Women Endorse TUEL Unity Meet', *Daily Worker*, 20 May 1929, 3.

109 'Women Workers Back Red Ticket at Mass Rally: Over 1.000 Militants Present', *Daily Worker*, 5 November 1928, 4; 'Speakers Urge All to Support Workers Party', *Daily Worker*, 28 August 1928, 2.

110 Joan Wallach Scott, 'Reply to the Hilden Critique', *International Labor and Working-Class History*, 16 (1979), 12–17.

111 Jane Humphries, 'Class Struggle and the Persistence of the Working-Class Family', *Cambridge Journal of Economics*, 1:3 (1977), 241–58, at 241.

112 Susan Himmelweit and Simon Mohun, 'Domestic Labour and Capital', *Cambridge Journal of Economics*, 1:1 (1977), 15–31.

113 Silvia Federici, 'The Reproduction of Labour-Power in the Global Economy, Marxist Theory and the Unfinished Feminist Revolution', *Caring Labor: An Archive*, 25 October 2010, https://caringlabor.wordpress.com/2010/10/25/silvia-federici-the-reproduction-of-labour-power-in-the-global-economy-

marxist-theory-and-the-unfinished-feminist-revolution/ (accessed 22 October 2016).
114 'The Bankers Club', *The Crusader*, 1:8 (September 1919), 23.
115 Grace (Lamb) Campbell, 'High Rents, Vile Houses is Negro's Lot in Harlem', *Working Woman*, May 1929, 10.
116 Campbell, 'High Rents, Vile Houses is Negro's Lot in Harlem'.
117 'Harlem Tenants to Meet Tonight', *Daily Worker*, 15 April 1929, n.p.: 'Protest End of Rent Law: Negroes Parade and Urge Tenants to Unite for Protection', *New York Times*, 2 June 1929, 23.
118 'Call for Unite Tenants' Fight: Harlem Mass Meeting Plans Wide Activity', *Daily Worker*, 10 August 1929, 5.
119 Grace [Lamb] Campbell, 'Negro Women In Industry', *Daily Worker*, 17 May 1929, 1.
120 David E. Staples, *No Place Like Home: Organising Home-based Labor in the Era of Structural Adjustment* (New York and London: Routledge, 2006), 4.
121 'Friends of Freedmen Meet in Capital', *Afro-American Baltimore*, 4 June 1920.
122 'Radical Church Will Open New Year's Work', *The Call*, 30 September 1922, 11.
123 McDougald, 'The Double Task'.
124 'Harlem Mass Meet to Hit Exploitation of Negro Working Women', *Daily Worker*, 14 June 1929, 5.
125 According to the 1920 United Census 24,438, or 60 per cent of all the black women working in New York, were either laundresses or servants. And in work requiring contact with the public in the capacity of saleswoman or representative, blacks were infrequently employed if they were known to be black, except in black businesses. Charles S. Johnson, 'Black Workers in the City', *Survey Graphic* 'Harlem' number, 6 (March 1925), 641–643, 718–721, http://etext.virginia.edu/harlem/JohWorkF.html (accessed 25 May 2006).
126 Grace P. Campbell, 'Tragedy of the Colored Girl in Court', *New York Age*, 25 April 1925, 3; Erik S. McDuffie, *Sojourning for Freedom: Black Women, American Communism, and the Making of Black Left Feminism* (Durham, NC: Duke University, 2011), 50.
127 McDuffie, *Sojourning for Freedom*, 45; Justin, 'Making a Success'.
128 Justin, 'Making a Success'.
129 McDuffie, *Sojourning for Freedom*, 45; Justin, 'Making a Success'.
130 Casefile 10110–1683: Bulletin of Radical Activities 1920–1921: 1 January 1920–31 December 1921.
131 Minkah Makalani, 'An Apparatus for Negro Women: Black Women's Organising, Communism, and the Institutional Spaces of Radical Pan-African Thought', *Women, Gender, and Families of Color*, 4:2 (2016), 250–273, at 251.
132 'Early Years and Political Parties', n.d., Box 1, Folder 21, Otto Edward Huiswoud Papers, Tamiment Library and Robert F. Wagner Labor Archive, New York University; Turner, *Caribbean Crusaders and the Harlem Renaissance*, 25.

133 Justin, 'Making a Success'.
134 'Early Years and Political Parties'; Turner, *Caribbean Crusaders and the Harlem Renaissance*, 25.
135 FBI Negro Activities, 6 March 1921, www.Fold3.Com/image/#4803619 (accessed 20 January 2015).
136 Turner, *Caribbean Crusaders and the Harlem Renaissance*, 78.
137 Letter to Theodore Draper in New York from Cyril Briggs in Los Angeles, 17 March 1958 [long extract], Theodore Draper Papers, Hoover Institution Archives, Box 31, www.marxists.org/history/usa/groups/abb/1958/0317-briggs-todraper.pdf (accessed 30 November 2014); Turner, *Caribbean Crusaders and the Harlem Renaissance*, 56.
138 Negro Activities, Investigative Case Files of the Bureau of Investigation 1908–1922, 2/3/21–4/2/21.
139 Casefile #61 -50: African Blood Brotherhood, Department of Justice–Bureau of Investigation Surveillance of Black Americans, Freedom of Information Act Retrievals, 1923, 18 September 1923–12 September 1923.
140 Casefile #61 -50: African Blood Brotherhood, Department of Justice–Bureau of Investigation Surveillance of Black Americans, Freedom of Information Act Retrievals, 1923, 27 November 1923–24 November 1923; FBI Marcus Garvey and the African Blood Brotherhood, 31 August 1923, Reel 1; 'A.B.B. Activities', *The Crusader*, 4 (July 1921), 1181.
141 Casefile #61 -50: African Blood Brotherhood, Department of Justice–Bureau of Investigation Surveillance of Black Americans, Freedom of Information Act Retrievals, 1923, 27 September 1923–29 September 1923, 24 August 1923–27 August 1923.
142 FBI Negro Activities, 2 March 1921, www. Fold3.Com/image/#8704288; FBI Negro Activities, 29 March 1921, www. Fold3.Com/image/#8704186; FBI Negro Activities, 4 April 1921, www. Fold3.Com/image/#8704129; FBI Negro Activities, 6 May 1921, www. Fold3.Com/image/#8704081 (accessed 20 January 2015); Turner and Turner, *Richard B. Moore*, 29–30.
143 'Manhattan YWCA', *New York Age*, 16 April 1921, 8.
144 'A.B.B. Activities', *The Crusader*, 4 (July 1921), 1181.
145 Casefile #61 -50: African Blood Brotherhood, Department of Justice–Bureau of Investigation Surveillance of Black Americans, Freedom of Information Act Retrievals, 1923, 13 November 1923–10 November 1923; L.F. Coles, Editorial, *Pittsburg Courier*, 20 August 1937, 2.
146 *The Appeal*, 30 December 1922, 2; 'Bolshevism for Negroes', *Northern Advocate* [New Zealand], 12 June 1922, 7; 'Radicals Plan to Invade South Fails of Materialisation', *Wilmington Morning Star*, 18 December 1922, 1.
147 'Soviets Took Advantage Riots to Urge Up Rising', *New York Herald*, 12 December 1922, 8; 'The African Blood Brotherhood's Position', *Richmond Planet*, 23 December 1922, 4.
148 Letter to Theodore Draper in New York from Cyril Briggs in Los Angeles, 17 March 1958; Negro Activities, Investigative Case Files of the Bureau of Investigation 1908–1922, www.fold3.com/image (accessed 20 January 2015);

'Program of the African Blood Brotherhood', *Communist Review* [London], 2:6 (April 1922), 449–454.
149 RGASPI 534/3/167: 2222 K. Karatov, 'Work Among the Negro Toilers: The Northern Part of the United States', Negro Bureau, n.d.
150 Letter to Theodore Draper in New York from Cyril Briggs in Los Angeles, 17 March 1958; '*Crusader Magazine* Appears', *Chicago Defender*, 21 August 1918.
151 Advertisements 'United Now for Equal Rights' Hamitic League of the World, in *The Crusader*, 1918–22; Mark Solomon, *The Cry Was Unity: Communists and African Americans, 1917–1936* (Jackson, MS: University Press of Mississippi, 1998), 6.
152 Letterhead Crusader News Agency, FBI Marcus Garvey and the African Blood Brotherhood, 5 June 1923, 27 August 1923, Reel 1; Solomon, *The Cry Was Unity*, 61.
153 Letter to Theodore Draper in New York from Cyril Briggs in Los Angeles, 17 March 1958; Casefile #61 -826: African Blood Brotherhood, Department of Justice–Bureau of Investigation Surveillance of Black Americans, Freedom of Information Act Retrievals, 1923, 1 January 1923–31 December 1923.
154 'New Raid on Reds Discloses "Rules" for Fight on US', *New York Times*, 1 May 1921, 1.
155 FBI Negro Activities, 1921, www. Fold3.Com/image/#4079560 (accessed 20 January 2015); The 1920 United States Census: Manhattan Assembly District 19, New York, New York; Roll: T625_1221; Page: 9B; Enumeration District: 1352; Image: 1146. Table of Contents, *The Crusader*, 2:2 (October 1919), 1; Turner, *Caribbean Crusaders and the Harlem Renaissance*, 37.
156 'Negro Business', *The Crusader*, 2:8 (May 1920), 8–9.
157 'Roll of Honor', *The Crusader*, 1:1 (Sept 1919), 23, 34.
158 Makalani, 'An Apparatus for Negro Women', 251.
159 FBI Marcus Garvey and the African Blood Brotherhood, 27 August 1923, Reel 1; Casefile #61 -50: African Blood Brotherhood, Department of Justice–Bureau of Investigation Surveillance of Black Americans, Freedom of Information Act Retrievals, 1923, 16 August 1923–10 August 1923.
160 FBI Marcus Garvey and the African Blood Brotherhood, 24 August 1923, Reel 1; Claude McKay, *Harlem: Negro Metropolis* (New York: Harcourt Brace Jovanovich, 1968), 223–224; Joanne Grant, *Ella Baker: Freedom Bound* (New York: John Wiley, 1998), 36; Memo from the Pure Food Co-operative Grocery Stores, Inc., New York City, n.d., Ella Baker Papers, Schomburg Center for Research and Black Culture, Box 2, Folder 3; 'New Food Store to Open on Lenox Avenue', *New York Age*, 23 February 1935; 'Issues Appeal for Co-Operative Store', *Amsterdam News*, 1 June 1935, 3.
161 Negro Actives, USMI Reports, 20 November 1920, Reel 17, frame 565; RGASPI 534/3/2: 37, 'Resolutions of the Convention of the Friends of Freedom', 25–30 May 1920.
162 Claude McKay, *Harlem: Negro Metropolis* (New York: Harcourt Brace Jovanovich, 1968), 223–224.

163 FBI Negro Activities, 6 May 1921, www. Fold3.Com/image/#8704061 (accessed 20 January 2015); FBI Marcus Garvey and the African Blood Brotherhood, 31 August 1923, Reel 1.
164 FBI Negro Activities, 6 July 1921, www. Fold3.Com/image/#8705284 (accessed 20 January 2015).
165 Negro Activities, Investigative Case Files of the Bureau of Investigation 1908–1922, 12–14 August 1921, www.fold3.com/image/#8703602 (accessed 20 January 2015); Negro Activities, Investigative Case Files of the Bureau of Investigation 1908–1922, 28 June–2 July 1921, www.fold3.com/image/#8703602 (accessed 20 January 2015). When Briggs joined the party, there were only two other blacks in it, Otto Huiswoud and Hendricks. Hendricks dropped out of the party – and the ABB – during an organising tour for the Brotherhood. In a report in *The Worker* on 11 August 1923, Huiswoud said that both Huiswoud and Hendricks joined the Brotherhood after Briggs had entered the Party. See Letter to Theodore Draper in New York from Cyril Briggs in Los Angeles, 17 March 1958.
166 'Grace Campbell: Dead Old CP Member', *Daily Worker*, 10 June 1943, 3; Philp Bart and William Weinstone, 'The Founding of the Communist Party in America', *People's World*, 1 September 2017, www.peoplesworld.org/article/the-founding-of-the-communist-party-in-america/ (accessed 19 November 2018).
167 Memo on Workers Party from J.R. Procter, Colonel, General Staff, Headquarters 2nd Corps Area, Governors Island, New York City, 27 March 1922, US Military Intelligence Reports, Reel 20, frame 908; 'Harlem West Side Branch, NY Action', *Chicago Daily Worker*, 5 August 1922.
168 Casefile #61 -50: African Blood Brotherhood, Department of Justice–Bureau of Investigation Surveillance of Black Americans, Freedom of Information Act Retrievals, 1923, 30 November 1923–26 November 1923.
169 FBI Marcus Garvey and the African Blood Brotherhood, 8 September 1923, Reel 1.
170 Letter to Theodore Draper in New York from Cyril Briggs in Los Angeles, March 17, 1958; FBI Marcus Garvey and the African Blood Brotherhood, 8 September 1923, Reel 1; FBI Marcus Garvey and the African Blood Brotherhood, 6 September 1923, Reel 1; FBI Marcus Garvey and the African Blood Brotherhood, 4 October 1923, Reel 1; FBI Marcus Garvey and the African Blood Brotherhood, 9 September 1923, Reel 1.
171 Casefile #61 -50: African Blood Brotherhood, Department of Justice–Bureau of Investigation Surveillance of Black Americans, Freedom of Information Act Retrievals, 1923, 21 November 1923–17 November 1923.
172 FBI Marcus Garvey and the African Blood Brotherhood, 9 September 1923, Reel 1; Casefile #61 -50: African Blood Brotherhood, Department of Justice–Bureau of Investigation Surveillance of Black Americans, Freedom of Information Act Retrievals, 1923, 13 September 1923–8 September 1923.
173 RGASPI 534/3/167: 2222 K. Karatov, 'Work Among the Negro Toilers', n.d.
174 Claude McKay, *A Long Way From Home* (New Brunswick, NJ: Rutgers University Press, 2007), 161.

175 *Ibid*.
176 'ANLC Opens Negro Labor Center In Harlem', *Pittsburgh Courier*, 1 September 1928, 4 section 1.
177 RGASPI 534/3/104: 1366 Negro Commission, 15 November 1928.
178 RGASPI/ 515/1/139/3367 Draft Plan Ethiopian Mutual Aid League for the South, [n.d.] CPUSA.
179 RGASPI, 515/1/1130/1687 Campbell, 'An analysis of the Negro Question in the USA'.
180 'Lovestonites' 'is a designation for the "Right Opposition" led in the United States by Jay Lovestone from the time of their collective expulsion from the Communist Party in 1928 to their formal dissolution in 1941', Paul Buhle, 'Lovestonites' in Mari Jo Buhle, Paul Buhle, and Dan Georgakas (ed.), *The Encyclopedia of the American Left* (Chicago: St James Press, 1990), 435–437, at 435.
181 RGASPI 515/130/1685 Minutes of Negro Commission, 11 September 1929.
182 'School Gives Post to Oakley Johnson', *Amsterdam News*, 4 October 1933, 16; 'Conference Called On Workers' School', *Amsterdam News*, 27 December 1933, 11; 'What's Doing in the Workers' Schools of the US', *Daily Worker*, 11 April 1934, 5; 'Negro History Taught New York', *Daily Worker*, 24 August 1934, 2; 'Officers Course In History', *Amsterdam News*, 25 August 1934, 16; 'Harlem Love Girls Get 25 Cents, Whites $5', *Afro-American*, 29 January 1938, 21; 'Harlem Holds Second Annual Legislative Meet Saturday', *Amsterdam News*, 24 December 1938, 7.
183 'National Scottsboro Committee of Action', *Daily Worker*, 3 May 1933; United States. Congress. House. Special Committee on Un-American Activities, *Investigation of Un-American Propaganda Activities in the United States* (Washington, DC: Government Printing Office, 1938–40), 1309; Elizabeth Dilling, *The Red Network: A Who's Who and Handbook of Radicalism for Patriots* (Chicago, 1934), 227, www.archive.org/stream/rednetworkwhoswh 00dillrich/rednetworkwhoswh00dillrich_djvu.txt (accessed 1 January 2011); 'Harlem Leaders Will Organise Scottsboro Defense Committee', *Pittsburgh Courier*, 9 October 1937, 37; Letter from A. Clayton Powell, Jr, Temporary Chairman, to Friends, Harlem Provisional Scottsboro Defense Committee, Rm. 204, 200 West 125th Street, New York City, 21 October 1937, NAACP, Scottsboro, Part 6, Reel 2, Frame 987; Flyer Harlem Provisional Scottsboro Defense Committee, William Patterson Papers, Box 208–22; Sponsored by Harlem Provisional Scottsboro Defense Committee, October 1937, NAACP, Scottsboro, Part 6, Reel 2, Frame 996.
184 James A. Miller, Susan D. Pennybacker, and Eve Rosenhaft, 'Mother Ada Wright and the International Campaign to Free the Scottsboro Boys', *American Historical Review*, 106 (2001), 387–430, at 388, 389, 399, 410, 421, 422, 428; Vron Ware, *Beyond the Pale: White Women, Racism and History* (London: Verso, 1992).
185 Audley Moore, because of the racism she encountered within the party, eventually resigned. Moore continued her political activity by fighting for education for

the poor and becoming a leader in the movement demanding reparations from the federal government for the labour of blacks under slavery. Moore promoted Pan-Africanism and was one of the founders of the Universal Association of Ethiopian Women. See Eugene Gordon, 'Negro Women Fight for Freedom in 1942 as their Sister did in "61"', *Daily Worker*, 8 March 1942; 'Women Who Lead the Way to Progress', *Daily Worker*, 8 March 1939; 'Negro Woman Urges Amter Support', *Daily Worker*, between 28 August and 18 November 1938; 'Woman Freed in Harlem Pool Petition', *Daily Worker*, 25 August 1938; William J. Maxwell, *New Negro Old Left: African-American Writing and Communism Between the Wars* (New York: Columbia University Press, 1999), 126, 136.

186 Letter to Comrade Foster from Claudia Jones, 6 December 1955, Howard 'Stretch' Johnson Collection, Tamiment Collection, New York University; Claudia Jones, Handwritten Autobiographical Notes, Civil Rights Congress (CRC), Part V, Reel 3: 0001–15, CRC Reel 58, Box 102 w46; Louise Patterson Interview by R.F. Prago, Side A, Box 27, Folder 8, Louise Thompson Patterson Papers, Special Collections, The Robert W. Woodruff Library, Emory University, Atlanta, Georgia.

187 'Mass Meeting', *Amsterdam News*, 11 May 1940, 5.

188 RGASPI 534/3/167: 222 'A statement of Several Negro Comrades Concerning Negro Work Particularly in the LSNR, Central Committee in Negro Work, 1930s; Oral Interview between Maude White Katz by Ruth Prago, OHAL Tape I, Side 1, 18 December 1981, Tamiment Library, NYU; Louise Thompson, 'Negro Women in Our Party', *Party Organizer*, 10 (August 1937), 25–27; RGASPI 515/1/1336 Mary Adams, 'Negro Work has Not Been Entirely Successful Because', 3 August 1928. In 1927, Margaret Cowl, Secretary Women's Department New York, NY District Workers Party, spoke to the work that was not being done among women. RGASPI 515/1/1136 Margaret Cowl, Secretary Women's Department New York, NY District Workers Party, Program for Communist work Among Women in the United States, The Fifth National Convention of the Communist Party of America, 31 August 1927.

189 *Fourth Annual Report of the Colored Woman's League of Washington, DC*, for the year ending 1 January 1897. Daniel Murray Pamphlet Collection (Library of Congress). Created [Washington, DC]: Printed by the F.D. Smith Printing Company, [1897].

190 'Early Years and Political Parties', n.d., Box 1, Folder 21, Otto Edward Huiswoud Papers, Tamiment Library and Robert F. Wagner Labor Archive, New York University.

191 Letter to Claude McKay from Grace Campbell, 25 February 1935, Claude McKay Collection, Yale Collection of American Literature, Beinecke Rare Book and Manuscript Library, JWJ MSS 27, Box 1, Folder 34.

192 Series 15029 Civil Services Employee History Card: Grace Campbell CK# 3421, New York State Archives, Cultural Education Center Room 11D40, Albany, NY.

193 'Grace Campbell: Dead Old CP Member'.

194 Some of the other fifty women include Mary Church Terrell, Ida B. Wells-Barnett, Marie C. Lawton, a Nannie Burroughs, Mary McLeod Bethune, G. Elise Johnson McDougald, Alice Dunbar-Nelson, Gwendolyn Bennett, Jesse Redmon Fauset, Lucy Slowe, Charlotte Hawkins Brown, Augusta Savage, Addie W. Hutton, Emma Ranson, Eva D. Bowles, Sadie T. Alexander, Florence Mills, Ethel Waters, and A'Lelia Walker. See Ruth R. Dennis, 'New York Radio Speech Praises 50 Race Women', *Pittsburg Courier*, 17 September 1927, 3.

# II

Interwar intersections of Red and Black

# 5

# Clements Kadalie, the ICU and the transformation of Communism in Southern Africa, 1917–31

*Henry Dee*

On 17 December 1926, the executive of the Industrial and Commercial Workers' Union of Africa (ICU) – the world's largest black trade union – sat up through the night.[1] Amid heated debate, they hammered out the union's position vis-à-vis Russia and the Communist world revolution. Mirroring heightening divisions between moderates, socialists and Communists across the world, numerous ICU officials wanted to ban organisers from simultaneously being leaders of the trade union and the Communist Party of South Africa (CPSA), fearing co-optation by the latter's predominantly white revolutionary leadership.[2] In the early hours of the morning the executive decided, on an alleged share of six votes to five, to enforce the ban. After the announcement, the ICU's four prominent Communist officials – James La Guma, Johnny Gomas, Eddie Khaile and Thomas Mbeki – stormed out, lustily singing the Red Flag.[3] In the following weeks, the ICU's newspaper, *The Workers' Herald*, denounced Communists as 'political murderers' intent on leading workers into 'an ambush well laid for them for years by the "boss' class".[4] The CPSA's *South African Worker*, in turn, declared that the national secretary of the ICU, Clements Kadalie, and his 'clique' had 'publicly declared their policy to be a reformist one'.[5]

For decades after the expulsions, South African Communists castigated ICU leaders as 'petty-bourgeois', 'anti-strike' 'good boys'.[6] These politicised interpretations have heavily influenced the historiography of Southern African radicalism: ICU leaders have been accused of making a sudden and irreversible shift towards anti-Communism in 1926 (ignoring earlier tendencies), while the interwar CPSA has monopolised South Africa's early 'radical tradition'.[7] Helen Bradford, Allison Drew, David Johnson, Tom Lodge, Sylvia Neame and Lucien van der Walt have demonstrated that syndicalists and Communists had important radicalising influences on leaders of the ICU, the African National Congress (ANC) and the Industrial Workers of Africa (IWA), a syndicalist black trade union active between 1917 and 1920, sharpening their ideas about capitalism and class.[8] This chapter, however, demonstrates that influences worked both ways.

Through its socialist rhetoric and mass mobilisation of up to 250,000 members, the ICU had a transformative effect, not only on the CPSA, Southern African trade unions and the ANC, but also at a global level. In 1927, Nikolai Bukharin, Comintern's general secretary in Russia, insisted that Communists in South Africa should 'only ask one question, namely the question of our policy with regard to the black trade union' – the ICU.[9] In America, black workers drew direct inspiration from the ICU's 'sterling leadership', at the same time as 'drinking deep from the inspiring well of the great workers' revolution of "Red Russia".'[10] And in Britain, George Padmore and C.L.R. James emphasised the 'immense importance' of the ICU.[11] Influencing radicals across the world, the ICU demonstrated both the possibility and importance of black leadership and unionised black workers, and in doing so transformed ideas about race, radicalism and revolution for Communists and non-Communists alike.

This chapter makes three arguments. First, the influence of Communists in Southern Africa, and the real difficulties that they faced, need to be contextualised against enduring anti-Communist tendencies within the ICU and other local organisations. This was particularly important towards the end of the 1920s, when global divisions between Communists and socialists became pronounced, and previously pluralist 'big-tent' organisations like the ICU fragmented. Second, the ICU's leadership transformed the priorities of Communists in Southern Africa by demonstrating the possibility, necessity and significance of organising black workers in their hundreds of thousands. It was ICU successes that led the CPSA to see the mass organisation of the black working class, rather than the local white labour aristocracy, as the 'instrument' of historic change – and throughout the second half of the 1920s, Communists spent considerable energy trying to gain control of the trade union. Third, ICU criticisms show that the CPSA was severely weakened by the influence of white labourism and top-down 'dictatorial' tendencies within its leadership. ICU leaders continued to work with, and join, the CPSA into the 1930s, but many Communists actively undermined the trade union from 1926, catalysing factional divisions that would contribute to a weakened labour movement in subsequent decades.

## The ICU's 'peaceful and constitutional' mass organisation

Clements Kadalie arrived in Cape Town in February 1918, following in the footsteps of his older brother and thousands of other Malawian immigrants.[12] Along with twenty-three other black workers and a handful of white trade unionists, he founded the ICU on 17 January 1919 in the Cape Town docks. In 1920, the ICU amalgamated with the syndicalist

IWA. The politics of the combined union drew most heavily, nonetheless, on the transnational race-pride of Marcus Garvey's Universal Negro Improvement Association (UNIA) – actively publicising the organisation's millions of members, ideas and conventions. Like the UNIA in America, the early ICU was internationalist and cosmopolitan, drawing its leadership and membership from West African, Central African, Southern African and Caribbean immigrant workers, as well as local South Africans.[13] Both Kadalie and James La Guma, the ICU's coloured assistant secretary, penned Garvey-inspired poetry, calling out across the diaspora: 'Ye dusky sons of Ham/Now is the time, arise.'[14] The ICU's Caribbean-born president James Gumbs was an 'out-and-out Marcus Garvey'.[15] At UNIA meetings, Kadalie called on audiences to 'unite with racial pride that at last Africa will be redeemed and all her sons return where nature first put them'.[16] And in personal letters, he confided his wish to become a 'great African Marcus Garvey'.[17] After the ICU won a wage increase on the Cape Town docks in September 1920, Kadalie attributed the success to the fact that the trade union had bridged local divisions of race and

> created a new theory of race consciousness in that both the native and colored people realised [...] that no victory could be accomplished by either in the struggle for existence unless they had accepted in toto the fact that as workers [...] a united front had to be presented.[18]

As highlighted by Lucien van der Walt, there were numerous complementary currents within the ICU's syncretic ideology.[19] The ICU integrated Garvey's opinions about race-first organising with syndicalist ideas about organising all workers into 'One Big Union', British notions of imperial citizenship and Mohandas Gandhi's non-violent philosophy of passive resistance. Combining these strands, one of the ICU's leading Garveyites, James Thaele, called on black workers to imbibe a 'Garveyan Gandhi philosophy' and set out 'on the warpath [to] self-determination[,] social, economic and religious'.[20] A notable number of ICU radicals, including Stanley Silwana and Thomas Mbeki, were heavily influenced by Garveyism, in particular. In Thaele's Garveyite newspaper, *African World*, Mbeki denounced how black people were 'denied even the rudimentary rights of citizenship – to say nothing of self-determination', while Silwana addressed UNIA meetings and insisted that the 'Bantu of today are not the Bantus of a decade ago, they are wide awake'.[21]

Despite early connections with white trade unionists, the ICU soon developed an antagonistic relationship with the broader white labour movement. Kadalie condemned how white workers scabbed during the IWA and ICU's joint strike at the Cape Town docks during December 1919, and 'assisted the police to mow down the defenceless men and women with guns' during black worker protests in Port Elizabeth in October 1920.[22] Tensions heightened after the 1922 Rand Revolt, an armed insurrection of white miners in Johannesburg. Banners inscribed with the slogan 'Workers of the World, Unite and Fight for a White South Africa' indicated the prejudices of white miners, and strikers shot forty-four black residents dead after rumours of a 'native rising' swept white communities.[23] Kadalie asserted that when 'white workers declared war on the black workers', the revolt 'was no longer an ordinary industrial upheaval', but an 'illogical' struggle defined by the 'brutal slaughter of the innocent black men and women'. He condemned 'the strikers, not as strikers, but as murderers'.[24] In the aftermath of the shootings, the South African army intervened and crushed the strike.

In the context of white vigilantism, failed white worker insurrection and the earlier failure of black anti-colonial resistance, the ICU insisted on 'peaceful and constitutional industrial organisation'.[25] Kadalie told black workers at ICU mass meetings: 'This is no time for sticks and guns, but for brains. Give us the financial support, the brain[s] we have got.'[26] In particular, ICU leaders tried to 'convince the white workers that our movement does NOT aim at a 'Native Rising'.'[27] In the ICU's newspaper, *The Workers' Herald*, poet Tembekile Kofi captured these sentiments, writing:

> Peacefully, let it be noted,
> We shall have our 'day' and 'say',
> Though we're met with guns and sabres.
> We shall provoke no senseless fray [...]
>
> Union means an all-in movement,
> None outside to scab upon us;
> With folded arms we'll stand like statues,
> Sing our songs but make no rumpus.
>
> That is how we'll win our battles,
> Make good our claim to rights;
> We have no weapons left us,
> Brains, not bombs, will win our fights.
>
> Forward then, in one big union,
> All in which we're organised,
> Solid phalanx undivided,
> No more shall we be despised.[28]

While the white labour movement was dominated by racist tendencies, ICU leaders argued that interracial co-operation was impossible. Highlighting the racialised limits of trade union solidarity, Kadalie recounted how 'the white man here in Africa theoretically constitutes himself as an "aristocrat" and forgets all his responsibilities as a workingman' – 'no direct or indirect support was ever accorded [to us] by the white workers'.[29] In supporting 'colour bars', white workers instead stood 'for a "White Empire" or a "White Commonwealth of Nations"', an Empire where the millions of darker skins must remain forever hewers of wood and drawers of water'. As such, the black worker was 'surrounded by two enemies – capitalism and his fellow white workers'. Organising coloured and African workers separately into 'One Big Union', the ICU was 'a deliberate challenge' to white trade unionism, and 'the defeat of white labor in Africa [was] inevitable unless the white workers change their attitude toward the aboriginals'.

Having consolidated its base among black railway, factory and dock workers in the Cape Province and Namibia, the ICU targeted Johannesburg's black miners from 1924. Kadalie recognised 'the Witwatersrand was the industrial backbone of South Africa', and that the ICU would 'not be in any way complete' until it organised workers on the mines.[30] Central to this shift was the need to break the mining sector's infamous transnational recruitment system – which was recognised as the key stumbling block to effective trade union organisation. As *The Workers' Herald* made clear, the recruitment system supplied 'scab labour' when workers downed tools and 'debarred [migrant workers] from forming themselves into an industrial union'.[31] By mid-1925, *The Workers' Herald* was reporting that thousands of miners were attending meetings in Johannesburg addressed by Kadalie and presided over by the Zulu leader Allison Wessels George Champion, a former mine official. The ICU also had some success organising Johannesburg's industrial workers. When ICU members at Maytham's Ltd, a Johannesburg tin works, demanded longer breaks in September 1925, the management locked sixty workers out. After members struck and marched to the ICU Workers' Hall, Kadalie intervened and the management conceded an hour's break. The *Johannesburg Star* reported it as the 'native trade union's first strike on white lines'.[32]

Organising the previously unorganised, the skilled and unskilled, men and women, Africans and coloureds, locals and immigrants into 'One Big Union', the ICU's syndicalist-inspired general trade union methods were recognised around the world as a globally significant development. South African trade unionists Ernest Gitsham and James Trembath, for example, championed the ICU's adoption of general trade unionism, and noted that like 'the striking rise to power of the unskilled English worker, beginning with the famous [1889] London Dock Strike, the Native worker also has begun to enter the Trade Union arena in startling fashion', through the ICU.[33] By 1926, Charles Freer Andrews, the president of the All-India Trade Union Congress (AITUC), likewise believed that, under the leadership of the ICU, black workers in South Africa were 'making more rapid progress than any other people in the world'.[34] And in 1927, A. Philip Randolph's newly formed Brotherhood of Sleeping Car Porters, the first black trade union in the United States, heralded the ICU as the 'largest economic organisation of black men in the world, having nearly 100,000 members'.[35] *The Chicago Defender*, similarly, described the ICU as 'the strongest organisation of Race workmen that has ever been formed in this section of the globe'.[36] And *The Pittsburgh Courier* portrayed the ICU as 'the largest Negro labor union in the world', representative of 'the more advanced thought and opinion' of 'New Negroes' in both 'the United States and Africa'.[37]

Johannesburg's capitalist elite, however, were quick to respond to ICU organisation. As Keith Breckenridge and Phil Bonner have demonstrated, already by August 1925, it was clear that ICU organisers had effectively been locked out of the gold mines.[38] Through the mine compound system, effective private policing, a strict policy of non-recognition, and a network of informers, ICU members soon found themselves dismissed from mine employment and refused entry to the mines.[39] ICU shop steward Thomas William Thibedi reported that mine workers were 'always threatened with expulsion or dismissal if they are observed to associate with the Workers' Union – the ICU'.[40] And at the start of 1926, Henry Daniel Tyamzashe, the subeditor of *The Workers' Herald*, reported that in Johannesburg members had been 'very slow, and even indifferent'.[41] Over 200,000 black mine workers and 100,000 domestic servants were employed on the Witwatersrand, but the ICU had only organised 8,000 local members by 1926.[42] In response to the ICU's setbacks, Kadalie told members in September 1925:

> We must organise the mine natives and it must be done in their homes and through their chiefs [...] The ICU movement has spread all over the country and now we have thousands of followers, but not enough; we want hundreds of thousands – enough to make a big noise [... the mine management] must not sleep.[43]

Sending ICU officials out into the Transkei, Pondoland, colonial Lesotho and Zimbabwe, as well as feelers into colonial Malawi and Mozambique, the ICU explicitly responded to the transnational nature of the Southern African labour market. ICU branch secretary Theodore Ramonti led combined meetings of South African and Mozambican workers at Witbank, emphasising that 'all present must work together to organise, report all grievances and attend all meetings in future'.[44] And Kadalie made contact with Mozambican radical, Brown Dulela, whose newspaper, *O Brado Africano* [The African Roar], severely criticised how Mozambicans did 'not have the right to choose the employer, the freedom to work for whom one wants' under the recruiting system.[45] With the ICU's Theo Lujiza also actively organising migrant workers in the Eastern Cape, Kadalie felt assured that '[o]nce we succeed to capture the Transkei and convince the chiefs with our aims and objects we can rest assured that we are drawing nearer to the time when this Organisation shall be dreaded by the Mine Owners of the Rand'.[46] As set out in Helen Bradford's now classic study of the ICU in rural South Africa, it was at this point that the trade union spread 'like veldt fire' and became a mass member organisation with over 100,000 members. Importantly, however, this expansion exemplified the ICU leadership's emphasis on general unionism as much as it represented a 'bottom-up' spontaneous rural revolt. Pioneering new ideas about race and mass organisation, the ICU emphasised that local and immigrant black workers needed to be organised in their hundreds of thousands across Southern Africa in order to effectively challenge capitalist interests.

### 'Fighting Bolshevism': black moderates and the ICU

The ICU was far from the only black trade union in Southern Africa, and it faced considerable condemnation over the course of the 1920s from more moderate workers' leaders. In July 1920, trade unionists in Bloemfontein hosted an abortive conference that hoped to bring together all black workers into 'one great union of skilled and unskilled workers of South Africa, south of the Zambesi'.[47] The meeting proved to be a disaster with two general trade unions, rather than one, emerging from the debacle. The first was Kadalie's Cape Town-based ICU. The second became known as the Industrial and Commercial (Amalgamated) Workers' Union (or ICWU), under the leadership of anti-Communist moderates Impey Ben Nyombolo, Bennet Ncwana and Henry Selby Msimang. Divisions between the ICU and ICWU quickly emerged, not least over whether to pursue a radical internationalist or moderate nationalist agenda. Particularly opposed to the global influence of Communism and Garveyism, Msimang promised that 'if the ICWU continues as it has begun, the end of industrial repression will soon be seen, and communism will languish and die'.[48] In contrast to the internationalist aspirations of the ICU, Msimang asserted that 'help from without is in itself disadvantageous in that it destroys energy and self-reliance – it is the shortest road to economic slavery and moral degeneration'.[49]

Communism, generally, had an ambiguous reception in South Africa. Hamilton Kraai, an IWA leader, told workers during the Johannesburg bucket strike of May 1918, 'we should today do as these workers of Russia did'.[50] Almost all black newspapers, however, including *Ilanga lase Natal* [The Natal Sun], *Imvo Zabantsundu* [Black Opinion] and *Umteteli wa Bantu* [Mouthpiece of the People] were anti-Communist. *Umteteli* described Communism as a 'dangerous creed', alleging that Africans were 'not yet mentally in a position to grasp the principles of Socialism'.[51] *Ilanga* similarly saw Communism as an 'insidious invasion', and its founder – former ANC president John Dube – wrote to the MP, John Sydney Marwick, in 1927: 'We, the moderate section of the Bantu people, feel just as you do that communism, whether among white or black, is a real danger to the community.'[52]

Wary of being labelled 'Bolshevists', and sceptical about the promise of Communism, the early ICU itself was also anti-Communist. In 1920, leaders insisted that the growth of the ICU 'could not, under any circumstances, be attributed to Bolshevist propaganda'.[53] The first issue of *The Workers' Herald* similarly asserted, in May 1923, that the ICU 'repudiates the Third International and the horrors associated with it'.[54] And when, in September 1923, ICWU leaders attacked the ICU for being 'Bolshevist', Gumbs, Kadalie and La Guma queried how 'in any shape or form we have neglected the interests of the African workers and worshipped any other gods[,] such as [the] Bolshevism of Russia'.[55]

Because they had practised 'communalism' for generations, many ICU leaders believed that they did not need the derivative, imported theories of the CPSA. Kadalie, for example, argued that the 'doctrines of Bolshevism do not in the least attract the attention of the true aboriginal', because 'since the creation of the world, the Native knows no other system of government than that of communism'.[56] He wrote to his cousin in 1923 'that we as Africans have practiced the communal cooperation so that it is not the whiteman's civilisation to teach that life amongst us people'. For generations in colonial Malawi, they had already 'practically adopted socialism, [rather] than the promotion of socialism in theory which is characteristic amongst the white races of the world'.[57] Champion similarly asserted that the 'Zulus are more communistic than anybody else, even the communists of Russia, because we in our lifetime had everything in common'.[58]

As such, ICU leaders believed that the CPSA had 'no intelligent policy – except murder – to place before the workers'.[59] In 1923, Kadalie contended that he had 'never come across any Native man who has become a Communist'.[60] The same year, *Umteteli* concurred that although the CPSA had 'preached Communism for years and many thousands of Natives have listened to their perfervid pronouncements', the 'Natives have gone unimpressed, and the Native communist is rare'.[61] The CPSA's own Eddie Roux was later frank that 'right up to the split [with the ICU] there was no appreciable following of Africans in the Party'.[62] He reflected:

> It was difficult to recruit any Africans into the Party. Africans were often, and with reason, suspicious of the white man. The few that came to our meetings felt strange and uncomfortable.[63]

At least in part, this open rejection of Communism reflected the broader anti-Bolshevik public sphere that dominated interwar South Africa. In 1926, Kadalie told audiences that he had to 'speak of conditions in Britain, because if I refer to conditions in Germany, France or Russia I will be called a Bolshevik'.[64] But it also reflected entrenched white labourism within revolutionary circles.

### 'Workers of the World Unite!': black Communists and the ICU

White Communists somewhat hubristically believed that the ICU 'ought by rights to become related to the Communist Party'.[65] Notably, however, almost every black radical was initially ambivalent about the white-dominated CPSA. This included organisers like John Gomas, Reuben Cetyiwe and Hamilton Kraai who had been active in syndicalist organisations that brought together white, coloured, African and Indian radicals during the 1910s, such as the International Socialist League (ISL). Only one black radical, T.W. Thibedi, was present at the formation of the CPSA on 30 July 1921.[66] Thibedi was often 'sworn at when he puts his head in' during executive meetings, and Bill Andrews, the CPSA's secretary between 1921 and 1924, held the view that

> there is no Native Worker we know in S[outh] Africa in whom we have absolute confidence, the educated ones are as you know under the influence of Missionaries or the Church or the Native Affairs Department and one is just as likely to send out a spy as a genuine comrade.[67]

Although the CPSA denounced racism, white workers were projected as the 'advanced guard' of the struggle at the CPSA's 1921 inaugural conference.[68] The same year, David Ivon Jones blamed the CPSA's 'exclusively white character' on the 'heavy social disabilities and political backwardness' of black workers, with the 'immediate needs of white trade unionism' throwing 'the more difficult task of native emancipation into the background'.[69] As such, the CPSA actively supported the 1922 Rand Revolt and defended 'colour bars' up to 1923, leading to 'spirited interchanges' with the ICU in Cape Town.[70] In 1924, white CPSA members like Frank Glass continued to assert that black workers 'could not possibly appreciate the noble ideals of Communism'.[71] Gomas, who became an ICU shop steward in 1924 and joined the CPSA in 1925, later reflected:

> Most of the people in the party at that time were anti-black, except for [Sidney] Bunting; they felt that the white workers were the revolutionary potential for the future; they felt that it was the white workers who were the

force for socialism. They were anti-African [...] We had to find some excuses for the double dealings of our white comrades.[72]

Another ICU Communist, Albert Nzula, similarly wrote that, initially, 'the Communist Party, as a whole, did not have much influence over the [ICU] movement owing to the then opportunist, chauvinist, character of its leadership'.[73] It was not until the CPSA's December 1924 conference, when the so-called 'nigrophilist' faction led by Sidney Bunting, Eddie Roux and Willy Kalk narrowly beat Andrews's white labourist faction, that the organisation performed a crucial pivot. Bunting, a former ISL leader, had prioritised the organisation of black workers for some time, helping the IWA in the 1910s. And he continued to insist into the early 1920s that black workers 'will eventually become far more powerful instruments of revolution than the white workers [in South Africa] can ever be'.[74]

It was arguably in response to ICU successes, however, that the CPSA eventually abandoned its focus on white workers and its support for 'colour bars'.[75] After addressing ICU meetings on the Rand and developing a close relationship with Mbeki, Silwana and Kadalie, Roux, in particular, adopted 'a kind of revolutionary nigrophilism.' He 'thought and cared less about Russia, the workers of the world and all the communist theories, and ever more about the national aspirations of the oppressed blacks of Africa'.[76] At the crucial 1924 CPSA conference, Roux insisted that the ICU was the 'most important factor for the Communist Party in the present situation'; while Silwana, attending as a fraternal delegate, emphasised that the CPSA had 'to prove to the masses that it is different'.[77] In 1926, the CPSA paper championed the ICU as the only militant trade union in South Africa, distinct from its stagnant or pro-capitalist counterparts.[78] And two years later, the CPSA explicitly echoed ICU ideas when arguing that the 'black peasantry constitute[d] the basic moving force of the revolution' – albeit, 'in alliance with and under the leadership of the [predominantly white] working class'.[79]

Between 1925 and 1926, the ICU had a complicated and often intimate relationship with the CPSA. La Guma and Gomas became Communists after Solomon Buirski of the Cape Town CPSA asked them for assistance during the 1925 International Seamen's Strike. Robert de Norman, Doris Pierce and James Shuba of the Cape Town ICU soon also joined the CPSA. Other ICU leaders, including Silwana and Mbeki, studied at the CPSA night school in Johannesburg run by Thibedi, while the secretary of the ICU's Port Elizabeth branch, Eddie Khaile, had joined the CPSA by the end of 1925.[80] From September 1925, the ICU's headquarters in Johannesburg had the slogan 'Workers of the World Unite! You have nothing to lose but your chains!' written on its doors, while *The Workers'*

*Herald* flirted with revolutionary slogans and printed numerous pro-Communist articles.[81]

The influence of the CPSA led many ICU radicals to drop their race-first approach to worker organisation. Silwana came to believe that ICU members had 'to learn from Russia', where 'all the workers, irrespective of what the colour of their face is, have to drink the spirit of class-consciousness'. He insisted that the 'ultimate goal of every trade union, be it of white or black workers, is to destroy capitalism and its children and bring about a state – a communistic state in which "he who does not work shall neither eat"'.[82] Having 'been largely influenced by Garveyism', the ICU's Jameson Gilbert Coka similarly discovered 'some fallacies in the "redemption of Africa" methods', and came to believe that Communism offered workers 'knowledge and [an] understanding of the way out of their oppression'.[83] Gomas, rapidly rising from ICU shop steward to provincial secretary, similarly regretted the fact that working class unity 'irrespective of colour or creed, is a considered tactic by an almost insignificant minority of the black and white workers of this country', and called on the 'African proletarians [to] unite, you have nothing to lose but slavery and a fruitful and wealthy Africa to win'.[84] La Guma, who hung a picture of Lenin addressing the Petrograd workers in his bedroom, likewise came to believe that the 'solution of the coloured problem and the elimination of racial antagonism lay in the uprooting the present economic system'.[85]

Importantly, however, black Communists nevertheless remained cognisant of the importance of race and black worker organisation. ICU member Joseph Phalane insisted at a 1926 CPSA meeting, 'we want a black Communist Party'.[86] Mbeki noted that because 'the foundation of South Africa is based on colour discrimination and racial animosity[,] stumbling blocks [remained] in advocating our pure class policy'.[87] And ICU Garveyite-turned-Communist Robert Dumah continued to believe that 'Garveyism teaches self-consciousness', while Communism 'teaches the worker the values of revolutionary determination and achievement'.[88] A hybrid document, combining syndicalist and Garveyite influences, the ICU's 1925 constitution opened with an extract based on the preamble of the Industrial Workers of the World (IWW) – asserting 'that the interests of the worker and those of the employer are opposed to each other' – at the same time as banning Europeans from holding office.[89]

The emerging Communist faction within the ICU, most notably La Guma, Khaile, Mbeki, Thibedi, Silwana and Gomas, alongside white Communists such as Bunting, Roux and Solly Sachs, regularly appeared on ICU platforms throughout the mid-1920s, and were actively supported by Kadalie.[90] Indeed, it was later alleged that Kadalie himself was the reason why 'Communists flooded the Workers' Hall'.[91] He also called on black and white workers to 'unite for the purpose of attacking capitalism throughout, and substitute the present system of society with a Socialistic Commonwealth on the Russian model'.[92] And at 'monster' open-air meetings in early 1926, he asserted that 'the people who knew real civilisation were the natives in their ordinary tribal life, and the people of Russia'.[93] Kadalie also fostered international connections with the Communist-financed American Negro Labor Congress (ANLC). He sent articles to its paper, the *Negro Champion*, and was only blocked from attending its inaugural conference in Chicago in October 1925 by the ICU's lack of finances.[94]

As recruitment and subscriptions on the Rand stalled, however, ICU leaders became divided over how to move forward and how money should be managed. After arriving in Johannesburg in early 1926, La Guma was soon working 'stealthily with the Communists to have the Union transferred into a hot-bed of Communism'.[95] Communists focused, in particular, on organising Johannesburg's railway workers and quickly built a 'healthy membership' while campaigning for higher pay.[96] With CPSA-member Ben Mazingi as its chairman, the Johannesburg ICU branch was critical of how substantial sums were spent on the legal defence of Kadalie, individually, and called for a mass campaign that focused on the ICU's broader membership. Subsequently, after touring ICU branches throughout South Africa, La Guma produced a damning report – condemning Kadalie, in particular, for his lavish expenditure, lax organisation and increasing dictatorial leadership style.[97] At the ICU's April 1926 annual conference, many Communists insisted on the need for a general strike. La Guma emphasised how the 'Russians have succeeded in wresting from the capitalists their labour's worth, and they now enjoy these fruits'. Most conference delegates, however, recognised the limited unionisation of mine workers and questioned the viability of a general strike. For Kadalie, the strike was 'the only weapon of the workers of modern times', but it was only useful when workers were 'properly organised'. The ICU's moderate senior vice president, Alexander Mac Jabavu, insisted that a '[s]trike should be the last word, and should not be thought of until all other constitutional methods were exhausted'. Notably, even CPSA veteran Thibedi 'agreed with Comrade Jabavu that the strike weapon should only be used as a last resort'.[98] Nothing came of the motion.

Significantly, although Kadalie became more amenable to Communists during the mid-1920s, substantial Garveyite and moderate factions within the ICU retained the trade union's early anti-Communist scepticism. Into the mid-1920s, ICU Garveyites remained a powerful group that threatened to transform the trade union into an 'auxiliary' of the UNIA.[99] The ICU's Garveyite president, James Gumbs, in particular, was 'naturally opposed to anything in which Europeans were in the ascendancy', in particular the CPSA.[100] Having also been influenced by the ideas of Marcus Garvey, the ICU's rising star, A.W.G. Champion, 'taught himself never to trust a European whether he was a missionary or a Communist'.[101] And within two months of Kadalie penning his explicitly pro-Russian article, James Thaele challenged him to a public debate over his newfound 'communistic tendencies'.[102] The Jewish-American bookstore owner, Jack Barnard, South Africa's only supplier of Marcus Garvey's *Negro World* and an 'honorary member' of the ICU, was likewise staunchly anti-Communist. Allegedly it was through Barnard's efforts that the Communists were 'chucked out, neck and crop, bag and baggage, from Prospect Township in Johannesburg'.[103] In response to the CPSA night school, Barnard started his own evening classes, asserting that workers were 'damn fools' for reading the Communists' *Young Worker*.[104] At ICU annual conferences throughout the 1920s, Jabavu, likewise, 'countered with an energetic denial' the 'propriety' of radicals, and 'vigorously objected to the association of the ICU with Communist propaganda'.[105] He was joined by ICU moderates such as Tyamzashe, Lujiza, James Dippa, John Mzaza, Doyle Modiakgotla and Jacob Sesing who 'had their way' at numerous ICU conferences, dominating proceedings.[106]

The result was an increasingly fractious relationship by the second half of 1926. In August, Thibedi was dismissed from his position as an ICU shop steward because he had been sending reports on to the CPSA's *South African Worker* rather than the ICU's *Workers' Herald*.[107] In late October, Kadalie blocked the Johannesburg branch from celebrating the anniversary of the Russian Revolution – though Mazingi, Thibedi and La Guma went ahead with festivities anyway.[108] A CPSA-owned press printed *The Workers' Herald* from February 1926, but a spat over payments saw the manager of the press 'very seriously' insult ICU officials and throw a batch of unprinted copy into the street. At a CPSA meeting on 29 October 'differences between members of the ICU and the Communist Party were discussed at considerable length', and from November the paper was printed elsewhere.[109] By the end of 1926, La Guma was facing increasing criticism from other officials for spending too much time in the office. And at the start of December, Kadalie attacked the pass laws, explicitly, 'as a Trade Unionist and not as a Communist'.[110]

Local tensions between the ICU and CPSA were exacerbated by global divisions. Between 1924 and 1928, previously healthy relations between socialists and Communists in Europe and Asia rapidly deteriorated.[111] In February 1926, Kadalie was 'sorry to observe' the global division between socialist and Communist trade unions, and championed the fact that 'Russia gave a new lead to the workers of the world' in 1917. He criticised the fact that the 'efforts of the British Labour movement to bring about international solidarity of the working class has been somewhat handicapped by the officials of the Amsterdam International'.[112] The split, however, forced Kadalie to make a choice between the Communist-led Red International of Labour Unions (RILU) based in Moscow and the predominantly socialist International Federation of Trade Unions (IFTU) based in Amsterdam. While La Guma was in close touch with RILU and the newly formed League Against Imperialism (LAI), Kadalie chose to affiliate the ICU with the IFTU in October 1926. British socialists such as Winifred Holtby and Mabel Palmer certainly influenced this choice.[113] But Kadalie's decision was also informed by an enduring anti-Communist sentiment within the larger ICU, particularly among powerful leading officials such as Gumbs, Champion, Jabavu and Tyamzashe. Despite the ICU's formal affiliation with the IFTU, La Guma insisted on going to the LAI's first international conference at the start of 1927 in Belgium as a CPSA representative – against the explicit wishes of Kadalie – even though he was paid to work full-time for the ICU.

Having alienated a number of other leaders, La Guma and other black Communists were forced to choose between the CPSA and the ICU in December 1926. Kadalie attacked the two coloured Communists, La Guma and Gomas, in particular, for not being 'full-blooded Africans' and having dual loyalties between the ICU and the 'European Communist Party'. Alexander Maduna and Champion subsequently moved the motion that 'no officer of the Union be permitted to become a member of the Communist Party'.[114] Lingering scepticism of white revolutionaries undoubtedly played a key role in the split. The white-dominated CPSA leadership was accused of having 'under its wing a Colour Bar even more deadly and [un]desirable than that contained in any Government measure'. Criticising the controlling ambitions of white Communists, *The Workers' Herald* called on 'all the workers [to] give a decided reply to these foreign adventurers' who had 'diabolicly endeavoured to reap the fruits planted by sons of the soil'.[115] The expulsions, however, also reflected personality struggles within the ICU. Some ICU moderates believed that La Guma was expelled for being too honest.[116] Gomas, similarly, felt that the expulsions were only 'ostensibly for their political opinions', and had far more to do with the criticisms La Guma had launched against Kadalie, Maduna and Champion over the course of the previous year.[117]

## Industrial unionism and failed strike action at the end of the 1920s

The CPSA was caught on the hop by their unexpected expulsion, and for over a year Communists hoped that rank and file support would facilitate their reinstatement and eventual control of the ICU. *The South African Worker* asserted that 'Kadalie and Co must not be allowed to smash native industrial organisation', and believed 'the best way to safeguard against this is by refusing to be deluded into starting rival trade unions, but to work for making the ICU the real organisation of the struggling workers'.[118] The Comintern, similarly, insisted that the CPSA's efforts, 'whatever the manoeuvres of the reactionary leaders, must be carried on under the flag of revival of the unity of the Industrial and Commercial Workers' Union and the demand for the right of workers of all tendencies to express their views within the general trade union organisation'.[119] Most CPSA members within the ICU, including Mbeki, de Norman, Mazingi, Silwana, Pierce, Johannes Nkosi and James Shuba (at least initially) remained in the trade union.[120] Gomas and Thibedi were frustrated that these leaders did 'not get tanned by the Party principles' and were, instead, only 'surface Socialists'.[121] The CPSA later blamed its lack of open support on the fact that 'the African people have not yet thrown up that degree of capable, fearless, class-conscious, honest, self-sacrificing, steadfast and incorruptible leadership'.[122]

Inevitably, however, money was also an important factor. Up to the end of the 1920s, the CPSA depended on unpaid, 'self-sacrificing' voluntary work. Roux was frank that the party struggled because it did not collect money and 'was never in a position to offer big salaries'. This may have 'discouraged the entry of African opportunists', but it also 'tended to make all black intellectuals fight shy of the movement'.[123] In stark contrast, full-time ICU branch secretaries commanded a £4 monthly wage, provincial secretaries received £10 a month, and ICU shop stewards got a percentage commission from the subscriptions they raised.[124] ICU leaders, in turn, readily co-operated with the CPSA when they were reimbursed for their time and labour. Kadalie's enthusiasm for Communism peaked in the mid-1920s when he was allegedly being paid £5 per month by Bunting.[125] And it was only at the end of the decade, as the ICU struggled to pay its organisers, that leaders like Nzula, Nkosi, Silwana and Shuba left the ICU to join the CPSA, partly 'tempted' by the offer of regular salaries.[126] Roux, in turn, fretted that these leaders only joined the CPSA because the ICU failed to pay them, and feared they would leave if ICU finances improved.[127]

For most of 1927 and 1928, La Guma, the former ICU general secretary, consumed himself with Comintern-related work and heavily contributed towards drafting the 'Native Republic Thesis' – travelling twice to Russia and back. The thesis called for 'an independent native South African Republic as a stage towards a workers' and peasants' republic with full rights for all races, black, coloured and white'. Its most biting assertion – replicating arguments made by Kadalie and the ICU throughout the early 1920s – was that white workers 'soaked as they were with imperialist ideology were not of primary revolutionary importance in this country'.[128] The thesis was initially rejected by the white-dominated CPSA for being anti-white, anti-internationalist and strikingly close to the ideas of Marcus Garvey.[129] La Guma, the thesis' chief advocate in South Africa, was backed by Douglas and Molly Wolton, but many, including Bunting, Roux, Thibedi, Ben Weinbren and Gana Makabeni, insisted that the CPSA should work with both white and black workers, and not alienate the former. Amid these factionalised debates, the basis of the ICU's success became highly contested. Bunting argued that the ICU 'has a greater expectation of life than the ANC because its foundation is class rather than race unity'. Douglas Wolton, in contrast, contended that the 'main-spring' of the ICU's 'astounding development was its appeal to the national sentiments of the African people'.[130] An exasperated La Guma complained that

> [most] European members of our party do not consider it 'practical politics' as they call it, to launch even a National Revolutionary movement amongst the blacks until such time as our lords and masters, the white worker, bestows his blessing upon us.[131]

Comintern, similarly, criticised Bunting and other opposers, asserting that their reservations were based on 'white chauvinism'.[132] The thesis was not officially adopted until early 1929.

After returning to South Africa, La Guma was parachuted in to become the general secretary of the new Communist-led Federation of Non-European Trade Unions (FNETU) in Johannesburg, a body established by Thibedi and Weinbren in March 1928 as an explicit challenge to the ICU.[133] Officials in Russia continued to insist that 'one of the objects of the Party is to strive for a united trade union of native workers'.[134] Bukharin, in particular, argued, 'what are we supposed to do with this issue, if we do not succeed in the struggle against these expulsions?'[135] Roux, however, contended that the Comintern 'should perhaps visualise the complete disbanding of the ICU' as 'favourable to the further growth of the Communist Party'.[136] He believed in breaking up the ICU 'as speedily as possible by appealing to all honest members to join the Communist Party, at the same time of course co-operating with it on any progressive policy it may still adopt'.[137] By 1929, FNETU was claiming over 3,500 members, concentrated in Johannesburg's clothing, mattress and furniture factories, and laundry works.[138] La Guma never showed much enthusiasm for the largely paper-based organisation, however, and as late as October 1928 still followed Comintern directives, insisting that the ICU had to be 'kept intact at all costs'.[139] Disillusioned by the initial rejection of the 'Native Republic' slogan, La Guma left for Cape Town in December 1928.[140] By September 1929 he had left the CPSA entirely.[141] Eddie Khaile also left the CPSA to concentrate on work in the ANC.[142]

Just like the ICU, FNETU's new industrial unions soon faced difficulties. Black workers in Johannesburg's expanding clothing industry were among the first organised by Communists into the South African Clothing Workers' Union (SACWU) – an industrial union that was 'parallel' to the white-only CPSA-organised Garment Workers' Union (GWU).[143] In May 1928, SACWU workers struck in support of the GWU after the dismissal of three white workers. When SACWU itself went on strike a month later over the dismissal of its organiser, however, the GWU failed to even issue a message of sympathy. After hundreds of SACWU workers paraded through the centre of Johannesburg, 'marching in column-of-fours, carrying banners, and wearing red tabs on their sleeves', Clements Kadalie addressed a strike meeting at 41 Fox Street, the CPSA's headquarters.[144] Thibedi and Makabeni, the secretary and chairman of the new trade union, were soon arrested for intimidation, and a hundred striking workers were charged for desertion and conducting an illegal procession. Strikers were allowed to return to work, but sentenced to ten days imprisonment or a £1 fine.[145] A subsequent CPSA-led strike of mattress workers in September also failed to win any gains.[146] At the end of 1928, Tyamzashe asserted that all the CPSA-led strikes on the Rand had 'fizzled out at the expense of the handful of misguided Natives who had placed their trust in men who obviously used them as dupes for propaganda purposes'.[147] Comintern concurred that:

> Until recently, the Federation did not have even embryonic forms of organisation. Its finances were hopelessly neglected and there was the danger that another Kadali[e] affair would arise. New members were recruited without any plan or purpose. The organisation of the trade union apparatus in the locals and in the factories made no headway.[148]

The ICU was at the forefront of a final spate of direct action in October 1928, when members at the government agricultural laboratory in Onderstepoort called a 'lightning strike' over poor working conditions.[149] After workers lost their case and were sacked, former ICU official-turned-CPSA leader, Albert Nzula, condemned how 'timidity has been allowed to have a say in [ICU] methods of fighting against Capitalist oppression', insisting that the 'African worker does not want a begging Union, but a fighting Union'.[150] Communists hoped that strike action led by 'fighting' unions would be a consciousness-raising stepping stone towards imminent nationalist revolution. But for many in the ICU, the CPSA's weak, ineffective, poorly organised strikes were a costly distraction – a 'native rising' or revolution were not imminent, and white Communists like Roux simply wanted to create martyrs.[151]

## The aftermath of the ICU

Despite the divisions emphasised by many historians, as noted by Tom Lodge, the break between the ICU and CPSA was far from clear cut.[152] Andrews and Thibedi appeared on ICU platforms soon after the expulsions in early 1927, while the CPSA's Fanny Klennerman continued to teach at the ICU's night school.[153] Kadalie wrote for the Communist Party of Great Britain's *Labour Monthly* in October 1927, regretting the split between Moscow and Amsterdam, and spoke in support of CPSA-led clothing strikers in 1928.[154] In mid-1928, *The Workers' Herald* denounced the fact that there were 'two rival Internationals and many important working class organisations stand outside both', insisting that it was 'the first duty of the working class to secure a united political International and a united industrial International'.[155] After quitting the collapsing 'Mother ICU' in January 1929, Kadalie's Independent ICU was soon in touch with the LAI, the Socialist Party of America and La Ligue Universelle de Defense de la Race Negro, as well as the CPSA.[156] On 16 December 1929, at the head of a combined Independent ICU-ANC-CPSA Dingaan's Day protest, Kadalie strode through the streets of Johannesburg backed by a 4,000-strong rally and a jazz band jamming to the tune of the workers' anthem, the Red Flag.[157] The CPSA's John Beaver Marks recalled that there were 'very cordial relations between some of us and Clements Kadalie' at the end of the 1920s, and that Kadalie regularly called into the Fox Street office.[158] Police reports from 1930, similarly, indicate that Kadalie and Tyamzashe were part of a 'Joint Committee of Action' with CPSA leaders in Johannesburg, investigating the possibility of taking over the ANC's *Abantu Batho* newspaper and running it 'on revolutionary lines'.[159]

Amid the fragmentation of the ICU, numerous former leaders joined CPSA-led trade unions. By 1930 ICU-turned-CPSA member James Shuba led the 'remnants of Kadalie's union' in Cape Town under the Stevedoring and Dock Workers Union.[160] In Pretoria, former ICU leader George Daniels became secretary of the Laundry Workers Union.[161] In Johannesburg, former ICU leaders Thibedi and Makabeni led the SACWU.[162] In Bloemfontein, Isaiah 'Ntele, D. Taabe and G. Matete left the ICU to lead the local CPSA branch. In Cape Town, Gomas and La Guma organised garment workers and the unemployed. And in Durban, approximately 6,000 ICU members led by Abraham Nduweni went over to the CPSA.[163] At the start of the 1930s, the CPSA and FNETU briefly flourished as a hub for these dissident, militant former ICU leaders and members, and in this sense, Kadalie was justified in his later claim that many black trade unions 'owe[d] their existence to the pioneering work of the "mother ICU" which blazed the trail in the industrial field'.[164] Even at its peak in 1929–30, however,

FNETU's claimed membership of 3,500 was tiny when compared to the scale of support commanded by the ICU, and by the end of 1930, top-down Stalinisation had decimated the organisation, with Thibedi, Makabeni and others expelled.[165]

In contrast to the ICU's 'big-tent' approach in the mid-1920s, the smaller, more fragmented black trade union movement of the 1930s was defined by bitter factionalism. Many leading Trotskyists believed that the IWA and 'famous' ICU 'had been, for the most part, little more than movements of political protest, with little, if any, genuine trade union content'.[166] The Stalinised CPSA was, likewise, highly critical of ICU organising, asserting that it 'would be a serious political error' for 'the Party merely to repeat the tactics of the political adventurer Kadalie'.[167] The CPSA's Moses Kotane emphasised that 'graft in the ICU was terrible. Money was squandered like water.'[168] Marks – who was a member of the ANC and the ICU before joining the CPSA – likewise wrote in 1935 that 'thousands

'Please Baas!', *Umsebenzi*, 16/01/1931

**Figure 5.1** A linocut cartoon by CPSA leader Eddie Roux, depicting Clements Kadalie and AWG Champion of the ICU and Abdullah Abdurahman of the African People's Organisation, from the front cover of *Umsebenzi*, 16 January 1931

of workers who once comprised the ranks of the ICU and ANC still suffer painful recollection[s] of the exploitation and misdirected energy under the [ICU and ANC's] false leadership'.[169] Kadalie and Thaele were depicted as sell-out collaborators in cartoons by Roux.

The ICU undoubtedly had its flaws. At both a local and global level, however, the trade union challenged Communists to rethink conventions about race and class. Despite his criticisms, Marks acknowledged that Kadalie was 'a very great demagogue' who caught 'the imagination of many people'.[170] Gomas, who remained staunchly loyal to the CPSA, fondly remembered the ICU as 'the biggest organisation we've ever had'.[171] While studying in Russia, Albert Nzula recognised the 'chauvinist' character of the early CPSA and argued that the ICU's unique success lay in its dual emphasis on both class and race.[172] Many black Trotskyists admired the ICU for similar reasons. Isaac B. Tabata and Ben Kies in Cape Town highlighted how the ICU united African and coloured workers, and broke the dominance of reformist black elites.[173] Meanwhile, within global black radical networks, Trinidadian compatriots George Padmore and C.L.R. James championed the 'profoundly important' ICU as the modern-day equivalent of the Haitian Revolution from the 1930s – with 'the same instinctive capacity for organisation, the same throwing-up of gifted leaders from among the masses'. Padmore and James rehabilitated both the UNIA and ICU to demonstrate 'fires that smoulder in the Negro world, in America as in Africa', at the same time as criticising Communist 'infiltrators' for causing 'deep disruption'.[174] In light of their own experiences, Communists' overbearing, top-down tendencies were all too obvious.

Significantly, then, influences worked in numerous ways. The ICU drew on the successes of both the UNIA and the Russian Revolution, at the same time as accounts of Garvey in America and Kadalie in Southern Africa shaped the policies of Communists and non-Communists alike. The Russian Revolution certainly inspired a select number of black militant leaders, most notably James La Guma and John Gomas. But Clements Kadalie and the wider ICU gave black workers in Southern Africa – and beyond – a vivid instance of black leadership and mass worker organisation, important early victories and powerful critiques of white labourism, in a far more tangible manner.

# Notes

1 For the history of the ICU, see Sylvia Neame, *The Congress Movement: The Unfolding of the Congress Alliance* (Cape Town: HSRC Press, 2015), vols 1–3; Lucien van der Walt, 'The First Globalisation and Transnational

Labour Activism in Southern Africa: White Labourism, the IWW and the ICU, 1904–1934', *African Studies*, 66:2–3 (2007), 223–251; Helen Bradford, *A Taste of Freedom: The ICU in Rural South Africa, 1924–1930* (Johannesburg: Raven Press, 1987); P.L. Wickins, *The Industrial and Commercial Workers' Union of Africa* (Cape Town: Oxford University Press, 1978).

2  For the interwar CPSA, see David Johnson, *Dreaming of Freedom in South Africa: Literature Between Critique and Utopia* (Edinburgh: Edinburgh University Press, 2019); Allison Drew, *Between Empire and Revolution: A Life of Sydney Bunting, 1873–1936* (London: Pickering & Chatto, 2007); A.B. Davidson, I. Filatova, V.P. Gorodnov and S. Johns (eds), *South Africa and the Communist International: Socialist Pilgrims to Bolshevik Foot Soldiers 1919–1930* (London: Frank Cass, 2003); Allison Drew, *Discordant Comrades: Identities and Loyalties in the South African Left* (Aldershot: Ashgate, 2000); Allison Drew (ed.), *South Africa's Radical Tradition* (Cape Town: UCT Press, 1996), vol. 1; Robin D.G. Kelley, 'The Religious Odyssey of African Radicals: Notes on the Communist Party of South Africa, 1921–1934', *Radical History Review*, 51 (1991), 4–24. Tom Lodge outlines the flaws in Mia Roth's recent scholarship in Tom Lodge, 'The Communist Party in South Africa, Racism, Eurocentricity, and Moscow', *South African Historical Journal*, 68:4 (2016), 675–677.

3  The exact events of this meeting are contested, see Neame, *Congress Movement*, vol. 2, 219–221.

4  'ICU Manifesto', *Workers' Herald*, 12 January 1927, 1–2.

5  James La Guma, Eddie Khaile and Johnny Gomas, 'Open Letter from the Expelled ICU Members', *South African Worker*, 24 December 1926, 1.

6  'Communists and Good Boys', *Umsebenzi*, 13 June 1930, 1–2; Edward Roux, *Time Longer Than Rope: A History of the Black Man's Struggle for Freedom in South Africa* (Madison, WI: University of Wisconsin Press, 1972), 247.

7  See for example Drew, *South Africa's Radical Tradition*; Mohamed Adhikari (ed.), *Jimmy La Guma: A Biography by Alex La Guma* (Cape Town: Friends of the South African Library, 1997), 48.

8  Bradford, *Taste of Freedom*, 114–118; Drew, *Discordant Comrades*, 46–57; T. Lodge, 'The Communist Party of South Africa and the Industrial and Commercial Workers' Union, 1923–1931', paper presented at the Southern African Historical Society, Makhanda, June 2019; Neame, *Congress Movement*, vol. 1, 296–307, 467–479, 541–586; van der Walt, 'White Labourism and the ICU', 150–154.

9  Davidson et al., *South Africa and the Communist International*, 154–156.

10  A. Warreno, 'Letters to the Editor', *Workers' Herald*, 28 July 1926.

11  George Padmore, *Pan-Africanism or Communism?: The Coming Struggle for Africa* (London: Dennis Dobson, 1956), 348–351; C.L.R. James, *A History of Negro Revolt* (London: FACT, 1938).

12  Henry Dee, 'Central African Immigrants, Imperial Citizenship and the Politics of Free Movement in Interwar South Africa', *Journal of Southern African Studies*, 45:6 (2019) 319–337.

13 Lara Putnam, *Radical Moves: Caribbean Migrants and the Politics of Race in the Jazz Age* (Chapel Hill, NC: University of North Carolina Press, 2013), 17; Robert Trent Vinson, *The Americans Are Coming!: Dreams of African American Liberation in Segregationist South Africa* (Athens, OH: Ohio University Press, 2012).
14 'Coloured' here refers to 'mixed' European-Malay-African ancestry. J.A.G. [James Arnold La Guma], 'A Call to Thee', *Black Man*, 1:6 (December 1920), 2.
15 Clements Kadalie, *My Life and the ICU: The Autobiography of a Black Trade Unionist in South Africa* (London: Frank Cass, 1970), 99.
16 'Universal Negro Improvement Association', *Black Man*, 1:2 (August 1920), 3.
17 Neame, *Congress Movement*, vol. 1, 157.
18 Clements Kadalie, 'A Call From Macedonia', *The Messenger*, 5:9 (September 1923).
19 Lucien van der Walt, '"One Great Union of Skilled and Unskilled Workers, South of the Zambezi": Garveyism, Liberalism and Revolutionary Syndicalism in the Industrial and Commercial Workers' Union of Africa, 1919–1949', paper presented at the European Social Science History Conference, Vienna, 2014.
20 J.S. Thaele, 'Non-Co-Operation with White Churches', *Workers' Herald*, 2 April 1925, 7.
21 T. Mbeki, 'The Spirit of Self Determination', *African World*, 4 July 1925; 'Big Black Problem', *Umteteli*, 19 August 1922, 2; S.M. Silwana, 'A Plea for Privilege', *Umteteli*, 30 September 1922, 9.
22 Clements Kadalie, 'Organised White Labour in Empire', *Workers' Herald*, 20 July 1925, 3.
23 Keith Breckenridge, 'Fighting for a White South Africa: White Working-Class Racism and the 1922 Rand Revolt', *South African Historical Journal*, 57:1 (2007), 228–243.
24 Clements Kadalie, 'The Aristocracy of White Labor in Africa', *The Messenger*, 6:8 (August 1924).
25 'Native Rising', *Workers' Herald*, 15 June 1926, 2.
26 South African National Archives, Pretoria (SANA) JUS 916 1/18/26 'The African World: Police Reports: Part 5', report on ICU meeting in Port Elizabeth on 28 November 1926.
27 Clements Kadalie, 'National Secretary's Report for 1925', *Workers' Herald*, 28 April 1926, 3.
28 T. Kofi, 'Maritzburg Musings on the ICU', *Workers' Herald*, 27 March 1926, 3.
29 Kadalie, 'Aristocracy of White Labour'; Kadalie, 'Organised White Labour'.
30 SANA JUS 915 1/18/26 'The African World: Police Reports: Part 3', report on ICU meeting at Springs on 25 July 1926.
31 'Recruiting System', *Workers' Herald*, 21 July 1923, 2.
32 Kadalie, *My Life*, 86; Kadalie, 'National Secretary's Report for 1925'.
33 Ernest Gitsham and James F. Trembath, *A First Account of Labour Organisation in South Africa* (Durban: EP & Commercial Printing, 1926), 122–124.
34 John W. Brown, *World Migration and Labour* (Amsterdam: International Federation of Trade Unions, 1926), 18.

35 'July Activities', *The Messenger*, 9:9 (September 1927).
36 'Laborers in South Africa Rise in Arms', *Chicago Defender*, 26 June 1926, 13.
37 'African Leader Coming to the United States', *Pittsburgh Courier*, 10 September 1927, 7; 'Alarm in South Africa', *Pittsburgh Courier*, 9 February 1929, 8.
38 Philip Bonner, 'The Decline and Fall of the ICU: A Case of Self-Destruction?', *South African Labour Bulletin*, 1:6 (1974), 38–43; Philip Bonner, 'Division and Unity in the Struggle: African Politics on the Witwatersrand in the 1920s', African Studies Seminar Paper, University of Witwatersrand, 9 March 1992, 14.
39 Keith Breckenridge, '"We Must Speak for Ourselves": The Rise and Fall of a Public Sphere on the South African Gold Mines', *Comparative Studies in Society and History*, 40:1 (1998), 71–108.
40 Thomas William Thibedi, 'Workers' Life', *South African Worker*, 23 July 1926, 4.
41 Henry Daniel Tyamzashe, 'Rand Activities', *Workers' Herald*, 15 January 1926, 4.
42 Gitsham and Trembath, *A First Account of Labour Organisation in South Africa*.
43 Breckenridge, 'We Must Speak for Ourselves'.
44 SANA JUS 916 1/18/26 'The African World: Police Reports: Part 6', report of ICU meeting in Witbank on 23 January 1927.
45 Elaine A. Friedland, 'Mozambican Nationalist Resistance: 1920–1949', *Civilisations*, 27:3/4 (1977), 332–344, at 340.
46 Clements Kadalie, 'General Secretary's Report for 1924', *Workers' Herald*, 15 May 1925, 3.
47 Van der Walt, 'White Labourism and the ICU', 240.
48 'Native Trade Union', *Umteteli*, 6 August 1921, 2.
49 Henry Selby Msimang, 'How We can Help Ourselves', *Umteteli*, 5 November 1921, 2.
50 Drew, *Discordant Comrades*, 46.
51 'Bolshevism', *Umteteli*, 11 June 1921, 2; R.V. Selope Thema, 'Bolshevism and the Africans', *Umteteli*, 6 January 1923, 2.
52 'An Insidious Invasion', *Ilanga*, 16 November 1928; Killie Campbell Manuscripts (KCM) Marwick Papers File 73, John L. Dube to John Sydney Marwick, 24 February 1928.
53 'South African Government and Native Workers', *Black Man*, 1:5 (November 1920), 1–2.
54 'The Workers' Herald', *International*, 18 May 1923, 4.
55 'ICU Manifesto', *Ilanga*, 12 October 1923.
56 Clements Kadalie, 'African Labour Congress', *Workers' Herald*, 21 December 1923, 1.
57 Malawi National Archives (MNA) S2/71/23 'Censored correspondence between Clements Muwamba and Clements Kadalie', Clements Kadalie to E.A. Muwamba, 29 April 1923.
58 Wits Historical Papers (WITS) A2744 A.W.G. Champion, *Autobiography*, 87–88.

59 'Communists', *Workers' Herald*, 17 May 1927, 5.
60 Clements Kadalie, 'The ICU', *Umteteli*, 3 March 1923, 4.
61 'Man from Moscow', *Umteteli*, 3 November 1923, 2.
62 WITS A2729 Sylvia Neame Papers, Sylvia Neame interview with Eddie Roux, July 1962.
63 Eddie Roux and Winifred Roux, *Rebel Pity: Life of Eddie Roux* (Bungay: Penguin, 1972), 50.
64 'ICU National Secretary at Maritzburg', *Workers' Herald*, 27 March 1926, 3.
65 'Trade Unions and the SALP', *International*, 4 April 1924, 6.
66 Drew, *Discordant Comrades*, 54.
67 Allison Drew, 'Will the Real Sidney Bunting Please Stand Up? Constructing and Contesting the Identity of a South African Communist', *English Historical Review*, 118 (2003), 1235; Davidson et al., *South Africa and the Communist International*, 66–68.
68 Kelley, 'The Religious Odyssey of African Radicals', 9.
69 Davidson et al., *South Africa and the Communist International*, 74–77; Brian Bunting, *Moses Kotane: South African Revolutionary* (London: Inkululeko Publications, 1975), chapter 2.
70 SANA JUS 289 3/1064/18 'Bolshevism in SA', Commissioner of Police to Secretary for Justice, 28 February 1922; 'The Workers' Herald', *International*, 18 May 1923.
71 Kelley, 'The Religious Odyssey of African Radicals', 9.
72 WITS A2729 S. Neame interview with J. Gomas, September 1962.
73 Albert Nzula, 'Struggles of the Negro Toilers in South Africa', *Negro Worker*, 5:5–6 (May–June 1935), 20–22.
74 Davidson et al., *South Africa and the Communist International*, 111–117.
75 Neame, *Congress Movement*, vol. 2, 468–470.
76 Roux and Roux, *Rebel Pity*, 47–48.
77 Bunting, *Moses Kotane*, chapter 2.
78 'For Militant Trade Unionism', *South African Worker*, 1 October 1926, 2.
79 Bradford, *Taste of Freedom*, 2.
80 Neame, *Congress Movement*, vol. 1, 473–475.
81 Bradford, *Taste of Freedom*, 141; 'Dawn of African Revolution', *Workers' Herald*, 20 February 1926, 2.
82 S. Silwana, 'Revolutionise Capitalism Out of State!', *Workers' Herald*, 14 August 1926, 3.
83 J.G. Coka, 'The Story of Gilbert Coka' in Margery Perham (ed.), *Ten Africans* (London: Faber and Faber, 1936), 273–321, at 313–314.
84 J. Gomas, 'The Workers and the Capitalists at Loggerheads', *Workers' Herald*, 15 October 1925, 5.
85 'Colour Bar and Segregation', *Star*, 1 February 1926.
86 'Education and Native Trade Unionism', *South African Worker*, 6 August 1926, 4.
87 Bradford, *Taste of Freedom*, 116.

88 R.A. Dumah, 'South African Native Farm Tenants', *Negro Worker*, 1:4–5 (1931), 10–13.
89 Bradford, *Taste of Freedom*, 114.
90 Kadalie, *My Life*, 179.
91 'Seventh African Labour Conference', *Workers' Herald*, 17 May 1927, 1–6.
92 Musa [C. Kadalie], 'Am I My Brother's Keeper?', *Workers' Herald*, 20 February 1926, 1.
93 'Colour Bar and Segregation', *Star*, 1 February 1926.
94 Kadalie, 'National Secretary's Report for 1925'; Clements Kadalie, 'British Color Bar Provokes Workers' Rebellion Among Negroes in South Africa', *Negro Champion*, June 1926; Minkah Makalani, *In the Cause of Freedom: Black Internationalism from Harlem to London* (Chapel Hill, NC: University of North Carolina Press, 2011), 122–124.
95 Henry Daniel Tyamzashe, 'Summarised History of the ICU' (East London, unpublished, 1941).
96 Neame, *Congress Movement*, vol. 2, 207–208; Kadalie, *My Life*, 80.
97 Neame, *Congress Movement*, vol. 1, 571–578.
98 Henry Daniel Tyamzashe, 'Fourth African Labour Congress', *Workers' Herald*, 28 April 1926.
99 Kadalie, *My Life*, 220.
100 Ibid., 71, 220–221.
101 SANA JUS 915 1/18/26 'The African World: Police Reports: Part 3', report on ICU meeting in Johannesburg on 4 July 1926.
102 KCM Marwick Papers File 73, Letter from J. Tandy to J. Marwick, 13 April 1927.
103 'Mr Jack Barnard', *Workers' Herald*, 15 September 1927, 5.
104 SANA JUS 916 1/18/26 'The African World: Police Reports: Part 7', report of ICU meeting in Johannesburg on 27 February 1927.
105 'ICU Congress', *Umteteli*, 17 April 1926, 3.
106 Tyamzashe, 'Fourth African Labour Congress'.
107 Neame, *Congress Movement*, vol. 2, 209.
108 Ibid., vol.2, 212–213.
109 Davidson et al., *South Africa and the Communist International*, 146–148; 'ICU Manifesto', *Workers' Herald*, 12 January 1927.
110 Neame, *Congress Movement*, vol. 2, 210–211; SANA JUS 916 1/18/26 'The African World: Police Reports: Part 4', report on ICU in Johannesburg on 5 December 1926.
111 Daniel F. Calhoun, *The United Front: The TUC and the Russians, 1923–1928* (Cambridge: Cambridge University Press, 1976); Carolien Stolte, 'Bringing Asia to the World: Indian Trade Unionism and the Long Road Towards the Asiatic Labour Congress, 1919–37', *Journal of Global History*, 7:2 (2012), 257–278, at 265–266.
112 Musa, 'Am I My Brother's Keeper?'
113 Neame, *Congress Movement*, vol. 2, 94–99.
114 Ibid., vol.2, 218–223.

115 'ICU Manifesto', *Workers' Herald*, 12 January 1927.
116 G. Lenono, *Mr Allison Champion, Provincial Secretary (Natal) and the ICU Funds* (Durban, 1927).
117 'Rousing Welcome to Brussels Delegate', *South African Worker*, 15 April 1927.
118 'No Breakaway Unions', *South African Worker*, 25 February 1927, 2.
119 Davidson et al., *South Africa and the Communist International*, 157–158, 166–172.
120 Drew, *Discordant Comrades*, 81; Neame, *Congress Movement*, vol. 2, 228. Nzula did not become a Communist until around September 1928, see Albert Nzula, 'Letter from the Workers', *South African Worker*, 24 October 1928, 3.
121 Neame, *Congress Movement*, vol. 2, 228; Drew, *Discordant Comrades*, 81.
122 'Russia and Africa', *South African Worker*, 4 November 1927, 1.
123 Roux, *Time Longer Than Rope*, 214–215.
124 Bradford, *Taste of Freedom*, 71; Neame, *Congress Movement*, vol. 1, 553.
125 SANA BNS 1/2/46 A1787 'Clements Kadalie', Commissioner of Police to Secretary for the Interior, 8 May 1925.
126 Warwick Modern Records Centre MSS.292/968/14 'Correspondence with and regarding the Industrial and Commercial Workers' Union of Africa', W. Holtby to J. Sassenbach, 31 July 1929.
127 KCM 99/6/1 E. Roux to N. Leys, 16 September 1928.
128 Kelley, 'The Religious Odyssey of African Radicals', 259.
129 Drew, *South Africa's Radical Tradition*, 20–21.
130 Bunting, *Moses Kotane*, chapter 2.
131 Davidson et al., *South Africa and the Communist International*, 173–174.
132 Roux and Roux, *Rebel Pity*, 74.
133 'Trade Union Notes', *South African Worker*, 25 May 1928, 6.
134 Davidson et al., *South Africa and the Communist International*, 197–199.
135 Davidson et al., *South Africa and the Communist International*, 154–156.
136 Drew, *South Africa's Radical Tradition*, 60–64.
137 KCM 99/6/1 Roux to Norman Leys, 16 September 1928.
138 James W. Ford, 'The Affiliation of the Federation of Non-European Trade Unions of South Africa to the RILU', *Negro Worker*, 2:1 (January–February 1929), 2–8.
139 J. La Guma, 'Disrupters in ICU', *South African Worker*, 24 October 1928, 8.
140 'SAFNTU to affiliate to RILU', *South African Worker*, 24 December 1928, 8.
141 'La Guma Suspended', *South African Worker*, 30 September 1929, 6.
142 'Communism Repudiated', *Umteteli*, 20 August 1927, 2.
143 'Trade Union Notes', *South African Worker*, 30 March 1928, 8; Leslie Witz, 'Separation for Unity: The Garment Workers Union and the South African Clothing Workers Union, 1928–1936', *Social Dynamics*, 14:1 (1988), 34–35.
144 KCM AWG Champion Papers 99/6/1, E. Roux to N. Leys, 16 September 1928.
145 'Strike of Native Factory Hands', *Rand Daily Mail*, 8 June 1928; Witz, 'Garment Workers' Union', 18–19.
146 'Strike at Mattress Factory', *South African Worker*, 24 October 1928, 1.

147 H.D. Tyamzashe, 'Communists Futile Attempt to Capture the ICU', *Workers' Herald*, 30 November 1928, 3.
148 Davidson et al., *South Africa and the Communist International*, 213–221.
149 H.D. Tyamzashe, 'Lopsided Policy', *Workers' Herald*, 31 October 1928, 5.
150 A.N. [Albert Nzula], 'Lesson of Onderstepoort Strike', *South African Worker*, 30 November 1928, 3.
151 Tyamzashe, 'Communists Futile Attempt'.
152 Lodge, 'CPSA and ICU'.
153 Drew, *Discordant Comrades*, 81–82.
154 Clements Kadalie, 'The Old and the New Africa', *Labour Monthly*, 9:10 (October 1927).
155 'Manifesto Urging International Unity', *Workers' Herald*, 12 May 1928, 1.
156 SANA NTS 7215 'League Against Imperialism'.
157 Edward Koch, 'Doornfontein and its African Working Class, 1914–1983', MA thesis, University of Witwatersrand, 1983, 172.
158 WITS A2729 S. Neame interview with J.B. Marks, August 1969.
159 SANA JUS 923 1/18/26 'Native Agitation Reports On: Part 27', CID Report, 16 July 1930.
160 Harold J. Simons and Ray E. Simons, *Class and Colour in South Africa, 1850–1950* (Harmondsworth: Penguin, 1969), 383–384.
161 'Pretoria Laundry Workers', *South African Worker*, 30 September 1929, 2.
162 For Makabeni's ICU connection, see Ken Luckhardt and Brenda Wall, *Organise or Starve: The History of the South African Congress of Trade Unions* (London: Lawrence and Wishart, 1980), 51.
163 Lodge, 'The CPSA and ICU'; 'Communist Leaders Deported', *Umsebenzi*, 6 February 1931, 3.
164 Kadalie, *My Life*, 223–224.
165 Drew, *South Africa's Radical Tradition*, 34.
166 Peter Abrahams, *Tell Freedom: Memories of Africa* (New York: Knopf, 1954), 306.
167 'Trade Unions and National Struggle', *Umsebenzi*, 20 February 1931.
168 Ralph J. Bunche, *An African American in South Africa* (Athens, OH: Ohio University Press, 2001), 68–70.
169 'Natives and Organisation', *Umsebenzi*, 4 May 1935, 2.
170 WITS A2729 S. Neame interview with J.B. Marks, August 1969.
171 WITS A2729 S. Neame interview with J. Gomas, September 1962.
172 Nzula, 'Negro Toilers'.
173 Isaac B. Tabata, *The Awakening of a People* (Johannesburg: People's Press, 1950).
174 Padmore, *Pan-Africanism or Communism?* 349–351; James, *A History of Negro Revolt*, 62, 71. In stark contrast, Padmore was highly critical of the ICU in his earlier book, George Padmore, *The Life and Struggles of Negro Toilers* (London: R.I.L.U. Magazine for the International Trade Union Committee of Negro Workers, 1931).

# 6

# Pan-Africanism and Marxism in interwar France: the case of Lamine Senghor

*David Murphy*

During the interwar period, France often appeared to be a haven of racial enlightenment for black people, especially those African Americans who had discovered the relative freedoms the country had to offer in the aftermath of the First World War. By the mid-1920s, Paris was awash with black culture: from jazz bands to the dance reviews featuring Josephine Baker to the growing obsession with Africa among contemporary artists. More astute visitors to France, however, were highly conscious that there were limits to the freedoms afforded by the French Republic to its transatlantic visitors: and these freedoms were generally not extended to black subjects from the French colonies. Adventurous visitors – not least, the Jamaican novelist and poet Claude McKay – who departed from the beaten track of the jazz clubs and cafes of the Latin Quarter and Montparnasse, might even have encountered some of the radical black men (for this was a largely, if not exclusively, male world) who were active in the nationalist, anti-colonialist and revolutionary movements in Paris, Bordeaux and Marseilles.[1] For, as the historian Michael Goebel has argued, Paris in the interwar period was the great 'anti-imperial metropolis', which attracted many radicals from around the world, including many black militants who sought to marry the causes of black internationalism and Communism.[2] Over the past few decades, a growing body of research has sought to look beyond jazz, artistic modernism and the elite black writers of the Negritude movement to uncover the writings and activism of a hitherto largely forgotten group of black militants from the 1920s who sought to fuse Pan-Africanist and Marxist thought.[3] One of the most important but still curiously neglected black militant figures of this period is the decorated Senegalese veteran of the First World War, Lamine Senghor (1889–1927) who, for a few short years, was perhaps the best-known and most influential black anti-colonial activist of his time.[4]

This chapter will chart the complex political trajectory of Senghor's short career as an activist before his early death in November 1927, aged just 38. Senghor's death came about as a result of serious injuries that he had sustained during the war. He had volunteered to serve the imperial homeland and he received the Croix de Guerre in recognition of his bravery in combat. He survived a gas attack, just outside Verdun in late 1917, but lost a lung, and subsequently contracted tuberculosis. This personal experience of the traumatic effects of modern, mechanised warfare would shape his activism in complex ways: on the one hand, it would lead him to focus on the rights of African war veterans, while on the other, it would lead to a persistent sense of anxiety about his health and the welfare of his family. He was a committed militant but one who was consistently plagued by doubts. Indeed, as will be discussed below, the archives reveal that his initial encounters with the radical anti-colonial movements of the time were almost certainly a result of his recruitment as an informer by the Ministry for the Colonies: the colonial authorities quite literally led him to become a radical anti-colonialist. Giving voice to his experience as a veteran and a colonised black African, he discovered and embraced Communism's critique of empire, but he also sought to forge a shared sense of black identity across disparate groups both within France and more globally. The call of both the Red and the Black were consistently to be found at the heart of his activism.

## Reading against/along the archival grain

One of the ironies of researching the career of Lamine Senghor and other militants from the French Empire during the interwar period is that the archival trace of their actions and writings has largely been preserved by the colonial establishment that sought to police, contain and, at times, suppress them. As the colonial population in France grew dramatically in the aftermath of the First World War, the Ministry for the Colonies established a *Service de contrôle et d'assistance aux indigènes* (generally abbreviated as the CAI). As its title indicated, the CAI was designed to offer assistance to those in need, but its key function was one of surveillance (*contrôle*). The CAI managed to infiltrate virtually every association of colonial subjects that was established in France, from radical anti-colonialists to the most anodyne mutual assistance groups: indeed, as we shall see below, it would appear that Lamine Senghor himself was initially recruited as an informer. The CAI's informers and agents reported on a monthly, weekly, sometimes daily basis, allowing us to build a picture of the actions, motives, achievements of, and tensions within, black, anti-colonial groupings, but always seen and read through the filter of the 'colonial mindset', with its complex and often contradictory political and racial hierarchies.

The issue of how to engage with the colonial archive has been the subject of intense debate over the past few decades. There has been an understandable desire on the part of many historians to read the colonial archive 'against the grain', to reveal the stories that the archive actively sought to suppress. This 'extractive' approach has, however, been criticised by prominent figures such as Ann Laura Stoler who advocates reading the archive 'along the grain', as a process of mining the archives for the epistemological and political anxieties of the colonial establishment, rather than for historical fact.[5]

Stoler is correct in stating that colonial archives have much to tell us about the mindset of colonialism and my approach to this archive always attempts to be conscious of the fact that I am, on one level, primarily engaging with how the colonial state understood the actions of Senghor and his comrades. However, I also firmly believe that the constructed, partial, incomplete nature of this and indeed all archives leaves cracks in the narrative through which alternative stories of those observed, policed and documented can emerge, as subaltern studies has amply demonstrated over recent decades.[6] My own approach here is guided by the work of Ferdinand de Jong (and also Paul Basu) on the potential, in recent work by artists and activists, in particular, for colonial archives to become 'sites for performative reappropriations'.[7] Such work points to 'the potential of forgotten pasts and unanticipated futures lingering in the imperial archive'.[8] The 'full story' of Lamine Senghor is not lying dormant in the archive waiting to be found: only through a creative reimagining can we try to revive his story and outline the contours of the future he sought to create.

The story of Lamine Senghor is one of those histories that has been silenced by the very process of historical production, as Michel-Rolph Trouillot has argued:

> Silences enter the process of historical production at four crucial moments: the moments of fact creation (the making of *sources*); the moment of fact assembly (the making of *archives*); the moment of fact retrieval (the making of *narratives*); and the moment of retrospective significance (the making of *history* in the final instance.[9]

Senghor and the other largely working-class activists in his milieu did not write memoirs or leave copious trails of correspondence. Unlike the highly educated writers of the Negritude movement that followed them a decade later, who wrote for mainstream French publishers, their writings appeared in ephemeral newspapers with a limited circulation. If we can piece together the collected writings of Lamine Senghor today, it is primarily because the CAI compulsively collected and archived those 'seditious' publications that they wished to suppress. The very fact, however, that we have access to

Senghor's articles and speeches, to some of his correspondence with the colonial state, to accounts of his private dealings with fellow activists and ordinary members of the black community allows us to imagine a different story about him than the one the colonial authorities attempted to impose on him.

## From loyal servant of France to anti-colonial militant

On 24 November 1924, Lamine Senghor, a hitherto largely unknown African veteran of the First World War, appeared as a witness for the defence in a libel trial at the Tribunal de Paris. The trial pitted the two most (in)famous black Frenchmen of their day against one another. The plaintiff, Blaise Diagne, was a deputy in the French parliament representing the four communes of Senegal, who had played a key role in the recruitment of African soldiers during the recent war; the main defendant, the Franco-Caribbean author René Maran, was a controversial figure in French public life, after he was awarded the prestigious literary prize, the *Prix Goncourt* in 1921 for his 'anti-colonial' novel, *Batouala*. At the heart of the case was an alleged slander of Diagne by Maran in an unsigned article, 'The Good Apostle', for the reformist black newspaper *Les Continents*. The author of the article claimed that Diagne had received 'a certain commission for each soldier recruited'.[10] Similar accusations had previously appeared in the mainstream French press, but Diagne regarded the publication of such claims in a 'black' newspaper as a danger to his reputation as an advocate for equality.[11] In the legal proceedings that followed, Maran acknowledged authorship of the article, but recent research on Maran's correspondence with the African-American critic Mercer Cook has cast considerable doubt on this version of events. Instead, it would appear that Maran took the blame so that Jean Fangeat, the newspaper's editor and true author of the article, might be spared a prison sentence.[12]

In many ways, Diagne and Maran were unlikely enemies: both were highly educated figures who believed profoundly in France's *civilising mission*, and they argued for the full assimilation of black people into French culture. In practical political terms, the trial gave Diagne the opportunity to strike a blow against a potential black rival for his seat in parliament as the deputy for Senegal. More significantly, they found themselves on either side of the fault line created by the issue of the 'blood debt' that France was deemed to owe to its colonial troops who had played such a vital role in the First World War. Over 130,000 black African troops had participated in the war with over 34,000 killed. Diagne had been sent to French West Africa in early 1918 with the grand title of High Commissioner for the Republic and had been greeted by the colonial establishment with all the pomp and ceremony usually reserved for visiting white dignitaries. This unprecedented celebration of a black African initially enhanced Diagne's reputation among France's many black subjects and its few black citizens. By the time of the libel trial, however, his star was on the wane, in some quarters at least: promises made about black participation in the war leading to reform of the colonial system, as well as increased access to rights and citizenship, had proven illusory. For many reformist and radical black groups, Diagne had quite simply sold out to colonial interests.

By the mid-1920s, the First World War and France's 'blood debt' towards its colonial troops had emerged as an issue on which the PCF [*Parti communiste français*] hoped to capitalise in recruiting colonised subjects to its cause. At the time of the trial, Senghor had been a member for just a few short months of the *Union Intercoloniale* (UIC), an organisation created by the French Communist Party in 1921 with the aim of providing a forum in which a broad transcolonial front against empire might develop. Nominally an independent group run by and for representatives of the colonised peoples (Nguyen ai Quoc, the future Ho Chi Minh, was one of the most active members of the group in its early stages), the UIC was in fact controlled by the PCF's Colonial Studies Committee. In the columns of the UIC's newspaper, *Le Paria* (The Pariah), were to be found some of the most violent denunciations of empire of the period, and it often linked the brutality of the First World War with brutality in the colonies.

Deploying Lamine Senghor as a key figure in its propaganda efforts was, in this respect, a clever strategy. The fact that Senghor had fought loyally and bravely for France made it that much more difficult for the French authorities to dismiss him as a subversive: and Senghor's status as a war veteran would remain central to almost every article and speech he would write over the next three years. The strategy also made sense in the immediate context of the Diagne–*Les Continents* trial, as it was an opportunity for the Communists to reach out to other anti-colonial forces. In 1924, the Comintern had called on Communists to seek alliances with all anti-colonial nationalist movements, and the trial was perceived as an opportunity to create a united anti-colonial front. This united front would only last a few years, but it is in this context that Lamine Senghor's activism should be situated.

We have thus far explored the reasons why the PCF were keen to deploy Lamine Senghor as part of its anti-colonial strategy: but what motivated Senghor himself? The question of why this once loyal colonial soldier became a leading anti-colonial militant is difficult to answer with certainty, but it is clear that the Diagne libel trial was a turning point in his life. Just a few months previously, he had been a member of *La Fraternité africaine* (also referred to in the CAI's records as *La Fraternelle sénégalaise*), one of many, small, largely apolitical community groups created to cater for the growing number of African colonial subjects on French soil. Early in the autumn of 1924, Senghor was recruited by the CAI as an informer and told to infiltrate the more radical *Union Intercoloniale*. As was often the case with the recruitment of informers, the CAI most likely played on Senghor's financial worries: this sickly young Senegalese man had a French wife and a young child, both of whom he wished to bring to his homeland, but he lacked the resources to do so on his modest salary as a postman. When his wife wrote to the leading black lawyer and activist, Kojo Tovalou-Houénou (who was, ironically, the owner of *Les Continents*, indicating the very small world of the black community at the time) to request financial help with their return to Africa, the letter was passed on to the Ministry for the Colonies, which seems to have used Senghor's financial predicament as leverage.[13] Within weeks, however, the Diagne libel trial erupted and Senghor was thrust forward as a defence witness, pressured by his new comrades in the UIC to take part, despite his misgivings about being involved in such a high-profile case.[14] The young militant suddenly found himself face to face with the man who had promised so much to the African soldiers who had fought in the First World War. We do not have access to Senghor's actual testimony but, shortly after the trial, he would write a general account of it for *Le Paria*:

> Instead of attempting to prove precisely how much the great slave trader [Diagne] received for each Senegalese he recruited, they should have brought before him a whole procession of those blinded and mutilated in the war. [...]
> All of these victims would have spat in his face the infamy of the mission that he had undertaken.[15]

For Olivier Sagna, Senghor's testimony during the trial reveals that 'more than the UIC militant, it is the war-wounded veteran whose wounds have been reopened who speaks'.[16] This, it would seem, was the moment he began his transformation into a genuinely radical activist, the part that the CAI had initially asked him to play.

The context of Senghor's entry into the world of radical, black anti-colonialism understandably raises questions about his individual actions and motivations, but also more widely about the marginal position of black radicals in this period. It seems evident from the colonial archives that, well into 1925, Senghor retained the hope that he would be repatriated to Senegal by the colonial authorities, even writing to the governor general of French West Africa on 9 March to request this. However, he changed his mind before a response had been sent, fearing that the radical turn he had taken over recent months would lead to brutal repression upon a return to his homeland.[17] Regarding the wider issues for black radicals, Senghor's case underlines their marginal position on French soil, both politically and personally: indeed, all through the interwar period, the CAI was hugely successful in recruiting informers within black groupings of all stripes. Most radical movements are to some extent vulnerable to state infiltration, but these black groupings seem to have been particularly exposed as the CAI preyed on the financial concerns of individuals without an extended family or social network to support them in hard times; in addition, black Communists were deeply conscious that their peripheral position within the PCF might lead to support being abruptly curtailed whenever the ideological winds from Moscow changed direction.

## L'Union intercoloniale: the rise and fall of a transcolonial front against imperialism

In the aftermath of the trial, Lamine Senghor quickly became a mainstay of UIC activities. He had joined the UIC at a moment when its geographical focus was evolving: initially dominated by representatives from French Indochina, it had gradually integrated North Africans, Caribbeans and, now with Lamine Senghor, it reached out to sub-Saharan Africa. Throughout 1925, Senghor was a regular contributor to *Le Paria*. He wrote about strikes in French West Africa projecting a vision of black and white workers united against their capitalist bosses, while condemning forced labour in the colonies as a new form of slavery, and, yet again, he decried the failure of France to deliver on its promises to those African troops who had served the country so loyally during the Great War. In an article on forced labour, Senghor denounced what was essentially a 'system of slavery'. Outside of the four communes in Senegal (whose inhabitants enjoyed French citizenship), it was the code of *indigénat* that governed relations between coloniser and colonised, and forced labour was a permanent threat for any colonial subject. In denouncing this injustice, Senghor reminded his readership of the 'blood debt' and the promises that had been made to the colonised. The sacrifice made by the *tirailleurs sénégalais* was supposed to bring an end to forced labour and other forms of injustice:

> So, that's the recognition shown by the 'Motherland' to its children who served as 'cannon fodder' from 1914–18; under Painlevé's premiership when 6,000 negroes were sacrificed in 3 days on 16, 17, 18 April 1917 at the Chemin des Dames! So, that's the reality of the promises made by the recruiters Diagne and Angoulvant in 1917–18?[18]

What is more, instead of compensating African soldiers for their sacrifice, they were then sent to fight in colonial wars in Morocco and Syria 'where 75% of the French army are negroes'; and, for those who might escape these conflicts, all they will be offered is the 'shameful slavery' of forced labour.[19]

On 10 February 1925, the PCF opened its Communist Colonial School, envisaged as a forum in which leading UIC members might learn the basics of Marxist ideology so as to ensure a certain level of orthodoxy in their writings and speeches. Classes were mostly led by the experienced Algerian Communist Hadj-Ali Abdelkader, and the topics covered included: imperialism in Africa; the development of capitalism; primitive Communism; capitalist production; class struggle; and the trade union movement. Even though classes were held late on weeknights from 9 p.m., Senghor attended quite assiduously – far more assiduously, in fact, than most of his UIC comrades. Many of these militants were better versed than Senghor in Communist ideology and may well have resented Jacques Doriot's insistence that they return to evening school.[20] The classes staggered on until mid-April but were eventually cancelled due to persistent low attendance. Although the classes might have failed in their overall purpose, they clearly succeeded in allowing Senghor to place his ideas about injustice within a broader ideological framework. His writing for *Le Paria* bears the imprint of this ideological training: essentially, the nationalist anti-colonial movements were cast as the prelude to a global world revolution. However, as will be shown below, Senghor's anti-colonialism deployed a rather heterodox form of Communist ideology. The most important issue (as with Ho Chi Minh before him) was the attempt to imagine an anti-colonial discourse capable of mobilising all colonised peoples: Communist orthodoxy counted for far less than the ability to unite the colonised of the world.

'Transcolonial' movements such as the UIC or the League Against Imperialism (discussed below) would all eventually splinter into nationalist anti-colonial groupings, but that should not lead us to dismiss the former too hastily. Long after Senghor had left the UIC, Indochinese anti-colonialists with whom he was friendly would continue to attend meetings of his various black groups in a show of 'transcolonial' solidarity. Equally, at the inaugural meeting of the League Against Imperialism in Brussels in February 1927, Senghor appears to have developed close ties to Messali Hadj and the Algerian delegation from the Étoile Nord-Africaine, based on bonds of religion and a shared colonial oppressor.[21] The UIC and the Brussels Congress can thus be seen as sites where the political and the personal coalesced, venues in which one's own often lonely struggle against the might of empire could find support from like-minded souls. Indeed, the CAI report on the Brussels Congress notes ruefully that it had been an inspirational event for many of those present: one delegate described it as 'the dawn of the great day' that they had been waiting for.[22]

In late 1924 and throughout 1925, the PCF carried out its most sustained anti-colonial campaign when it sought to organise resistance to the colonial war in the Rif Mountains of Morocco.[23] The PCF-UIC campaign against the war was led by Jacques Doriot who saw in the resistance of the Moroccan indigenous leader, Abd El-Krim, against Spanish and French domination of the Rif region the perfect occasion for the PCF finally to prove its anti-colonial credentials to an increasingly impatient Comintern. When Abd el-Krim won a remarkable victory over the Spanish colonial army in September 1924, Doriot and Pierre Semard sent a congratulatory telegram on behalf of the *Jeunesses communistes* (published on the front page of the Communist Party's newspaper, *L'Humanité*, the following day), which expressed the wish that 'after its definitive victory over Spanish imperialism, the people of the Rif will continue, together with the French and European proletariat, the struggle against all imperialists, until Moroccan soil has been fully liberated'.[24] It seemed at last as though the PCF was fully embracing the Comintern's anti-colonial agenda but, in reality, much of the PCF hierarchy was reluctant to lend the campaign its full support.

Senghor threw himself wholeheartedly into the campaign against the Rif War, appearing at countless rallies alongside French Communists, particularly Doriot and Paul Vaillant-Couturier, the latter of whom he may have known through the pacifist *Association Républicaine des Anciens Combattants* (ARAC), as well as other prominent UIC members. Another speaker with whom Senghor often shared a platform at rallies was the novelist Henri Barbusse, author of the great anti-war novel, *Le Feu* (Under Fire), and a war veteran who, like Vaillant-Couturier, gravitated from ARAC to the PCF. We have little evidence regarding Senghor's personal relations with French members of the PCF hierarchy, but it does not seem entirely coincidental that many of those with whom he collaborated most closely were from the pacifist, anti-war wing of the Communist movement. Their shared experiences of the First World War provided them with the common ground upon which to construct a shared politics.[25]

It was during this intense period that Senghor transformed himself into a powerful orator – a fact agreed upon by both his friends and his enemies – capable of addressing audiences both large and small (at one rally in May 1925 at Luna Park in the Parisian suburbs addressing a crowd of 15,000). Beyond the significance of his actual words, Senghor's presence on stage at mass rallies and political meetings was often deployed as a form of political theatre that positioned Communism as an international brotherhood of all nations and races. For instance, as he took to the stage at the Lille Workers' Congress on 12 July 1925, Senghor was embraced by a woman named Klaweiss who was there to address the gathering as the mother of a young soldier who had been killed in the fighting in Morocco. A few weeks later, on Sunday 2 August, the largest protest against the Rif War was held when 60,000 workers took to the streets of the Parisian suburb of Clichy, a left-wing stronghold. As the march reached its destination in the central square, the Communists stage-managed a moment of 'fraternisation' between a disabled war veteran, a (white) Parisian worker, a black man and an Arab who appeared arm in arm on the steps above the crowd. This sight was met, according to *L'Humanité*, with the now standard crowd response of a spontaneous and rousing rendition of *L'Internationale*. The black man chosen for this choreographed spectacle of transnational Communist unity was none other than Lamine Senghor. He was not one of the speakers, however: that right was reserved for major PCF dignitaries such as Marcel Cachin.[26]

After loyally serving the PCF and the UIC throughout the Rif campaign, Lamine Senghor had gradually come by early 1926 to resent the limited space devoted by the Communist movement to black questions in general as well as to his own marginalised status in particular. There were only so many times he could accept the non-speaking role or being asked to deliver the 'fraternal salute' of his black brothers to PCF gatherings. Apparently, the final straw came when the PCF was invited to send two representatives to the Congress of Black Workers in Chicago in October 1925.[27] They selected Senghor and the Antillean lawyer Max Bloncourt but, at the last minute, informed them that they would have to pay for the journey out of their own pockets. When Senghor objected, it was suggested that he either work his passage to America or stow away: he refused. Senghor decided that in order to promote the interests of black people, it was necessary to create independent black organisations, and in early 1926, with the creation of the *Comité de Défense de la Race Nègre* (Committee for the Defence of the Negro Race, CDRN), that is just what he did.

## From Red to Black? Or the Red and the Black?

In March 1926, Lamine Senghor officially registered his new association and embarked on a tour of France's port cities (Marseilles, Bordeaux, Le Havre) in order to encounter the small working-class black community and attempt to convince them that the CDRN would defend their collective interests. He also frequently visited the African military camp at Fréjus, in southern France, to try and convert the troops to his cause. His skills as a public speaker, honed during the Rif campaign, served him well, and by the summer of 1926 it was estimated by the agents of the CAI, the secret police of the Ministry of the Colonies, that he had recruited close to 900 members (in a black population numbered at less than 20,000).[28] Throughout the rest of the year, it often appeared that Senghor had broken entirely with the PCF and had decided to devote himself to defending the black community, initially embracing a moderate, reformist position. The CDRN's initial moderation was perhaps best symbolised by the involvement in the group of Camille Mortenol, a black, former navy officer, who had been a protege of the French abolitionist, Victor Schoelcher. Indeed, one of the CDRN's highest profile events was a procession in July 1926, led by Mortenol, to lay a wreath on Schoelcher's grave.

Senghor's split with the PCF was only ever partial, however, and issues of race and class were consistently intertwined in his speeches and his writing. The colonial authorities often assumed that Senghor was a Communist seeking to hide his political affiliations from the black community, in an attempt to subjugate the cause of combating racial and colonial oppression to the cause of promoting global Communism. In reality, this revealed more about the colonial authorities' attitude towards Communism than it did about Senghor's fundamental beliefs. It also revealed their attitude towards the mental capacities of black Africans: for they believed that Senghor was merely a stooge, parroting ideological sound bites that he surely could not understand: the CAI surveillance notes regularly and sarcastically asserted that his speeches must have been written for him, most usually, it was claimed, by the Antillean lawyer, Bloncourt (as Antilleans were placed higher than Africans in the racial hierarchies of French colonialism).[29]

The CDRN may, ultimately, have proven to be a short-lived organisation that did not achieve its goals, but, during the twelve months of its existence, it experimented in intriguing and productive ways with issues of racial and political solidarity. In particular, as Christopher Miller and Brent Hayes Edwards have both demonstrated, it sought to foster a critical reflection on the language of race, exploring the forms of self-definition available to black people.[30] The CAI records indicate that there had been much internal discussion within the CDRN about whether to use the term 'noir' or 'Nègre' in their title, and Lamine Senghor played a decisive role in pushing the committee towards the latter term. In his article, 'The Negroes have Awoken', published in *Le Paria* in April 1926, Senghor articulates a racial identity based not on shared racial characteristics but on a shared sense of oppression: 'To be a Negro is to be exploited until one's last drop of blood has been spilt or to be transformed into a soldier defending the interests of capitalism against those who would dare try to stop its advance.'[31]

In passing, the fact that the article announcing this change of direction appeared within the UIC's own newspaper is yet more evidence that there had not been a radical split between Senghor and French Communism. This does not mean that the creation of the CDRN was simply a case of Senghor the Communist masquerading as a black internationalist. It seems far more likely that the PCF's continued funding of Senghor's activities after the creation of the CDRN was the expression of their desire not to lose a talented and effective militant; and, in the context of mid-1920s Communist flirtation with anti-colonial nationalists of various hues, it was deemed politically expedient.

In the mid-1920s, to call for 'the awakening of the negro' evoked a set of ideas and a vocabulary that had been rendered popular by Marcus Garvey. In the course of his seemingly inexorable rise as a major leader of black America (until his conviction for mail fraud in 1925), Garvey had consistently called for the black world to wake from its long sleep, and his calls for black people to take pride in themselves had resonated around the world.[32] The influence of Garvey on black politics in interwar France has commonly been underplayed, as the general assimilationism that marks these French groups seems in many ways to be the antithesis of Garvey's identitarian discourse, and the Jamaican's anti-Communist stance meant that it would have been difficult for Senghor and other militants to embrace him openly.

Black French activists of the interwar period were, however, partly operating (consciously or not) within a discursive space opened up by Garvey when they argue for the dignity of 'le Nègre' and call for the rejection of the white world's stereotypical and racist vision of the black world. In the case of Lamine Senghor's articles written in his capacity as president of the CDRN, he fuses Garvey's call for racial solidarity with a Leninist interpretation of imperialism as the supreme form of capitalism. The 'Nègre' constitutes a specific category within a wider landscape of global capitalist exploitation: s/he shares the suffering of the working-class as a whole, but this condition is not reducible to that of the white proletariat.

The CDRN's use of the term 'Nègre' as a proud badge of self-identification (just as Garvey had proclaimed himself a 'Negro') was a departure from the emerging norms of the period. In an era when the term 'noir' was widely gaining prominence as a more dignified replacement for 'Nègre', seen as derogatory and demeaning, Senghor and the CDRN deliberately choose 'Nègre' as the term that encompassed all black people. The 'nègre' is an individual who has been downtrodden and oppressed through slavery, colonialism, segregation: the terms 'noir' and 'homme de couleur' [person of colour] were seen merely as escape routes for educated blacks seeking a place in a dominant white society. The first step towards liberation was to embrace one's identity as a 'nègre': for only then could one perceive the true nature of Western oppression of the black world.

## No more slaves!

From its creation in March 1926, the CDRN had loudly and regularly proclaimed its intention to publish a newspaper, *La Voix des nègres* (The Voice of the Negroes), which would act as 'the voice' of the black community. Ironically, by the time it finally appeared in January 1927, proudly and insistently proclaiming the unity of 'les nègres', the CDRN was in fact in the middle of a long and protracted schism that would, a few months later, lead to the break up of the organisation. It is difficult to identify a single cause for the split, which involved a complex and overlapping set of divides between Communists and reformers, between working-class black members and an educated black (largely Caribbean) grouping, and part of it was no doubt a personal struggle between Senghor and Joseph Gothon-Lunion, the general secretary of the CDRN.[33] Gothon-Lunion had made a famous trip to Moscow in 1924 as a Communist delegate at a meeting of the Comintern, and a celebrated photograph of him sitting on the Tsar's throne had been widely circulated. By late 1926, however, he was now presenting himself as the true face of black moderate reformism with Senghor cast as a puppet of the PCF. After several months of rancour and dispute, Senghor and his fellow radicals deserted en masse to create the *Ligue de Défense de la Race Nègre* (League for the Defence of the Negro Race, LDRN), leaving not just the name CDRN to the reformers but also a legal claim from the CDRN's typist for unpaid wages (a claim that the LDRN heartily supported).

In the latter half of 1926, a young Malian, Tiémoko Garan Kouyaté, had emerged as one of Senghor's key lieutenants within the CDRN and, subsequently, the LDRN. Kouyaté travelled to France to train as a teacher in Aix-en-Provence, but had been expelled in 1924 for expressing anti-colonial sentiments.[34] He gravitated towards the Communist movement as Africa's best ally, and he was strongly supportive of Senghor during the struggles that convulsed the CDRN from November 1926 onwards. However, as 1927 wore on and Senghor's health faltered, leading him to be absent from Paris for long spells, Kouyaté came to bemoan what he perceived as the malign, underhand influence of the PCF, constantly manoeuvring in the background to retain its influence over the LDRN. Little did Kouyaté realise that, in the aftermath of Senghor's death, he would be faced with the same dilemmas as his erstwhile mentor, seeking to maintain the independence of a black movement, while relying on PCF financial and organisational clout.

In the midst of the CDRN infighting, Senghor was invited to speak at the inaugural Congress meeting of the League Against Imperialism (LAI) in Brussels (10–14 February 1927), the organisation of which was led by Willi Münzenberg, the German Communist. In many respects, Senghor's speech at the Congress was the moment that sealed his reputation as the leading black anti-colonialist of his day. The LAI was largely a Communist initiative, but in its initial phase it sought to rally all anti-colonial forces together, and Senghor shared a platform in Brussels with prominent nationalist leaders including Jawaharlal Nehru (India), Mohammed Hatta (Indonesia), as well as Henri Barbusse whom he had worked with on the Rif campaign.[35]

In his speech at the Congress, Senghor was liberated from the moderation that had marked most of his contributions to the CDRN, and he launched into a vehement attack on imperialism as a renewed form of slavery. At the heart of the speech was an impassioned denunciation of European imperialism in Africa: 'What is colonisation? It is the violation of the right of a people to organise itself as it sees fit.'[36] Senghor here seeks to forge a unity between those suffering from each of the many distinct forms of Western domination of 'colonised' lands. He also tests a vocabulary for defining colonialism that he would most likely have been developing at the time for his anti-colonial fable, *La Violation d'un pays* (The Rape/Violation of a Land, 1927), which would be published just a few months later.

In the remainder of the speech, he deployed many of the standard rhetorical and ideological tropes of the French radical anti-colonial left in the mid-1920s. He attacked the injustice in the treatment of those colonial soldiers who had fought for France in the First World War. He denounced the cruel treatment of the colonised, citing examples from colonial reports of extreme physical punishments meted out to Africans. Inverting the trope of African savagery, he identified French imperialism as the true source of barbarism: 'Who could fail to shudder at the thought that today, in the twentieth century, the French are still committing such horrific acts, worthy of the ferocity of the middle ages?'[37] Imperialism could not hope to bring civilisation to the colonies for it was an inherently unjust system of domination and French claims of a civilising mission were, in fact, deeply insincere: '[The French] say "Oh no, we must not teach the negroes" because, if they are educated, they will be civilised and we will no longer be able to do what we wish with them.'[38] Forced labour was a lynchpin in his argument that European imperialism was merely a renewed form of slavery:

> Slavery. We are told it has been abolished. We might accept that the retail sale of individuals has been outlawed [...]. But we can see that the imperialists reserve the very democratic right to sell an entire negro people to another imperial power. It is not true, slavery has not been abolished. On the contrary, it has been modernised.[39]

The trope of twentieth-century colonialism as a modern form of slavery – common in PCF discourse of the period – sought to undermine the civilising rhetoric of the European powers and, in the black world, to promote a transcolonial unity between Africans and members of the diaspora. Senghor concluded by proclaiming in Leninist terms that imperialism was a product of capitalism which imposed its domination on the colonised 'over there' and the workers 'over here' (as Sartre would later write in *Colonialism and Neocolonialism*):

> Those who suffer from colonial oppression must take each other by the hand and walk shoulder to shoulder with those who suffer from the misdeeds of metropolitan imperialism; they must bear the same weapons and destroy the universal evil of global imperialism. Comrades, we must replace it by the union of free peoples of the earth. No more slaves![40]

The speech was a great success in the hall, and was met with acclaim by the other delegates. Indeed, many of the photographs of the Congress show Senghor at the centre of the shot, the arms of fellow delegates draped around him (echoing the stage management of a racially diverse anti-colonial movement that the PCF had deployed during the Rif campaign). As Kasper Braskén's work has shown, Willi Münzenberg was a key figure in developing connections between anti-colonialism and anti-fascism in this period, and this choreographing of multi-ethnic workers and militants bears his imprint.[41]

The speech was also a success far beyond the confines of the Congress. It was immediately translated into English and reproduced in various journals in the United States.[42] W.E.B. Du Bois's *The Crisis* reported Senghor's words approvingly in its July 1927 edition, the author having discovered a translation of the speech in the 15 May edition of *The Living Age*.[43] The author states that Senghor 'vigorously challenges the superiority of Caucasians and says that their present colonisation of Africa is nothing more or less than the usurpation of the right of a nation to direct its own destinies'.[44] In a fascinating article published just a few months after the Congress, Roger Baldwin, director of the American Civil Liberties Union, who was present in Brussels and, like Senghor elected to the executive committee of the LAI's international committee, cited the Senegalese as one of the most eminent of the 'men without a homeland', those political exiles who had made Paris their home. Little more than two years after his first public appearance, this young man from Senegal had managed to carve out a position as a radical spokesman not only for black people in France but also internationally.

Senghor's speech in Brussels was in effect a distillation of the key ideas he had developed since the Diagne trial. It would be misleading to make claims for Senghor as a groundbreaking political theorist, for his speeches and his articles did not seek to provide in-depth analysis of the links between capitalism and empire. He was, rather, a brilliant communicator of ideas, driven by moral outrage at the injustices of capitalist imperialism. A passionate public speaker, he was able to energise audiences, large and small, and distil complex political ideas into a series of resonant images. At certain points in history, the actions and personality of key individual actors can be deployed to seize opportunities created by a complex set of political and economic factors.

## Conclusion

Lamine Senghor continued the exploration of colonialism as a modern form of slavery in *La Violation d'un pays*, which he published in June 1927. This slim volume of about thirty pages relates in polemical fashion the bloody history of slavery and colonialism. It is a deeply hybrid text that mixes the form of the fable with a highly didactic approach, utilising the political language of revolutionary Communism: the text is also accompanied by five simple line drawings designed to reinforce the political message. It concludes with the overthrow of the colonial regime by a world revolution that liberates not only the colonies but also the metropolitan centre from the yoke of capitalist imperialism. The resolution of Senghor's story acts as a form of ideological wish fulfilment: we might usefully describe it as the 'performance' of an international anti-colonialism, imagining the overthrow of empire, even if the means to achieve independence escaped them. Within weeks of its publication, however, Senghor's health faltered, and he would pass away just a few months later with the LDRN in turmoil, once again arguing about funding and political orientation.

Upon Senghor's death, the anti-colonial cause lost one of its most prominent figures and it is debatable whether the black community in France has ever known a more effective political leader. Initially, it was his Red comrades who mourned his passing, as *L'Humanité* published a fulsome obituary just days after his death. In a telling indication of the estrangement between Senghor and his erstwhile comrades in the LDRN, the members of the committee only learned of his death upon the publication of *L'Humanité*'s obituary. His deputy, Tiémoko Garan Kouyaté, would finally publish a glowing obituary in the LDRN's newspaper, *La Race Nègre*, which appeared in May 1928, six long months after Senghor's death.

For its part, the League Against Imperialism viewed Senghor's untimely demise as a useful propaganda opportunity, transforming the Senegalese into a martyr whose death had been caused, it claimed, by vile French imperialists. It is the LAI's version of his passing that has proven most enduring. Willi Münzenberg is the source of the myth, wilfully spread by the League, that Senghor had died in prison after months of incarceration, arrested as 'punishment' for his part in the Brussels LAI Congress: Senghor had, in fact, spent just one night in prison in March 1927, after an altercation with an overzealous gendarme. Writing in the first issue of the LAI's journal, *The Anti-Imperialist Review*, in 1928, Münzenberg stated that:

> Some Governments became nervous and irrational as a result of the Congress. In France, the African Lamine Senghore [sic], the brave representative of his suffering race, who was elected a Member of the Executive Committee of the League Against Imperialism, and whose speech at the Congress was a passionate and mordant denunciation of French imperialism, fell a victim to the rancour of the authorities. He was arrested and cast into prison, where he died a few months later of tuberculosis.[45]

Senghor's early death thus allowed him to join a pantheon of Communist and anti-colonial martyrs, the purity of their devotion to the cause proven by their ultimate sacrifice.

As this chapter has sought to demonstrate, however, the reality of his life was far more complex than this political mythology allows. He was, by turns, a loyal servant of France, an informer, a Communist, a black internationalist and anti-colonialist and, through it all, a concerned father of two young children constantly fretting about how he might provide for his family. In political terms, he spent the period between 1924–27 exploring different potential ways of rallying various forces against empire, while recognising the specificity of the racial oppression suffered by black people.

Throughout the interwar period, black activists from the US, the Caribbean, and Africa were drawn to the Communist movement as a potential ally, but many eventually became disillusioned at what they perceived as the lack of attention paid to the specificity of the racism endured by black people. It is unlikely that any of the white delegates at the LAI Congress in Brussels suffered the indignity of being turned away from their hotel rooms due to the colour of their skin, as reportedly happened to Senghor.[46] White, European Communists quite literally could not understand the racial concerns of their black comrades.

The political trajectory of anti-colonial figures such as Senghor is thus often cast as either a movement from nationalism to Communism or, more typically, its polar opposite – a recognition that Communism had no room for the black experience. Unlike Aimé Césaire or George Padmore, he was not obliged to make a choice between Pan-Africanism and Communism. The experience of Tiémoko Garan Kouyaté, who replaced him as leader of the LDRN and was constantly in conflict with the PCF hierarchy over the next decade, warns us that Senghor may well have struggled to maintain an affiliation to both the Red and the Black causes. But, throughout his brief career as an activist, Senghor believed that these two ideologies could complement each other in the quest for black liberation. This refusal to choose between Communism and nationalism was shared by many other key figures of the period, not least Ho Chi Minh. For the French historian Alain Ruscio, Ho Chi Minh's ultimate political stance can be described as 'communism because of nationalism' or 'nationalism plus communism'.[47] Equally, Lamine Senghor did not see his political options in dichotomous terms, forcing him to choose either *the Red or the Black*. On the contrary, no matter how unpromising the circumstances, he consistently maintained a commitment to both *the Red and the Black*.

## Notes

1 Claude McKay, *Banjo: A Story Without a Plot* (London: Serpent's Tale, 2008 [1929]); Claude McKay, *A Long Way from Home* (New Brunswick, NJ: Rutgers University Press, 2007 [1937]).
2 Michael Goebel, *Anti-Imperial Metropolis: Interwar Paris and the Seeds of Third World Nationalism* (Cambridge: Cambridge University Press, 2015).
3 Two key early texts on this subject are Philippe Dewitte, *Les Mouvements nègres en France 1919–39* (Paris: L'Harmattan, 1985) and Olivier Sagna, 'Des Pionniers méconnus de l'indépendance: Africains, Antillais et luttes anticolonialistes dans la France de l'entre-deux-guerres (1919–39)', PhD thesis, Paris 7, 1986. Important recent scholarship includes: Jonathan Derrick, *Africa's 'Agitators': Militant Anti-Colonialism in Africa and the West, 1918–39* (London: Hurst, 2008); Jennifer Anne Boittin, *Colonial Metropolis: The Urban Grounds of Anti-Imperialism and Feminism in Interwar Paris* (Lincoln, NE: University of Nebraska Press, 2010); Minkah Malakani, *In the Cause of Freedom: Radical Black Internationalism from Harlem to London, 1917–1939* (Chapel Hill, NC: University of North Carolina Press, 2011) looks at this radicalism in a wider Atlantic context.
4 For a general overview of Lamine Senghor's activism, see my article, David Murphy, '"Defending the Negro Race": Lamine Senghor and Black Internationalism in Interwar France', *French Cultural Studies*, 24:2 (2013), 61–73; and my edition of his collected writings: Lamine Senghor, *La Violation d'un pays et autres écrits anticolonialistes*, ed. David Murphy (Paris: L'Harmattan, 2012). My research on Lamine Senghor builds on the pioneering work of other scholars, not least: Christopher L. Miller, *Nationalists and Nomads: Essays on Francophone African Literature and Culture* (Chicago, IL: University of Chicago Press, 1998); Brent Hayes Edwards, *The Practice of Diaspora: Literature, Translation and the Rise of Black Internationalism* (Cambridge, MA: Harvard University Press, 2003); and, in particular, Sagna, 'Des Pionniers méconnus de l'indépendance'.
5 Ann Laura Stoler, *Along the Archival Grain: Epistemic Anxieties and Colonial Common Sense* (Princeton, NJ: Princeton University Press, 2009).

6 In her recent study of the 17 October 1961 massacre of Algerians in Paris, Lia Brozgal has argued that the archive of this event must be interpreted in light of the 'anarchive' – a diverse collection of cultural texts representing that night in Paris. Lia Brozgal, *Absent the Archive: Cultural Traces of a Massacre in Paris, 17 October 1961* (Liverpool: Liverpool University Press, 2020).

7 See Ferdinand de Jong, 'At Work in the Archive: Introduction to Special Issue', *World Art*, 6:1 (2016), 3–17, at 13. See also Paul Basu and Ferdinand de Jong, 'Utopian Archives, Decolonial Affordances: Introduction to Special Issue', *Social Anthropology*, 24:1 (2016), 5–19.

8 De Jong, 'At Work in the Archive', 14.

9 Michel-Rolph Trouillot, *Silencing the Past: Power and the Production of History* (Boston, MA: Beacon Press, 1999), 26.

10 'Le bon apôtre', in Senghor, *La Violation d'un pays*, 109. All translations are mine. Senghor, *La Violation d'un pays*, 40.

11 For a brilliant account of this landmark trial, see Alice L. Conklin, 'Who Speaks for Africa? The René Maran-Blaise Diagne Trial in 1920s Paris' in Sue Peabody and Tyler Stovall (eds), *The Color of Liberty: Histories of Race in France* (Durham, NC: Duke University Press, 2003), 302–337.

12 See Roger Little, 'Du nouveau sur le procès Blaise Diagne-René Maran', *Cahiers d'Etudes Africaines*, 60:1 (2020), 141–150.

13 For a more detailed account of the CAI's recruitment of Senghor, see my article, David Murphy, 'La courte vie militante de Lamine Senghor (1924–1927)', *Les Cahiers d'histoire*, 126 (January 2015), 55–72, at 61.

14 Archives Nationales d'Outre-mer (ANOM), 5 Slotfom 6. Note by Agent Désiré, 10 November 1924.

15 'Un procès nègre' [A Negro Trial], in Senghor, *La Violation d'un pays*, 33–34.

16 Sagna, 'Des Pionniers méconnus de l'indépendance', 311.

17 Murphy, 'La courte vie militante de Lamine Senghor (1924–1927)', 62.

18 'En A.O.F. – Le travail forcé pour les indigènes', in Senghor, *La Violation d'un pays*, 40.

19 Senghor, *La Violation d'un pays*, 40.

20 A series of surveillance notes by Agent Désiré lists the classes of the Ecole Coloniale Communiste. ANOM 3 Slotfom 63. Full outlines of the content of the classes are available from the National Archives in Dakar. ANS 21 G 27 (17).

21 See Dónal Hassett, 'An Independent Path: Algerian Nationalists and the League against Imperialism' in Michele Louro, Carolien Stolte, Heather Streets-Salter and Sana Tannoury-Karam (eds), *The League Against Imperialism: Lives and Afterlives* (Leiden: Leiden University Press, 2020), 79–105.

22 ANOM, 3 Slotfom 145: Monthly CAI report, February 1927, 50.

23 For an overview of the campaign against the war, see David H. Slavin, 'The French Left and the Rif War, 1924–25: Racism and the Limits of Internationalism', *Journal of Contemporary History*, 26:1 (1991), 5–32.

24 *L'Humanité*, 11 September 1924; cited in Senghor, *La Violation d'un pays*, 121.

25 Gregory Mann has studied the ways in which a shared experience of the battlefield had the potential to bring French and African veterans together. See Gregory

Mann, *Native Sons: West African Veterans and France in the Twentieth Century* (Durham, NC: Duke University Press, 2006). The possibility that ARAC played a role in forging bonds between left-wing French and African militants is a topic that requires further exploration.
26 *L'Humanité* devotes much of the first two pages of its issue of 3 August 1925 to the march. Lamine Senghor is not identified here as the black man in question. He identifies himself as this figure, however, in an article published in *L'Humanité* ten days later on 13 August.
27 Makalani discusses the Chicago congress in his book, *In the Cause of Freedom*, 120–126.
28 The CAI consistently cast doubt on the CDRN membership numbers cited by Senghor and other members of the executive and it appears evident that there was a problem in ensuring that signed-up members actually paid their membership dues. A monthly CAI report for October 1926 accepts, however, that a figure of 900 members is probably only 'slightly inflated'. ANOM, 3 Slotfom 144: CAI monthly report, October 1926, 8.
29 See, for example, Note by Agent Désiré, 31 March 1925. ANOM 3 Slotfom 3.
30 See Miller, *Nationalists and Nomads*; Edwards, *The Practice of Diaspora*.
31 'Le réveil des nègres', in Senghor, *La Violation d'un pays*, 41–42.
32 Indeed, although not directly acknowledging his influence, the CDRN clearly owed a lot to Garvey – in terms of iconography (the shooting star in the naive and romanticised image of Africa featured on the association's headed paper, and the black star of its official stamp) and of language, especially the repeated appeals to black pride and solidarity.
33 Dewitte, *Les Mouvements nègres*, 106–108.
34 *Ibid.*, 35.
35 The LAI has lately been the subject of significant scholarly attention. See, in particular, the recent edited volume, *The League Against Imperialism: Lives and Afterlives*. My contribution to this volume provides a detailed analysis of Lamine Senghor's speech: David Murphy, 'No More Slaves! Lamine Senghor, Black Internationalism and the League Against Imperialism' in Michele Louro, Carolien Stolte, Heather Streets-Salter and Sana Tannoury-Karam (eds), *The League Against Imperialism: Lives and Afterlives* (Leiden: Leiden University Press, 2020), 211–235.
36 Senghor, *La Violation d'un pays*, 58.
37 *Ibid.*, 60.
38 *Ibid.*, 59.
39 *Ibid.* 60–61. The reference to 'the very democratic right to sell an entire negro people to another imperial power' alludes to fears at the time that France might sell its Caribbean colonies to the US in order to pay off part of its war debts.
40 Senghor, *La Violation d'un pays*, 63.
41 Kasper Braskén, '"Whether Black or White, United in the Fight": Connecting the Resistance against Colonialism, Racism, and Fascism in the European Metropoles, 1926–36', *Twentieth Century Communism*, 18 (2020), 126–149.

42 For details on the reception of the speech, see Brent Hayes Edwards, 'The Shadow of Shadows', *positions: east asia cultures critique*, 11:1 (2003), 11–49.
43 'A Black Man's Protest', *Living Age*, 332:4306 (15 May 1927), 866–868; 'The Browsing Reader', *The Crisis* (July 1927), 160.
44 'The Browsing Reader', *The Crisis* (July 1927), 160.
45 Willi Münzenberg, 'From Demonstration to Organisation', *The Anti-Imperialist Review*, 1:1 (July 1928), 4–10, at 5. Given Münzenberg's close connections with Communists across Europe, it is inconceivable that he was unaware of the true circumstances of Senghor's death: indeed, Senghor's obituary in *L'Humanité* clearly stated that he had passed away in a friend's home in the southern town of Fréjus, and not while languishing in a prison cell. Münzenberg's propaganda has certainly had some long-lasting effects, and the myth of Senghor as anti-colonial martyr was spread so assiduously that it still regularly resurfaces, even in the work of some highly respected contemporary scholars. To cite just one example, Vijay Prashad states that 'a leading light, Lamine Senghor of the Committee for the Defense of the Negro Race, died in a French prison shortly after the conference'. Vijay Prashad, *The Darker Nations: A People's History of the Third World* (New York: New Press, 2007), 23.
46 Dónal Hassett cites Messali Hadj's *Mémoires* as the source for this incident. Hassett, 'An Independent Path'.
47 Alain Ruscio, 'Nguyên Ai Quôc/Hô Chi Minh: portrait d'un "Bolchevik jaune" (1917–1923)' in Hô Chi Minh, *Le Procès de la colonisation française et autres textes de jeunesse*, ed. and presented by Alain Ruscio (Paris: Le Temps des Cerises, 2012), 7–28, at 8.

# 7

# Black Americans in Russia: Ira Aldridge and Paul Robeson

## Lisa Merrill and Theresa Saxon

When I sing the 'spirituals' and work songs of the Negro people to Soviet audiences, I feel that a tremendous bond of sympathy and mutual understanding unites us.

*Paul Robeson, 1937.*[1]

Borders are more than political lines separating countries and territories, signifying economic, cultural and linguistic dimensions. In this chapter, we explore the careers of Black American actors Ira Aldridge and Paul Robeson, both of whom, while subject to oppression and racism in the United States, were received warmly as performers in Russia, where they were renowned for their artistry. We examine the history of their engagement in activism, and ways they were appropriated for political principles, crossing material and symbolic borders and boundaries in Imperial Russia and the post-revolutionary Soviet Union.

Aldridge and later Robeson visited Russia within very different political climates. Ira Aldridge first travelled from America to England in 1824. Then, after two decades performing to mixed reviews in England, in the 1850s he toured extensively across Europe, including several visits to Russia, and Poland in the 1860s as the boundaries between those nation states were shifting under pressure from imperial conquest and resistance. Aldridge's first visit to Imperial Russia, in 1858, coincided with official discussions around the emancipation of serfs, and the connection between the systems of slavery and serfdom were noted in press reports of Aldridge's performances. Aldridge's conscious celebration of his African ancestry, and his apparent championing of the repressed in Russia, may have led authorities to fear his potential to disrupt.

More than seventy-five years later, actor, singer, and activist Paul Robeson travelled to England in 1927, and then extensively through the USSR starting in 1934. Paul and Eslanda Robeson's embrace of the Soviet Union as a place of liberation and equality for Black Americans was so all-encompassing that for over a year they chose to send their son to school there, rather than in the racist United States. Robeson's speeches in support of Soviet workers and of the Communist state led to his harassment by the right-wing US government that restricted his movements and denied his passport.

Though Robeson was more overtly political than Aldridge, and though the contexts of their visits were very different, they each were drawn to Russian culture and utilised by the Russian press as catalysts for political positions that they were seen to embody personally and represent with their artistry. Aldridge and Robeson's respective engagements with the Russian/Soviet political climates were noted by V. Rogov in an essay titled 'Othello in the American Theatre', which asserted that the 'acting of Aldridge in serf-ridden Russia sounded a clarion call', and that subsequently 'The acting of Paul Robeson during these years of war with humanity-hating fascism also goes far beyond the accustomed limits of theatrical activities.'[2]

## Ira Aldridge's European tours

In July 1852, Black American actor Ira Aldridge began touring and performing throughout Europe to great acclaim. Aldridge's European and later Russian tours were extensive and more rewarding critically and financially than he had experienced throughout his three decades in Britain. In mid-nineteenth century eastern Europe the actor was widely applauded, and reviews repeatedly referenced full houses and appreciative and enthusiastic audience reactions. Timing was key to his success. In 1848, just four years prior to Aldridge's first European tour, a series of revolutions of impoverished and oppressed populations reverberated throughout Europe and theatre had become a place where political activism could be covertly enabled.

Aldridge's first European tour included mostly western locations in Belgium and those then within the Prussian Empire. However, Aldridge also performed in Poland: in Poznań, Breslau, Gdańsk, Kraków, initially with an English-speaking company. But very soon, Aldridge nuanced his strategy, staging bilingual performances where he performed his roles as Othello, Shylock, Lear, and Mungo, in English, while the rest of the resident company performed in their native languages, or the official languages of the respective state. Hungarian, Polish, and Ukrainian audiences in lands respectively conquered by other imperial forces found themselves to be aliens in their own lands. Performances in their native languages, rather than those of their imperial rulers, therefore held great significance to them.

Thus, in the context of Aldridge's tours, language use signalled an acceptance of a deep-seated cultural as well as linguistic identity, which Benedict Anderson has referred to as 'linguistic nationalism'.[3] Conversely, Aldridge's performances with troupes using the language of the occupier reinforced borders and boundaries to understanding and empathy. Thus, Aldridge faced censorship from imperial officials in some regions and rejection in others depending upon whether the company appearing with him was performing in the national language, or the imperially imposed language.

On his first tour, Aldridge appeared in Poznań (known as Posen at the time) to acclaim, the local paper declaring that the actor in multiple roles was a 'great master in portraying feelings'. Commenting on Aldridge as Shylock in *The Merchant of Venice*, a German-language reviewer, Ludwig Sittenfeld, wrote: 'Being himself a representative of a despised race, he could strongly and truly portray the feelings of wronged Jews.'[4] Although Aldridge's collaboration was with the German theatre in the town, his performances were also attended by Polish speakers as well as German imperialists.[5] However, in a later tour, in Kraków, in January 1858, tensions between the powers of imperial occupation and local nationalist activists had escalated, and Aldridge's performances with a German-speaking theatre troupe were not reviewed by the local Polish papers, who had 'ceased to review plays staged at the German theatre'.[6]

Furthermore, in Hungary, Aldridge's performances of Shakespearean productions at the National Theatre in Pest were remarkable for being delivered by Aldridge in English – the language of the bard – and the remainder in Hungarian, rather than German – the language of the oppressor. While he did not overtly agitate against the political power of the various empires through which he toured, Aldridge's own advocacy against prejudice resonated with local centres of national activism in Hungary. While performing in Pest, Aldridge, at a post-performance dinner, praised the 'highly developed theater life' of Hungary.[7] Aldridge also declared: 'I see it as my mission […] to alert humanity and ask for their sympathy in this immense injustice on behalf of my race.'[8] Aldridge's acknowledged mission to speak out against slavery aligned with that of the Hungarian nationalists who were fighting for sovereignty and against imperial repression of national languages and cultures.[9]

On this tour, Aldridge had become the subject of surveillance by the Austro-Hungarian police, possibly because he was working with actor/stage manager Karl Rémay, a known amnestied political prisoner, suspected of liaising with Hungarian revolutionary leader Lajos Kossoth.[10] Moreover, in Hungarian theatres, Aldridge had been feted by an audience of nationalists who were known to be protesters against the control of the Austrian Empire. Significantly, Aldridge was subsequently banned from entry into Austria-Hungary. This first European tour, then, brought visibility for Aldridge as a theatre performer but also entangled him with European political intrigues.

Between 1852 and 1857, Aldridge undertook two more tours across Europe, which he found to be both financially and critically rewarding. In November 1858, with an invitation to perform in the state theatres of St Petersburg, Aldridge began touring in Baltic towns that were part of the Russian Empire, to generally positive acclaim, and as he recorded in a letter to the *Athenaeum*, for significant financial reward.[11] Aldridge's Russian tour seemed set to be as lucrative and critically regarding as his tours across Europe. Moreover, in Russia, Aldridge's presence, as an actor of African ancestry, became symbolically significant, as we discuss below.

## Pushkin and Aldridge: Black heritage in Russian culture

Although the renowned Russian poet Alexander Pushkin had died twenty years before Aldridge arrived in Russia in 1858, Pushkin's celebrated artistry, coupled with his pride in his own African ancestry, remained part of his fame. Furthermore, just months earlier, in December 1857, Imperial Russia's new tsar Alexander II had published a declaration announcing the intent to abolish serfdom. Both of these factors proved to be very auspicious for Aldridge, and influenced audiences reactions to him.

In *Eugene Onegin* Pushkin had signalled and celebrated his own African ancestry and current Russian locality: 'Beneath my Africa's warm sky, to sigh for sombre Russia's spaces / Where first I loved, where first I wept, and where my buried heart is kept.'[12]

Thus, Pushkin celebrated his mixed-race heritage as one who identified with both 'Africa's warm sky' and Russia's 'sombre' spaces. Perhaps not surprisingly, in Russia Aldridge's racial identity became a source of cultural capital, associating him with Pushkin. As Krystyna Courtney argues, through his publicity machinery, in Russia Aldridge billed himself (as he had in Britain and across Europe) as the African Roscius, thereby 'purposefully drawing attention to his race'.[13] In this way, Aldridge's own African heritage, like the distinguished Pushkin's before him, could be regarded a source of honour, not one of racist ignominy that had greeted him in the United States and in prestigious theatres in London.

Moreover, in his novel *Arap Petra Velikogo* (translated as *The Blackamoor of Peter the Great*), Pushkin speculated on the experiences of his African great-grandfather, 'Ibrahim Gannibel', identifying him as the son of an Ethiopian prince who was captured as a child and brought to Russia to serve Emperor Peter the Great.[14] Pushkin's Ibrahim was 'looked upon as a wonder', and 'an object of curiosity', which, though 'behind an appearance of benevolence, offended his self-esteem'.[15] However, while

Aldridge may have been regarded by some, at least initially, as a 'curiosity', his abilities as a performer of Shakespearean characters appealed to Russian audiences, who regarded the actor as an extraordinary talent.

Henry Louis Gates has noted that Russians knew that Pushkin's African great-grandfather Ibrahim became Chief Military Engineer in the Russian army.[16] Thus, poet Alexander Pushkin was regarded 'a resonant symbol of all that a person of African descent could achieve' when 'unfettered by the confining strictures of racism'.[17] In fact, it was because Pushkin embraced his African ancestry, argues Gates, that he became the most able poet and artistic voice of Russia. '[T]hat he stood a little apart from his countrymen', states Gates, 'gave Pushkin a clear-eyed vantage point from which to view his fellow Russians.'[18] In this way Pushkin became a prominent challenger to Tsarist Russian imperial codifications of society, life, and culture, criticising elite Russia's culpability in acts of prejudice against others, as well

**Figure 7.1** Ira Aldridge by Taras Shevchenko, 1858

as against the serfs of Russia. Pushkin's literary prominence since the early nineteenth century, and his acknowledgement of his African ancestry, may have contributed to the acceptance of both Ira Aldridge and Paul Robeson, who subsequently were lauded in Russia.

It was also in 1858 that Ukrainian artist and poet Taras Hryhorovych Shevchenko attended Aldridge's St Petersburg performances, and the two became close friends. Shevchenko, who had been born into serfdom, had been sentenced to nine years penal military service in Russia for writing poetry that condemned Tsarist imperialism and protested serfdom and oppression of ethnic minorities. Shortly after Shevchenko's release, thanks to the influence of Count Fyodor Petrovich Tolstoy, director of the St Petersburg theatres, he met and befriended Aldridge in St Petersburg.[19]

Although the two men did not speak each other's language, they shared experiences of persons who fought against the oppression of their respective people. According to Adriana Helbig, 'Those who knew both men noted that they often sang together.'[20] Helbig cited a Ukrainian Hour radio programme in which producer Irena Bell asserted that 'Aldridge greatly appreciated the sorrowful and melodic Ukrainian songs that captured the unfortunate plight of the people of Ukraine. Shevchenko, in turn, loved the songs of the Negro South for the same reason.'[21]

Both Aldridge and Robeson were moved by Russian folk songs, and performed them, although in very different contexts. Almost a century later, Paul Robeson would note the similarity between the two musical forms of each culture. As Aldridge's Russian biographer Sergei Durylin asserted, the affinity between Russian folk songs and the songs 'of Negro slaves did not seem odd at all;' Durylin claimed 'both were the songs of slaves, whether white or black'.[22]

In addition to his Shakespearean characters, in his tours across Russia Aldridge would sometimes play the character of Mungo, a Black slave in the house of a brutal master in Isaac Bickerstaffe's musical production, *The Padlock*. Durylin notes an account by Russian actor A.A. Alekseev, who remembered Aldridge telling him through an interpreter about performing 'a negro lackey', in a 'comic opera', most likely the character of Mungo. On Alekseev's benefit night Aldridge also added a Russian song, 'Vo piru byla, vo besedushke', to that evening's performance. Alekseev remembered that 'Aldridge sang the song in comical manner' and 'the audience encored endlessly'.[23]

Although *The Padlock* was billed as a comedy, it had generally been staged in England and America as a racist grotesque, starring a white actor in blackface make-up. In Kiev, one review seemed to grasp the significance of Aldridge in the role of Mungo, describing the play as a 'social tragicomedy', that, in depicting the Black slave the actor had dramatised the 'fate of the whole race'.[24] Moreover, in Lemberg (Lviv, Ukraine), Aldridge's appearance as Mungo was considered a moving contrast to his portrayal of Shylock, showing the range of his talent.[25] Perhaps audiences, aware of enslavement in the land of Aldridge's birth, recognised the poignance of this characterisation, particularly as it followed Aldridge's high culture performances of Shakespeare.

Most significantly, Russian audiences would have understood the cultural importance of Aldridge as a Shakespearean performer. By the 1800s, translations of Shakespeare were in circulation in Russia, though rarely performed outside Moscow and St Petersburg. Ira Aldridge, therefore, brought Shakespeare's characters alive on the stage, touring widely across the regions of the Russian Empire, as we discuss below.

### Ira Aldridge: connecting serfs and slaves in Imperial Russia

In press reports of Aldridge's first-Russian performances the connection between the systems of slavery and serfdom were noted. Reviewer K.I. Zvantsov, who attended a performance by Aldridge in St Petersburg, wrote: 'for us, at this time, the role of Othello performed by this artist of genius, with all its subtleties of tribal and climatic character, has great universal meaning [...] in that misery of the African artist is heard the far-off roars of the whole of suffering humanity'.[26]

Alexander Vasilievich Nikitenko, a former serf born in Ukraine, who ascended to the ranks of a professorship in Russia literature at the state university of St Petersburg, recorded in his diary the power of Aldridge's impact as a performer of Shakespeare:

> I can't speak or understand English, but since I know the play well, I went to the theatre – which I don't regret. Aldridge is a great artist. One can hardly go further than this actor in expressing strong and deep passions. In the third act, in the scene with Iago, he is so terrifying that it is difficult for people with weak nerves to bear, and you are choked with tears in the heartbreaking scene in the last act.[27]

Aldridge's performances as Othello in St Petersburg generally elicited receptive audiences and appreciative critics. However, in November, Count V.F. Adlerberg, at that time minister of the Imperial Court, refused permission to Aldridge to continue performing there. Adlerberg had warned Tsar Alexander II that 'in all revolutions private theatres served as a means for the excitement of the passions, and ... is the fruit of revolutions'.[28] Perhaps as a result of Adlerberg's determination Aldridge was refused permission to continue performing in St Petersburg, despite formal appeals made to the minister.

That Aldridge was lauded by theatre audiences and artists in St Petersburg yet sanctioned by the Tsar's minister demonstrates the fractures in Imperial Russia's political and social control at this time. Nevertheless, Aldridge was ordered to leave St Petersburg on 12 January 1859. So, despite protestations from his friends, including Taras Shevchenko, Aldridge headed along the Baltic coast and into Germany and from there back to England, concluding his first tour into Russia, shadowed by the spectre of empire and repressive political systems, but also attracting much critical praise from respected artistes and intellectuals.

In September 1862, on a subsequent Russian tour, Aldridge appeared for the first time in Moscow. By this time, the American Civil War, which was being fought over slavery, had become news across the globe, and in Russia serfdom had been abolished (in February 1861). Thus, although Aldridge performed widely and was the subject of many laudatory reviews, issues of the humanity and liberation of both Black people and serfs figured in the few racist reviews Aldridge received. In Moscow, a virulent letter to the editor by N.S. Sokhanskaya (pen name Kokhanovskaya) condemned the acceptance and accolades Aldridge's *Othello* received:

> The disgrace is truly ours if we are ready to accept that Aldridge's blackness helps us to penetrate deeper and more fully into the spirit of Shakespeare's poetry. If lips are thick and dark blue, are they able to express better the cries of a human soul? [...] it was as though this were not the Maly theatre in Moscow but an African jungle fueled with shrieks coming from this powerful howling black flesh.[29]

Perhaps not surprisingly, this vicious reaction, reducing the humanity of Black people to 'black flesh', and also, in grotesque language, questioning the right of such a person to be the arbiter of Shakespeare was similar to the rhetoric that had shrouded Aldridge's performance in London at the Covent Garden Theatre Royal in 1833, at the very time that Britain abolished slavery in its colonies.

However, Kokhanovskaya was 'unanimously rebuffed by the progressive press', since other theatre critics in Moscow protested such treatment of Aldridge, offered him accolades, and recorded enthusiastic audience reception.[30] Critic B.N. Almazov explained that Aldridge was 'a psychological actor' who excelled in 'portraying subtle movements of the soul in a character he plays', therefore 'only connoisseurs of art and of Shakespeare's plays can pass judgement about it'.[31] In this way Almazov highlighted the ignorance of Aldridge's critics, and stated that Aldridge 'concentrates all your attention only on the inner meanings of his speech'.[32] This Almazov attributed to Aldridge's 'highly truthful understanding of art, a deep knowledge of the human heart, and an ability to feel the subtlest spiritual movements indicated by Shakespeare and to bring them to life before the Public'.[33]

While Aldridge performed in English – it was the English of Shakespeare – and accordingly for audiences and reviewers in Russia, cultural capital associated adhered to Aldridge, for embodying Shakespeare's great characters. So, in Russia, it was his powerful artistic ability that led audiences to understand him, and therefore Shakespeare's characters, through the emotional and psychological dimensions he portrayed through his gestures and voice. Similarly, another review from Odessa highlighted Aldridge's non-verbal expressiveness, recounting that during a performance of *Othello*, as the tragic hero reacted to the discovery of Desdemona's innocence, the audience 'shrieked with horror', unable to 'bear it anymore', and in the closing scene, 'exploded with thunderous applause'.[34]

This was the case with other roles as well, and often responses to Aldridge's race featured in positive reviews. In Odessa, Ukraine, Aldridge's performance of *The Merchant of Venice* was reviewed in a Jewish journal, which noted that he 'amplified the expression of fatherly tenderness significantly', and also emphasised that 'such a Jew as Shylock could not so easily agree to change his religion', so the horror at the insistence he should do so was made manifest in 'facial expressions and in gestures' and 'a long mute scene that is in itself the height of the mimic art'.[35]

Indeed, across theatres of the Russian Empire, Aldridge had been praised as a performer of Shakespearean characters and had become noted as a model for other actors to follow. Although many did not understand Shakespeare's English, Aldridge's emotive expressiveness on stage clearly resonated palpably with audiences.[36] Thus, as Sergei Durylin noted, 'the Russian actors awaited such a one in order to learn how to master their art, and the Russian spectators in order to delve into the mighty feelings and thoughts of Shakespeare'.[37] Moreover, as Bernth Lindfors remarked of the enthusiastic reception Aldridge received by Russian critics and audiences: 'Aldridge's actions spoke as loudly as Shakespeare's words.'[38]

## Robeson and Russia

Three quarters of a century after Aldridge's highly lauded performances in Russia, Paul Robeson, another Black American performer, singer, and later Shakespearean actor, would find himself and his talent welcomed and celebrated in Soviet Russia. Unlike Aldridge, however, Robeson's facility for, and embrace of, the Russian language figured deeply in his attraction to Russia and his reception there. As with Aldridge, the time and political landscape of Robeson's travels to the then USSR were significant.

Paul and his wife, Eslanda Cardozo Goode Robeson, were not alone in being drawn to the Soviet Union. Jamaican-born poet Claude McKay was one of the first Black artists in this period to go there. McKay arrived in 1922, and was followed over the next few decades by numerous Black American writers, artists, and activists. Following the Bolshevik Russian Revolution in 1917, an interest in issues of race had been a feature in early Soviet culture as the Soviet Union enacted laws against racism and anti-Semitism. This impressed many Black Americans, particularly given the blatant discrimination they experienced in the US. By the early 1930s Black American artists saw in the Soviet Union possibilities for creative work and social acceptance that would be unencumbered by the blatant racism that restricted their lives and expressions of their art in the United States.

Cultural performances and narratives about race were of great interest in the new Soviet republic. In 1932, Langston Hughes and a group of twenty-one young Black Americans, led by Black activist Louise Thompson, came to Russia to participate in a film titled *Black and White*, that would depict racism and resistance in the United States. The film was never made, but progressive and socially conscious directors like Sergei Eisenstein, Vsevolod Pudovkin, and Dziga Vertov, in the then nascent Soviet film industry, appeared to present and offer opportunities for Black American performers that far exceeded those afforded them in the US at the time.[39]

Two years later, in 1934, singer and actor Paul Robeson came to Moscow at the invitation of Sergei Eisenstein, the film director behind such revolutionary classics as *Battleship Potemkin*, *Strike*, and *October*. Eisenstein had been inspired by the American writer John Vandercook's novel *Black Majesty*, about the King of Haiti Henri Christophe, and Eisenstein had invited Robeson to potentially star in a film about the Haitian Revolution.[40]

But, even before this invitation, like numerous other progressive Black American artists, Robeson had already been intrigued by the prospects of the Soviet Union. Moreover, having been studying Russian, he felt an affinity for the Russian language, Russian music, and the Russian people. As the *New York World-Telegram* reported on 30 August 1933, Paul Robeson 'may soon be singing to his audiences in Russian', and 'Hebrew', since Robeson was quoted as saying, 'I know the wail of the Hebrew and I feel the plaint of the Russian. I understand both [...] and I feel that both have much in common with the traditions of my own race.'[41]

Furthermore, Robeson's wife Eslanda had additional reasons to be interested in Russia. Her mother, who traced her descent in part from the Sephardic Jewish Cardozo family, had been fascinated with Russian culture since childhood and communicated her interest to Essie and her two brothers, both of whom moved to Russia. Essie's brother, John Goode, had arrived in Russia the spring before the Robesons' first visit, and several days before their arrival Essie's brother, Frank Goode, also came to Russia, where he eventually settled in the town of Gorky, married a Russian woman, and became a Russian citizen.

Robeson's attitudes towards the Soviet Union, and the prospect of a society free of the racism he experienced in the United States, were reinforced by his friendship with his close friend from his first days in Harlem, Black activist and lawyer Bill Patterson, who was residing in Russia at that time and later would become a leading figure in the US Communist Party.[42] In addition, Robeson met early on with Eisenstein's assistant, Herbert Marshall, an expatriate British director then working in Russia. Marshall, who, like Patterson was also fluent in Russian, greeted the Robesons when they first arrived in Russia, just before Christmas in 1934, and Marshall provided Robeson with 'an entrée into Russian culture'.[43] Upon his arrival, Robeson was received ecstatically by the Soviet theatrical establishment, and invited to sing an aria onstage from Mussorgsky's opera *Boris Godunov*. Marshall found that Robeson's songs in concert 'became more international than any other singers in history'.[44] This endeared Russian audiences to Robeson. Despite Soviet policies promoting atheism, he was asked to sing negro spirituals over the radio and at government parties as this music represented the folk art of a people oppressed by a particularly vicious kind of capitalism.

In 1933, even before the Robesons came to the Soviet Union, Paul's moving rendition of the spiritual 'Sometimes I Feel Like a Motherless Child', became emblematic for Russians of Black Americans' attitudes about the racism in the United States. The Soviets powerfully deployed the image of Black Americans abandoned by their 'mother' country by placing Robeson's recording of the song 'over an animated short film about racism and labour exploitation in the American sugar industry'.[45] The film used stereotypical primitivist images in animated depictions of oppressed Black workers in the capitalist US. Jennifer Wilson has asserted that, 'Soviet writers and illustrators too often perpetuated a lot of the harmful stereotypes ... that they were ostensibly trying to dismantle'.[46] However, Robeson's plaintive rendering of the song served to reinforce the message that in a socialist system like the Soviet Union, Black workers would have a welcome home. Robeson and other Black Americans championed internationalism and the spread of proletarian consciousness to nations who had been oppressed by capitalism and colonialism and saw in the Soviet Union possibilities for an embrace of other egalitarian possibilities denied Black people in the US.

As was the case a century earlier, when Aldridge was considered by some to embody the cause of the serfs in Imperial Russian, the presence of another captivating Black American performer was illustrative to many of the revolutionary impulses seen to be allied with now-Soviet Russia. Robeson's own political leanings, as a socialist, as well as a Black artist, no doubt influenced his attraction towards the Soviet Union, and helped cement the reception he received there. In an interview with Robeson by Vern Smith for the *Daily Worker*, Smith noted the 'tone and feeling of the workers and artists of the Soviet Union towards this visiting Negro singer, son of a slave in the United States – to show the wholehearted appreciation of these Russian sons of serfs who are now freed by their own efforts'.[47] And increasingly at this time, Robeson saw the connections between capitalism, colonisation, and racism in global contexts and brought this awareness to his trips to the Soviet Union.

What attracted Essie and Paul Robeson to the Soviet Union was the institutionalised rejection of racism. Together and separately, the Robesons made several other trips to Russia, over the next three decades, and for over a year they elected to educate their son, Paul Jr, in Moscow, where they felt he would not be exposed to the racist taunts he had encountered in schools in the Jim Crow era United States. Robeson returned to the Soviet Union in 1935 and again for a concert tour in 1937. During his 1937 tour, Robeson discussed the revolutionary impact of the Soviet constitution for Black people, noting 'Everywhere else, outside of this Soviet world, black men are an oppressed and inhumanely exploited people.'[48] But in the Soviet Union, Article 123 of Chapter X of the Soviet Constitution stated: 'The equality of the right of citizens of the USSR, irrespective of their nationality or race, in all fields of economic, state, cultural, social and political life is an irrevocable law.'[49] This made a profound impression on both of the Robesons, and for a time they considered moving there, as both of Essie's brothers had.

Unlike Aldridge, Robeson was fluent in Russian, which endeared him to audiences in the Soviet Union. Of the Russian language, Robeson conjectured, 'I would probably be able to do plays better in Russian than in modern English because I find the language richer, warmer, more fully expressive, more colourful than modern English.' Moreover, Robeson went further to assert that 'the Russian language today is comparable to Shakespearean English – young, forceful and rich'.[50] For Robeson, that connection was also musical as he claimed to find 'the same note of melancholy, touched with mysticism' in the songs of the Russian serfs and 'Negro spirituals'.[51] As Gerald Horne asserted, 'for Robeson, language was not just a tool of communication, but also a way to forge a deeper connection with social and political consequence'.[52]

For Aldridge, the deployment of the different languages performed by his local casts – and the cultural identities they represented and reinforced for specific local audiences – accounted for much of his reception in eastern Europe and throughout the Russian Empire. But since multilingual Robeson chose to speak and sing in the languages of the people in his audience, Robeson's own facility with languages coupled with his interest in the universality of musical forms and the common etymologies of different linguistic systems served for him as evidence of a universal human connection between peoples that he advocated politically as well as culturally. As he asserted in a speech to the Central Conference of American Rabbis, on 25 November 1945, '[t]he Soviet Union stands today as a concrete demonstration that it is possible to abolish completely, and in a very short time, long established habits of discrimination and oppression based upon differences of race, creed, color, and nationality'.[53]

While Robeson's linguistic abilities endeared him to most audiences in the Soviet Union, that facility could also be deployed as a political and social tool. 1949 was the 150th Anniversary of Pushkin's birth, and an important occasion in the Soviet Union. Robeson concluded his 14 June 1949 concert in Moscow's Tchaikovsky Hall with a controversial performance of the 'Song of the Warsaw Ghetto Uprising'/*Zog Nit Keynmol*, which he sang in the original Yiddish. The song celebrated and memorialised the courage of those Jews targeted by the Nazis that Russia had fought so valiantly against during the Second World War. But by 1949 the position of Jews in the Soviet Union was extremely vulnerable, and so Robeson's choice to introduce the song in Russian and sing it in Yiddish was seen by many as a political statement.

Robeson may have concluded his concert in this way as an implicit protest against Stalinist anti-Semitism, which had erupted violently in 1948 and had led to the murders of close friends of Robeson, including actor/artistic director of the Moscow State Jewish Theatre Solomon Mikhoels, whom Robeson had first met along with poet Itzik Feffer in America in 1943 as members of the Soviet Jewish Anti-Fascist Committee. According to Martin Duberman and Christopher Silsby, prior to the Moscow concert, Robeson met with Feffer, and learned from him of the atrocities against Jewish citizens taking place in the Soviet Union, and the threat on Feffer's life as well.[54]

While Robeson's son, Paul Jr, later speculated that his father may have been largely silent on this matter because he was concerned that any overt interference may have caused more damage to his Jewish friends in the Soviet Union, both Robeson's decision to conclude his concert with *Zog Nit Keynmol*, a song celebrating the heroism of the oppressed Jewish people, and to sing that song in the original Yiddish was

Figure 7.2 Paul Robeson in front of Pushkin, 1949

a powerful choice.⁵⁵ Moreover, Robeson first recited the song lyrics in Russian, so that the Moscow audience would understand these words of resistance:

> Never say that you have reached the very end,
> When leaden skies a bitter future may portend;
> For sure the hour for which we yearn will yet arrive,
> And our marching steps will thunder: we survive!

Listening to a recording of this concert, Tayo Aluko has described the 'unmistakable anger' in Robeson's voice when singing, in Yiddish, the 'Warsaw Ghetto Uprising' song. Aluko speculated that the anger apparent in Robeson's voice in the recording 'was probably anger at the Soviet purges against his Jewish friends – and thousands of others; at his country for the historic and continuing maltreatment of Blacks, and at both Moscow and Washington for squandering the gains made when Nazi Germany was defeated – crucially, with Soviet help'.[56]

Perhaps Robeson's feelings on this occasion resembled what an anonymous Russian critic said a century earlier of Aldridge's Russian performances as Othello and Shylock – characters tragically destroyed by white prejudice. At the time the Russian critic claimed Aldridge, 'deeply feels the insults being inflicted on colored people by whites in the New World. In Shylock he sees not just a Jew, but a human being afflicted by the hatred of his fellow human beings and expresses this feeling with amazing truth and passion.'[57]

Similarly, Lois Potter has asserted that, like Aldridge in his performances as Shylock, Robeson 'came to identify the cause of European Jews and the proletariat with that of Black Americans, and felt an immediate love for Russia, where his excellent knowledge of the language added to his popularity'.[58]

Language choices in performance or song affected the reception of both of these Black American artists, as we have seen. At times both Aldridge and Robeson were subject to severe travel restrictions when their statements, performances, and very presence appeared to threaten the authoritarian impulses of the various empires or nation states through which they travelled, or, in Robeson's case, of which he was a citizen. For both, the use of language – their own, or that of their cast – signalled an affiliation with either imperial forces or with other oppressed peoples such as serfs, Jews, or colonised Ukrainians and Hungarians, as well as with revolutionary sympathisers who saw analogies between the oppression of enslaved Black Americans and the plight of landless serfs.

As we noted above, Aldridge faced restraints when his company was performing in a national language (Hungarian, Polish, Ukrainian) as opposed to the imperial language. He was challenged over the lack of a permit stamp in his passport in Austria-Hungary and was barred from performing in St Petersburg. Nevertheless, in eastern Europe and the Russian Empire, Aldridge enjoyed a lifelong theatre career that never could have been possible in the United States.[59] In 1867, Aldridge died on tour, in Lodz, Poland (then part of the Russian Empire) where he was buried in such a style that one report stated, 'we cannot remember ever having seen a funeral procession that matched this one in grandness'.[60]

For Robeson, travel constraints by the US government were far more extreme, as the United States blacklisted him and cancelled his passport from 1950–58. It was during this time that he published a fifteen-page pamphlet entitled 'The Negro People and the Soviet Union'.[61] Although

Robeson's passport was eventually restored, he paid a heavy price in the US for his lifelong fight against fascism, his equation of Nazism with white supremacy in America, and his consistent commitment to socialist principles. In public, and even when called before the United States House of Un-American Activities Committee during the Red Scare, Robeson chose to defend and not to criticise the Soviet Union, particularly when US audiences might interpret such critique as further grounds for an anti-socialist policy that would favour right-wing capitalist interests in the US over those of a country that had constitutionally guaranteed equality to people of all races.[62] Gerald Horne has contended that 'part of what made Robeson a revolutionary was his rejection of narrow nationalism and his uplifting of a radical internationalism ... in pursuit of racial equality domestically and the socialist community globally that would guarantee it'.[63] In his memoir, *Here I Stand*, Robeson quoted Karl Marx, who wrote: 'Labour in a white skin can never be free while labour in a black skin is branded.'[64]

Robeson embodied these convictions and demonstrated them publicly with speeches as well as his musical performances. In both contexts, Robeson was performing respect for cultures through speaking or singing these sentiments in their languages, embodying and vocalising through public address and performance his creative potential to build bridges and break down barriers.

## Connections: Aldridge and Robeson

Interestingly, there were several personal and ideological connections and contrasts between Aldridge and Robeson in Russia / the Soviet Union. Aldridge was generally not well known in the US, either in his lifetime or after his death in 1867, while Robeson was an international celebrity. Robeson would have most likely first heard about Aldridge in London in 1925 where the Robesons were living and Paul was performing in *Emperor Jones*. Aldridge's daughter, Amanda Ira Aldridge, was a singing teacher in London at the time, and she and the Robesons became friends. Amanda Aldridge passed on to Robeson the earrings that her father wore when he performed Othello, in the hope that Robeson would someday wear them 'when he, too, played the role'.[65] These were most certainly the earrings Aldridge wore during the Russian performances we have discussed here. Although Robeson never played the part in the Soviet Union, he did later perform it in London and New York; and like Aldridge before him, Othello became a signature role. For both men, in both times and places, the remarkable phenomenon of a Black man playing this role (rather than a white actor in blackface) with a white actress as Desdemona, challenged white racist responses.

When the Robesons first went to Russia, in 1934, Paul's friendship with British director Herbert Marshall, then working in Russia, provided a further connection between Aldridge and Robeson. 1934 was the year that the Union of Soviet Writers was formed, and Russian director and theatre historian Sergei Durylin was an early member. In that same year Durylin delivered a lecture at Moscow State University on 'Ira Aldridge, A Great Negro Tragedian', and wrote the first full-scale biography in Russian in 1940. Marshall translated Durylin's biography of Aldridge and Marshall later co-authored another biography of Aldridge in English. When Marshall and Mildred Stock's, *Ira Aldridge: The Negro Tragedian*, was published in Ukraine, Robeson wrote a preface, stating that Aldridge brought to life, for Russians, 'the great Shakespearean characters'.[66] But, as Robeson wrote, 'Aldridge brought more than Shakespeare to the people' since 'he understood and was especially sensitive to the serfdom of Tsarist society, and the oppression of national minorities.'[67] Clearly, for both Robeson and Marshall, Aldridge was an actor who had made a deep impact on Russia, and on each of them. In 1958, Marshall suggested Robeson consider narrating a Russian film about Aldridge, to be written by Marshall. That film was never made, but as Lois Potter has asserted, 'Aldridge was not only a role model, but also a contributing factor in the passionate love of Russia that was to be so significant in Robeson's life.'[68]

The presence and positive reception of these two remarkable Black artists in both Tsarist Russia and its neighbours for Aldridge, and later, in the Soviet Union, for Robeson, were seminal in both performers' careers. Their presence also arguably had potentially propagandist value to various classes at various times in Russia, while also affording them the acceptance and acknowledgement denied to them in the country of their birth. As Black American artists in Russia, Ira Aldridge and Paul Robeson are pivotal figures for discussions of attitudes globally that continue to inform contemporary critical approaches to race and representation, and the ways performance can be a tool of social change, and art can be a medium through which common humanity can be recognised and expressed.

## Notes

1 Philip S. Foner (ed.), *Paul Robeson Speaks* (Secaucus, NJ: Citadel Press, 1978), 115.
2 V. Rogov, 'Othello in the American Theatre', *Literatura I Iskustvo*, 2 September 1944, translation in Margaret Webster papers, Library of Congress, cited in

Lindsey R. Swindall, *The Politics of Paul Robeson's Othello* (Jackson, MS: University of Mississippi Press, 2011), 106.
3 Benedict Anderson, *Imagined Communities: Reflections on the Origin and Spread of Nationalism* (London: Verso, 1983), 55.
4 Ludwig Sittenfeld cited in Krzysztof Sawala, '"Othello's Occupation's Gone!" The African Roscius in Poland, 1853–67' in Bernth Lindfors (ed.), *Ira Aldridge: The African Roscius* (Rochester, NY: University of Rochester Press, 2007), 243–266, at 250.
5 Cited in Bernth Lindfors, *Ira Aldridge: Performing Shakespeare in Europe, 1852–1855* (Rochester, NY: University of Rochester Press, 2013), 86.
6 Cited in Bernth Lindfors, *Ira Aldridge: The Last Years, 1855–1867* (Rochester, NY: University of Rochester Press, 2015), 73.
7 Cited in Lindfors, *Ira Aldridge: Performing Shakespeare in Europe*, 115.
8 Cited in *ibid.*, 115.
9 A story frequently reprinted at this time asserted that Aldridge 'interceded actively' in the emancipation for enslaved African Americans, having paid for the manumission of a recaptured family, who were to be sold, separately, back into enslavement. Though this story has not been corroborated, it circulated widely in towns and cities where Aldridge performed. *Theater-Vereins-Zeitung*, 14 January 1854, cited in Lindfors, *Ira Aldridge: Performing Shakespeare in Europe*, 171.
10 The police report in full, states 'I have had my eye on him constantly, but although I was offered no occasion to intervene directly against him it is quite possible that in the case of his return to London he will undertake verbal commissions for Kossuth, or otherwise mediate a connection with him.' In Lindfors, *Ira Aldridge: Performing Shakespeare in Europe*, 161.
11 Of Aldridge in *Othello* in Riga (now Latvia), one reviewer reported that 'though his language is foreign', the audience was 'nonetheless carried away to the storms of admiration'. W.A.G., 'Aldridge in Riga', *Rigasche Zeitung*, 9 October 1858. Aldridge's letter to the *Athenaeum* recorded that he had been given a 'magnificent present' of silver from the Ural mountains, by the Governor General of the east Provinces. Cited in Lindfors, *Ira Aldridge: The Last Years*, 102, 104, 128.
12 Alexander Pushkin, *Eugene Onegin: A Novel in Verse*, trans. James E. Falen (Oxford: Oxford World Classics, 1990), 26.
13 Krystyna Kujawinska Courtney, 'Ira Aldridge, Shakespeare and Color-Conscious Performances in Nineteenth-Century Europe' in Ayanna Thompson (ed.), *Colorblind Shakespeare: New Perspectives on Race and Performance* (Abingdon: Routledge, 2006), 103–124, at 108.
14 The national identity of Pushkin's great-grandfather has been subjected to repeated revision, but evidence indicates that Ibrahim Gannibel was originally from Logon (now Cameroon) and was purchased at a slave auction by one of Tsar Peter's ambassadors. In T.J. Binyon, *Pushkin* (New York: Alfred A. Knopf, 2002), 4.
15 In the Russian title of Pushkin's unfinished novel, *Arap Petra Velikogo*, Pushkin used the word 'Arap' or Arab, translated as 'Moor'. Translations frequently

use the term 'Blackamoor'. Citations in this article are taken from Alexander Pushkin, 'The Blackamoor of Peter the Great' [1828], *Complete Works of Alexander Pushkin*, trans. Paul Debreczeny (Stanford, CA: Stanford University Press, 1983), 11–40, at 13.

16 Henry Louis Gates, 'Foreword' in Catharine Theimer Nepomnyashchy, Nicole Svobodny and Ludmilla A. Trigos (eds), *Under the Sky of My Africa: Alexander Pushkin and Blackness* (Evanston, IL: Northwestern University Press, 2006), xi–xiv, at xi.

17 Gates, 'Foreword', xi.

18 *Ibid.*, xii.

19 Shevchenko was also an acclaimed artist who produced several portraits of Aldridge in St Petersburg. One is now at Howard University.

20 Adriana Helbig, *Hip Hop Ukraine: Music, Race, and African Migration* (Bloomington, IN: University of Indiana Press, 2014), 38.

21 *Ibid.*, 38.

22 Sergei N. Durylin, *Ira Aldridge*, trans. Alexei Lalo, ed. Bernth Lindfors (Trenton, NJ: Africa World Press, 2014), 39.

23 A.A. Alekseev, *Vospominaniya Aktyora A.A. Alekseev* (Moscow: Artist, 1894), 136–139, cited in Durylin, *Ira Aldridge*, 155.

24 *Kievski Telegraf*, 91 (16 September 1861), cited in Lindfors, *Ira Aldridge: The Last Years*, 164.

25 *Lemberger Zeitung* (15 May 1861) cited in Lindfors, *Ira Aldridge: The Last Years*, 161.

26 K.I. Zvantsov, 'Ira Aldridge: *Othello*', *Teatralny i Muzikalny Vestnik*, 28 November/ 10 December 1858, 351, cited in Lindfors, *Ira Aldridge: The Last Years*, 169.

27 Aleksandr Nikitenko, *The Diary of a Russian Censor*, ed. Helen Saltz Jacobson (Amherst, MA: University of Massachusetts Press, 1975), 180.

28 Report from Adlerberg to the Minister of Internal Affairs, 19 May 1868, in which he reproduces his report of 1858. Cited in Murray Frame, '"Freedom of the Theatres": The Abolition of the Russian Imperial Theatre Monopoly', *Slavonic and East European Review*, 83:2 (2005), 254–289, at 266.

29 N.S. Sokhanskaya (pen name Kokhanovskaya), cited in Durylin, *Ira Aldridge*, 140–141.

30 Durylin, *Ira Aldridge*, 143.

31 B.N. Almazov, 'Aldridge on the Moscow Stage', 40:12, cited in Durylin, *Ira Aldridge*, 121.

32 Errol Hill, *Shakespeare in Sable: A History of Black Shakespearean Actors* (Amherst, MA: University of Massachusetts Press, 1984), 20.

33 *Ibid.*, 20.

34 De-Ribas, *Staraya Odessa*, 93–94, cited in Lindfors, *Ira Aldridge: The Last Years*, 164.

35 *Zion*, 21 (14 November 1861), 336, cited in Lindfors, *Ira Aldridge: The Last Years*, 166. In the nineteenth century, Ukraine was part of a region of the Russian Empire included in the Pale Settlement, where Jewish communities were confined by prejudiced court regulation.

36 Lindfors cites an unpublished account by actor P.M. Nadimov-Shamsjenko of Odessa, that Aldridge would use specific gestures to cue in his supporting cast so 'there would be no pause and no interruption'; Lindfors, *Ira Aldridge: The Last Years*, 167. In a letter to his first wife, from Stockholm during his 1857 European tour, Aldridge also stated confidently that any language barrier is 'easily got over'. Cited in Herbert Marshall and Mildred Stock, *Ira Aldridge: The Negro Tragedian* (London: Rockliff, 1958), 209.

37 Marshall and Stock, *Ira Aldridge*, 223. Although attributed to Durylin, this quotation is uncited.

38 Bernth Lindfors, 'Mislike Me Not For My Complexion: Ira Aldridge in Whiteface' in Bernth Lindfors, *Ira Aldridge: The African Roscius* (Rochester, NY: University of Rochester Press, 2007), 180–190, at 188.

39 Evelyn Louise Crawford and MaryLouise Patterson (eds), *Letters from Langston: From the Harlem Renaissance to the Red Scare and Beyond* (Berkeley, CA: University of California Press, 2016).

40 See Charles Forsdick and Christian Høgsbjerg, 'Sergei Eisenstein and the Haitian Revolution: "The Confrontation Between Black and White Explodes Into Red"', *History Workshop Journal*, 78 (2014), 157–185, which details the full story of this episode.

41 'Robeson Spurns Music He "Doesn't Understand"', *New York World-Telegram*, 30 August 1933. In this article he compared the music and languages of Hebrew, Russian, and Chinese to the European languages of French, German, and Italian which he said had 'nothing in common with the history of my slave ancestors'.

42 Crawford and Patterson, *Letters from Langston*.

43 Jonathan Karp, 'Performing Black-Jewish Symbiosis: The "Hassidic Chant" of Paul Robeson', *American Jewish History*, 91:1 (2003), 53–81, at 67.

44 Cited in Gerald Horne, *Paul Robeson: The Artist as Revolutionary* (London: Pluto Press, 2016), 63.

45 'Animated Soviet Propaganda S01: American Imperialist Black and White, 1933, directed by I. Ivanov-Vano and L. Amalrik. Mezrabpomfilm', www.youtube.com/watch?v=ZmCpKYk_ARM (accessed 26 July 2021). Jennifer Wilson, 'When the Harlem Renaissance went to Communist Moscow', *New York Times*, 21 August 2017, www.nytimes.com/2017/08/21/opinion/when-the-harlem-renaissance-went-to-communist-moscow.html (accessed 3 August 2021).

46 Wilson, 'When the Harlem Renaissance went to Communist Moscow'.

47 '"I am at home," Says Robeson at Reception in Soviet Union', *Daily Worker*, 15 January 1935, in Foner, *Paul Robeson Speaks*, 94.

48 Paul Robeson, 'When I Sing', broadcast *Sunday Worker*, Moscow, 7 February 1937, in Foner, *Paul Robeson Speaks*, 116.

49 Robeson, 'When I Sing', 116.

50 Horne, *Paul Robeson*, 54.

51 Karp, 'Performing Black-Jewish Symbiosis', 69.

52 Horne, *Paul Robeson*, 9.

53 Karp, 'Performing Black-Jewish Symbiosis', 63. This remark suggests that Robeson was unaware of the anti-Semitism in the Soviet Union at the time.
54 Martin Duberman, *Paul Robeson* (New York: Knopf: 1988), 353. Christopher Silsby, 'Spirituals, Serfs, and Soviets: Paul Robeson and International Race Policy in the Soviet Union at the Start of the Cold War' in Christopher Balme and Berenika Szymanski-Düll (eds), *Theatre, Globalisation and the Cold War* (London: Palgrave Macmillan, 2017), 45–57.
55 There has been much debate over Robeson's intention and the degree to which he may have been aware of the plight of Jews and dissidents at that time under the Stalin regime. See Duberman, *Paul Robeson*, 353–354; Andrew Stewart, 'Robeson's Message from the Grave', *Independent*, 22 December 1997, www.independent.co.uk/life-style/robesons-message-from-the-grave-1290185.html (accessed 26 July 2021).
56 Tayo Aluko speaking on 'Zog Nit Keynol' as part of his programme, *Paul Robeson in Five Songs*, BBC Radio 3, 2 April 2020. English translation of 'Zog Nit Keynol' from Aluko's broadcast. See www.bbc.co.uk/programmes/m000gv2w (accessed 3 August 2021).
57 Anon., 'Phelka', 259:1089, cited in Durylin, *Ira Aldridge*, 72.
58 Lois Potter, *Othello* (Manchester: Manchester University Press, 2002), 122.
59 At the time of Aldridge's death, he had received invitations to perform in Boston and New York, though no plans had been made. In summer 1858, before his first European tour, Aldridge had turned down a request from the Academy of Music in New York. See Lindfors, *Ira Aldridge: The Last Years*, 95.
60 *Ibid.*, 259.
61 Horne, *Paul Robeson*, 125.
62 Tom Perucci, 'The Red Mask of Sanity, Paul Robeson, HUAC and the Sound of Cold War Performance', *TDR/The Drama Review*, 53:4 (2009), 18–48.
63 Horne, *Paul Robeson*, 10.
64 Paul Robeson, *Here I Stand* (Boston, MA: Beacon Press, 1958), 82. The famous quote from Marx can be found in *Capital*, vol. 1, chapter 10.
65 Duberman, *Paul Robeson*, 91.
66 Herbert Marshall (ed.), *Bulletin for the Center for Soviet and East European Studies*, 18 (1976), n.p., held in Morris Library Special Collections Research Center.
67 Paul Robeson, draft (unpublished) 'Preface for Ira Aldridge for Shevchenko Anniversary', for Herbert Marshall (1963), Paul Robeson Collection, Moreland-Spingarn Research Centre, Howard University, cited in Swindall, *The Politics of Paul Robeson's Othello*, 106.
68 Potter, *Othello*, 107.

# III

Politics and poetics

# 8

# Raya Dunayevskaya: the embodiment of the Red/Black Atlantic in theory and practice

*Chris Gilligan and Nigel Niles[1]*

Raya Dunayevskaya (1910–87) was a profound thinker, who worked in an intellectual tradition, Marxism, that has been dominated by men. She was one of the most important thinkers of the twentieth century, and one of the most neglected. She deserves to be better known, not *because* she was a woman (although the role of women in the development of Marxism is often underappreciated), but because the Hegelian-Marxism (Marxist-Humanism) that she recovered in the 1940s, and developed in the following decades, is a vital resource for our own age of mounting social contradictions.

Dunayevskaya was an avowed Red. In her teenage years she was a member of the youth wing of the Workers (Communist) Party. When the party became Stalinised, she was expelled. She went on to work with the (Transatlantic Trotskyist) left opposition. At the beginning of the Second World War she was part of the minority who split from the (Trotskyist) Socialist Workers Party (SWP) in protest at its defence of the Soviet Union. After the war she rejected the vanguardist conception of the revolutionary party and was central to establishing the News and Letters Committees (NALC) as an organisation based in the philosophy of Marxist-Humanism.

Dunayevskaya was a Red, but the Black struggle was always integral to her conception of Marxism. From her early years, when she was active in radical Black politics in Chicago, until her dying days, she insisted on the integrality of the Red and Black struggles. For her, the Red and Black struggles were not separate struggles, but were different moments in the same struggle: the struggle to overthrow capitalism and establish a new society, on fully human grounds.

Dunayevskaya was also a transatlantic figure. She was born in Tsarist Russia but based in the USA throughout her adult life. Though based in the USA, she engaged in correspondence with revolutionaries in Africa and Europe (as well as Asia and Latin America), and visited both continents to engage with revolutionaries there.

Throughout her life she was critical of leftists who neglected, or downplayed, the Black dimension of the struggle for a new society. She was also, however, critical of radical Black figures who relegated, or downplayed, the class dimension of the struggle for human freedom. Throughout her life she acknowledged her intellectual debts to leading theoreticians in both the Marxist and Black freedom movements. Her highest praise, however, was always for the masses. She argued that the masses' struggle for freedom, as both means and end, was an essential precondition for the creation of a new society. Intellectuals, she persistently argued, unless they were engaged in a process of mutual self-development with movements from below, always ended up frustrating movements for human freedom.

Despite her many achievements and her contemporary relevance, however, she is relatively unknown. For this reason, we have sought to both introduce her life and work, and outline some of her work on the Red/Black theme. Given the range and depth of her life's work, it is difficult to do justice to both, especially in the space of a relatively short chapter. In making choices about what to include and exclude, and what to emphasise, we have been guided by two things: this book's theme of the Red/Black Atlantic; and the two key turning points in Dunayevskaya's own thought and political 'career'. The Red/Black Atlantic theme has meant that we have said little or nothing about her important writings on Hegel and dialectics, on Marx's *Capital*, on women's liberation, on Stalinist Russia, on Mao and China, or on a whole host of other topics that she wrote about during her lifetime. We have only touched on these topics in so far as they illuminate her Red/Black theory and practice. The chapter is organised around two key moments in her own political development and provides (in the footnotes) a selective introduction to the online Raya Dunayevskaya archives.[2] The first section provides an introduction to her 'early' life, including the period when she worked with Trotsky. The second section outlines her break with Trotsky and her cofounding, with C.L.R. James, of the State-Capitalist Tendency. The third section outlines her philosophical breakthrough, on theory and practice, her subsequent break with James, and the founding of Marxist-Humanism. These Marxist-Humanist years of her life were when she produced her richest work, including on Black freedom movements. In this section we provide a flavour of this work by focusing specifically on two aspects of the Red/Black Atlantic in her theory and practice: her work on what she referred to as 'the American roots of Marxism', and her work on African liberation movements.

## The early years

Raya Dunayevskaya (birth name Rae Spiegel) was born on one side of the Atlantic and spent most of her adult life on the other side of the Atlantic.

She was born in 1910, into a Jewish family, in the Ukraine, which at that time was part of the Russian Empire. She was 7 years old when the Russian Revolutions, February and October, shook the world. She witnessed, firsthand, the turmoil and excitement of the revolutionary upheaval of society. She witnessed the immense power of human action, when the masses were gripped by the idea of freedom, and felt their own power to achieve this freedom. She also witnessed, first-hand, the brutal backlash against the masses striving for freedom, in the shape of the counter-revolutionary White Army. The Russian Revolution both emboldened the Jewish struggle for emancipation, and emboldened antisemitic pogroms against Jews. Caught up in this explosive mix of emancipation and repression, her family chose to flee – across the Atlantic, to the United States of America.

In 1922, aged just 12, Raya Dunayevskaya stepped off a boat in Chicago, with her mother and siblings. They came to join her father, who had arrived in Chicago a few years earlier.[3] Chicago, at that time, was a centre of radical Black politics. A few years earlier, in 1919, the city had been one of the many across the United States that had been convulsed by Black uprising against racial oppression. These uprisings gave birth to the 'New Negro' and turned Garveyism into a mass movement. In the same year, Lenin met with 'American Marxists [and] formulated the first Marxist thesis on the "Negro Question"'.[4]

From almost the moment she arrived in Chicago, Dunayevskaya plunged into the midst of the Black/Red struggle. As a high school senior, she was instrumental in organising a student strike against her school's segregationist policy.[5] In 1925, aged just 15, she attended the founding convention of the American Negro Labor Congress (ANLC), which has been described as 'the first national meeting of Negro workers ever convened in the Western world'.[6] She worked in the offices of the *Negro Champion*, the publication of the ANLC, and wrote book reviews for its pages, until it was moved to New York in 1928. She was also in correspondence with some of the leading African-American intellectuals of the New Negro movement.[7] In these same years, she was also a member of the Young Workers League, the youth section of the Workers (Communist) Party, and wrote for its publication the *Young Worker*.[8]

Dunayevskaya was expelled from the youth wing of the Workers Party in the late 1920s and spent the next decade working for Trotskyist organisations, including writing for the *New International* and the *Militant*. During this period, she maintained the transatlantic flow of ideas through her work with the *Russian Bulletin of the Opposition*.[9] And she continued to play a role in the Red/Black dimension in the USA. She was, for example, a member of the Washington Committee to Aid Agricultural Workers, that was established to support sharecroppers' struggles in the South. She has said that her work with the Committee 'opened the two-way road between the US and Africa for me, especially since Nnamdi Azikiwe was then in the US writing his *Renascent Africa*'.[10] After her application to go to Spain, to fight against the fascists, was refused, she went to Mexico and offered her services to the exiled Leon Trotsky. In Mexico she acted as Trotsky's Russian language secretary. She, for example, translated some of Trotsky's writings on the Spanish Civil War into English, for publication in the English language Trotskyist press.[11] She returned to the USA in early 1938 to attend the funeral of her father, and remained in the USA after that. In the USA she resumed her work with the Trotskyist movement, and maintained a correspondence with Trotsky.[12] In May 1939 she met C.L.R. James, the Trinidadian radical who became a Trotskyist while living in England in the early 1930s. At the time James was developing ideas about a separate organisation for Black radicals, as a way to involve them in the Trotskyist movement. Dunayevskaya found his arguments persuasive, partly because it chimed with her own experience. She wrote to Trotsky that 'even those Negroes, who are very close to us and have a fair smattering of Marxism ..., still can only be aroused to activity when you speak to them of the conditions of their own race and of definite program towards their liberation'.[13] By the end of 1939 she had handed on her work on the *Russian Bulletin* to other Trotskyists, and wrote to Trotsky that she was 'concentrating all of my [her] time for work in the Negro field'.[14]

## Dunayevskaya and the Johnson-Forest Tendency

Dunayevskaya has identified two fundamental turning points in the development of her own thinking. The first of these moments came at the outbreak of the Second World War. As Dunayevskaya herself described it:

> To my utter shock and disbelief, I realised that with the outbreak of the war, Trotsky, who had been fighting the Stalinist bureaucracy for over a decade, would now turn to the workers and ask them to defend Russia, because it was a 'workers' state though degenerate'. Here was this man who had helped make two great revolutions, the 1905 and the 1917 Revolutions, and I couldn't believe that I was saying to Trotsky, 'You are wrong and I am right'. Actually I lost my power of speech for two days.[15]

The realisation that 'the highest moment of her own development' was inherently flawed, was a profound shock to Dunayevskaya. A lesser person might have felt crushed by this realisation. Instead, as soon as she had recovered from her initial shock, Dunayevskaya set out to try to understand what it was about Trotsky's thinking that led him to call for a defence of the Soviet Union, even though he had been a resolute opponent of Stalin and Stalinism?

Her disagreement with Trotsky led her to formulate her theory of state-capitalism. She criticised Trotsky for his focus on the abolition of private property as key to understanding the nature of the Union of Soviet Socialist Republics (USSR). Against the idea that the USSR was a workers' state, although degenerate, she retorted that 'the ownership of the means of production by a state ... in no way resembles the Marxian concept of a workers' state, i.e. "the proletariat organised as the ruling class"'.[16] Dunayevskaya argued that although the form of property ownership in the USSR had changed, from private to state owned, the *relation of production* had not changed. In the USSR, just as everywhere else that capitalist relations of production dominated, the workers were both dominated by their (state or private) employers and alienated from their own labour. When Dunayevskaya and C.L.R. James discovered that they had, independently, arrived at a state-capitalist understanding of the USSR, they sought each other out and established the State-Capitalist Tendency, or Johnson-Forest Tendency (JFT), within the American Trotskyist movement.[17]

Dunayevskaya and James were later joined by Grace Lee (Boggs), a philosophy graduate, who was taking an interest in radical left politics. Over the course of a decade and a half the three of them enjoyed an incredibly creative collaboration. They sought to recover the Hegelian roots of Marxism. Dunayevskaya and Grace Lee, for example, translated some of the key sections of Marx's Economic and Philosophic Manuscripts of 1844 into English.[18] Dunayevskaya translated Lenin's notes on Hegel's *Science of Logic*.[19] And it was during this period that James wrote his study of Hegel, *Notes on Dialectics*.[20] They also further developed their state-capitalist theory. Dunayevskaya, for example, undertook an extensive study of empirical data on the economy of the USSR, and drew on her deep understanding of Marx's *Capital* to analyse this data.[21] They also developed a critique of the vanguard party, as a form of organisation.[22]

The JFT also engaged in significant debate and organisational activity around what was then referred to as the Negro Question. Dunayevskaya played a prominent role in this activity. In June 1944 she produced a twelve-page discussion document, 'Marxism and the Negro Problem', which placed the Black struggle in the USA in the context of Lenin and Trotsky's writings on the National Question.[23] During 1945 and 1946 Dunayevskaya entered into a polemical debate with Coolidge (Ernest Rice McKinney), the leading Black spokesperson for the Shachtmanite majority in the Trotskyist Workers Party (WP).[24] In this debate she defended Trotsky's writings on the Negro Question from attack, and reiterated the case for the WP giving the Black struggle an independent significance within the WP. She argued that white workers needed to see the Black struggle as integral to their own struggle, and that failure to do so weakened the workers' own struggle.

In 1951 the JFT made their final break with Trotskyism, and they went on to form their own organisation, the Correspondence Publishing Committees (CPC).

## Dunayevskaya and the founding of Marxist-Humanism

The second fundamental turning point in Dunayevskaya's intellectual development came after the formation of the CPC. The JFT had rejected vanguardism – the idea that the role of the party was to *lead* the masses to revolution and on to socialism – but they were still grappling with the question of the alternative to the party. They formulated the problem as the issue of the dialectics of the party.[25] The JFT had rejected vanguardism, but Dunayevskaya was not satisfied with its opposite: spontaneism – the idea that the masses would create a new society through their own (spontaneously developed) revolutionary ideas and actions. At the heart of the question of 'the dialectics of the party', as Dunayevskaya saw it, was the question of the relationship between theory and practice. She argued, drawing on Hegelian-Marxist dialectics, that the struggle to transcend capitalism required a transcendence of these opposites: spontaneism and vanguardism. In order to overcome the division between mental and manual labour, and establish fully human relations, there needed to be a *two-way* movement between theory and practice. Both vanguardism and spontaneism, she suggested, sundered this two-way movement.

During the rest of her life Dunayevskaya worked to develop and apply this insight. She rejected the vanguardist separation of theory and practice, as involving a division of labour between party (theory) and masses (practice). She argued that the turning of the Russian Revolution, from an emancipatory revolution to a totalitarian counter-revolution, showed the dangers of this division of labour. She argued that the process of overcoming the separation between mental and manual labour was something that had to come about as part of the process of *making* a revolution. It could not wait until *after* the revolution. She argued that the masses do articulate theory, through their actions. This form of theory she was to come to refer to as 'the movement from practice that is itself a form of theory'.[26] Spontaneists suffered from a different shortcoming. In rejecting any role for theoreticians, they denied the *two-way movement* between theory and practice. Dunayevskaya argued that the movement from practice that arises from the masses is an *essential* element in any successful overcoming of capitalism, but it was an *insufficient* element. The movement from practice had to be met by a movement from theory, in order for the *partial* nature of each movement to be overcome. When the masses were struggling for freedom, she argued, they reached for theory as a means to overcome their own, partial, experience of the world and a means to make conscious their own self-understanding of their struggle.

C.L.R. James did not endorse Dunayevskaya's conception of the relationship between theory and practice. He maintained a spontaneist orientation.[27] In 1955 Dunayevskaya, along with a significant number of members of the CPC, split from James and went on to form News and Letters Committees (NALC) on Marxist-Humanist grounds.

Dunayevskaya's conception of the relationship between theory and practice, and between the Red and Black, underpinned the workings of NALC from its inception. The integral nature of theory and practice, and the Red and Black, can be seen in the appointment of Charles Denby, a Black autoworker, as worker-editor of the NALC's monthly publication, *News & Letters*.[28] Denby continued to work in the car plant and undertook his role as editor, in close collaboration with Dunayevskaya, outside of his wage-labour hours. Her commitment to combining theory and practice in the Red/Black struggle can be seen in the Red/Black conference, organised by NALC at the end of the 1960s, to discuss some of the themes that Dunayevskaya was working on, for the book that became *Philosophy and Revolution*.[29] It can also be seen in her active engagement with the civil rights movement in the USA.[30]

The crucial role of Black struggles as part of the 'movement from practice that is itself a form of theory' was a recurring feature of Dunayevskaya's theory and practice. The Red/Black theme can be seen in her regular ('Two Worlds') column for *News & Letters* (1955–81)[31] and in her three major works: *Marxism and Freedom: From 1776 Until Today* (1958), *Philosophy and Revolution: From Hegel to Sartre and from Marx to Mao* (1973) and *Rosa Luxemburg, Women's Liberation and Marx's Philosophy of Revolution* (1981) (she sometimes referred to these books as her 'trilogy of revolution'). Her Red/Black writings covered a host of different themes, across the whole of her Marxist-Humanist period (1955–87). She wrote extensively on the relationship between 'race' and class.[32] She wrote about the interrelationship between women's liberation, Black liberation and the emancipation of the working-class.[33] She wrote about the significance of the Black liberation struggle in the United States as the leading edge of the struggle for human freedom in the USA.[34] She wrote about 'the two-way road from African to America and back, indeed the triangular – African–West Indian–Black American – development of ideas' (her conception of the Red/Black Atlantic).[35]

There isn't the space in this chapter to do justice to the full range and depth of Dunayevskaya's work on the Red/Black struggle for freedom in the period from the founding of Marxist-Humanism in 1955, to her death in 1987. In the remaining space we will give readers a taster of some of her activity and thinking through a brief outline of two elements of her practical and theoretical contribution to the *transatlantic* Red/Black struggle. Firstly, we will provide an elaboration of a section of *Marxism and Freedom*, where she examined Marx's contribution to the transatlantic Red/Black struggle. And, secondly, we will look at her engagement with the national liberation struggles in Africa in the early 1960s.

## The American roots of Marxism and the Red/Black Atlantic

One of the key decisions NALC made at their founding convention in 1955 was to commission Dunayevskaya to write *Marxism and Freedom: From 1776 Until Today*.[36] In *Marxism and Freedom* she aimed 'to re-establish Marxism in its original form, which Marx called "a thoroughgoing Naturalism, or Humanism"'.[37] The book provided the philosophical foundations of Marxist-Humanism. One of the fundamental points that she was at pains to establish, as the basis for a renewal of the humanist foundations of Marxism, was that Marx's Marxism was rooted in, and developed alongside of, the struggles of the masses to realise human freedom. She notes that Marx's transcending of the limitations of both materialism (Feuerbach) and idealism (Hegel) happened in the context of the ferment of 1840s Europe, struggles that found their fullest expression, and greatest defeat, in the revolutions of 1848. She also notes that the defeat of the revolutions led to a period of quiescence among the masses, and a period of 'academic' intellectual labour on the part of Marx.

By the end of the 1850s, however, revolts began to stir again. Black struggles in the USA, against slavery, were one of the stirrings that signalled a new period of freedom struggle. As Marx noted in a letter to Engels, written on 11 January 1860:

> In my opinion the biggest things that are happening in the world today are on the one hand the movement of the slaves in America started by the death of John Brown and, on the other, the movement of the serfs in Russia.[38]

Dunayevskaya noted that the struggles surrounding the Civil War in the USA led *both* to Marx becoming engaged once again in practical revolutionary activity *and* to his greatest period of creative intellectual work. On the activist front, Marx played a leading role in helping to found and run the International Working Men's Association (IWMA), the First International

(1864–74). In 1958, when *Marxism and Freedom* was published, Marx's role in the IWMA was already well known, including the fact that the IWMA aided the North in the Civil War.[39] Dunayevskaya, however, was the first to observe that 'under the impact of the Civil War, and the subsequent struggles for the eight-hour day, Marx completely reorganised the structure of his greatest theoretical work, CAPITAL'.[40] In doing so, she suggested that Marx's theory (in *Capital* and in his writings on the Civil War) and practice (in the IWMA) was an element in the Red/Black Atlantic.

Dunayevskaya argued that it was the *activity* of the masses that inspired Marx's reworking of *Capital*. 'As the proletariat began to move positively towards their own emancipation', she argued, 'they illuminated all the studies Marx had undertaken in the previous period, and gave new insights into the development of capitalist production.'[41] And she points out that Marx distanced himself from left intellectuals and activists, such as Ferdinand Lassalle, who dismissed the significance of the Civil War, and the 'self-styled American Marxists who evaded the whole issue of the Civil War by saying they were opposed to "all slavery, wage and chattel"'.[42] In opposition to these leftists, Marx argued that the emancipation of slaves in America was a necessary precondition for the emancipation of all workers in the USA. As Marx put it, in a widely cited passage from *Capital*:

> In the United States of North America, every independent movement of the workers was paralyzed so long as slavery disfigured a part of the Republic. Labor cannot emancipate itself in the white skin where in the black it is branded.[43]

As long as workers tolerated the enslavement of African Americans, Marx suggested, they were holding back their own emancipation. This link between the emancipation of slaves and the freedom of workers was not just recognised by Marx. It was recognised by the Lancashire mill workers and the Liverpool dock workers who, despite the great hardships they suffered as a result, refused to handle 'slave' cotton. As Dunayevskaya put it, it wasn't Marx 'who decided that the Civil War in the United States was a holy war of labor. It was the working class of England.'[44] These workers, through their actions, established a new transatlantic dimension to the Red/Black struggle.

The passage from Marx's *Capital*, about labour in white skin and black, is often cited in works on Marxism and racism. The next part of the passage, however, is rarely cited. Marx went on to say that:

> out of the death of slavery a new life at once arose. The first fruit of the Civil War was the eight hours' agitation, that ran with the seven league boots of the locomotive from the Atlantic to the Pacific.[45]

Dunayevskaya drew particular attention to the second part of the passage. This second part illustrates other dimensions of Red/Black struggle. The victory against slavery was an inspiration for workers in America, which immediately gave rise to a struggle to limit the working day to eight hours. This historical moment provides an illustration of what Dunayevskaya refers to as 'Black masses as vanguard' of the struggle for human emancipation in the USA.[46] In the USA, Dunayevskaya argued, the Black struggle has *led* the struggle for human emancipation. The Black struggle has inspired other struggles. This Black struggle, and the workers' struggle for emancipation, she argued, are not separate struggles, but different aspects of the *same* struggle – the struggle for *human* emancipation.

Dunayevskaya did not just point to parallels between the freedom struggles in the USA and the transatlantic class solidarity, on the one hand, and Marx's theorising on the other. She showed how the two are inextricable in Marx's greatest work, *Capital*. Dunayevskaya noted that during the 1850s Marx had been working on his *Critique of Political Economy*. Marx, however, was dissatisfied with it and he only allowed the first few chapters to be published. The *Critique*, Dunayevskaya suggested, was:

> an intellectual, that is, a remote work; a theoretical answer to an actual problem. Or, to put it differently, it was an *application* of dialectics to political economy, instead of the *creation* of the dialectic that would arise out of the workers' struggles themselves.[47]

This distinction, between an *application* of dialectics and the *creation* of the dialectic, is crucial to grasping what Dunayevskaya meant by the movement from practice to theory *that is itself a form of theory*.

Dunayevskaya is not saying that the *Critique* has no merit. She says that Marx, through an *application* of dialectics, subjected the whole of classical political economy to profound criticism. This criticism, however, was academic because Marx was adopting the 'ordinary procedure for an *intellectual* [which is] to study the history of other theories and to separate himself from them on *their* ground'.[48] Marx, in the *Critique*, did lay bare the inner logic of the most theoretically rigorous attempts to understand the inner workings of capitalist society (principally in the work of Smith and Ricardo). This critical analysis, however, was remote because it was dealing with the work of the classical thinkers on *their* ground, as theory.

In the 1860s Marx radically reworked the *Critique* to produce the work that we know as *Capital*. In 1863 he reorganised the structure of the work. Previously history and theory had been separated, 'with a historical explanation attached to each theoretical chapter'.[49] Now he moved the material on the history of theory and made this material – *Theories of Surplus Value* – appendices to the three volumes of *Capital*. Then, in 1866, a year before publication, he created an entirely new, and substantial (seventy pages), section on 'The Working Day' (chapter 10).

This reorganisation of the material, Dunayevskaya argued, was not simply a matter of editing or presentation. It was, more profoundly, a case of fusing a unity of theory and practice – of rooting an understanding of capitalism in the struggles of the working class. When Marx moved the material on the history of theory to the appendices, Dunayevskaya suggested, he was simultaneously shifting his focus from political economy (theory) to the laws that govern capitalist production *itself*. Capitalist production, however, is not something governed purely by objective 'economic' laws. The worker, the source of the capitalists' profit, is both an objective (a *labourer* who produces commodities), and subjective (a living *human being* who thinks their own thoughts), factor in capitalist production. Capital is a social relationship, not a mechanical process, and the worker, unlike the other factors of production (machinery and raw materials), has a mind of their own. They can think their own thoughts, they can imagine a world that is organised differently and they can assert their own interests. The slaves, in their struggle against slavery in the South, were showing that they thought their own thoughts and desired their own freedom. The American workers, in their struggle for an eight-hour day, were asserting their own interests by attempting to place a limit on their exploitation by capital. It is these struggles that *created* a new dialectic, a struggle between Capital and Labour. The slaves and wage-labourers in America did not need to be aware of, let alone understand, Marx's concept of surplus value, in order to know that the wealth of the capitalist was being extracted from their surplus labour (i.e. that part of the working day, beyond which the workers have created the value required to reproduce themselves as labourers). It took the workers' struggle for the eight-hour day, however, Dunayevskaya argued, to enable Marx to deepen his understanding of surplus value.

'The concept of the theory of surplus value', Dunayevskaya noted, 'includes the division of the working day into paid and unpaid labor. But that still leaves the exact analysis of the working day, for the most part, undetermined.'[50] The working day has *logical* limits, which can be determined. Workers need to eat and sleep and therefore cannot persistently work a twenty-four hour day without collapsing from exhaustion. The *actual* length of the working day, and the proportions which are made up of paid and unpaid labour, cannot be worked out though the application of logic to the problem. It is worked out through the class struggle, between capitalists and workers. It was the struggle of the workers in America that illuminated this insight for Marx and led to him including a whole chapter on the working day in *Capital*.

The workers' struggle for the eight-hour day was a movement from practice to *theory*, because this practical struggle helped to illuminate theory. It enabled Marx to gain a deeper understanding of the inner workings of capitalism. As Dunayevskaya puts it, 'the thinking of the theoretician is constantly filled with more and more content, filled by workers' struggles and workers' thoughts'.[51] The struggle of the workers is also a *form* of theory. The workers' activity was not mindless activity, it was *consciously* aimed at securing limits to the time that 'belonged' to the capitalist, and to expanding the time that 'belonged' to the worker. The workers' activity was a form of *theory* because, like theory 'proper', it attempted to grasp the objective reality underlying the surface appearance. It is a movement from practice *to* theory, because workers are also striving to *comprehend* the world that confronts them, and in doing so they are striving to overcome the division between mental and manual labour.

Dunayevskaya argued that her Marxist contemporaries, unlike Marx in his day, were not listening to theory that was coming from freedom struggles of their day. 'There is a crying need', she said, 'for a new unity of theory and practice which begins with where the working people are – *their* thoughts, *their* struggles, *their* aspirations ... Where the workers think their own thoughts, there must be the intellectual to absorb the new impulses. Outside of that there can be no serious theory.'[52] In 1958 she discerned a movement from practice to theory in 'the struggles the world over for freedom', including 'the actions of the Negro school children in Little Rock, Arkansas, to break down segregation, [and] the wildcats in Detroit for a different kind of labor than that under present-day Automation'.[53] In 1958, this movement from practice was not, she argued, being met by a movement from theory. Instead, she argued, the vanguardists were attempting to impose their already worked out theory on the masses, and the spontaneists were acting as cheerleaders for those in struggle. Both were guilty of abdicating their responsibility to develop the theory that was coming from the freedom struggles of the masses, so that this theory could play its necessary role in the process of liberation.

### African liberation and the transatlantic Red/Black struggle

A year after *Marxism and Freedom* was published, NALC published a pamphlet, written by Dunayevskaya, on national liberation struggles in the 'Third World'. In the pamphlet – *Nationalism, Communism, Marxist-Humanism and the Afro-Asian Revolutions* (NCM-HAAR) – Dunayevskaya drew explicit links between liberation struggles in Africa and workers struggles in the USA. 'Truly the Afro-Asian revolutions', she said, 'are not "over there" ... while we are "over here" safe, sound and unconcerned ... the new struggle for freedom in "backward" lands is very close to the hearts, minds and aspirations of workers in advanced countries'.⁵⁴ Dunayevskaya pointed out that 'the Korean war was the most unpopular war in American history' and that French youth, who had been sent to fight in Algeria, had mutinied.⁵⁵ She pointed to the possibilities for world revolution, immanent in the revolts against 'Communist' totalitarianism in Hungary and in the Afro-Asian revolutions.

She contrasted these popular working-class responses with those of 'the old radicals [who] seem inclined to dismiss this revolution with "sympathy" and a knowing look that betokens their belief that there is no road open to Afro-Asia but that of capitalist industrialisation'.⁵⁶ She also drew attention to a similar separation between the Afro-Asian masses and 'leaders' of the revolutions. 'The greatest obstacle to the further development of these national liberation movements, she wrote, 'comes from the intellectual bureaucracy which has emerged to "lead" them.'⁵⁷ And she, again, drew parallels between the 'Third World' and the industrialised economies, when she compared this intellectual bureaucracy and the way in which 'the greatest obstacle in the way of the working class overcoming capitalism comes from the Labour bureaucracy that leads it'.⁵⁸

In 1962, Dunayevskaya went on a two-month tour of four countries in West Africa – Nigeria, Ghana, Senegal and the Gambia. In advance of the tour she had made contact with some African exiles in England, and with some leaders and activists in Africa.⁵⁹ During her tour she met with Nnamdi Azikiwe (Governor General of Nigeria, 1960–63) and Léopold Senghor (the poet and cultural theorist who became the first president of the Republic of Senegal in 1960).⁶⁰ Her greatest enthusiasm, however, was displayed in her comments on the masses. In a letter to NALC, for example, she wrote earnestly about an anti-austerity rally that she was invited to in Lagos. She drew attention to the Nigerian masses' continuous movement for freedom when she noted that 'it is, after all only 1½ years since independence, and yet they [the protesters at the rally] are already openly opposed to the new government'.⁶¹

Dunayevskaya attempted to maintain the transatlantic Red/Black connection on her return to the United States. A Nigerian activist, Emé, organised a series of classes on Marxist-Humanism and also wrote some articles on Nigeria that were published in *News & Letters*.⁶² Dunayevskaya also, for example, corresponded with a Ghanian activist, Kofi, who also provided at least one article for *News & Letters*.⁶³ Dunayevskaya also wrote articles for publications – *Africa Today* and *Présence Africaine* – with an extensive African readership.⁶⁴

Dunayevskaya's transatlantic Red/Black engagement was not simply a case of promoting the NALC, or Marxist-Humanism as a philosophy, it involved a two-way dialogue. Dunayevskaya reported back to the NALC Convention that:

> We have much to learn from Africa and peculiarly enough (this bears repeating) it included the one subject we consider ourselves more expert on than anyone else, i.e. the role of the party ... The very fact that the worst features of single party-ism in Africa appear in Ghana where there are opposition parties shows that the evil is not in the single party-ism per se so much as it is in the limitations of speech, independent organisations of the workers, and the narrowing of their horizons to 'productivity'.[65]

Where state-capitalism in the USSR, and subsequently in Mao's China, suggested the single party as something authoritarian, Dunayevskaya's visit to Africa sensitised her to the idea that it was not the particular party *form*, single party or party and opposition, that was the issue at stake. Rather it was the relationship between theory and practice. In this regard she contrasted the situation in Ghana with that in Guinea. In Ghana, she argued, Kwame Nkrumah's call for the single-party state was an attempt to consolidate the power of a new elite. In Guinea, by way of contrast, Ahmed Sékou Touré's one-party state involved a mass party, with significant devolution of power to the local level and the involvement of the masses in decision-making at the local level.

The flaw with the movement in Guinea, as Dunayevskaya saw it, was that at the local level there was no discussion of Marx's philosophy, only practical discussions about 'whether to build a bridge or a school, where to build it and who and how to do it ... thereby once again re-establishing the division between mental and manual work'.[66] The African masses, she argued, needed to be engaged not just as 'hands' that would build a new society, but as whole people. The masses, she argued, were people with minds as well as bodies: people who thought their own thoughts and were striving to participate in the remaking of Africa *as whole people*, not just as helping hands.

Her engagement with African activists helped to inform her theorising and writing. It provided one of the sources for the NALC pamphlet on the Black struggle in the USA, *American Civilisation on Trial* (1963), and her second major work, *Philosophy and Revolution* (1973).

## Conclusion

We have only had the space here to give readers a taste of Dunayevskaya's theory and practice on the Red/Black Atlantic. We have also only had the space to explicate a few pages from the first of her major works, *Marxism and Freedom*. That text is a good starting point for gaining an understanding of Dunayevskaya's profound contribution to rescuing and developing Marx's Marxism. For readers with a specific interest in the Black dimension of her Red/Black theory, *American Civilisation on Trial* may be an easier way into her work. Her thinking developed throughout her lifetime, and readers can find almost all of her published work, and much that was unpublished in her lifetime, at the Raya Dunayevskaya online archives (her three major books, the 'trilogy of revolution', are not available on the archive). Selections of her most important articles and pamphlets are also available online.[67]

We hope that we have demonstrated that Dunayevskaya was the embodiment of the Red/Black Atlantic, in both her theory and practice. As a 'Red', she made some major contributions to the development of Marxist thought. The 'Black' dimension of her theory and practice was both integral to, and flowed from, her Marxism. This does not mean that the Black dimension was subordinate to the struggle for a new, socialist, society; it meant that the Black dimension was only one element in that struggle. Dunayevskaya, from the early 1950s, long before the celebration of new social movements in the late 1960s, identified women, youth, rank-and-file workers and Black masses as both revolutionary Force and Reason in the struggle for a new society. This is because these sections of society were struggling (Force) against their subordination and had ideas (Reason), rooted in their own specific experience of the world, about what was wrong with capitalist society and how those wrongs might be challenged. The Black dimension was, in Dunayevskaya's view, one dimension of the struggle for a new society. The Black struggle, she pointed out, was often at the vanguard of the struggle for human freedom in the USA. All oppressions, however, had to be transcended, before there could be a new society based on fully human grounds. In an age in which the far right are once again on the rise, an age in which racist and xenophobic ideas and activity are being legitimised, on both sides of the Atlantic, the Red/Black theory and practice of both Marx and Dunayevskaya are invaluable resources in the struggle for a new, human-centred, society.[68]

## Notes

1 The authors benefited from audience comments at the 'Red and the Black: The Russian Revolution and the Black Atlantic' conference, held at the Institute for Black Atlantic Research, 13–15 October 2017. We also appreciate the feedback from Ravi Bali. Anne Jaclard and Andrew Kliman, of the Marxist-Humanist Initiative, provided helpful comments on earlier drafts of the chapter. Any errors which remain are our own.

2  The archives have been digitised and are available online at https://rayadunayevskaya.org/ (26 November 2021). Every page of the archives has an archive page number. In the footnotes of this chapter we indicate sources from the archive by the prefix # followed by the page number or numbers being referred to (e.g. a 1985 interview with Dunayevskaya in the *Chicago Literary Review* is archived at #10228–10233).
3  Eugene Gogol, *Raya Dunayevskaya: Philosopher of Marxist-Humanism* (Eugene, OR: Resource Publications, 2004), 6.
4  Lou Turner, 'Origins of Black Marxism', *News & Letters*, April 1985, #10225.
5  'Marxist-Humanism, an Interview with Raya Dunayevskaya', *Chicago Literary Review*, 15 March 1985, #10232.
6  Turner, 'Origins of Black Marxism', #10226.
7  For some of this correspondence see #8511–8517.
8  On Dunayevskaya's early years see Volume 12, Section 1.A of the Raya Dunayevskaya Collection.
9  The *Bulletin* was a Russian-language publication, that carried articles by members of the Left Opposition (including, for example, Leon Trotsky, Christian Rakovsky and Karl Radek) and news of events that were happening in the Soviet Union. A sample copy, in Russian, is available in #2319–2341.
10 Raya Dunayevskaya, 'Introduction to Volume XII' of the *Raya Dunayevskaya Collection*, https://rayadunayevskaya.org/volume-12-section-breakdown/ (accessed 3 August 2021).
11 Her translation of some of Trotsky's writings on the Spanish Civil War can be found in the archives, #8792–8808.
12 For some of this correspondence see #2211–2240.
13 Dunayevskaya letter to Trotsky, 21 May 1939, #2239.
14 Dunayevskaya letter to Trotsky, 10 November 1939, #2240.
15 *Chicago Literary Review*, 'Interview', #10229.
16 Raya Dunayevskaya, *The Union of Soviet Socialist Republics is a Capitalist Society* (1941), #51. The Marx/Engels quote is from the *Communist Manifesto*.
17 The JFT was named after their Party names, J.R. Johnson (James) and Freddie Forest (Dunayevskaya).
18 Dunayevskaya's translations, from the early 1940s, of sections of Marx's *Economic and Philosophical Manuscripts* are at #8845–8858.
19 V.I. Lenin, *Notebook on Hegel's Science of Logic*, #1492–1584.
20 C.L.R. James, *Notes on Dialectics* (New York: Lawrence Hill, 1981).
21 See e.g. various articles at #69–163.
22 The summation of their work in the JFT, including their critique of the vanguard party, was published in *State-Capitalism and World Revolution*, #1333–11412.
23 Freddie Forest, 'Marxism and the Negro Problem', 18 June 1944, #259–270. A follow-on discussion article, with the same title, was published in the JFT's internal bulletin in April 1946, #286–295.
24 See F. Forest, 'Negroes in the Revolution: The Significance of Their Independent Struggles', #282–285; F. Forest, 'Abstract of Com. Coolidge's Document

on Negro Question', #296–310. A collection of her writings on the 'Negro Question' from this period is available at #9008–9046.
25 See e.g. Dunayevskaya's 'May 1953 letters' to Grace Lee, RCD, #1797–1812.
26 See e.g. Dunayevskaya, 'The Emergence of a New Movement from Practice that is Itself a Form of Theory', in *A 1980s View: The Coal Miners' General Strike of 1949–50 and the Birth of Marxist-Humanism in the US* (Detroit, MI: News & Letters, 1984), 33–43.
27 See e.g. C.L.R. James and Grace Lee (with Cornelius Castoriadis), *Facing Reality* (Detroit: Correspondence, 1958).
28 Denby was his party name; his birth name was Simon P. Owens and he also wrote under the name Matthew Ward. For more on Denby read his autobiography, *Indignant Heart: A Black Worker's Journal* (Detroit, MI: Wayne State University Press, 1989).
29 N&LC, 'A Report on the Black–Red Conference', #4338–4354.
30 Mary Hamilton et al., *Freedom Riders Speak for Themselves* (1961); National Editorial Board of News & Letters, *American Civilisation on Trial* (1963); Mario Savio, Eugene Walker and Raya Dunayevskaya, *The Free Speech Movement and the Negro Revolution* (1965); Mike Flug, *The Maryland Freedom Union, Workers Doing and Thinking* (1969). All available in #3369–3563.
31 The complete collection of these (approximately 180) articles is at #6561–7089.
32 See e.g. Raya Dunayevskaya, 'Revisiting "Black Power", Race and Class', *News & Letters*, January 1967, available at: http://libcom.org/library/black-power-dunayevskaya (accessed 3 August 2021).
33 See e.g. Raya Dunayevskaya, *Rosa Luxemburg, Women's Liberation and Marx's Philosophy of Revolution* (Atlantic Highlands, NJ: Humanities Press, 1982).
34 See e.g. *American Civilisation on Trial*.
35 The quote was taken from the introduction, co-written with Charles Denby, to Lou Turner and John Alan's *Frantz Fanon, Soweto and American Black Thought* (Detroit, MI: News & Letters, 1976) (#5305–5362), #5310, but it appears elsewhere in her writings.
36 See #2637–2645.
37 Raya Dunayevskaya, *Marxism and Freedom: From 1776 until Today* (Amherst, NY: Humanity Books, 2000), 21. The Marx quote is from 'Critique of the Hegelian Dialectic', in Marx's *Economic and Philosophical Manuscripts of 1844*.
38 Cited in Dunayevskaya, *Marxism and Freedom*, 81–82.
39 See e.g. G.M. Stekloff, *History of The First International* (London: Martin Lawrence, 1928), available on the Marxist Internet Archive at: www.marxists.org/archive/steklov/history-first-international/ (accessed 3 August 2021). For a more recent, and detailed, study of Marx and the American Civil War see Robin Blackburn, *An Unfinished Revolution: Karl Marx and Abraham Lincoln* (London: Verso, 2011).
40 Dunayevskaya, *Marxism and Freedom*, 21.
41 *Ibid.*, 87.

42 *Ibid.*, 84.
43 Cited in *Ibid.*, 84.
44 *Ibid.*, 91.
45 Cited in *Ibid.*, 84.
46 'Black masses as vanguard' is the subtitle of Dunayevskaya's 1963 pamphlet, *American Civilisation on Trial*.
47 Dunayevskaya, *Marxism and Freedom*, 87; emphasis in the original.
48 *Ibid.*, 90–91; emphasis in the original.
49 *Ibid.*, 89.
50 *Ibid.*, 88.
51 *Ibid.*, 89.
52 *Ibid.*, 286.
53 *Ibid.*, 287.
54 Dunayevskaya, *Nationalism, Communism, Marxist-Humanism and the Afro-Asian Revolutions* (#2688–2722), #2699.
55 *Ibid.*, #2698.
56 *Ibid.*, #2698.
57 *Ibid.*, #2703.
58 *Ibid.*, #2703.
59 See, e.g., her reports on meetings with the Africa Forum in England in 1959, at #9433 and #9467–9468. For correspondence with Africans, see e.g. #9608–9613, #13819–13821, and #13830–13831.
60 For notes on these meetings and on other aspects of her Africa trip, see #9573–9604.
61 See #9575.
62 See #9675–9677.
63 See #9635–9674.
64 The articles in *Africa Today* are at #3184 and #3189. The *Présence Africaine* articles are at #3193 and #9622.
65 Dunayevskaya, *Draft Resolution on Perspectives* (#3204–3219), #3210.
66 *Ibid.*, #3211.
67 See e.g. Marxist Internet Archive, http://bit.ly/2JeyNHk and Marxist-Humanist Initiative 'Archives of Marxist-Humanism', http://bit.ly/2BCmWP0 (accessed 3 August 2021).
68 For a contemporary example of the Red/Black Atlantic, in a Marxist-Humanist tradition, see the Marxist-Humanist Initiative pamphlet *Resisting Trumpist Reaction (and Left Accommodation): Marxist-Humanist Initiative's Perspectives for 2018* (the pamphlet was the outcome of transatlantic collaboration between Marxist-Humanists in the USA and the UK), http://bit.ly/32EBbPt (accessed 3 August 2021).

# 9

# European Marxist or Black intellectual? C.L.R. James and the advancement of Marxism beyond Russian-Leninism

*Tennyson S.D. Joseph*

The work of Trinidad-born Caribbean intellectual C.L.R. James has made a distinct contribution to global Marxist thought which remains relevant to twenty-first-century global politics. Specifically, James's work offers a post-Leninist reading of the character and future potential organisational forms of working-class revolt. In his major theoretical work, *Notes on Dialectics*,[1] and his more popular works, *Facing Reality*[2] and *The Invading Socialist Society*,[3] a central concern was to identify the ways in which the material conditions of capitalism shaped the level of consciousness and the organisational forms of the global working class, and had rendered obsolete the organisational imperatives proposed in Lenin's *What is to Be Done?*[4] In concrete terms, James was able to show how the new revolutionary upheavals – such as in Hungary in 1956 – had meant that '1945–1956 is finished' and that 'the future is with revolution after all'.[5]

It is safe to argue that the period following the early 1990s collapse of Soviet Union, Eastern European and other global Communist projects, and which has continued to witness the eruption of spontaneous mass movements independent of centrally organised vanguard parties, has largely confirmed James's perspective. Thus, new twenty-first-century movements like Occupy, the Arab Spring, the 2008 Barack Obama election campaign,[6] Black Lives Matter and Me Too movements, the yellow vests (gilets jaunes) in France, and Fees Must Fall student uprisings in South Africa, though still embryonic, all conform to James's expectation of the transcending of Lenin's vertical, hierarchical, centralised, vanguardist organisational form.

However, perhaps because of his mastery of Hegelian-Marxist dialectics, and despite his work and association with Pan-Africanism and Caribbean politics, James is often treated as a 'European' thinker, particularly by those who see a conflict between race and class, and between Pan-Africanism and Marxism. This has also arisen because of James's own avowed Europhilism, as reflected in the tensions in *Beyond a Boundary*, for example, where his infatuation with the culture of the quintessential English game cricket was contradictorily intermingled with his anti-colonial impulse to overcome class and racial boundaries.[7]

Relatedly, James's radicalism is often seen as being relevant to the advanced capitalist regions, rather than to the formerly colonised Caribbean states of the Black Atlantic, and his writing on Marxism, treated as separate from his reflections on Pan-African and Caribbean politics. While it is impossible to deny James's Pan-Africanist credentials, his Pan-Africanism is often treated as being separate from, and subordinate to, his Marxism. With the exception of the reviews of his 'The Revolutionary Answer to the Negro Problem in the USA',[8] very few writers see James's theoretical reflections on Marxist organisation as being linked to the possibilities of Pan-African liberation.

It is the failure of scholars to appreciate the conceptual concerns uniting the two perspectives which this chapter seeks to address. The chapter re-examines and assesses the contemporary relevance of James, as a Marxist and a pan-Africanist, to the development and application of Marxist ideas one hundred years after the Russian Revolution, and as a critique of global capitalism in the twenty-first century.

This is not to suggest that James was the only black, Caribbean Marxist who addressed the tensions between Marxism and Pan-Africanism, and black liberation. Indeed, a central question problematising the relationship between Marxists and Pan-Africanists has been the relative weight which should be given to class versus race considerations, both as an explanation of black and colonial oppression and as an organisational response to such oppression. This question has been widely studied, with many interventions offered by the black left,[9] of which two of the most important contributions by Caribbean intellectuals being the work of George Padmore[10] and that of Walter Rodney.[11]

However, James's contribution to resolving the race/class dilemma is specifically original and uniquely relevant to a reflection on Marxism in the Black Atlantic, when compared to the reflections of Rodney and Padmore. Only James is accused of being a 'black European' especially since he consciously embraced the label. Both Rodney and Padmore, it can be argued, accommodated Marxism to their Pan-Africanism as distinct from James, whose Pan-Africanism can be seen as fitting within his overarching Marxist interpretation of social and political change. Further, and relatedly, it is only James who consciously seeks to advance Marxism theoretically, by deliberately shifting and transcending the analytical categories of Lenin and Trotsky and applying his new analytical categories to the problems of the late twentieth century.[12] As a result, it is James who makes a more theoretically advanced contribution to Marxism one hundred years after the Russian Revolution, and relevant to understanding the challenges of black oppression and anti-capitalist revolt in the early twenty-first century.

This chapter therefore has four main aims. First, it will present the basis upon which James has been problematised as a 'European' thinker and will seek to extricate him from the charge of being a 'black European'. Secondly, the chapter will show how James's approach was consciously aimed at resolving any lingering tensions between the two perspectives. Thirdly, the chapter will engage briefly in how other black-Caribbean Marxists, George Padmore and Walter Rodney, addressed the problem of the treatment of race in Marxist thought, in order to allow for a comparative discussion of James's own treatment of the question. Finally, the chapter closes by examining how James's organic resolution of the race/class dilemma assisted in advancing Marxist theory of revolutionary organisation beyond its Leninist expression and by showing how James's ideas are reflected in twenty-first century revolts.

## Extricating James from the charge of 'Black European'

The relationship between C.L.R. James's Marxism and his Pan-Africanism is a complex issue. This is reflected in the widely varying analyses among scholars who have sought to assess where James's Pan-Africanism fits within his Marxism. On one side of the spectrum sits a scholar like Anthony Bogues, who views the very idea of James as a Pan-Africanist in the 1930s as problematic since 'James had a long way to go to come to terms with the distinctive African contributions to human civilisation'.[13] At the other end sits a writer like Christian Høgsbjerg, who has researched deeply into James's earliest years in Britain, and has scoured the archives to show that James had a commitment to Africa, as a counterargument to those who point to the 'under-development' of his Pan-Africanism.[14] While Høgsbjerg does not 'claim to offer any final analysis of James's early Pan-Africanism, or claim in some hagiographic fashion that James was at all times in all ways free from any kind of intellectual elitism with respect to Africans', he maintains that the 'label of Pan-Africanist itself is a meaningful one to apply to James, and that it is fundamentally mistaken to see James – and James's Marxism and Trotskyism – as "Eurocentric"'.[15]

There is however much in James's own self-assessment and open admissions of his intellectual influences which explains the difficulty among Afrocentrists with accepting James as anything other than a European Marxist intellectual. Given the importance of James to twenty-first-century post-Stalinist understandings of Marxism, and in the context of the Black Lives Matter global uprising, an examination of how James resolves the tension between Pan-Africanism and Marxism is important for advancing Marxism as relevant to radical politics of the early twenty-first century.

The context of James's early education neither equipped him with the historical knowledge of the anteriority of ancient African political philosophy to European thought,[16] nor with the tools to grasp the political implications of such a reality. In contrast, James's fascination with antiquity was largely confined to its Greco-Latin aspects. In *Every Cook can Govern*[17] for example, C.L.R. James, in diametrical contrast to the Africa-first perspectives presented by writers like Diop,[18] Martin Bernal[19] and George G.M. James,[20] wrote glowingly of the intellectual contribution of the early Greeks to global development:

> Today, when we speak of politics, democracy, oligarchy, constitution, law; when we speak of oratory, rhetoric, ethics; when we speak of drama of tragedy and comedy; when we speak of history; when we speak of sculpture and architecture; in all these things we use the terms and build on the foundations that were developed and discovered by the Greeks.[21]

Similarly, James's famous description of Garveyism as 'pitiable rubbish'[22] (despite his more respectful obituary to Garvey),[23] his description of himself as a 'black European'[24] and his frequent claims that the experience of European-directed West Indian slavery had transformed the Caribbean into a 'fully Europeanised People',[25] all help to explain his rejection by more Afrocentric black intellectuals and activists.

Further, even in those instances where he attempts to extricate himself from the charge of Europhilism, James succeeds only in further understating Africa's contribution, and crediting Europe for modern civilisation. For example, James in *'The Making of the Caribbean Peoples'* states:

> I denounce European colonist scholarship, but I respect the learning and profound discoveries of Western civilisation. It is by means of the great men of ancient Greece; of Michelet, the French historian; of Hegel, Marx, and Lenin; of Du Bois; of contemporary Europeans and Englishmen likes Pares and E.P. Thompson; of an African like Chisiza, that my eyes and ears have been opened and I can today see and hear what we were, what we are, and what we can do.[26]

By his own admission therefore, James credits 'the opening of his eyes and ears' to European scholarship.

Despite this, however, it is impossible to discount James's Pan-Africanism since his intellectual and political activity was closely connected to the struggles of blacks globally. The association of James in the International African Friends of Ethiopia and the International African Service Bureau, as well as his earliest public speeches in Britain in defence of liberation movements in Africa, so well documented by Høgsbjerg,[27] provide ample proof of his appreciation of black racial struggle as linked to proletarian liberation. It is no accident that James's magnum opus was his history of the Haitian Revolution,[28] which consciously sought to challenge the Eurocentric accounts which were 'always talking about West Indians as backward, as slaves, and continually oppressed and exploited by British domination ... So I decided that I would write a book that showed the West Indians as something else.'[29] James achieves this by, among other things, demonstrating the success of the Haitian ex-slaves in establishing an independent black state, successfully resisting and defeating the most powerful European power of the day in the process.[30]

Significantly, in *Black Jacobins*, James puts forward his clearest statement on the relationship between race and class: 'the race question is subsidiary to the class question, and to think of imperialism in terms of race is disastrous. But to neglect the racial factor as merely incidental is an error only less grave than to make it fundamental.'[31]

This assertion conforms to the central Marxist idea, and emerges as James's dominant conception eclipsing a 'race first' perspective. Later, in a 1967 speech entitled 'Black Power',[32] James defended the focus on race by Black Power advocates like Stokely Carmichael in the US civil rights movement, and he criticised some Marxist groupings for not embracing the Black Power movement:

> the independent struggle of the Negro people for the democratic rights and equality ... not only had to be defended and advocated by the Marxist movement. The Marxist movement had to understand that *such independent struggles were a contributory factor to the socialist revolution* ... The American Negroes in fighting for their democratic rights were making and (*sic*) indispensable addition to the struggle for socialism in the United States.[33]

This view approximates very closely that of Harold Cruse who, though presenting a contentious rejection of James and other Caribbean intellectuals, claims that 'the Negro movement represents an indirect challenge to the capitalist status quo not because it is programmatically anti-capitalist, but because full integration of the Negro in all levels of American society *is not possible within the present framework of the American system*' (emphasis in original).[34]

James's clearest statement on the role of the black struggle and its significance for the attainment of socialism, however, can be found in his 1948 article 'The Revolutionary Answer to the Negro Problem in the USA'. There, James is adamant that the black struggle should be seen as the vanguard of the revolutionary struggle in the USA, and should not be subordinated to the dictates of the Marxist parties since the Negro struggle 'is able to exercise a powerful influence upon the revolutionary proletariat, that it has got a great contribution to make to the development of the proletariat in the United States, and that it is in itself a constituent part of the struggle for socialism'.[35]

This perspective was formulated by James in his 1939 meeting with Russian revolutionary leader Leon Trotsky, during the latter's ultimately ill-fated exile in Mexico. In the meeting, James reinforced his emerging commitment to his later notion of 'free creative activity' by expressing support for black autonomous revolutionary organisation and activity. Despite being lukewarm to the demands for black nationalist territorial separation in North America, a position opportunistically adopted by the official Communist parties, James was willing to support such a move once it had the support of the majority of the blacks.[36] Richards observes that James

> rejected any Marxist approach which failed to distinguish between black and white workers regarding both as simply the victims of class oppression ... James supplanted the call for black territorial self-determination with the demand that black Americans control their own political affairs and organisations – a demand which he regarded as expressive of their fight for equality and democratic rights within American society.[37]

In reflecting on James's pro-Marxist stance, it should be noted that the widely held claim of Marx's denigration of the black and anti-colonial struggle in preference for the spread of capitalism and the eventual proletarian revolution in advanced capitalist countries, has been challenged by a number of writers who have offered strong arguments against the 'Eurocentric' Marx.[38] James's readiness to accept the autonomous activity of black nationalists, his awareness that such activity could advance, rather than retard the socialist cause, as well as his rejection of attempts by Marxists to dominate and stifle the black movement, while remaining a committed Marxist, all demonstrate his willingness to revise the Marxian categories to allow the 'most oppressed section of American society and the most discriminated against' to become 'the very vanguard of the proletarian revolution'.[39]

Further, James's reformulation of Marxism to accommodate the race question was not confined to the realities of the USA. Indeed, his most original and profound ideas on the race question were expressed in relation to anti-colonial developments in the Caribbean. James's analysis of the development of plantation slavery in the Caribbean, for example, building on Trotsky's theory of uneven and combined development,[40] led him to the conclusion that a modern, totally Westernised proletariat had been created in these territories. This, he felt, explains the level of rebelliousness which has characterised Caribbean populations, from the slavery period to the present.[41] Discussing James's Marxist analysis of West Indian slavery, A.W. Singham remarks that James

> made his own unique and important modification in dealing with a special variant of imperialism, the Caribbean states. While Marx, Lenin and even Trotsky and Luxemburg saw the traditional states of Africa and Asia as reflecting the 'Oriental' peculiarity, James showed how the Caribbean was the first modern society to arise outside Western Europe, where both institutions and populations had been transplanted. It was to be a replica of Europe outside Europe. The settlers bought with them a 'modern' socio-economic organisation to exploit agriculture ... There was a commitment to the principles of hierarchy and rationality, which characterised the modern capitalist states.[42]

Singham further demonstrates the implications of James's analysis when applied to the concrete historical experiences of Caribbean peoples, as seen in his study of the Haitian Revolution. Singham argues that

> James was demonstrating concretely that not all national revolutions followed the same patterns, nor did all colonial societies have the same type of economic structure. In San Domingo a new type of hybrid had emerged from the imposition of a capitalist form of economic organisation, the plantation, on the pre-feudal structure of slavery. This bore no relation to Marx's Asiatic mode of production, but had produced a new kind of contradiction. Thus, San Domingo under Toussaint was able to 'leap over the stages of national development'. Like Lenin, but with more concrete evidence James stressed the flexibility in the stages of history of different societies.[43]

This novel application of Marxist theory to the experience of Caribbean slavery and Caribbean political development foreshadows Cheikh Anta Diop's analysis of the differences between European and African slavery.[44] In his rejection of Marx's universalising of 'stages of development', Diop posits the view that historically it was only the specific features of European slavery which created the conditions for dialectical conflict and radical transformation of society. This fact, to Diop, is captured in Marx's rejection of the 'generalised slavery' of the Asiatic mode of production, since it did not conform to his dialectical theory of the constant overcoming of contradictions.[45] In 'The Making of the Caribbean Peoples', James emphasises that it was the experience of slavery which created the seeds for the transformation of Caribbean society:

> liberty means something to us that is very unusual. There were many generations of slaves in Africa, of that we are quite sure ... But when we made the 'middle passage' and came to the Caribbean we went straight into a modern industry – the sugar plantation – and there we saw that to be a slave was the result of our being black. A white man was not a slave. The West Indian slave

was not accustomed to that kind of slavery in Africa; and therefore in the history of the West Indies there is one dominant fact and that is the desire for liberty; the ridding oneself of the particular burden which is the special inheritance of the black skin.[46]

In a strikingly similar mode of thought, Cheikh Anta Diop makes the following observation:

> The Greek city-state was founded from birth on slavery and the intangibility of private land ownership. In contrast, the appearance of a state with an Asiatic economic system, as described by Marx and Engels, shows that it did not spring abruptly from the brutal contact of two races one of which enslaved the other and thus created, from the outset, the conditions for the development of the class struggle and private property ... In sum, it suffices for societies with an Asiatic mode of production to be reduced into slavery ... for them to insert themselves into the historic cycle of humanity. The worldwide emancipation of all the former European colonies, which, without exception were dependent on that mode of production, illustrate the idea.[47]

As noted earlier, this generally held assumption of the inherent Eurocentrism of Marxist theory and of Marx himself has been challenged by Anderson,[48] who has explored Marx's less publicised writings on the possibility of revolution outside the main capitalist centres. Among Marx's works explored were those concerned with 'his theorisation of a number of non-Western societies of his day – from India to Russia and from Algeria to China – and their relation to capitalism and colonialism', his 'writings on movements for national emancipation ...', his 'theorisation of race and ethnicity in relation to class, with respect to both Black labour in America during the Civil War and Irish labour in Britain', and his 'writings on societies that were for the most part peripheral to capitalism during his lifetime'.[49] Anderson's main conclusion is that, when taken as a whole, Marx was far more open to the possibilities of non-European socialist revolution than has commonly been assumed.[50]

It is perspectives such as Anderson's which create spaces for the creative application of Marxist analytical categories to the treatment of black struggles, and which assist with countering the charges of Eurocentrism levelled at James. Indeed, no absolute and final label can be attached to James when assessing his consciousness of, and his commitment to, fighting racial oppression. James's theoretical treatment of the race question becomes progressively more sophisticated as he matures. In his later years, he accepted Garvey's call for black pride and racial consciousness as one of the leaps necessary for the emancipation of the black race.[51] In a similar vein, he expressed greater awareness of the dominant culture of Caribbean peoples as being African. To James, genuine independence – an independence which breaks completely with the European past – can only be achieved by returning to the African past. This 'return to Africa' was, to James, one of the most significant achievements of the Haitian Revolution:

> after the successful revolution for Haitian independence in 1802, the Haitian intelligentsia tried for nearly a hundred years to build a model French civilisation and culture in the West Indies. Their failure is of great importance to us today ... Recognising this failure to make themselves French, they turned back home. What they found and built up was the African heritage which the Haitian peasants more than all others in the West Indies had preserved.[52]

## Marxism and the race/class problematic

There is little doubt that the tensions between Marxism and Pan-Africanism can be sourced in a sometimes too rigid and formulaic interpretation of Marx's supposed emphasis on class, both as an explanation for human oppression as well as an organisational impulse against oppression. Indeed, the general labelling of racial consciousness as 'false consciousness' accounts for much of the difficulty by radicals to embrace Marxism as relevant to the Caribbean. Relatedly, it is the unwillingness to accept Marxism's class-centrism which has resulted in the emergence of several new theories growing out of a 'race first', 'gender first' or 'Caribbean exceptionalism' perspective. The Garvey movement,[53] Black Power,[54] Pan-Africanism,[55] and plantation economy theory[56] all grew out of a conscious effort to develop political theories which would make race and culture more central and to develop indigenous theories that would address more directly the problems of Third World, non-white societies. They were all attempts to create an alternative explanatory theory, more consciously tailored to the specific modes of oppression confronting persons of African descent in the periphery. Before examining James's response to the race/class question it is useful to reflect briefly on the scholastic debate on Marx's Eurocentrism.

Those who argue against the relevance of Marxism to black struggle claim that much can be found, both in the original Marxist theory and in the practical expression of Marxist movements, to justify the perception of Marxism as 'white man's ideology'.[57] For example, A.W. Singham,[58] remarking on the question of racism in Marx's thought, has described Marx as being 'hopelessly confused and little informed on the colonial question'. He accuses Marx of 'introducing a novel but hardly scientific concept' and 'non-analytical term' – the Asiatic mode – 'to explain the traditional colonised societies of Africa and Asia'. He argues that:

Historically this is not surprising, for Marx shared the contempt of most bourgeois intellectuals of Western Europe at that time for non-Western, non-White cultures. At one point, for example, Marx wrote quite contemptuously that 'India had no indigenous history, but was rather a tale of successive invaders who found their empires on the passive basis of that unresisting and unchanging society'. The dialectic apparently worked for Europeans but not for Asians.[59]

As noted above, however, such claims have been forcefully countered by Anderson. Responding specifically to the supposed Eurocentrism in Marx's 'Asiatic' category, Anderson observes that:

> Marx examined the different course that these developments had taken in Asia as opposed to Western Europe. Although these issues were to generate much discussion in the twentieth century under the rubric of the Asiatic mode of production, Marx never actually uses this term in the *Grundrisse*. He uses the term 'Oriental despotism' in his 1853 India writings. In 1859, however, in the preface to the *Critique of Political Economy*, he does employ the term 'Asiatic mode of production'. Marx writes of 'the Asiatic, ancient, feudal and modern bourgeois modes of production', which 'may be designated as epochs marking progress in the economic development of society'. Since he characterises modern capitalism as 'the last antagonistic form', part of 'the prehistory of human society', a socialist future is also implied, as was some type of early stateless form preceding both the Asiatic and the ancient modes of production. Adding these two implied modes of production would yield a six-fold list: (1) early stateless (2) Asiatic (3) ancient (4) feudal (5) bourgeois or capitalist, and (6) socialist.[60]

Further challenges have been raised in relation to Marx's 'economic determinism', and his emphasis on the causal relationship between infrastructure and superstructure. As the argument goes, by relegating racial prejudice to the sphere of the superstructure Marx downplays its potential for revolutionary transformation. As C.W. Mills has observed:

> the aprioristic commitment to the view that ethnicity is largely constructed, and ultimately decomposable in class terms, needs to be reconsidered as a corollary of Marx and Engels' questionable 'universalism' which, like its Hegelian antecedent, represents as supranational and colourless what is really European and white. Correspondingly, the crucial psychic dimension of the struggle for black personhood ... with its links to historical reclamation and redemption, rests crucially on the assumption that ethnicity is part of one's identity, a claim difficult to handle within a Marxist conceptual framework in which 'class', 'economic' and the relation to the 'means of production' are truly the 'objective' and 'determining'.[61]

Given these criticisms, therefore, an important step in the merger of the Red and the Black (black Marxism) has been the resolution of the claims to

Marxism's Eurocentrism, and the creative application of Marxist theory to the struggles of African and colonial peoples. A comparative examination of how this is achieved in two other notable black Caribbean Marxists, George Padmore and Walter Rodney, can help in clarifying why James can be seen to have made perhaps the more deeply original advance to Marxism, and the more complete resolution of the race/class dilemma.

Padmore's treatment of the race/class problematic evolved over time according to the shifting nature of his relationship to the official Communist parties. In the moments when he is closely associated politically, organisationally and intellectually to the Communist International, he discusses racial oppression as being tied to the oppression of blacks given their specific locations in the global capitalist system. Thus, in *The Life and Struggles of Negro Toilers*, Padmore suggests that the 'oppression of negroes assumes two distinct forms: on one hand they are oppressed as a class, and on the other as a nation ... this national oppression has its basis in the social-economic relation of the Negro to Capitalism'.[62] Through these lenses, Padmore sees blacks as carrying a twofold burden: class and race. Their exploitation as workers is more brutal due to their colonial status, and their super-exploitation allows capitalism to offer better terms to white workers, further splitting the working class along racial and national lines and frustrating the emergence of a 'class-for-itself' consciousness.

However, following his formal break with the Communist International, Padmore proposes a more overtly race-based interpretation to the problems of black emancipation, and a more deliberate race-centric organisational response. Thus, Padmore's solution to the race/class problem, particularly in *Pan-Africanism or Communism*, is to remove black political struggles from the leadership of European-led political organisations. Indeed, in his later years, Padmore's Pan-Africanism assumed tendencies of petit bourgeois nationalism borne out of his anti-Communism. This was seen, for example, as argued by Leslie James, in Padmore's adoption of a distinctly anti-Communist line, joining petit bourgeois Caribbean leaders like Eric Williams in abandoning Prime Minister Cheddi Jagan of British Guiana, when that country's constitution was suspended by Britain in the 1950s. Leslie James reports that Padmore went as far as informing his readers that British Guiana should serve as a warning 'to colonial nationalists and trade union leaders to keep clear of communist affiliations'.[63] Similarly, in a review of *Pan-Africanism or Communism* by Daniel Guérin, Padmore was told that

> sometimes you are very much anti-communist and sometimes you behave like a genuine Marxist ... I am a little worried about a 'pan-Africanism' which could be an empty slogan without much more contents than

anti-communism ... How to go beyond bourgeois nationalism? The answer is socialism, Marxism, communism, but not the caricature of Marxism and communism offered by Stalin and his agents.[64]

It is clear from this that Padmore does not achieve an appropriate synthesis between race and class. What he achieves is the abandonment of the previous practice of the pursuit of black liberation under subordination to European Communist leadership. Beyond the practical question of independent black political leadership, however, there is no perceptible movement beyond Lenin's theory of imperialism as an explanation of the colonial problem, and there is no qualitative contribution to Marxist theory. Indeed, what Padmore confirms is the relevance of Lenin's theory of imperialism to colonial conditions. This is seen clearly, for example, in his compilation of *How Russia Transformed Her Colonial Empire*, written long after he had 'broken' with the Soviet Union, but in which he praised Lenin and the Soviet Union's nationalities policy for achieving 'more than any other Great Power has achieved in centuries'.[65] Given his emphasis, therefore, Padmore's response lies in the tactical realm: blacks must organise themselves as blacks, while remaining conscious of their struggle against capital (economic oppression) which is the basis of their condition.

Similarly, Walter Rodney, a Black Power scholar and Marxist, also engages in reflections which are aimed at resolving the tensions between race and class. While Rodney maintains a more consistent pro-Marxist analytical frame, he nevertheless sublates race into class, and treats one as indistinguishable from the other. Rodney sees imperialism as being historically racist and white: 'that association of wealth with whites and poverty with blacks is not accidental. It is the nature of the imperialist relationship that enriches the metropolis at the expense of the colony, i.e. it makes the whites richer and the blacks poorer.'[66] This conflation of race into class is also seen in Rodney's expansion of 'black power' as a concept relevant to the political aspirations of all non-white people of the globe:

> When a Pakistani goes to the Midlands he is as coloured as the Nigerian ... The black people of whom I speak are non-whites – the hundreds of millions of people whose homelands are in Asia and Africa, with another few millions in the Americas. A further subdivision can be made with reference to all people of African descent whose position is clearly more acute than that of most non-white groups. It must be noted that once a person is said to be black by the white world, then that is usually the most important thing about him[67]

However, despite, or perhaps because of, Rodney's comfort with Marxism as a body of ideas that is not overturned by the reality of a world built on racial inequality, his work does not show strong evidence of theoretical expansion of Marxism, as seen in a theorist such as Charles

Mills. Mills, 'in attempting to bring out the possible insights provided by a "black", or at least racially informed Marxism', can be said to have advanced '(a modified) historical materialism'.[68] This limited contribution to Marxist theorising is seen too in Rodney's work on the Russian Revolution, published posthumously in 2018 from his compiled lectures while at the University of Dar es Salaam in the late 1960s. There, his main approach is to show how Marxist theory and the concerns of the Russian Revolution can be applied to the problems of racism and black nationalism, rather than to theoretically build on Marxism.[69]

As a result of this emphasis Rodney, like Padmore, can also be seen as presenting a weaker theoretical advancement of Marxism when compared to C.L.R. James. Indeed, Rodney indicates explicitly that Marxism's principal value resides in its utility as a tool or method, and as a tool it may have contextual applicability. Rodney believes that Marxism, if viewed as a method,

> would exist at different levels, at different times, in different places and retain its potential as a tool [since] a methodology would, virtually by definition be independent of time and place. You will use the methodology at any given time, and any place. You may get quite different results, of course, but the methodology itself would be independent of time and place.[70]

Rodney also argued that being a Marxist placed upon him the obligation to speak for the working class, and to interpret social reality in the interest of the working class rather than the bourgeoisie.[71] Like Padmore, he accepts the Marxist reading of imperialism and applies it to the black condition. Thus, to Rodney, there was no race/class dilemma, since, in every country in the world, blacks fell into the ranks of the proletariat.

Similarly, in his reflections on the Russian Revolution, Rodney argues that 'Marx's position demonstrates that his historical or dialectical materialism is a method that can be applied to different situations to give different answers.'[72] Rodney made similar claims about Lenin's application of Marxism. He argued that 'Lenin saw that nationalism was always associated with capitalist development, but was not always favourable to the bourgeoisie'. Rodney notes that Lenin felt 'on the contrary, the struggle in the colonies could be expected to assume national forms, which would challenge the bourgeoisie of the imperialist countries' and he 'called the colonies a vast reservoir of potential allies of socialism against imperialism'.[73] Rodney argued further that 'Lenin was right because he applied Marxist analysis to the relevant facts, but few Marxists are consistent with this, and it is significant that the black revolt has been treated similarly.'[74]

None of this, however, is to deny the great skill with which Rodney marshals Marxist methodology to explain race and class relations in the periphery as he does in the case of Guyana,[75] and as demonstrated and argued by David Austin in his discussion of Rodney's contribution to the Black Writers conference in Montreal in 1968.[76] What Padmore and Rodney achieve, however, is the application of Marxism to the struggles of Africans, rather than a new and original contribution to Marxist theory as can be seen in the case of James. In Padmore's case, Marxism is valuable as an explanation of imperialism and the colonial question, while in Rodney's case it is a Marxism as valuable methodical tool which informs explanation and guides action. It is C.L.R. James, however, who approaches the Pan-African question by theorising anew the analytical and organisational imperatives of Marxism beyond their Leninist expression.

## The Jamesian synthesis: class, race, democracy and socialism

C.L.R. James's political thought can best be appreciated for its contribution to the resolution of the problems created by the race/class schism among radical political thinkers. James expresses an overriding commitment to Marxist class analysis, while at the same time acknowledging the social contradictions of societies structured along racial configurations. In 'The Revolutionary Answer to the Negro Problem in the USA', James asks:

> On the question of the state, what Negro, particularly below the Mason-Dixon line, believes that the bourgeois state is a state above all classes, serving the needs of all the people? They may not formulate their beliefs in Marxist terms, but their experience drives them to reject this shibboleth of bourgeois democracy.[77]

More importantly, however, James was able to merge Pan-Africanism with socialism in his critique of Lenin's vanguard party and his proposal of new organisational forms more relevant to the technological age of the late twentieth century, in which Lenin's assumptions about the relationship between leadership and mass no longer held true. This important contribution to Pan-African politics is often missed by scholars who tend to read James's socialist discussions on the Soviet Union as separate from his discussions on African and Caribbean politics. However, a close reading of James shows that his Pan-Africanism and his discussions on Caribbean politics were never separate from his criticism of Lenin's vanguardism and his prescriptions for 'free creative activity' as an alternative to Leninism.

Perhaps one of the least understood aspects of C.L.R. James's political thought is why he devised the mass party and proposed it as a concrete structure or model for a post-colonial West Indies seeking to establish independence and democracy. James's mass party has been viewed as a retreat from his socialist perspective and that it is 'inconsistent with, and indeed contradicts, his more general theoretical principles concerning social and political change'.[78] Similarly, Lai has described James's discussions of the mass party as being 'somewhat more conventional and more liberal democratic than social revolutionary'.[79]

However, James's contribution to Pan-Africanism can only be grasped by understanding the essential unity of his ideas. Indeed, James's mass party was the logical outcome of his synthesis of democracy and socialism. While it is generally assumed that James's proposal of the 'mass party' arose out his specific political struggles in the People's National Movement (PNM) in Trinidad and Tobago, a more thorough analysis suggests that it was consistent with his theorising on 'free creative activity' as an alternative to the extreme centralism of Communist Russia. It was a mechanism designed to foster socialist participatory democracy, similar to that established by the short-lived Soviets and workers' councils of which James had written extensively elsewhere, in the conditions of the Third World.

It is because of James's awareness of the colonial question that he recognises the role of party organisation in the limited task of overcoming colonialism as a logical step to the struggle for socialism. This view was expressed unambiguously in *Modern Politics*:

> the party, adapted to local conditions and basing itself upon a careful examination of both the Second and Third Internationals, is still valid for countries which are under-developed, that is to say, where industry and therefore the proletariat is not dominant. One proof of the continuing validity of the party in those areas is the continuing victories they are winning in country after country.[80]

When James speaks of 'victories', he is thinking only in terms of the anti-colonial struggle, and not the attainment of socialism.

Further, James's concept of the party is in keeping with his dialectical logic which recognises that organisational forms are dependent upon the objective development of underlying material conditions. James's mass party had transcended the initial anti-colonial struggle and was designed to facilitate an advanced form of democracy in a post-colonial society whose political history had been devoid of the practice and experience of democracy. It was a mechanism appropriate for the self-activity of party members, not their domination and direction from above. It was consistent with his concept of spontaneity and 'free-creative activity'. It is on this basis that James saw it necessary to propose a new model of party organisation for the PNM as a counter to the inherited and inherent authoritarian tendencies in West Indian political parties. James in *Party Politics in the West Indies*, where his concept of the mass party was outlined, observes that 'the people of underdeveloped countries cannot themselves form the government. But by "independent political activity" they find out what they can do, their privileges and their responsibilities'.[81]

James's theory, by focusing on the struggles of 'under-developed countries', was also by extension providing a post-Lenin organisational model which could embrace black, Pan-Africanist, anti-colonial democratic struggles and anti-capitalist socialist struggles. It was designed to ensure a continuous flow of decisions from the bottom upwards and not from the top downwards. Moreover, it was aimed at widening the decision-making structure to include every member of the rank and file of the party and to break the decision-making monopoly of the leadership – or, more accurately, the party leader. It was a deliberate post-Leninist prescription.

One of the challenges to James's relevance is the claim that it is difficult to identify concrete evidence of a Jamesian praxis, either programmatically or organisationally, in any of the post-1950 political developments in the globe. It is also not likely to find a movement explicitly describing itself as 'Jamesian' or 'Jamesite'. However, what is often missed is the extent to which late twentieth to early twenty-first-century political movements have vindicated James's expectation of the growth of independent mass-based 'free creative activity' moving beyond organised political groups and existing independently of authoritarian leadership.

James's notion of 'free creative activity' and his post-vanguardist prescriptions are reflected in contemporary struggles of the global underclass as seen in the Occupy Movement, environmental struggles, Black Lives Matter, student struggles in present-day South Africa as seen in the Rhodes Must Fall and Fees Must Fall campaigns, the yellow vests in France, the Me Too movement and the general shift away from centralist Leninist organisational forms. It is in this way that James escapes the label of European Marxist, since his critique of Lenin and his theory of self-organisation never excluded the black struggle, but placed it at the centre of the global struggle against capitalism. Indeed, while many of these movements can be seen as 'episodic' and in some cases 'short-lived', there is little doubt that they carry in themselves sharp deviations from the Leninist-type of twentieth-century movements that James had argued against. There is little doubt too that these movements have been offering radical and effective responses to capitalism in the age of globalisation and neo-liberalism. There is certainly little doubt that the Black Lives Matter movement, though still in its infancy, has been having the most profound impact on global politics in the forms of radical anti-racist, anti-authoritarian and anti-capital mass mobilisations, in the midst of a public health and economic crisis associated with the COVID-19 pandemic, in the third decade of the twenty-first century. It is therefore likely that the early to mid-twenty-first century may produce more fertile Jamesian moments than the last five decades of the twentieth.

## Notes

1 C.L.R. James, *Notes on Dialectics: Hegel–Marx–Lenin* (London: Allison and Busby, 1980).
2 C.L.R. James, Grace Lee, and Pierre Chaulieu, *Facing Reality* (Detroit, MI: Bewick Editions, 1974).
3 C.L.R. James, Freddie Forest, and Ria Stone, *The Invading Socialist Society* (Detroit, MI: Bewick Editions, 1972).
4 V.I. Lenin, *What is to be Done?: Burning Questions of Our Movement* (New York: International Publishers, 1969).
5 Christian Høgsbjerg, 'Facing Post-Colonial Reality? C.L.R. James, the Black Atlantic and 1956', in Keith Flett (ed.), *1956 And All That* (Newcastle: Cambridge Scholars Publishing, 2007), 181–201, at 192.
6 Horace Campbell, *Barack Obama and Twenty-First-Century Politics: A Revolutionary Moment in the USA* (London: Pluto Press, 2010).
7 See Christian Høgsbjerg, 'C.L.R. James's "British Civilisation"? Exploring the "Dark Unfathomed Caves" of *Beyond a Boundary*' in David Featherstone, Christopher Gair, Christian Høgsbjerg, and Andrew Smith (eds), *Marxism, Colonialism, and Cricket* (Durham, NC: Duke University Press, 2018), 51–71.
8 C.L.R. James, 'The Revolutionary Answer to the Negro Problem in the USA' in Anna Grimshaw (ed.), *The C.L.R. James Reader* (Oxford: Blackwell, 1992), 182–189.
9 Charles W. Mills, 'Race and Class: Conflicting or Reconcilable Paradigms?', *Social and Economic Studies*, 36:2 (1987), 69–108. See also Tony Martin, 'C.L.R. James and the Race/Class Question' in *The Pan-African Connection: From Slavery to Garvey and Beyond* (Dover, MA: The Majority Press, 1984), 165–178.
10 George Padmore, *Pan-Africanism or Communism* (New York: Doubleday, 1972).
11 Walter Rodney, *The Groundings with My Brothers* (London: Bogle-L'Ouverture Publications, 1969); Walter Rodney, *Walter Rodney Speaks: The Making of an African Intellectual* (Princeton, NJ: Africa World Press, 1990); Walter Rodney, *The Russian Revolution: A View From The Third World* (London: Verso, 2018).
12 George Belle, 'The Collapse of the Soviet System: Implications for the Caribbean Left', in Allan Cobley (ed.), *Crossroads of Empire: The Europe–Caribbean Connection 1492–1992* (Bridgetown: Department of History, University of the West Indies, 1994), 94–110. See also Tennyson S.D. Joseph, 'C.L.R. James and the Grenada Revolution: Lessons Learned and Future Possibilities', in Wendy Grenade (ed.), *The Grenada Revolution: Reflections and Lessons* (Jackson, MS: University of Mississippi Press, 2015), 152–178.

13 Anthony Bogues, *Caliban's Freedom: The Early Political Thought of C.L.R. James* (London: Pluto Press, 1997), 46.
14 Christian Høgsbjerg, *C.L.R. James in Imperial Britain* (Durham, NC: Duke University Press, 2014); Christian Høgsbjerg, '"The Most Striking West Indian Creation Between the Wars": C.L.R. James, the International African Service Bureau and Militant Pan-Africanism in Imperial Britain', in Shane Pantin and Jerome Teelucksingh (eds), *Ideology, Regionalism, and Society in Caribbean History* (Cham, Switzerland: Palgrave Macmillan, 2017), 99–130.
15 Høgsbjerg, '"The Most Striking West Indian Creation Between the Wars"', 103.
16 Cheikh Anta Diop, *The African Origin of Civilisation: Myth or Reality* (New York: Lawrence Hill, 1974).
17 C.L.R. James, *Every Cook can Govern and What is Happening Every Day* (Jackson, MS: New Mississippi, 1986).
18 Diop, *The African Origin of Civilisation*. See also Cheikh Anta Diop, *Civilisation or Barbarism?: An Authentic Anthropology* (New York: Lawrence Hill, 1991).
19 Martin Bernal, *Black Athena Afro-Asiatic Roots of Classical Civilisation: The Fabrication of Ancient Greece 1785–1985*, Vol.1 (New Brunswick, NJ: Rutgers University Press, 1987).
20 George G.M. James, *Stolen Legacy* (Trenton, NJ: Africa World Press, 1988).
21 James, *Every Cook can Govern*, 8.
22 C.L.R. James, *A History of Pan-African Revolt* (London: Drum and Spear Press, 1969).
23 J.R. Johnson [C.L.R. James], 'Marcus Garvey', *Labor Action*, 4:11 (24 June 1940), 3, www.marxists.org/archive/james-clr/works/1940/06/garvey.html (accessed 26 November 2021).
24 John Bracey, 'Nello', *Urgent Tasks: Journal of the Revolutionary Left*, 12 (1991), 125–126, at 125.
25 C.L.R. James, 'The Making of the Caribbean Peoples', Lecture delivered at the 2nd Conference on West Indian Affairs, Montreal (Detroit: Facing Reality, 1966).
26 Ibid., 7.
27 Høgsbjerg, *C.L.R. James in Imperial Britain*.
28 C.L.R. James, *The Black Jacobins: Toussaint L'Ouverture and the San Domingo Revolution* (New York: Random House, 1963).
29 MARHO – The Radical Historians Organisation (eds), *Visions of History* (Manchester: Manchester University Press, 1983), 267.
30 More recent scholarship has accused *Black Jacobins* of elements of Eurocentrism. Clinton Hutton, for example, has pointed to the book's title, and the centring of the contribution of Toussaint Louverture, the educated, privileged freed black, as evidence of James's treating the Haitian Revolution as a by-product of the French Revolution. Also, while James acknowledges the role of Vodou in the early organisational stages of the revolution, Hutton's work strongly centres the political philosophy and the religious cosmogony of the black slaves themselves as a key factor in the philosophy, practice and eventual outcome of the Haitian Revolution. See Clinton Hutton, *The Logic and*

*Historical Significance of the Haitian Revolution and the Cosmological Roots of Haitian Freedom* (Kingston: Arawak Publications, 2005).
31 James, *The Black Jacobins*, 183.
32 C.L.R. James, 'Black Power' in Anna Grimshaw (ed.), *The C.L.R. James Reader* (Oxford: Blackwell, 1992), 362–374.
33 *Ibid.*, 372.
34 Harold Cruse, *Rebellion or Revolution?* (New York: William Murrow, 1968), 100.
35 James, 'The Revolutionary Answer to the Negro Problem in the USA', 183.
36 See Martin, 'C.L.R. James and the Race/Class Question'; and Glenn Richards, 'C.L.R. James and the Question of Black Self-Determination in the United States', paper presented at 17th Annual Third World Conference, 4–6 April 1992, Third World Conference Foundation, Detroit.
37 Richards, 'C.L.R. James and the Question of Black Self-Determination in the United States', 146.
38 Kevin B. Anderson, *Marx at the Margins: On Nationalism, Ethnicity and Non-Western Societies* (Chicago, IL: University of Chicago Press, 2010).
39 James, 'The Revolutionary Answer to the Negro Problem in the USA', 188.
40 See Høgsbjerg, *C.L.R. James in Imperial Britain*.
41 James, 'The Making of the Caribbean Peoples'.
42 Archie W. Singham, 'C.L.R. James on the Black Jacobin Revolution in San Domingo: Towards a Theory of Black Politics', *Savoucou*, 1 (1970), 86–87.
43 *Ibid.*, 85.
44 Diop, *The African Origin of Civilisation*; Diop, *Civilisation or Barbarism?*
45 Diop, *The African Origin of Civilisation*, 225.
46 James, 'The Making of the Caribbean Peoples', 4.
47 Diop, *The African Origin of Civilisation*, 225.
48 Anderson, *Marx at the Margins*.
49 *Ibid.*, 1–4.
50 *Ibid.*, 1–4.
51 C.L.R. James, *Party Politics in the West Indies* (San Juan: Inprint Caribbean, 1984), 167.
52 *Ibid.*, 167.
53 Marcus Garvey, *Philosophy and Opinions of Marcus Garvey*, ed. Amy Jacques Garvey (New York: Atheneum, 1969).
54 Rodney, *The Groundings with My Brothers*.
55 Padmore, *Pan-Africanism or Communism*.
56 Lloyd Best, 'Outlines of a Model of a Pure Plantation Economy', *Social and Economic Studies*, 17:3 (1968) 283–326; George Beckford, *Persistent Poverty: Underdevelopment in Plantation Economies of the Third World* (Kingston: UWI Press, 1994).
57 Ian Cummins, *Marx, Engels, and National Movements* (London: Croom Helm, 1980).
58 Singham, 'C.L.R. James on the Black Jacobin Revolution', 84.
59 *Ibid.*

60 Anderson, *Marx at the Margins*, 155.
61 Charles W. Mills, 'Marxism and Caribbean Development: A Contribution to Rethinking' in Judith Wedderburn (ed.), *Rethinking Development* (Mona, Jamaica: Consortium Graduate School, 1991), 14–35, at 28.
62 George Padmore, *The Life and Struggles of Negro Toilers* (London: R.I.L.U Magazine for the International Trade Union Committee of Negro Workers, 1931), 5.
63 Leslie James, *George Padmore and Decolonisation from Below: Pan-Africanism, the Cold War and the End of Empire* (Basingstoke: Palgrave Macmillan, 2015), 129.
64 Cited in James R. Hooker, *Black Revolutionary: George Padmore's Path from Communism to Pan-Africanism* (New York: Praeger, 1967), 129.
65 George Padmore with Dorothy Pizer, *How Russia Transformed Her Colonial Empire: A Challenge to the Imperialist Powers* (London: Denis Dobson, 1946), ix.
66 Rodney, *The Groundings with My Brothers*, 19.
67 Ibid. 16–17.
68 Charles W. Mills, *From Class to Race: Essays in White Marxism and Black Radicalism* (Boulder, CO: Rowman & Littlefield, 2003), 124.
69 Rodney, *The Russian Revolution*.
70 Walter Rodney, 'Marx in the Liberation of Africa' (edited transcript of a speech delivered at Queen's College, New York, 1975) (Georgetown: Working People's Alliance, 1981), 4.
71 Rodney, *Walter Rodney Speaks*, 98.
72 Rodney, *The Russian Revolution*, 49–50.
73 Ibid., 164.
74 Ibid.
75 Walter Rodney, *A History of the Guyanese Working People, 1881–1905* (London: Heinemann Educational Books, 1981), 174–189.
76 David Austin (ed.), *Moving Against the System: The 1968 Congress of Black Writers and the Making of Global Consciousness* (London: Pluto Press, 2018), 18–21.
77 James, 'The Revolutionary Answer to the Negro Problem in the USA', 183.
78 Denis Benn, *Ideology and Political Development: The Growth and Development of Political Ideas in the Caribbean, 1774–1983* (Kingston: Institute of Social and Economic Research, UWI, 1987), 122.
79 Walton Look Lai, 'Trinidadian Nationalism' in Paget Henry and Paul Buhle (eds), *C.L.R. James's Caribbean* (Durham, NC: Duke University Press, 1992), 174–209, at 183.
80 C.L.R. James, *Modern Politics* (Port-of-Spain: PNM Publishing, 1960), 92.
81 James, *Party Politics in the West Indies*, xix–xx.

# 10

# Poetry and Walter Rodney's unfinished revolution

## David Austin

Some of our finest comrades will fall, have fallen, in struggle, and we don't set about to get the best of our workers and revolutionaries killed just so that we can write poetry to celebrate them subsequently. When they are lost, they are lost, it's an irreparable loss and may in fact qualitatively affect the development of struggle in another phase. And even for those whom we might not remember in poetry and song, what about their lives, their decision to risk all? As materialists we have to say that they are risking all. If we had some other philosophical belief we could say that they are going to a better life, but from a materialist point of view we say that they are prepared to end this particular material existence with no compensation except their own feeling that the society which they are recreating will hasten towards socialism.

*Walter Rodney*

When History sleeps, it speaks in dreams: on the forehead of the sleeping people, the poem is a constellation of blood. When History wakes, image becomes act, the poem happens: poetry moves into action.

*Octavio Paz*

We must understand that we are still locked in struggle, and we are saying we are ready to proceed. We are moving forward, we are not intimidated, we recognise the pressures but are far from bending under those pressures.

*Walter Rodney*

'Reggae fi Radni' was first published in the black British political journal *Race Today* and then appeared on Linton Kwesi Johnson's 1984 LP *Making History*. The elegy is one of his most poignant mediations of the demands of revolutionary struggle. Johnson has written a number of elegies over the years. In fact, it is fair to say that elegies have been a central part of his oeuvre, and even his early 'blood poems' deal with death, even when it is a kind of collective death of sorts, in ways that might be described as elegiac. So what, then, makes 'Reggae fi Radni' unique? The answer lies in Walter Rodney's biography. He was a singular figure, a remarkable intellectual and political voice whose ideas, intellect, and actions influenced his generation in the Caribbean and its diaspora, in Africa, and among Afro diasporic peoples in general. He was also a powerful voice for socialism and was internationally recognised as a historian and a political thinker. In other words, because Rodney was such an exceptional historical figure, the gravity of his death still lingers in the present. His life and work continue to capture our imaginations, and his ghost still haunts us because the revolution he anticipated, committed himself to, and ultimately paid for with his life, remains unfinished in Guyana, the Caribbean, Africa, and the world at large.

Rodney was a historian, but as Alissa Trotz has argued, for him, 'History was not an inert set of documents gathering dust on the shelves of archives', because Rodney 'was interested in a living history, in the ways in which it could offer us insights that could transform our contemporary condition'.[1] And while gender was not central to his work, as Trotz points out, along with his wife Pat Rodney, the feminist and Marxist Selma James was an important influence on him. History was about movement and possibility for Rodney as it was for James Baldwin, who described a process in which a weary history emerges from the terror of the times as 'A slow, syncopated/relentless music begins'.[2] Rodney did not write history as someone who was concerned about history for history's sake or as a mere academic exercise; nor was he solely preoccupied with revolutionary theory. He was a historian who took his craft seriously, but ultimately, he was concerned with revolutionary change as an active participant in the making of history.

## Kindred souls

In 'Reggae fi Radni', the poet captures tragic circumstances that surrounded this seminal figure's death, a death that, like his life, deserves to be considered alongside the likes of Frantz Fanon, Malcolm X, and other figures whose lives were cut short early. The lives of Johnson and Rodney intersected in various ways, almost as if the poet was destined to elegise the historian. Their connections speak to an informal but deeply embedded transnational social network of writers-artists-intellectuals, channels of communication, conversation and affiliation through which political ideas and art have been exchanged in mutual appreciation and critical reflection.

The poet and the historian were part of a shared political and artistic circle and Johnson admired Rodney's politics, convictions, and eloquence.[3] And while the poet was very familiar with Rodney's work, there is a particular link between C.L.R. James and Johnson's elegy: 'Reggae fi Radni' is in part a versification of James's posthumous presentation on Rodney's life and work in much the same way that Johnson's 'blood poems' poeticise the poetics of Fanon's phenomenology of violence. This is not to say that the poem does not reflect the poet's independent assessment of Rodney or the conversations that Johnson would have contributed to in Caribbean, Pan-African, and African solidarity and socialist circles in London following Rodney's death,[4] nor does this view diminish the originality of the poem in any way. Rather, my point is to highlight the interplay between his poetry, Rodney's politics, and James's assessment of Rodney's praxis, intriguing connections that help to situate a poem in which Rodney's life becomes a political metaphor for exigencies of revolutionary politics.

Rodney and Johnson were active in the same informal political circles. Both moved to London from Jamaica in 1963 (Johnson to join his mother and Rodney to pursue a PhD). Though not dreadlocks Rastas, both had been closely associated with Rastafari as young men – Rodney with the dispossessed Rastafarians of Jamaica and Johnson in the concrete jungle of London where he performed with the group Rasta Love. Both were preoccupied with African liberation solidarity work and, despite their appreciation of African and Caribbean history, both eschewed the great king and queen's syndrome – that is to say that they avoided those romantic and mystical representations of an African past in lieu of confronting the weight of contemporary challenges.[5] Both admired the Guyanese poet and politician, Martin Carter, whom Johnson declared 'the political poet par excellence'[6] and whose *Poems of Succession* he described as 'the finest poetic response to historical change in the English speaking Caribbean' – poems that 'were born out of and reflect Carter's own involvement in the struggle of the Guyanese people for national sovereignty and the thwarted efforts to forge a socialist path'. Carter was once an ally of Rodney's nemesis Forbes Burnham, but he later became Burnham's staunch opponent, and as Johnson suggests, the poems written between 1951 and 1975 illustrate the shift in Carter's consciousness over time as the 'defiant, resolute mood of the earlier poems are counterpointed by the more philosophical, brooding, skeptical tone of later poems'.[7]

Here it is worth noting that Rodney's appreciation of literature extended beyond poetry and into fiction, and the Barbadian writer George Lamming was perhaps the writer he most appreciated (it was Lamming whom Rodney requested to write the introduction to *A History of the Guyanese Working People*). And in his lectures on the Russian Revolution – lectures that demonstrate both his extensive knowledge of historical and political literature on the Russian Revolution and, in sharp distinction to C.L.R. James, his sympathies for the Soviet Union despite its purges of its revolutionary leadership under Stalin – Rodney stressed the importance of pre-revolution Russian literature, including the writing of Tolstoy and Dostoyevsky, who in their various ways challenged Russia's ruling elite and, in the process, helped lay the foundation for the Russian Revolution.[8]

## Elegy for Rodney

'Reggae fi Radni' is part of an elegiac tradition that is perhaps as old as poetry itself. Elegy invokes the three m's of melancholy and mourning tied with memory – and in the case of Walter Rodney we might add another, martyrdom – as the living recall the dead as they lived. By choosing to remember them the dead are resurrected, their lives reproduced or reborn in a process of renewal in so far as their spirits are conjured up, fulfilling the living's need to keep the dead alive or to maintain an attachment to the deceased. Elegies are about the mourner's need to heal and feel whole and, in this spirit, they are as much about life and for the living – the mourner – as they are about death and the mourned. Great elegies capture, in J. Edward Chamberlain's words, 'a person's and a people's grief'[9] while setting 'the human imagination up against the overwhelming reality of death, and in so doing they embody both our resistance to it, and our acceptance'.[10] For the poet and theorist Fred Moten, the elegy is tied to tragedy that represents yearning, mourning, lament, a desire for home and a sense of belonging, and a reaction to a tragic state of affairs or a breach or radical interruption of the 'fragile singularity' as well as an invocation of the ghost of totality.[11]

As critic Peter M. Sacks has written, in the English poetic tradition elegies frequently shift from darkness into renewal or light, often invoking the life cycle of vegetation as a metaphor for the cycle of life, death, and rebirth in general. This is part of a process in which death is naturalised as if it is merely part of a season that has passed, only to return again.[12] For Sacks, elegies also serve to unleash the pent-up anger and frustration that is part of grieving while giving voice to protest and posing questions that shift from the mourner's preoccupations with the deceased to the larger social arena as a way of making sense out of a death, and life.[13] This is precisely what Johnson and the many other Rodney elegists attempt to do.

But Johnson's poem is more consistent with the more recent tendency within the elegiac tradition to offer a critical reflection and even criticism of the deceased,[14] and in this spirit, 'Reggae fi Radni' might also be understood as the poet's internal dialogue or engagement with Rodney, externalised in tone in the form of a conversational elegy. Here the poet meditates on Rodney's life and work from a critical distance in order that the ideals and spirit of Rodney's politics may continue despite what Jacques Derrida refers to as the 'ultimate interruption' of death.[15] In this spirit the poet combines respect, admiration, and even celebration of Rodney's life with critical questions about his praxis and the circumstances surrounding his assassination. In the process we encounter Rodney, not simply as a martyr or heroic figure, but a human being, someone who is vulnerable, forlorn, and even prone to doubt which, rather than diminishing him in our eyes, brings his struggle closer to us while at the same time elevating his humanity.

'Reggae fi Radni' is part of a larger tradition of elegies and tributes by and/or about Caribbean artists and revolutionary figures[16] and one of many Rodney elegies that were published in the aftermath of his murder, many of which were collected under the title *Walter Rodney: Poetic Tributes*. The poems vary considerably in content and style, but many of Rodney's elegies frame him as a martyr or a saviour and lament the loss of someone whose life embodied the aims and aspirations of the people of Guyana and the greater Caribbean and the Pan-African world. In keeping with the elegiac heroic martyr figure, Rodney is depicted as Jesus Christ, but in the spirit of Pier Paolo Pasolini's cinematic depiction of the revolutionary Jesus in *The Gospel According to St. Matthew*, as the Jewish prophet whose radical theology and deeds threatened established Judaism[17] and eventually spawned an entirely new faith. Rodney did not overturn tables of money in temples, but he did preach a radical revolutionary politics and paid the price of freedom with his life – an ordinary human being of exceptional intellect and deep political conviction who lives in the hearts and is remembered in the minds of his friends, comrades, and followers, and whose spirit lingers in those who have chosen to take up his call.

But of the many Rodney elegies, 'Reggae fi Radni' is by far the best known, in part because of Linton Kwesi Johnson's international stature, which is in turn tied to the fact that he combines verse and music, considerably expanding the reach of his art. The poem is sombre, meditative and repetitive and its use of counterpoint brings to mind Mahmood Darwish's elegy for his friend and fellow Palestinian, Edward Said. In the poem the Darwish-speaker engages in dialogue with his late friend on life, struggle, and the future of Palestine, shifting from agreement to disagreement and then ultimately back to agreement.[18] Like Darwish's 'Counterpoint', Johnson's poem goes beyond lament, hagiography, and celebration and into the realm of criticism-critique. Instead of opting for valorisation by recalling Rodney's many virtues it poeticises the politics surrounding his death, taking us beyond the romanticism that is so often attached to elegy and memory, beyond Rodney's life and death and into the praxis of revolutionary politics through a meditative reflection on the art of insurrection and social transformation as the poet attempts to glean meaning from the otherwise senseless killing of the revolutionary historian. By drawing on Rodney lore as a metaphor for politics the poet-narrator muses on the meaning of political struggle as Rodney's life becomes the personification and embodiment of eclipsed hopes and dreams and untapped potential.

'Reggae fi Radni' is best appreciated phonographically. Its simple monorhyme scheme, coupled with the haunting music of the Dennis Bovell

Dub Band that includes the melancholy melody of a mandolin, recalls the mournful music of Francis Ford Coppola's classic film, *The Godfather*. The mandolin sustains the poem's sombre sensibility while the playful tone of the xylophone hints at the possibility that, despite the tragic turn, there is still hope that better days are ahead. Meanwhile, the poem's refrain – the elegiac device of repetition[19] – creates a cyclical sense of continuity between past, present, and possible futures in a rhythmic lament that canalises grief while keeping the mourning in motion as if, only over time, it can be purged. Despite the poem's sensibility of sorrow, it is deeply spiritual, but not morose. Rodney's ghost haunts the poem just as duppies – a Jamaican word for ghosts – haunt the living in the Caribbean. The spirit world is omnipresent in the Caribbean and is embodied in the duppiness that is dubbed into the poem in ways that recall W.E.B. Du Bois's famous chapter in *The Souls of Black Folks*, 'Of the Songs of Sorrow'. The chapter captures the elegiac sensibility of 'Negro' spirituals or folk songs, elegiac in the sense that their spirit, the *geist* which reflects Du Bois's studies in Germany and his engagement with Hegel's dialectic, is conjured up from the same place as mourning, a place of lingering sorrow associated with that liminal space that former slaves occupy between death and the quest for human freedom in what Du Bois describes as the 'rhythmic cry of the slave'.[20] If, as Alexander G. Weheliye suggests, Du Bois was the original deejay dub mixer and *The Souls of Black Folks* the prototype for hip-hop in that it mixes, cuts, and collates African-American and European-American literary and musical genres,[21] then 'Reggae fi Radni' represents a three-dimensional contrapuntal elegiac mix that can only be genuinely appreciated in the totality of its aurality, that is to say in is orality and musicality, without privileging the scribal which is essentially a transcription of voices and soundscapes in our heads.[22] When we hear the poet's monotone baritone mourn and lament in rhythmic harmony with the music his voice haunts and taunts us, beginning with the refrain, 'Yuh no see', a common Caribbeanism that, in this context, both poses a rhetorical question and reinforces the sense that the speaker is searching for answers in the sonic scenarios that the poem presents for its readers and listeners.

In short, this mournful poem attempts to derive meaning from Rodney's death – the meaning of social change and the demands of revolutionary politics – and to proffer a politics by raising questions about his political life. It offers a friendly critique, devoid of romanticism and mystique, that ultimately hints that his tragic failure to patiently wait for 'the people' to take the lead in the transformative process in Guyana, to wait for that momentary pause or what Moten refers to as the break, the caesura, which engenders moments of innovation and improvisation, interruptions that are sometimes the result of tragedy which also breeds creativity, novelty and the demand for a fundamental shift or reorientation that represents a cut away from the mundane sense of continuity.[23] Revolution, like poetry, is about rhythm and repetition, that painstaking work that lays the groundwork for the coming struggle which emerges out of the ongoing struggle. Like poetry, it is about tempo, timing, and the turn, that moment of possibility embedded in the break – and the moment, that poetic-political cut, had yet to present itself in Guyana, it would seem.

In the poem's first stanza, Johnson employs the image of a cloud hovering over a dream 'like a daak silk screen' obscuring the speaker's anticipated vision. He moves in counterpoint with the 'some may say' refrain, juxtaposing various views and perspectives on Rodney's life and death, engaging in what we might call the three d's elegy – dialogue, debate and disagreement – in an effort to derive meaning from Rodney's death:

> some may say dat Waltah Radni
> woz a victim af hate
> some wi seh dat im gaan
> through heaven's gate
> some wi seh dat Waltah Radni
> shouldn tek-up histri weight
> an goh carry it pan him back
> like him did wear im anarack[24]

The poet's third person dialogical approach – 'some may say' and the Jamaicanised 'some wi seh' – facilitates the playful presentation of perspectives without committing to or compromising any of them. He contrasts the 'some' say Rodney 'woz a victim af hate' with the others who say he has 'gaan/through heaven's gate', while still others might say that Rodney 'shouldn tek-up histri weight' and carry it on his back in attempting expedite the revolutionary process. The poet-narrator's reference to the historian's carrying of history on his back like an anorak – which nonetheless fails to protect him from the coming storm – is perhaps an allusion to what C.L.R. James described as Rodney's attempt to take history into his own hands through armed struggle against the dictatorship of the government of Forbes Burnham's People's National Congress (PNC) before the actual conditions in Guyana were ready for it. In the aftermath of Rodney's killing there was a deluge of commentary on his life, death and politics as people sought answers to why such an important figure had been so callously eliminated. The most prominent voice among those who posed questions and attempted to provide clarity following Rodney's death was James, his old friend and mentor – if it can be said that he was mentored by anyone.

This was not the first time that James made a public intervention on Rodney's behalf. He had sat alongside him in Montreal at Sir George

William's University (now Concordia) following Rodney's expulsion from Jamaica in October 1968 where he argued that the Hugh Shearer government's desperate actions were part of the general misgovernment and decline in political leadership in the Caribbean. Rodney is highly respected in London and on the African continent for his scholarship, James told the audience, and he 'is in difficulties because he is telling the people there something about the history of Africa which has been so much neglected'.[25] When Rodney wrote a scathing critique of the African leadership and bourgeoisie as part of his contribution to the Sixth Pan-African Congress in 1974,[26] it was James who sounded the alarm and encouraged Rodney to exercise caution: 'We of the Caribbean cannot go to the Pan-African Congress and be the leading ones in putting forward these ideas. That would be a political blunder of the most primitive type.'[27] It was not that James did not agree with the sentiments outlined in Rodney's essay. He himself had written a critique of the leadership of his old friend Kwame Nkrumah when he came to the conclusion that the president had lost touch with the people of Ghana,[28] and he did not attend the Pan-African Congress because it had been co-opted by state officials who prevented the participation of the non-governmental – not to be confused with NGOs – Caribbean delegation.[29] Moreover, James consistently wrote about and spoke of the active role that the general population can and should play in governing Africa and the Caribbean, in fact in all societies. James was not admonishing Rodney, but making a statement on his tactics: that Rodney, from the Caribbean, was not in a position to lay such a devastating critique of the African petty bourgeoisie in a public forum, particularly given that at that time he was living in Tanzania and might be subjected to undue pressure as a result of his criticisms. James was always looking out for his younger friend. In other words, James was not raising questions about the validity of Rodney's political position, but about his political tactics.

The next time that James would have occasion to publicly discuss Rodney, and to pose similar tactical questions, was during a Rodney memorial symposium held at the University of California at Los Angeles where he addressed Rodney's politics and the factors that he believed contributed to his death. It is worth noting that James was living in England, removed from the eventual crime scene as events leading up to Rodney's death unfolded in Guyana. It is also important to consider the intense and incessant political pressure, repression and violence that Rodney and other leaders of Working People's Alliance (WPA) – the socialist and multiracial political party that mounted serious opposition to the PNC – were subjected to by the Burnham government, including the imminent threat of death.[30] That said, James offers an analysis that, whether or not his narrative entirely reflects Rodney's reality in the months, weeks and days leading up to his death, provides several political insights on the dynamics of social change. James's thesis is simple: Walter Rodney did not sufficiently appreciate the exigencies of taking power. In presenting his argument, he cites Lenin's 22 January 1917 lecture on the 1905 Russian Revolution. Speaking to young Swiss workers in Zurich, Lenin stated, 'We of the older generation may not live to see the decisive battles of this coming revolution.' Nonetheless, 'I can, I believe, express the confident hope that the youth which is working so splendidly in the socialist movement of Switzerland, and of the whole world, will be fortunate enough not only to fight, but also to win, in the coming proletarian revolution.'[31] Despite his own confident prediction that he would not see revolution in his time, by March of that same year the Russian Revolution was underway and Lenin was forced to hastily make his way to Moscow to catch up with it. For James, Lenin's speech suggests that you can never tell when the possibilities for change will present themselves. James argued that the role of the revolutionary and the proponent of social change is to patiently lay the groundwork and to be prepared to seize opportunities for change when they arise having taken the time to make the necessary preparation and planning for change. History is replete with examples of liberation movements that have waged struggles to seize power only to find that, once they have won it, the leadership is ill-prepared to lead. James believed that Rodney should have spent more time grounding with the people of Guyana (perhaps in much the same way that he had grounded or engaged in a political and cultural dialogue with the people of Jamaica, the black majority, before being expelled in 1968),[32] laying a foundation for the moment when political opportunities would arise, opportunities that Rodney's work itself would have helped to create, so that he and his co-conspirators would be well positioned to make the most of them. By devoting his energies towards solidifying ties with the working class, including agricultural laborers, while helping to develop the political consciousness of his political associates in relation to the art of revolutionary politics and organisation, Rodney and the WPA would have presented a more formidable threat to the Burnham government that could not be so callously crushed.

James believed that, despite the repression of the PNC government, the climate in Guyana was not ready for an immediate and direct insurrectionary challenge for power. Rodney had not exhausted all the political channels available to him and the population was not at a stage at which they would endorse open insurrection and, regardless of the circumstances, he should not have found himself in a position where he was handling an explosive device. For James, 'a revolution is made by the revolutionary spirit of the great mass of the population. And you have to wait' until the people and the social circumstances are ready[33] because revolution 'comes, as Marx says, like a thief in the night'.³⁴ So again, when the speaker in 'Reggae fi Radni' suggests that Rodney 'shouldn tek-up histri weight' and carry it on his back he is suggesting that Rodney was attempting to take the struggle in Guyana to a place it was not ready to go; that the people were not prepared for insurrection, yet. In this spirit James argued that, although Rodney was aware of what James described as the lack of revolutionary political experience among the WPA's leadership, he did not spend sufficient time training them on the art of taking power, an art that is rooted in the knowledge that the opposition is preparing to eliminate you.³⁵ Ultimately James's critique hinges on the view that Rodney lacked the patience and perhaps temperament to build a revolutionary movement in which the population would play the central role.

Once again, the poet-narrator invokes the image of a cloud sitting on top of his dream, but this time the cloud is 'like a shout ar a scream/ar a really ugly scene/dat awake mi fram di dream/an alert mi to di scheme'. The scheme is Rodney – the 'prizinah af fate', which implies that his fate was tragically sealed once he decided to confront Burnham's power – being killed.³⁶ Again, for 'some', Rodney has gone 'through the heroes gate' while others suggest that he fell victim to the pressures of the moment, 'couldn tek histri weight'.

Deploying a clever rhythmic rhyme scheme, the poet writes: 'soh im tek it awf im back/an goh put it pan im lap/an goh fall in a trap/an soh Burnham get e drap.'³⁷ Rodney carried the weight of history on his back, but the load, the burden, proved to be too heavy to carry, and so he put it on his lap, which is where the bomb that killed him was detonated. But rather than attempting to carry this weight on his own, the poet-narrator implies, the load should have been shared with the mass of the population in order that they too could make history.

The cloud overshadows the speaker's dream, foreshadowing an untoward scheme – Rodney's death – before the dream reaches its climax, the point where the true protagonists, 'di people', enter the dream's 'crucial scene'. The dream has a two-fold meaning: on the one hand, Walter Rodney is the dream personified, a leader in the people's struggle in Guyana who was physically eliminated by a bomb; on the other hand, the dream represents the struggle itself, which is 'blown to smidahreen', or destroyed, before the people, the workers and peasants, can take their place at the forefront of the struggle. In killing Rodney, an embodiment of the hopes and aspirations of his people, Guyana's dreams of liberation are momentarily extinguished.

'Walter found himself in a car with a member of Burnham's army', says James, 'making some arrangement about some gadget that turned out to be an explosive. *He should never have been there.*'³⁸ For James, this is a case of the road to hell being paved with the best of intentions: 'No political leader had the right to be there', and 'Not only should he never have been there, the people around him should have seen to it that he was not in any such position. That was a fundamental mistake, and it was a political mistake ... because he was doing all sorts of things to show them that a revolutionary is prepared to do anything.' Fully aware that Burnham was prepared to physically destroy his opponent, James says he warned Rodney to beware of assassination, a warning that was not sufficiently heeded.[39] Here James takes his cue from the Russian Revolution where the Bolshevik leaders fled to Finland in order to avoid arrest and persecution, but if he were to take Cuba as the model, as it was for many Caribbean revolutionary figures, Rodney's actions were consistent with those of Fidel Castro and other key leaders of the Cuban Revolution, all of whom were on the frontlines of Cuba's revolutionary struggle in the 1950s.

Rodney took the study of revolutionary struggle and its history – and this is obvious in his lectures on the Russian Revolution – seriously, and he was conscious of the risks, the potential real-life consequences involved in armed struggle. He was young, but he had a history of political involvement in the Caribbean, dating back to his youth in Guyana, where he canvassed for the People's Progressive Party, and his student days and his groundings in Jamaica as a professor at the University of the West Indies. He was well respected throughout the Caribbean, even by those who did not share his political ideals. With all of these factors working in his favour, he represented a serious challenge to Burnham. At some point, and given the level of political repression and violence carried out by the state against the Working People's Alliance (WPA) and other oppositional figures, Rodney and other WPA members appear to have quietly arrived at the conclusion that armed struggle was the only political option available to them. And Rodney was not shy about the potential use of arms as an instrument of politics. As early as 1968, during the Montreal Congress of Black Writers, he pressed psychiatrist Alvin Poussaint on Fanon and the revolutionary nature of violence, during an exchange.[40] In his 1969 essay on Black Power he poetically posed the question: 'By what standards can we equate the violence of blacks who have been oppressed, suppressed, depressed and repressed for four centuries with the violence of white fascists. Violence aimed at the recovery of human dignity and at equality cannot be judged by the same yardstick as violence aimed at maintenance of discrimination and oppression.'[41] And as he remarked in the spring of 1975, any decision to engage in armed struggle would involve taking stock of the political situation in a given context and arriving at the conclusion that change would not be possible under the leadership of the ruling government.[42]

Rodney went even further in 1976: armed struggle 'is often associated with the greatest revolutionary heights which people have reached', but this is not as a result of some reverence for it or the result of romantic notions of violence, but 'because it is in those contexts that the political struggle has been most highly evolved' because the 'depth and extent of political mobilisation which accompanies and precedes armed struggle in so many places, most recently in Angola, Mozambique and Guinea-Bissau, is really what accounts for its success, rather than the fact of arms itself'. This said, the decision to engage in armed struggle can only be made by 'the people already engaged in struggle, because it is really when people have engaged in struggle historically through a variety of forms that they settle upon the most effective' form of struggle, including the possibility of armed struggle.[43] Given the circumstances that led to Rodney's death and his subsequent immortalisation in verse, the following dread statement by him sends an eerie echo into the present: 'we don't set about to get the best of our workers and revolutionaries killed just so that we can write poetry to celebrate them subsequently' as the loss of revolutionaries in armed conflict can lead to 'an irreparable loss and may in fact affect the development of struggle in another phase. *And even for those whom we might remember in poetry and song, what about their lives, their decisions to risk all?*' This is why '*people move very slowly and only finally towards armed struggle*', only when other means are exhausted.[44] Armed struggle was not an absolute for Rodney, and he had no romantic illusions about the kind of martyrdom that is expressed in Johnson's verse play *Voices of the Living and the Dead* ('Our singers will sings songs about you/Our poets will write poems about you in memoriam/Flowers will bloom on your graves'[45]). He rather expressed his faith that the people of the Caribbean were capable of determining their mode of struggle as they organised against government repression for a more egalitarian society.[46] His philosophically sobering assessment of revolution, martyrdom, death and elegy as well as his openness to the possibility of armed struggle, while cautioning against hasty and even callous decisions to engage in it, demonstrate his complex understanding of the dynamics of revolution, which he acquired from both his deep appreciation of revolutionary history and practical experience.

Rodney had followed the Cuban Revolution closely and delivered seminars on it while teaching in Tanzania (he also assisted in seminars on China).[47] While in Tanzania he also began preparations for a manuscript on the Russian Revolution, which he outlined in the form of a series of lectures that demonstrate the depth and breadth of his study of literature on the revolution in general. His familiarity with contemporary Russian academic literature on the subject is particularly noteworthy, a body of work for which James, the Hegelian-Marxist who, going back to his days within the international socialist movement and his association with Leon Trotsky, would have cared little. But in addition to Lenin, Rodney also shows his appreciation of the work of Leon Trotsky who had been denigrated and discarded by Moscow and official Communism.[48]

Like George Lamming, Horace Campbell has argued that Rodney and James shared an experience as West Indians who, as a people, were forged out of an encounter between the peoples of Africa, Europe, Asia, and the Indigenous peoples of the Americas – a worldly, cosmopolitan experience that catapulted figures such as Aimé Césaire, Claude McKay, René Depestre, Frantz Fanon, and George Padmore[49] – to which we can add Suzanne Césaire and Claudia Jones, among others – onto the international stage. But Rodney came of age after these figures had set a foundation of intellectual-political inquiry and he benefited immensely from his predecessors, a luxury that James's generation did not have.

Like Johnson, Rodney likely would have been initially familiar with the Algerian liberation struggle through the work of Fanon and he was attuned to the various revolutionary movements in Africa from his first-hand familiarity with African history and politics.[50] And while James's impact on Rodney has at times been overstated, we also know that he was very familiar with the history of the Haitian Revolution through James's *The Black Jacobins*, a revolutionary study of revolution. In other words – and this is important in terms of tempering accusations that he was an adventurist who carelessly and naively attempted to artificially ignite an armed movement – Rodney was well acquainted with revolutionary theory and history, had put a great deal of thought into the social, political and individual cost of armed struggle, and genuinely believed that the working class – 'the people' – would come to their own conclusions to take up arms if and when they deemed it necessary. Revolution and armed struggle was not something to play with, and it was only after careful consideration that he reasoned in 1976 that, while 'above-ground struggle' may still be a viable option in much of the Caribbean, this may no longer be a viable option in Guyana, the obvious implication being that, given the level of repression by Burnham's government, armed struggle was not only inevitable, but imminent.[51]

For Anthony Bogues, James's critical remarks on Rodney failed to appreciate that, by putting his own life on the line, 'Rodney was more *preoccupied* with defining a new kind of revolutionary political leadership' in which 'the gap between the highly educated and the mass of the population would not be reproduced in a political hierarchy where the educated did the thinking about political programs while members of the oppressed class did the doing, the mundane work which sometimes places their lives in danger'.[52] This leadership approach was partly reflected in the WPA's unconventional rotating chair, which essentially meant 'that there was no single leader, and the maximum leader, appointing and disappointing, unaccountable in all essential matters was discarded', according to Tim Hector. Along with the WPA's biracial leadership, this approach 'could better represent the society itself and escape the racialism which plagued Guyana's politics. Few things were more novel or more creative in Caribbean politics.'[53] Rodney and the WPA were attempting to do something new in Caribbean politics and for Bogues, playing with the title of poet and historian Edward Kamau Brathwaite's 1973 review of *How Europe Underdeveloped Africa*, Rodney endeavoured to integrate 'the local dialect with the dialectic' in his praxis, to flexibly apply Marxist theory to Guyana's local cultural-political realities,[54] and to encourage the leadership to do for 'the people' what the leadership was asking of them. This was the model that was applied during the Cuban Revolution against the Batista regime, and Rodney's respect for what he described as the Cuban Revolution's dynamism in the 1960s outstripped even his admiration for the dynamism of Jamaican society.[55]

For Rupert Roopnarine, who worked closely with Rodney in the WPA, James's analysis was not up to his usual standards, and he attributes this lapse to James's deep sense of loss of one of his 'disciples'. Yet he acknowledges that Rodney had grown impatient following his return from Zimbabwe's independence celebrations in the spring of 1980 where, perhaps due to the necessities of nation-to-nation diplomacy (Zimbabwe and Guyana) politics, he unsuccessfully attempted to acquire assistance from the new Southern African government. The movement in Guyana appeared to be ebbing at this point and Rodney felt the urgent need to get things moving and to regain momentum in the direction of insurrection,[56] to perhaps 'heighten the contradictions'. This reality may have unduly influenced Rodney's decision-making at the time, but Roopnarine believes that James failed to appreciate the dynamics on the ground in Guyana in relation to the details of the secret efforts to unseat Burnham. He does acknowledge Rodney's desire to demonstrate that he was willing to lead by example, but also that Rodney found himself in the position of acquiring arms because he was trusted, and in a relatively small and close-knit society where news travels fast through informal networks, trust was paramount in order to minimise the danger.[57]

Andaiye, a key figure in WPA, has argued that it was not Burnham that Rodney misread but the so-called 'lumpen' in Guyana. Rodney was drawn to this group and it was an alleged member of this class who handed Rodney the walkie-talkie that killed him.[58] Andaiye's analysis raises pointed issues about the poor, dispossessed and the working class, and the often facile and romantic ways in which they are portrayed, ignoring that the dispossessed can also be as conservative or even reactionary as the political elite. In essence she suggests that, despite his deep theoretical and historical understanding, in this instance Rodney was perhaps too trusting, even careless, in the political relations he fostered. Her view veers somewhat towards James's and recalls Johnson's refrain 'some may say' which ultimately suggests that Rodney could have been more cautious and discerning in his assessment of Guyana's political context and that in taking on Burnham he perhaps 'woz noh shaak fi di sea' (was no shark for the sea) and 'like a fish to di ook' he fell prey to Burnham.

'Reggae fi Radni' ends when the dream is blown to bits in the middle, 'before di really crucial scene' which is 'wen di people dem come een'.[59] The narrator's dream, Rodney's revolutionary aspirations, and the hopes of 'the people' are scattered (at least for the time being) along with Rodney, who is eliminated before the people of Guyana enter the stage and assume their role at the forefront of the struggle. Ultimately, the poem emphasises the idea that politics is about people, about ordinary people, the 'each and everyone' that is so important to Johnson's later work; without popular participation in which 'the people' mount the stage of 'theatre of the oppressed', the final scene before the new beginning of the next scene, politics is essentially an empty shell, a ruse in a carnivalesque play in which politicians perform and their constituents passively observe or act as bit-part players as the political parade passes them by.

There is no easy road to freedom and Walter Rodney was clearly operating under very challenging circumstances. The logic and spirit of the circumstances appear to have been carrying him along, and once set in motion it appears as though the tragic end was inevitable. If it was going to be a choice between maintaining his grip on power and eliminating the opposition, then Rodney's tragic demise was inevitable, as he himself seems to have come to terms with. In 'Reggae fi Radni', his life becomes a metaphor for the eclipsed dreams of the Caribbean left and the poem itself is a meditation on the demands of social change. The eerie spirit of the poem is only enhanced by the knowledge that, according to Robert Hill, Rodney anticipated his death ('I won't be here')[60] a point that Jan Carew also hints at in his Rodney elegy. As the Kenyan-Kikuyu novelist Ngũgĩ wa Thiong'o has written about Rodney, 'in his death, he has come alive as part and parcel of those millions foreseen in one of the poems by Martin Carter, those wretched of the earth in Africa, the West Indies, the Third World, all over the world, "who sleep not to dream, but who are always dreaming to change the world"'.[61] This was Rodney's dream, ultimately beginning and ending with that corner of the world, the world that he knew best – Guyana.

During a 1995 African Liberation Day celebration in Montreal, Patricia Rodney implored us to think about her late husband 'not just as a political activist, but somebody who was a humanist who loved people, who enjoyed people – and I think that is the reason he was a revolutionary. Because a revolutionary wants to change the lives, the circumstances of people, to make them economically, socially, politically and spiritually better ... it is in that context I would like him to be remembered.'[62] Beyond his revolutionary image, 'Reggae fi Radni' humanises a committed revolutionary intellectual who was cut down in his prime, and seemingly before his time. We are all the wiser for Rodney's experiences and, despite his unseemly death, his work, spirit and, crucially, his life lessons persist in our ongoing struggles to bring about the freedom for which he lived and died. Rather than engage in the romance of martyrdom Johnson pays Rodney the highest tribute by critically deriving meaning from his politics for posterity.

## Notes

1 Alissa Trotz, 'Walter Rodney's Example: Lessons for Our Times', Symposium to Commemorate the 30th Anniversary of the Assassination of Walter Rodney, Queen's College Alumni Association, New York, and WBAI-Pacifica Radio, York College, Brooklyn, NY, 12 June 2010 (unpublished paper), 14.
2 James Baldwin, 'Staggerlee Wanders', *Jimmy's Blues and Other Poems* (Boston, MA: Beacon Press, 2014), 15.
3 David Austin, 'Interview with Linton Kwesi Johnson', 26 October 2004.
4 Austin, 'Interview with Linton Kwesi Johnson', 26 October 2004.
5 David Austin, *Fear of a Black Nation: Race, Sex, and Security in Sixties Montreal* (Toronto: Between the Lines, 2013), 23; David Austin, 'Introduction to Walter Rodney', *Small Axe*, 10 (2001), 64; Linton Kwesi Johnson, 'Reality Poem', *Mi Revalueshanary Fren: Selected Poems* (London: Penguin, 2002), 35–36.
6 Austin, 'Interview with Linton Kwesi Johnson', 26 October 2004. Linton Kwesi Johnson, 'Review Notes', *Race Today*, 9:7 (November/December 1977), 167.
7 Johnson, 'Review Notes', 167.
8 Walter Rodney in Robin D.G. Kelley and Jessie Benjamin (eds), *The Russian Revolution: A View from the Third World* (London: Verso, 2018), 65.
9 J. Edward Chamberlain, *Come Back to Me My Language: Poetry and the West Indies* (Urbana, IL: University of Illinois Press, 1993), 264.
10 J. Edward Chamberlain, *If This is Your Land, Where are Your Stories?: Finding Common Ground* (Toronto: Alfred A. Knopf Canada, 2003), 183.
11 Fred Moten, *In the Break: The Aesthetics of the Black Radical Tradition* (Minneapolis, MN: University of Minnesota Press, 2003), 68.
12 Peter M. Sacks, *The English Elegy: Studies in the Genre from Spencer to Yeats* (Baltimore, MD: Johns Hopkins University Press, 1985), 20–21.
13 *Ibid.*, 22.
14 For more on elegies as criticism see Tammy Clewell's reading of J. Ramazani in 'Mourning and Beyond Melancholia: Freud's Psychoanalysis of Loss', *Journal of the American Psychological Association*, 52:1 (2004), 53–56.
15 Jacques Derrida, 'Rams: Uninterrupted Dialogue – Between Two Infinities, the Poem' in Thomas Dutoit and Outi Pasanen (eds), *Sovereignties in Question:*

*The Poetics of Paul Celan* (New York: Fordham University Press, 2005), 139–140.

16 See, for example, Aimé Césaire's elegy for Frantz Fanon and his tribute to Wifredo Lam; various elegies for Bob Marley, including Rachel Manley's 'Bob Marley's Dead', James Berry's 'Sound of a Dreamer (*Remembering Bob Marley*)', John Agard's 'For Bob Marley', and Afua Cooper's 'Stepping to Da Muse/Sic (for Bob Marley)'; Mervyn Morris's 'Valley Prince', Lorna Goodison's 'For Don Drummond', and Norman Weinstein's 'Drummond's Lover Sings the Blues', 'The Ethiopian Apocalypse of Don', and 'The Migration of Drummond's Organs (*After Death*)' – all for the legendary Jamaican trombonist Don Drummond; Bob Stewarts 'Words is Not enough', ahdri zhina mandiela's 'Mih Feel It (*Wailin fih Mikey*)', Malik's 'Instant Ting', Norval Edwards's 'Poem for Michael', and Kamau Brathwaite's 'Stone (*For Mikey Smith stoned to death on Stony Hill, 1954–1983*)', which are dedicated to the memory of the Jamaican poet Michael Smith; and, among others, Andrew Salkey's homage to Grenada's Maurice Bishop (he also wrote an elegy for Guinea-Bissau's Amílcar Cabral).

17 For an account of the historical Jesus of Nazareth who became the theological Christ, see Reza Aslan, *Zealot: The Life and Times of Jesus of Nazareth* (New York: Random House, 2013).

18 Rebecca Dyer, 'Poetry of Politics and Mourning: Mahmoud Darwish's Genre-Transforming Tribute to Edward W. Said', *PMLA*, 112:5 (2007), 1450.

19 Sacks, *The English Elegy*, 23.

20 W.E.B. Du Bois, *The Souls of Black Folk* (New York: Dover Publications, 1994 [1903]), 156.

21 Alexander G. Weheliye, *Phonographies: Grooves in Sonic Afro-Modernity* (Durham, NC: Duke University Press, 2005), 100–102, 202.

22 Moten, *In the Break*, 180.

23 *Ibid.*, 98–99.

24 Linton Kwesi Johnson, 'Reggae fi Radni' in *Mi Revalueshanary Fren: Selected Poems* (London: Penguin, 2002), 47.

25 The 18 October 1968 speech is published as 'On the Banning of Walter Rodney from Jamaica' in David Austin (ed.), *You Don't Play with Revolution: The Montreal Lectures of C.L.R. James* (Oakland, CA: AK Press, 2009), 299–302, at 299.

26 Walter Rodney, 'Towards the Sixth Pan-African Congress: Aspects of the International Class Struggle in Africa, the Caribbean and America' in Horace Campbell (ed.), *Pan-Africanism: Struggle against Neo-Colonialism and Imperialism* (Toronto: Union Labour/Better Read Graphics, 1975), 18–41, at 19. Rodney's remarks are part of what remained a defining feature of his character throughout his short life. His uncompromising and no-nonsense political stance and his ability to pointedly articulate his political ideas, irrespective of whose feathers his convictions might ruffle, is one of the traits that separated him from many of his contemporaries.

27 C.L.R. James, quoted in Rupert Lewis, *Walter Rodney's Intellectual and Political Thought* (Detroit, MI: Wayne State University Press, 1998), 171.

28 C.L.R. James, *Nkrumah and the Ghana Revolution* (Westport, CT: Lawrence Hill, 1977).
29 Tim Hector, 'Walter Rodney, the Dread Scene, There and Here', *C.L.R. James Journal*, 8:1 (2000/2001), 79.
30 For an analysis of the history of left politics in Guyana see Nigel Westmaas, 'Firebrands, Trade Unionists and Marxists: The Shadow of the Russian Revolution, the Colonial State, and Radicalism in Guyana, 1917–1957' in David Featherstone and Christian Høgsbjerg (eds), *The Red and the Black: The Russian Revolution and the Black Atlantic* (Manchester: Manchester University Press, 2021), 157–173.
31 Cited by C.L.R. James, *Walter Rodney and the Question of Power* (London: Race Today Publications, 1983), 5.
32 Rodney's dialogical approach to education in Jamaica meant that he became both a student and a teacher among members of Jamaica's underclass. In essence, this was Rodney's attempt to engage in a 'politics from below' that would contribute to a mass political and cultural consciousness. This in turn helped to spawn a wave of oppositional politics, in the country's post-Rodney period. See Walter Rodney, *The Groundings with My Brothers* (London: Verso, 2019).
33 James, *Walter Rodney and the Question of Power*, 8.
34 James is certain that Rodney was aware that Burnham was prepared to use the army and the state apparatus in general against him ('prepare your wills') and 'became too anxious about it'. According to James, Rodney 'did not wait for the revolutionary people and the revolutionary class to be in conflict with the government before he could start the question of the insurrection', adding that 'The working class by and large was with Walter, the leader, but they were not in any mortal conflict with the government' and were unprepared to push the struggle to its limits. They were not ready to directly contest Burnham's power. James, *Walter Rodney and the Question of Power*, 8.
35 *Ibid.*, 9.
36 For an analysis of tragedy in relation to revolutionary politics see David Scott, *Omens of Adversity: Tragedy, Time, Memory, Justice* (Durham, NC: Duke University Press, 2014).
37 Johnson, 'Reggae fi Radni', 48.
38 James, *Walter Rodney and the Question of Power*, 9 (emphasis in original).
39 *Ibid.*
40 Austin, *Fear of a Black Nation*, 119.
41 Walter Rodney, *The Groundings with My Brothers* (London: Bogle-L'Ouverture Publications, 1990), 22.
42 Walter Rodney, *Walter Rodney Speaks: The Making of an African Intellectual* (Princeton, NJ: Africa World Press, 1990), 45.
43 Colin Prescod, 'Guyana's Socialism: An Interview with Walter Rodney', *Race & Class*, 18:2 (1976), 109–128, at 125.
44 Prescod, 'Guyana's Socialism', 125–126 (emphasis added).
45 Linton Kwesi Johnson, *Voices of the Living and the Dead* (London: Race Today Publications, 1988 [1974]), 31.

46 Prescod, 'Guyana's Socialism', 126.
47 Lewis, *Walter Rodney's Intellectual and Political Thought*, 168.
48 Rodney, *The Russian Revolution*, 79–89, 172–176.
49 Horace Campbell, 'C.L.R. James, Walter Rodney and the Caribbean Intellectual' in Selwyn R. Cudjoe and William E. Cain (eds), *C.L.R. James: His Intellectual Legacies* (Amherst, MA: University of Massachusetts Press, 1995), 407–408.
50 Prescod, 'Guyana's Socialism', 126.
51 Prescod, 'Guyana's Socialism', 126–127. In a recently declassified CIA memo documenting a late 1979 conversation between Rodney and a representative of the US embassy in Guyana, Rodney not only shares his view on Maurice Bishop and the revolutionary government of Grenada (he describes the government as a 'political embarrassment') but also appears to have, quite remarkably, shared his views on armed struggle. According to the memo, he told the representative that he was not sure whether or not the WPA would engage in acts of terrorism, which he abhorred, but that some kind of retaliation against the government would occur within the next year as all legitimate and legal channels of political opposition had been exhausted. The memo, *dated 13 December 1979*, is based on a conversation that appears to have taken place that month, six months before Rodney was killed, during which, in the classic Marxist conception of the highly industrialised state and socialism, he reiterated his view that the US would one day become the most successful socialist state, and expressed his appreciation for the country's democratic spirit and that a WPA-led government would seek to have friendly relations with the US. But he also expressed his admiration for Cuba, discussed the ideological inflexibility of the People's Progressive Party on economic matters, and gave the impression that his death was imminent and that he was resigned to that fate. If the memo is authentic – and here I do not simply mean in terms of an accurate recording of the conversation, but more an accurate record of the spirit and tone of the conversation – it portrays an image of a somewhat vulnerable and even forlorn Rodney who is fully aware that his death is imminent. He is concerned about what will happen to his family if he is eliminated and, as part of the transition of the WPA to a political party, is attempting to clarify its position on a number of issues in order to avert misunderstanding with the US, allaying fears and attempting to minimise the political and personal fallout that would ensue in the event of his elimination. This said, it is hard to imagine that Rodney did not at least anticipate that his conversation would likely be shared with the Burnham government and that, given his acknowledgement that the WPA was preparing for armed struggle of some kind – if this is in fact the case – the Burnham government would take steps to prevent this, including physically eliminating Rodney and other members of the WPA.
52 Anthony Bogues, *Black Heretics, Black Prophets: Radical Political Intellectuals* (New York: Routledge, 2003), 144 (emphasis in the original).
53 Tim Hector, 'Walter Rodney, Friend, Scholar and Caribbean Figure Extraordinary', *C.L.R. James Journal*, 8:1 (2000/2001), 67.
54 Bogues, *Black Heretics, Black Prophets*, 5.

55 Rodney, *Walter Rodney Speaks*, 10–11, 18–19.
56 Rupert Roopnarine in Clairmont Chung (ed.), *Walter A. Rodney: A Promise of Revolution* (New York: Monthly Review Press, 2012), 111.
57 Roopnarine in Chung, *Walter A. Rodney*, 112–113.
58 Andaiye, quoted in Rupert Lewis, *Walter Rodney's Intellectual and Political Thought*, 243.
59 Johnson, 'Reggae fi Radni', 48, 49.
60 During a 1979 conversation in the US, Robert Hill proposed plans for a speaking tour in 1980. Rodney ominously told Hill that he would not be around the following year, clearly suggesting that he would not be alive by that time. Hill in Clairmont Chung (ed.), *Walter A. Rodney: A Promise of Revolution* (New York: Monthly Review Press, 2012), 68.
61 Ngũgĩ wa Thiong'o, *The First Walter Rodney Memorial Lecture* (London: Friends of Bogle, 1987), 9.
62 Patricia Rodney, 'Walter Rodney and Black Liberation', Montreal, 25 May 1995 (unpublished).

# 11

# 'Hard Facts': Amiri Baraka and Marxism-Leninism in the 1970s

*David Grundy*

From 1974 until his death in 2014, poet, playwright, activist and critic Amiri Baraka was a committed Marxist. Baraka announced his transition to Communism in a series of speeches and essays from 1974 through to 1975. Influenced by his encounters with African leaders and intellectuals committed to socialism and by an older generation of African-American Communists, Baraka called on his organisation, the Congress of Afrikan People (CAP), to examine 'the international revolutionary experience [namely the Russian and Chinese revolutions] and integrate it with the practice of the Afrikan revolution'.[1] By October 1974, CAP was reorganised as a Marxist-Leninist-Maoist organisation, forming part of the New Communist Movement (NCM) – an understudied but vital attempt to build a vanguard revolutionary party in the United States during the 1970s and 1980s. CAP changed its name to the Revolutionary Communist League (RCL) in 1976, merging with the Asian-American and Chicano organisations I Wor Kuen and the August 29th Movement to form the League of Revolutionary Struggle (LRS) in 1979. LRS continued to organise throughout the 1980s, eventually disbanding in 1990. Following the dissolution of LRS, Baraka continued in political and artistic organising, though not a member of a particular party, remaining a resolutely anti-imperialist, anti-racist voice to the end.

This story is too little told. Baraka criticism still focuses almost exclusively on his earlier involvement with the New American Poetry and the Black Liberation Movement (BLM), perpetuating a wider erasure of African-American internationalist Marxist traditions. This chapter therefore has three primary objectives. First, it outlines Baraka's trajectory from cultural nationalism to Marxism and subsequent activism within the New Communist Movement. Second, it participates in recent NCM historiography, suggesting that we might learn not only from the NCM's failures – dogmatism, sectarianism and an emphasis on polemics over successful mass mobilisation – but also from its resolute commitment to anti-imperialism, anti-racism and to organising among communities of colour.[2]

Third, the chapter's second half introduces Baraka's Marxist poetry from 1974 to 1979, reading poems from his collections *Hard Facts* (1975) and *Poetry For The Advanced* (1977) alongside recordings with funk group The Advanced Workers, to show their combination of 'lyric necessity' with political agitation, their presentation of 'class struggle in music', and their surge towards a promise of revolution that at the time of writing seemed very much a present and realisable horizon.[3] All three aspects seek to challenge the legacies of historical forgetting that have rendered this work apparently unreadable to generations of critics, and that characterise the broader scholarly neglect of internationalist Marxism among black radicals in the United States. Remembering these writers' and activists' participation in global anti-fascism and anti-imperialism reminds us of revolutionary possibilities that are too often passed over. As Baraka himself put it, 'there is a gap in American history' – and, we might add, in the international and internationalist histories of the Red and Black Atlantic.[4] This chapter aims to help close that gap.

## From nationalism to Marxism: ideological development and early influences

Born Everett Leroy Jones in October 1934, in Newark, New Jersey, Baraka's father worked for the Post Office and his mother was a social worker. Encounters with the violent racism of US politics marked recent family history: Baraka's grandfather, Tom Russ, was first run out of Dothan, Alabama after he opened a supermarket, and then nearly killed when he ran against the Republican Party as an independent Assemblyman in Newark.[5] Nonetheless, Baraka described his class background as comfortably lower middle class, with his father aspiring to be a member of the 'black bourgeoisie'.[6] Baraka studied at the HBCU Howard University, where his teachers included the great poet Sterling Brown, before joining the Air Force, an experience he would later mockingly refer to as the 'Error Farce'. Tipped off by an anonymous letter accusing him of being a Communist, his superiors discovered Soviet writings in Baraka's possession, and he was dishonourably discharged.[7] However, while he'd read the *Communist Manifesto*, Baraka was not at this stage either a full-blown Communist or a political activist, his interests remaining predominantly literary.[8] Upon his discharge, he made his way to New York, renaming himself 'LeRoi Jones' and quickly becoming part of the city's blossoming literary intelligentsia, co-editing the little magazines *Yūgen* and *The Floating Bear*, and establishing friendships with poets such as Diane di Prima, Allen Ginsberg and Frank O'Hara. Baraka's 1959 visit to Castro's Cuba with a delegation of other writers was in some ways a political turning point, inspiring the essay 'Cuba Libre', published in *Evergreen Review* that year. His correspondence with the Cuban writer Rubi Betancourt, who challenged his bohemian claims to artistic autonomy, caused him to re-evaluate his political stance, and, during the early 1960s, Baraka was increasingly involved with political activism, first with the group On Guard for Freedom, who protested the assassination of Patrice Lumumba at the UN Building in New York in 1961, and then with his own Organisation of Young Men and In/Formation. Baraka was also becoming positioned as a literary spokesperson on the 'race issue', particularly with the success of his controversial play *Dutchman* in 1964.[9] Though many of his intimate relationships and friendships were with white writers, Baraka was increasingly attracted to the modes of black nationalism espoused most famously by Malcolm X, meeting to discuss politics with Malcolm X and Tanzanian politician Muhammad Babu in 1965. Following Malcolm X's murder in 1965, Baraka abruptly broke ties with his white friends, moving from Greenwich Village to Harlem and founding the Black Arts Repertory Theater/School (BART/S). Using government anti-poverty funds, BART/S produced classes, theatrical productions, concerts and street theatre with a militantly anti-white stance, urging the people of Harlem to revolution and declaring Harlem an independent black nation. Within the year, the BART/S experiment ended in violence, and Baraka moved back to Newark in December.

Baraka was now a leading figure in the Black Arts Movement (BAM) which spread across the nation through a series of grassroots artistic endeavours in cities like New York, San Francisco and Los Angeles. Teaching for a semester at San Francisco State in 1967, he come under the influence of the nationalist thinker Maulana Ron Karenga: Karenga's 'black value system', *Kawaida*, was a mode of thinking which borrowed from left-wing anti-imperialist thinkers such as Fanon and Mao, yet was explicitly hostile to Marxism. (It was around this time that he took on the 'Bantuised' Arabic name Imamu Amiri Baraka (literally, 'blessed prince', with the honorific 'Imamu' meaning 'spiritual leader').[10] Baraka soon became involved in political activism in his home town of Newark, New Jersey, with the United Brothers, Committee for a Unified Newark (CFUN) and Congress of Afrikan People.[11] Beaten and jailed by police in the 1967 Newark Rebellion, Baraka had first-hand experience of Newark's racialised inequality, which CFUN and CAP sought to challenge through developing educational institutions such as the African Free School, agitating for affordable housing with the Kawaida Towers project, conducting 'Stop Killer Cops' campaigns, and contributing to Kenneth Gibson's 1970 election as the city's first black mayor. Baraka was also emerging as a national voice in what Komozi Woodard calls the 'Modern Black Convention Movement', most notably through the 1970 CAP Congress in Atlanta, Georgia, and the 1972 National Black Power Assembly in Gary, Indiana. Dedicated to building a 'black united front' in the US, the Convention Movement helped elect black officials such as Gibson and Carl Stokes, and espoused Pan-Afrikan solidarity with African anti-colonial struggles, most notably through the 1972 African Liberation Day demonstrations in support of national liberation parties in Guinea-Bissau, Angola, Zimbabwe, Mozambique and South Africa.[12]

Strongly influenced by Maulana Ron Karenga's US Organization, Baraka was at this time one of the leading representatives of cultural nationalist politics in the United States. Adopting Karenga's Kawaida ideology, which stressed black self-determination and community control in Afrocentric and often patriarchal terms, he promoted Kawaida widely among his own organisations, authoring expositions of Kawaida such as *A Black Value System* (1970). Baraka had been involved with the Black Panthers in 1967, yet the FBI-provoked hostilities between the Panthers and the US Organization, following the murder of Panthers Bunchy Carter and John Huggins in December 1968, saw such connections downplayed.[13] Like Karenga, Baraka was hostile to the Panthers' Marxism and willingness to work with white organisations: while Karenga would, in Baraka's words, 'borrow and cop from some-a-everybody [...] Mao and even Lenin and Stalin and Marx', he 'hid the bits and pieces he had taken from the white revolutionaries', influencing Baraka, who'd read Marx and Mao, to 'excise [their] repeated references to communism'.[14] Aware of class divisions within the Black Liberation Movement, denouncing the 'black bourgeoisie' and figures such as Roy Wilkins and Whitney Young, and drawing on Marxist-oriented decolonial thinkers, Baraka was nonetheless wary of the white left's vocabulary of class struggle, disparaging the 'terrible Marx on the dirty Lenin black people have been given by some dudes with some dead 1930's white ideology as a freedom suit'.[15] In a 1970 speech marking the founding of CAP, he called for a 'nationalist, international, nationalist, pan Africanist political party', drawing parallels to the Marxist Vietcong and other 'Third World people', but rejected the terms 'revolution' and 'vanguard' as 'the white boy's thing', insisting that: 'I would rather make a coalition with Roy Wilkins or Whitney Young – with any of the most backwards upside-down Negroes in the world, because even they must be, in the jivist moment, committed to change.'[16]

Privately, however, Baraka was beginning to have reservations about such a strategy. CFUN broke with Karenga in 1970, and while Baraka still espoused 'revolutionary Kawaida', he distanced himself personally from Karenga, particularly after Karenga's arrest for kidnapping and torturing two female members of US Organization in 1971.[17] Beginning dialogue with more explicitly left currents within the Black Liberation Movement, Baraka's left turn was also shaped by the example of decolonising movements in Southern Africa. In 1971, Owusu Sadaukai (Howard Fuller), director of the Malcolm X Liberation University in Greensboro, North Carolina, travelled to Mozambique, meeting with guerrilla liberation organisation FRELIMO; Sadaukai subsequently established the African Liberation Support Committee (ALSC), which, along with CAP, organised African Liberation Day demonstrations nationwide the following May.[18] Sadaukai's encounters with FRELIMO warned him of the rise of an African neo-colonial bourgeoisie, and this analysis helped activists like Baraka find a framework to understand their betrayal by elected officials like Kenneth Gibson, whose neglect of the working-class black communities who had elected him Baraka saw as a form of domestic neo-colonialism.[19]

Key too was the influence of Amílcar Cabral, leader of the African Party for the Independence of Guinea and Cape Verde (PAIGC) in the independence struggle in future Guinea-Bissau, and one of the foremost anti-colonial leaders in the era of decolonisation. Cabral visited New York and dialogued with African-American activists in October 1972, several months before he was murdered, likely by Portuguese agents; in February 1973, Baraka gave a speech after Cabral's funeral in Conakry, Guinea-Bissau, drawing parallels between elected black officials such as Gibson in the States and neo-colonialist administrators in Africa, and emphasising the role of class in anti-colonial struggles. The funeral also spurred the poem 'Afrikan Revolution', published in leading US journal *Black World*, in which Baraka called on 'Afrikan People all over the world [...] yellow folks brown folks red' to unite against 'all capitalists, racists, liars, Imperialists', insisting that 'Capitalism must be destroyed./Imperialism will die'.[20] As Baraka noted later: 'We were finding out about an Africa of imperialist domination and class struggle. For [Kwame] Nkrumah and Cabral the enemy of Africa was imperialism, not just white people.'[21] CAP newspaper *Black Newark* was renamed *Unity and Struggle*, a phrase taken from Cabral's writings, in February 1974, and CAP began to publicly endorse Marxism that May.[22]

Following this, Baraka travelled with the American delegation to the Sixth Pan-African Congress ('Six Pac') held in Dar es Salaam, Tanzania, in June 1974.[23] This was the first Pan-African congress to be held in Africa itself, and Baraka held dialogue with Guyanese activist-historian Walter Rodney, Tanzanian president Julius Nyerere, President Sékou Touré of Guinea and Marcelino Dos Santos of FRELIMO.[24] Baraka had visited Tanzania twice before, where he had been shepherded by Marxist-Leninist Muhammad Babu, Minister of Economic Planning. Babu 'escorted me around to countless affairs, even though he was then Minister of Economics of Tanzania, and the two of us zoomed around Dar in his car, with Babu driving'.²⁵ Baraka first met Babu through Malcolm X as far back as 1965, at a time when X himself was shifting towards leftist internationalism with the Organisation of African-American Unity (OAAU); the meeting is recalled in the poem 'Class Struggle' from *Hard Facts*: 'you had come as/ambassador from new afrika, when the fumes/of revolution 1st opened our nose'.²⁶ The three 'swore oaths, with another,/of revolution'; visiting Babu some years later, Baraka remembers 'going into his study and wondering why he had all those volumes, some forty-five of them, of Lenin lined up in his bookcases'.²⁷ A consistent left critic of the rise of neoliberalism in former colonial African states, Babu rejected Nyerere's *Ujamaa* model of African socialism – at this stage an important influence on Baraka – for failing to address Tanzania's reliance on raw material exports (a colonial legacy) and for irresponsibly implemented nationalisation. Babu was jailed by Nyerere in 1972 for supposed involvement in the assassination of Vice President Abeid Karume, further alerting Baraka to tensions within newly independent nations and the messy entanglements of colonialism (Baraka saw Babu's arrest as a CIA frame-up).²⁸

Baraka's report on Six-Pac, published that October, advocated 'the anti-imperialist thrust of revolutionary socialism' over 'reactionary nationalism', and the July 1974 Afrikan Women's Congress, organised by Amina Baraka in Newark, 'marked [CAP's] clear evolution [...] toward becoming a vanguard revolutionary party'.²⁹ CAP became a Marxist organisation in October and the transition was publicly announced in December.³⁰ Baraka's return to America additionally saw him encounter a domestic tradition of black Communism. Notably, he learned the 'basics of Marxism – like surplus value' in a three-month dialogue with veteran organiser William Watkins, who 'taught him the fundamentals of political economy and tried to expose the limitations of cultural nationalism'.³¹ The following January, Baraka met with key NCM figure 'Black Bolshevik' Harry Haywood at the Black Women's United Front (BWUF) Conference in Detroit: the two spent an entire day in discussion, Baraka, who 'showed tremendous deference to Haywood', asking Haywood about Communist theory and giving him an overview of the last five years of the Black Liberation Movement.³² Haywood, who joined Cyril Briggs's African Blood Brotherhood in 1922, followed ABB members into the Communist Party of the United States of America (CPUSA), studying in Moscow in the 1920s (fellow students included Ho Chi Minh) and drafting the Comintern's 'Resolutions on the Negro Question' in 1928 and 1930, which stated that African Americans in the Black Belt of the United States constituted an oppressed nation, with the right to self-determination, including the right to secession (the so-called 'Black Belt South Thesis'). In the 1930s, Haywood organised campaigns for the Scottsboro Boys and with the National Miners Union and Sharecroppers' Union. Expelled from the CPUSA in the late 1950s, Haywood sided with Mao in the Sino-Soviet split, regarding the CPUSA's abandonment of the position of self-determination for African Americans, as well as Khrushchev's notion of 'peaceful co-existence', as a betrayal. Working with Malcolm X and with Harlem Rent Strikers, and with the Detroit Revolutionary Union Movement and the League of Revolutionary Black Workers in the 1960s, Haywood was a key figure in the NCM as it emerged from the confluence of anti-revisionist CPUSA dissidents and newer Maoist currents. Throughout his political career, he held to the 'Black Belt South Thesis' as a key element in US revolutionary struggle. Soon after meeting, this thesis would become a central and lasting tenet of Baraka's political thought.[33]

The influence of women of colour on Baraka's left turn was also hugely significant. It was the build-up to the Afrikan Women's Conference organised by Amina Baraka in July 1974 – and the subsequent establishment of a Black Women's United Front (BWUF) in 1975 – that definitely saw CAP move towards socialism, equally emphasising 'Use of Scientific Socialism – Marxism-Leninism and Mao Tse Tung Thought' and 'Struggle Against Male Chauvinism and Equality of Women Activists'.[34] As Dayo F. Gore, Jeanne Theoharis, and Komozi Woodard note in *Want to Start a Revolution?*, their vital work on 'radical women in the Black Freedom Struggle', historical studies of this period too often retain a '"leading man" master narrative that [...] minimises the contributions of women', 'centr[ing] men and locat[ing] women at the margins of great social change' (the 'men lead but women organise' model).[35] Amina Baraka had been central in one of CFUN's main initiatives, the African Free School in Newark, and many other aspects of CAP organising, and it was the influence of female activists within CAP which, more than anything, turned the movement away from the misogyny of the nationalist period.[36] As Amiri Baraka later noted: 'it was Amina who encouraged this study [of Marxism] and pressed for its public dissemination to the organisation as a whole'.[37] Likewise, Jamala Rogers was a key member of the St Louis branch of CAP, involved with the ALSC and National Black Assembly (NBA), and followed its members into the RCL and LRS. Another key figure, veteran Marxist-feminist activist Vicki Garvin, worked with Baraka in the BWUF and the National Black United Front: a former member of the CPUSA and the National Negro Labor Council, Garvin had worked with Malcolm X in Ghana in the 1950s, teaching English in Mao's China from 1960 to 1970, before moving first to Newark, then New York. And in the later 1970s and 1980s, Baraka worked with Mae Ngai, an important left organiser within Asian-American movements, as part of the LRS. (Ngai was an important commentator on the far right anti-migrant turn under US President Donald

Trump.)[38] Baraka's female comrades were essentially giving him a history lesson in lived experience. Through their influence, he could newly link anti-colonial movements, class struggle and the fight for women's equality to his existing focus on the black liberation struggle in America.

### 'The basis of the party yet to be built': from CAP to LRS

Baraka was now part of the New Communist Movement. Ignored and derided in much historiography, the NCM emerged from 1960s New Left, Black Power, and other formations, including Students for a Democratic Society, the League of Revolutionary Black Workers, the Black Workers Congress and the Young Lords. Its numerous, often small pre-party formations sought to create a vanguard Communist Party; their focus was internationalist, anti-racist and anti-imperialist, heavily influenced by Mao Zedong's thought and by the commitment to internationalism displayed by the pre-Cold War Communist movement.[39] Despite its often dogmatic 'anti-revisionist' Stalinism, the movement *was* a large, cross-racial left presence at a time of intense reaction: examining Baraka's role within it serves to illuminate not only our sense of his work but of this period within the left as a whole.

Baraka's involvement with the NCM began with the June 1974 Newark taxi drivers strike, organised by CAP, alongside the local Black Panthers and the mainly white Revolutionary Union.[40] At this stage, as Baraka suggests, 'we still had a lot to learn'. CAP activists became newly embroiled in heated ideological debates about the niceties of Leninist theory, and often felt disconnected from white left groups, whose struggles were conjunctural rather than structural.[41] Baraka expressed his frustrations at left sectarianism in *Unity and Struggle* that December:

> There are some organisations that spend more time plotting how to undermine other socialist organisations than how to struggle against monopoly capitalism [...] We do feel that it will be very positive when 'multinational' organisations face the fact of their not really being multi, but predominately white.[42]

Embroiled in 'academic word wars, super militant rhetorical battles, to see who has the most grasp of socialist theory', CAP 'repeated the mistakes of some of our new comrades in the new Left movement', losing 'dozens of valuable, experienced activists'.[43] Though Baraka initially envisaged transforming CAP into a vanguard party, he soon realised that Marxism-Leninism lacked black nationalism's popular base.[44] Compared to its earlier incarnation within the Black Convention Movement, CAP (subsequently

RCL and LRS) knew it was small: like all NCM organisations, a pre-party formation, rather than a vanguard party per se.[45] Yet it did much valuable work. More so than other NCM organisations, it organised among marginalised sectors of the labour force: migrant and undocumented workers in New York sweatshops, Los Angeles metal fabrication workshops, San Francisco, Honolulu and Boston hotels, and Carolina canning plants.[46]

The RCL/LRS conducted campaigns in Newark, Mississippi, Alabama and Georgia, within the anti-apartheid movement, against slumlords and for education reform, establishing a People's Committee on Education and protesting the 1978 Bakke decision which had effectively reversed affirmative action.[47] Perhaps its most effective campaign, 'Stop Killer Cops', founded through a mass demonstration against the murder of Claude Reese in Brooklyn in September 1974, 'mobile[zed] thousands of people around the country'.[48] During the 1980s, strategic debates on how to fight the rise of Reagan and the Ku Klux Klan led to involvement in Jesse Jackson's Rainbow Coalition, differences over which saw the LRS dissolve in 1990 (Baraka himself left in 1988).[49] One of the longest-lived NCM organisations, LRS's dissolution reflected the NCM's broader demise. But Baraka remained a Marxist until his death, continuing to organise in Newark (ultimately leading to the election of his son Ras as mayor in 2014) and stirring controversy with his 2001 poem 'Somebody Blew Up America' in 2001. Presently, I'll turn to Baraka's poetry from 1974 to 1979, in the pre-Reagan years when his Marxism was at its most fiery and immediate. First, I'll outline the legacy of historical forgetting affecting both Baraka's own late embrace of Marxism and existing historiography of this period.

## 'There is a gap in American history': black Marxism and historical forgetting

As Angel L. Martinez notes, Baraka 'arrived at [h]is commitment [to Marxism] considerably late compared to other revolutionary internationalist artists'.[50] 1960s cultural nationalism overlooked an earlier tradition of black Marxism that might have suggested an alternative direction, including Communist activists Cyril Briggs, C.L.R. James, Claudia Jones, Nelson Peery, James and Grace Lee Boggs, Paul Robeson, Langston Hughes, W.E.B Du Bois, Harry Haywood and Vicki Garvin. (As Lisa Merrill and Theresa Saxon's chapter in the present volume suggests, the silencing of Robeson and others in the McCarthy era was especially important in terms of the way this earlier tradition of black Marxism became overlooked.) Because of this, Baraka's highly publicised 'left turn' in 1974 caused consternation among large sectors of the nationalist movement he'd helped promote.[51] Before

Baraka left for Six-Pac in Tanzania that June, he gave three speeches, at the CAP Midwest Regional Meeting in Chicago, the Second National Black Political Convention in Little Rock, Arkansas, and the ALSC Conference at Howard University, which suddenly and polemically announced his transition to Marxism, leading to the resignations of activist-organiser Jitu Weusi and poet-publisher Haki Madhubuti from CAP, and secretary Elizabeth Atkins from the NBA – to be followed by Baraka himself that November.[52] These resignations led to a bitter polemical exchange in the black press.[53] In the succeeding months, the membership of both CAP and the NBA shrank dramatically, and *Black World* itself abruptly folded the following year, Baraka's turn away from the nationalist ideology he'd been so influential in promoting effectively leading to the collapse of the various organisations associated with it.[54] The controversy over Baraka's left turn reflected already-existing divisions within the Black Convention Movement, as certain elements moved away from independent politics and towards the Democratic Party, while others, such as Sadaukai's ALSC, endorsed Pan-Africanism and internationalist Marxism. But Baraka's individually significant role within the movement should also be stressed, and the way this transition was managed was arguably damaging. Baraka knew this. He initially attempted to balance the multiple influences of Karenga-influenced nationalism with African socialism and Marxism-Leninism: in the first of the three transitional speeches, at the Regional CAP meeting in Chicago, he called for a party simultaneously influenced by Marxism, Mao, Nyerere, Touré, Cabral and Karenga.[55] As indicated by his resolute commitment throughout the 1970s and 1980s to the 'black nation thesis' inherited from Haywood, Baraka's Marxist concerns were often outgrowths of, rather than sharp breaks from, his preceding political positions. Baraka initially insisted that a Marxist-Leninist vanguard party could work with nationalist organisations within a 'progressive Black United Front', citing James Boggs's arguments on the 'relative independence' of revolutionary and reformist movements.[56] This two-pronged strategy continued throughout the 1970s and 1980s, most notably in the League of Revolutionary Struggle's involvement with Jesse Jackson.[57]

Nonetheless, Baraka's handling of CAP's 1974 transition was dogmatic and heavy-handed, alienating nationalist elements rather than winning them over to the left. In particular, his attacks on Weusi and Madhubuti, serialised over eleven issues of *Unity and Struggle*, frequently took a personal tone.[58] Madhubuti recalls: '[Baraka] came out with both feet jumping on [me]. [...] He talked about my diet ... you know what I'm saying? It didn't have nothing to do with politics.'[59] And Michael Simanga notes: 'it was the source of a great deal of discussion and disappointment that Baraka's critique was so personal and [the] CAP [...] had chosen to publicly humiliate people who were as committed as we were'.⁶⁰ Baraka himself later admitted: 'While much of my criticism [...] was accurate, the tone and approach were like beating somebody in the head for disagreeing.'⁶¹ And, for CAP activist Jamala Rogers: 'The [...] evolving ideology [...] was problematic for some both inside and outside the organisation [...] I will be the first to admit that liquidation of CAP as a national-in-form mass organisation was a political error.'⁶²

Elevating one individual's contributions over those of others – not only 1970s activists comrades like Garvin, Amina Baraka, Jamala Rogers and Mae Ngai, but earlier black Marxists – leads to political errors and a distorted view of history. In its skewed focus on the pre-Marxist period, whether the 'New American Poetry' or black nationalism, Baraka criticism further erases traditions of black Marxist internationalism, presenting the Black Arts and Black Power movements as if they magically emerged with the death of Malcolm X, and just as magically disappeared by 1974. Such narratives reflect government-fostered internal divisions within Black Power organisations, such as the Panthers–US split; personality cult; McCarthyite historical erasure; the failure of the CPUSA; and the assassination of leaders propounding a left-leaning, internationalist united front strategy, most notably Malcolm X and Martin Luther King (both of whom were in talks with Baraka shortly before their deaths).⁶³ As Baraka put it in the 1977 poem 'Malcolm Remembered': 'when they killed you/it left a double vacuum/No communist party, no national/leadership'.⁶⁴ It was this in part that meant Madhubuti reacted with such shock to Baraka's Communist turn and that members of the NBA preferred to make alliances with racist Alabama governor George Wallace than with an 'avowed Communist'.⁶⁵

Likewise, earlier African-American socialist writing, most notably that of Langston Hughes, was 'very carefully hidden by American literary marshals [...] You always find out what [...] the literary "avant" of the Right [did], but what about the literary "avant" of the Left? There is a gap in American history.'⁶⁶ Baraka co-edited LRS magazine *The Black Nation* (1981–86) with Michael Simanga, publishing Hughes, Margaret Walker, Askia Touré and Marvin X alongside Jayne Cortez, Amina Baraka, Walter Rodney, Michael Smith and Linton Kwesi Johnson, and his own writing reflects this vibrant cross-cultural aesthetic: essays on Aimé Césaire, Ngũgĩ wa Thiong'o and Ousmane Sembène sit alongside the reggae poem 'Wailers' (1982), for Bob Marley and Larry Neal, and 'In the Tradition' (1980), whose revolutionary roll call includes Frederick Douglass, Harriet Tubman, Léon Damas, René Depestre, Jacques Roumain and Nicolás Guillén.⁶⁷ Young Lords founder Felipe Luciano calls this 'the Black Global Aesthetic' and Baraka's son, Ras, notes: 'There was always poetry read and great speeches given from dignitaries and artists from all over the world [...] I heard artists from Latin America, Africa, the Caribbean, Europe, and activists alike.'[68] Such work continued the collective, performance-based focus of the Umbra Workshop, BART/S and Spirit House, through the Nuyorican Poets Cafe, the Anti-Imperialist Cultural Union, Yenan Workshop, The Advanced Workers and Proletarian Ensemble.[69]

Baraka's own autobiography essentially stops 'somewhere in 1974', and we lack a comprehensive account of such activity.[70] Recent Black Power histories end with the movement's mid-70s decline, and literary critics frequently overlook Baraka's Marxist poetry. Yet critical judgements of the controversies within CAP and NCM dogmatism should not overshadow our evaluation of this work. Far from subordinating 'aesthetics' to 'politics', his work refuses such distinctions and, in the current climate of rising right-wing nationalism, has more to teach than ever. I'll now turn to Baraka's Marxist poetry, outlining its publication contexts and addressing individual poems on religion, family, music and revolution.

### 'A weapon of revolutionary struggle': Hard Facts (1975)

Baraka's Marxist political activism and poetry were most closely connected between 1974 and 1979: unfortunately, no single volume collects such work. Returning to the small press practices of the 'Beat' era, Baraka's People's War (formerly Jihad) 'put out an endless stream of inexpensive pamphlets', including most of his own contemporaneous writings and books by Sékou Touré, Cabral and Lenin.[71] Self-publishing was both virtue and necessity. Baraka sardonically notes: 'From the big publishers I published regularly until about 1970. This is probably when they thought it was good business.'[72] While Baraka's black nationalist work of the 1960s was marketed alongside texts by Fanon, Eldridge Cleaver and others, Marxism-Leninism during the 1970s was a less attractive proposition to publishers.[73] As Anthony Monteiro puts it, Baraka 'was whited out by the American mainstream'.[74]

Two major works of Marxist-Leninist poetry appeared during this period. Excerpts from *Hard Facts*, a collection written between 1973 and 1975 during the transition to Marxism, were first published as a People's War pamphlet in 1975, and appeared in full alongside its 1977 follow-up, *Poetry for the Advanced* in Baraka's *Selected Poetry* (1979), published by William Morrow. Written between October 1974, when CAP officially reformed as a Marxist organisation, and November 1975, *Hard Facts*' introduction takes its place alongside Baraka's earlier manifesto 'The Revolutionary Theatre' as a vital statement of revolutionary aesthetics:

> Yes, poetry should be a weapon of revolutionary struggle. And we say it again. Otherwise it is 'a teacup in Rocky's summer place,' a distraction, an ornament the imperialists wear to make a gesture toward humanity.[75]

Echoing the call from 'Black Art' (1965) for 'assassin poems, poems that shoot guns', Baraka newly emphasises revolutionary praxis and the study of socialist texts:

> [The people] need odes of strength, attack pieces, bomb, machine gun and rocket poems. Poems describing reality and methods of changing it. Rhythmic reading lists, objectivity, clarity, information, science, as well as love and concern.[76]

Calling for a 'new revolutionary art' and a new 'anti-imperialist cultural union', Baraka was still predominantly a cultural worker. As Robin D.G. Kelley notes:

> Despite his immersion in Marxist-Leninist-Maoist literature, his own cultural work suggests [...] he knew [...] that [political questions were] not going to be settled through reading Lenin or Stalin. If [they] ever could be settled, the battles would take place, for better or for worse, on the terrain of culture.[77]

For Kelley, cultural work can conduct political struggle; conversely, political work can manifest the same imaginative urge generally ascribed to culture.

> Progressive social movements do not simply produce statistics and narratives of oppression; rather, the best ones do what great poetry always does: transport us to another place, compel us to relive horrors and, more importantly, enable us to imagine a new society. [...] Social movements enable participants to imagine something different, to realise that things need not always be this way. It is that imagination, that effort to see the future in the present, that I shall call 'poetry'.[78]

In this vein, *Hard Facts* addresses current political struggles and reflects on those of the past with the benefit of a new-found Marxist perspective, addressing music, family and revolution. 'Red Autumn' reflects on the transition to Marxism-Leninism in October 1974, the month of Baraka's birthday, and one with Russian Revolutionary predecessors.[79] A personal reminiscence of this life-changing whirlwind of meetings, organising activities and ideological debates, the poem opens with a descriptive cityscape shot through with civic corruption, the headquarters of the gigantic Newark-based company Prudential, 'the largest life insurance company in the world', towering over the 'low houses' below.[80] Visiting Amina's family, the Barakas 'talk of the city's political corruption', 'readying to go to a women's conference' where 'some sisters/[are] pushing a proposal to call a multinational women's front together, by spring'. Such experiences are presented through the vocabulary of political organising, the specific task of creating a 'multinational women's front' leading to more general commentary on the need to move 'from the tactical to strategic, build the whole structure that will/change the century, change the social system, change the way we live, change the peoples / lives and the future of the world'. The movement from 'indian summer' to 'red autumn' – where redness is both seasonal and political symbol – from 'winter […] yet ahead' to the proposed multinational women's front 'by spring', both provide a metaphor for struggle, and the mundane yet urgent calendar of political work.

This double movement is reflected formally: the tension between the demands of prose statement or description, expressed in the form of the sentence, and the contours of sound patterning and the poetic line, give the poem an affective charge reflective of the movement of politics in the texture of lived experience. As Baraka noted of his recent work in 1977, while 'the content is always trying to talk about […] the necessity for change', 'the forms themselves are dictated by the time, place, and condition, like anything else'.[81] This has not been well understood. Werner Sollors, for instance, argues that the 'prosaic' qualities of Baraka's Marxist poetry represent the failure of 'literary logic', as 'politics wins out over aesthetics'.[82] While critics praise the contemporaneous 'New Sentence' and other Modernist challenges to conventional poetic forms, they tend to stop short when the 'prosaic' material is more explicitly polemical. In doing so, they also erase the internationalism of Baraka's influences. As well as Hughes, Baraka was influenced during this period by the concise polemical prose writings of Chinese writer Lu Hsun (Xun) to seek 'a deliberately wider line and a rhythm shaped by the ideological requirements of the statement itself'.[83] Hailed by Mao as 'the sage of modern China', Lu Xun's 1920s *zawen* (short essays) 'combined poetry and revolutionary observation'.[84] The word *zawen* connects *zagan* (miscellaneous impressions) and *zatan* (miscellaneous discussion), and these short satirical texts, 'a catch-all name for all kinds of prose pieces', responded to the miscellany of the moment (*za*: miscellaneous, cluttered, jumbled) with the clarity of immediate analysis.[85] Formerly a poet and short story writer, with the conceptualisation of *zawen*, Lu Xun moved away from reliance on existing literary forms or standards, finding a way to combine contingency, clarity and accessibility with a sense of personal aesthetic style.[86] Lu Xun's work often responds to the demands of a particular moment, and for Baraka the 'short essay form is really suited for the kind of daily struggle I'm engaged in – it's a kind of *struggle form*':

> It's *wider* than a poem, as far as I'm concerned. Because in poetry you usually have a rhythmic dynamic that you either have to force, if you don't have it with you, or if you have it with you, it flows and has a life of its own. But in the short essay form the rhythm flows from what you have to say.[87]

But Baraka's distinction between essay and poem perhaps oversimplifies his own negotiations between the two. While the introduction to *Hard Facts* is a clear example of the essay form, poems such as 'Red Autumn' also emerge from it. The rhythm of the poem 'flows from what you have to say', but this in turn is rhythmically guided by sound, by 'a rhythmic dynamic which flows and has a life of its own'. Intended as the 'necessary daggers and javelins' for the struggle (the title to Baraka's 1984 collection of essays), Lu Xun's *zawen* were also intended as 'a form of convalescence: a stage of preparation between toil and combat'.[88] 'Red Autumn', too, mixes apparently miscellaneous impressions with strategic discussions. It is also a 'convalescent' reflection, a preparation for the struggle ahead which freights apparently miscellaneous observations with a wider sociohistorical perspective. Baraka unites and structures these observations through techniques that are nothing if not 'poetic'. In the poem's opening lines – 'communist sparrows gnawing on a fire escape/together in bread lines flying off to the next low house' – 'communist sparrows' appears as an arbitrary, near-surrealist application of adjective to noun, but turns out to operate along a witty pun on 'bread lines', uniting observation of the city environment with its connotations of political corruption and poverty. The next two lines – 'cant get up to prudential, that high white, w/the stain glass eyes/while indian summer flutters, drunks mutters' – unite the movement of sound, through assonance and internal rhyme ('*high white* [...] glass *eyes*'; 'summer *flutters*, drunks *mutters*'), the movement of the eye (following the sparrows) and the movement of the mind. The sparrows stay among the 'low houses' of the poor, gnawing on fire escapes because they lack 'bread' (money), leading to the pun on 'bread lines' and social welfare, and 'cant get up to' the Prudential Building, leading Baraka to reflect on political corruption in the city. Perhaps the sparrows were seen at the moment of composition, triggering this reflection on the events of the red autumn; perhaps they were present at the visit to Amina Baraka's grandmother and father, neatly correlating with the discussion of the political discussion in Newark, and providing a symbol for urban spatiality and its power imbalances. What Baraka reveals is that urban space *already has* a poetics: the Prudential Building is a building designed and functioning as a symbol in day-to-day life, its expensive life insurance policies contrasting with those who starve through being unable to reproduce themselves, lacking the necessary 'bread' (money) to buy 'bread' (food). Social community here functions on four levels: Baraka and Amina Baraka (addressed somewhat patronisingly as 'the little girl') and her family; the political corruption against which they fight, concretised by the tenements and Prudential; the political organisations in which they are involved; and the movement of revolution across the world.[89] The relation between particular and general, poetry and prose, arises organically from the form of the poem itself, registering the social constitution of what the eye/I can see: a dialectic of observation, particular and general. Baraka furthers his existent, essentially autobiographical project, of situating his own struggle within the broader context of ordinary people's lives, the black struggle in America, and the global context of revolution to transform 'the whole world'.

### 'Class Struggle in Music': The Advanced Workers

Recalling Kelley on the black radical imagination, it makes sense that, in Baraka's poetry, the language of activism takes its proper place within a poetic context; likewise, the language of the aesthetic informs and feeds into politics. Perhaps the most important way in which Baraka's Marxist work links the contingencies of feeling with 'the motion of history' is its figuration of music. 'Literary Statement On Struggle!', which follows 'Red Autumn' in *Hard Facts*, opens with a line that might have come directly from Baraka's earlier work – 'A poem is/the naked advice of the heart' – before clarifying the combination of passion and political analysis – such a statement should 'try to make people progress/our life here go forward' – and ends by invoking Charlie Parker for the revolution: 'Nows the time, Charley Parker sd, Now's the time. Say do it, do it, we gon / do it [...] to say again revolution, and again revolution and again revolution [...] all that's bad and mad and won't be had.'[90] Baraka's Marxist poetry finds its key figure in music, which enacts the combination of universal and particular, cross-racial unity and particularised cultural experience, that formed the basis of his political organising. Music, as a bridge between individual and community, in which, as Baraka noted in his earlier work on blues, generic forms allow for 'completely personal' expression, 'as arbitrary and personal as the shout', is not only a *figure for* political modes of being, but *already enacts* the collectivity such movements group towards.[91] Baraka writes poems about music – notably 'Pres Spoke in a Language', 'AM/TRAK' and 'In the Tradition', for Lester Young, John Coltrane and Arthur Blythe – formally suffused with musicality – blues patterns, songlike refrains, sonic imitations of scat, be-bop and free jazz, actualised in dynamic performances, often within musical contexts. Manifesting a 'lyric necessity in my own self', these poems also constitute *lyrics*, their insistent aurality involving speech in its wider form, from spoken utterance to political speeches to song.[92] As Chris Stroffolino notes, 'the poem [...] turn[s] into a [...] prose argument' only 'if read on the page without hearing a live performance'.[93]

Given this, a pamphlet like *Hard Facts* only tells part of the story. It was, above all, in performance that Baraka's work really came alive, as attested by the stunning recordings of 'Dope', 'Against Bourgeois Art' and 'Afro-American Lyric' that appear on the album *New Music/New Poetry* and in readings given at Buffalo and Naropa Universities.[94] In 1976, Baraka recorded two 45 RPM sides with The Advanced Workers and the Anti-Imperialist Singers, a group including members of Parliament/Funkadelic and Kool and the Gang.[95] These singles, released by People's War, give a sense of what a viable Marxist pop music might sound like. More accessibly tied to the demands of the pop song than the experimental approach of bands as The Red Krayola, these two songs, 'Better Red Let Others Be Dead' and 'You Was Dancin Need To Be Marching So You Can Dance Some More Later On' are only fleeting artefacts of the cultural activity that bands such as The Advanced Workers carried out.[96] Such performances often went unrecorded, emerging out of specific social circumstances, and avoiding the marketisation of struggle that involvement with major record labels might have risked. On the 45s, Baraka's spoken contributions do not so much 'lead' the band – poet as lead singer – as form a galvanising interlude, a short political speech which the band members take up as a chant, somewhere between slogan, song lyric, and slogan, pulsing into and forming the song's principal, joyous riff: 'and when you asked what truths they party taught/they'd say Marxism-Leninism-Mao-Tse-Tung Thought'. Something of the power of this record was indicated when Paul Gilroy played it as part of his keynote address at the 2014 Baraka conference at the ICA in London, which took place shortly after Baraka's death. However incongruous the juxtaposition of Maoist slogans with funk, it's hard not to be exhilarated and inspired, not only by the music but by the conviction with which those slogans are delivered, and the hopes they contain.

### 'Can I get a, like they say, witness': Poetry for the Advanced (1977) *and beyond*

The Advanced Workers record was made in a period of revolutionary hope. New alliances were being made within the New Communist Movement, and the example of decolonial liberation movements in Africa, as well as struggles in southern Europe, still burned bright. It's easy to forget that this was an era in which the possibility of an international, anti-capitalist and anti-imperialist revolutionary movement was still a realistic possibility. While the Soviet Union had long since degenerated into a corrupt superpower, movements in Angola, Guinea-Bissau, Portugal, Spain and China threatened to dissolve the order of post-war capitalism and the remnants of the old colonial order.[97] In retrospect, this was the moment of Reagan, Thatcher and Deng Xiaoping: but at the time, this was by no means set in stone. As Baraka later noted:

> This was the era when Mao Tse-Tung said, 'Countries want independence, nations want liberation, and the people want revolution.' Remember that. For our generation, that was the cry. We used to say that all the time; we loved to hear that. We also used to quote him saying, 'Revolution is the main trend in the world today.' That's what we used to say.[98]

Baraka's work from roughly 1974–79 is intensely reactive, charting each new outrage and tactical response with a furious capacity for witness and desire for change. By the time his essay collection *Daggers and Javelins* appeared in 1984, he argued that the trend was now towards fascism. The NCM had largely disintegrated into faction fighting, and the rise of Ronald Reagan led to the very real fear of world war, increased Ku Klux Klan activity, police violence, the rolling back of affirmative action, and continuing exploitation of minority workers. This was 'a deeply reactionary right-wing period', in which the left was faced with 'disorder and splitting and failure', leaving 'only two choices, socialism or fascism'.[99] Its legacies are still with us. The long shadow of Reaganism, the triumphalism of the 'End of History' and the diminishing presence of visible mass struggles has made it difficult to remember the high level of class struggle and anti-imperialism to which Baraka's Marxist work attests. Yet, in this work, revolution is not something distant and far off, but an imminent horizon.

This horizon becomes especially apparent in Baraka's second book of Marxist poetry, *Poetry for the Advanced*. Completed in 1977, it appeared alongside *Hard Facts* as part of Baraka's 1979 *Selected Poetry*, published by William Morrow. As in *Hard Facts*, politics emerges from the texture of lived experience. But Baraka's poetic Marxism is here more honed, the swerve from lyric invective to lineated political argument and back assured, convincing and moving. These poems underscore both 'personal' and 'political' as *inter*personal: family, lovers, friends. They understand that life is lived socially, and that poetry, which affects life, is produced socially, whether on a wider or more intimate scale. The opening 'Poem for Anna Russ and Fanny Jones' addresses Baraka's maternal and paternal grandmothers. Anna Russ had lived with the Jones family in Newark when Baraka was a child: she and her husband, Tom, who suffered racialised violence after running against the Republican Party, figure throughout Baraka's work.[100]

> [...] This is the world. We are in it. We can live and survive
> at a higher level. We can advance all life to higher ground. And the quiet
>     grandmothers
> died

and went to 'heaven' could take note of the same feeling cause that's what
   they had to
mean
if the metaphysical cloak their times had draped on their world was
   translated. [...] There is a
better life, but its in the world, in the lives of the people, we just have to
   struggle, we
just have to care and take care and study, we just have to fight some more
   people's wars.
That wd be the hymn underneath, we will meet again on higher ground.
   That all society
will
be raised to higher ground, a more advanced life. And that feeling has
   burned in me
since
the dawn of my life.[101]

Despite denouncing 'metaphysics' – whether Christianity, Buddhism, Islam or Kawaida – the *social* function of religion remained important for Baraka and a spiritual discourse returns in his later work, in a distinct brand of poetic dialectics owing as much to Sun Ra as to Lenin, Monk as to Mao.[102] Critical of Christianity's 'metaphysical cloak', Baraka nonetheless notes its embedded political hopes, 'translat[ing]' 'the same feeling' which 'they had to mean': Marx's 'heart of a heartless world'.[103] As in the earlier 'Careers', which notes how Anna Russ, working as a domestic, 'stole things for jesus' sake', even if she 'probably asked for forgiveness on the bus', Baraka is aware that Russ's Christianity motivated her acts of quiet defiance.[104] Formally, Baraka's poems reflect Christianity's dialectical nature, appropriating its rhetoric for stinging critique in the abrasively hilarious 'When We'll Worship Jesus' and 'Dope'. Echoing Langston Hughes's 'Goodbye Christ', Baraka proclaims:

> We'll worship Jesus
> When jesus do
> Somethin
> When jesus blow up
> the white house
> or blast nixon down[105]

Likewise, 'Dope' literalises Marx's famous 'opium of the masses' metaphor. Opening with a kind of prelude – 'ray light morning fire lynch yet/uuuuuuu, yester-pain in dreams comes again. race-pain, people our people our people everywhere' – the poem turns into a dramatic monologue, complete with stage directions, satirising the pacifying 'common sense' explanations of an evangelical Christian preacher who refuses to face up to the causes of such pain:

It must be the devil
It must be the devil
it must be the devil
(shakes like evangelical sanctify
shakes tambourine like evangelical sanctify in heat)

[...] must be the devil, going to heaven after i die, after we die
everything gonna be different, after we die we aint gon be
hungry, ain gon be pain, ain gon be sufferin wont go thru this
again, after we die, after we die owooo! owowoooo!
after we die, its all gonna be good, have all the money we
need after we die, have all the food we need after we die
have a nice house like the rich folks, after we die, after we die, after we
die, we can live like rev ike, after we die, hallelujah, hallelujah, must be
the devil, it ain capitalism, it aint capitalism, it aint capitalism,
naw it ain that, jimmy carter wdnt lie, 'lifes unfair' but it aint capitalism
must be the devil, owow![106]

Ironised in this poem, incantation and repetition are more often used 'to raise and to popularise'.[107] This is the conclusion to the poem 'Like, This is What I Meant!'

So that even in our verse
the irresistible tide of revolution
is unleashed
yes
unleashed

So that even
   in our verse
this Red Explosion
   is unleashed

Yeh
unleashed
So that even
   in our
   verse
   even in
   our dancing           (repeat as song)
   even in
   our song
   yeh
   in our pure lover song

    REVOLUTION!!![108]

The performance instruction, 'repeat as song', attests to the temporal openness of this call: it could go on for as long as necessary, exacerbating the build-up to the final, capitalised 'REVOLUTION!!!' Eliding the verb emphasises the focus on action: art as verb rather than noun, process rather than product.[109]

Such action is fundamentally collaborative – this work needs an audience to confirm or deny its message. In the introduction to *Hard Facts*, Baraka writes: 'The question of the audience is key, is central to the work. "For Whom" is the problem as Mao Tse-tung sounded it. For whom does one write, the audience standing there as you compose, to whom, for whom, it is directed.'[110] Baraka's performative calls are ready to be actualised by their occasions of composition and performance: books, rallies, marches, addresses to college students, party meetings, political conventions. These poems urgently call to the audience to confirm or deny their claims: 'Get a quick consensus, on that', as he puts it in 'When We'll Worship Jesus'. In 'Against Bourgeois Art', Baraka repeatedly calls for 'someone' to join him in his observations of the white American art world, itself a tool in the American Cultural Cold War:

> [...] Is there somebody here to record this? [...] Is there someone, here, to get this down? Can I get a, like they say, witness. An eye that can see through this here.[111]

In a pose of mock-disbelief, Baraka's appeals for a revolutionary art and politics are appeals to common sense, hammering against the shibboleths of avant-garde art and the norms of late 1970s capitalism. While 'Revolution sweeps the world, Bourgeois artists stare at crumbs of dust in the light'; 'it is the state, bulshitting/on the wall'.

> As wild a motherfucking joint as america is
> somebody should get this shit down, otherwise no one will believe it.
> Get it down
> Get it on the record

The poems seek completion in their audience, and the translation of political aspirations to political action. In his 1964 essay 'Hunting is Not Those Heads on the Wall', Baraka denounced the separation of self-enclosed art objects from the live processes of thought, feeling, performance and creation.[112] A decade later, his Beat-influenced focus on spontaneity was developed and expanded by a mature conception of the relation between art and politics, 'unity gained thru struggle'.[113] Baraka's Marxist poetry is a vital contribution to debates on the political role of art, the building of cross-racial unity, and the relation of local struggles to world revolution. Given the recent scholarship and renewed interest in the New Communist

Movement, and in internationalist Marxisms and feminisms such as those of Walter Rodney, Claudia Jones, Rosa Guy and Sarah E. Wright, it is to be hoped that further work will be done in this field, to which the present volume forms a valuable contribution. Remembering these writers' and activists' participation in global anti-fascism and anti-imperialism reminds us of revolutionary possibilities that are too often passed over. Such work remains a necessary, reactive and passionate response to injustice, 'an eye that can see through this here'.

## Notes

1 Amiri Baraka, *Revolutionary Party, Revolutionary Ideology*, CAP (Congress of Afrikan People) Position Paper, CAP Midwest Regional Meeting, Chicago, 31 March 1974 (Newark, NJ: CAP, 1974). This chapter emerges from a paper at 'The Red and the Black – The Russian Revolution and the Black Atlantic' conference, Institute for the Black Atlantic, University of Central Lancashire, Preston, UK, October 2017. My thanks to David Austin, Asad Haider, Max Elbaum, Komozi Woodard, Michael Simanga and Daniel Widener for their insights.

2 For NCM historiography, see further the following (partial) list of examples: Max Elbaum, *Revolution in the Air: Sixties Radicals Turn to Lenin, Mao and Che* (London: Verso, 2018 [2002]); Asad Haider, 'Unity: Amiri Baraka and the Black Lives Matter Movements', *Lana Turner Journal*, 8 (2015), https://web.archive.org/web/20160308193224/http://lanaturnerjournal.com/contents/unity-amiri-baraka-and-the-black-lives-matter-movements (accessed 9 November 2021); Robin D.G. Kelley and Betsy Esch, 'Black Like Mao: Red China and Black Revolution' in Fred Ho and Bill V. Mullen (eds), *Afro Asia: Revolutionary Political and Cultural Connections between African Americans and Asian Americans* (Durham, NC: Duke University Press, 2008), 97–154; Mae Ngai, 'Democracy, Self-Determination, and Revolution: Baraka's Communist Writings in the 80s' in Haki Madhubuti, Michael Simanga, Sonia Sanchez, and Woodie King Jr with Gwendolyn Mitchell (eds), *Brilliant Flame! Amiri Baraka: Poetry, Plays & Politics for the People* (Chicago, IL: Third World Press, 2018), 428–438; Paul Saba (ed.), *The Encyclopaedia of Anti-Revisionism Online*. Marxists.org, www.marxists.org/history/erol/erol.htm (accessed 3 August 2021); and *Unity Archive Project: The Archive of the League of Revolutionary Struggle 1978–1990*, https://unityarchiveproject.org/ (accessed 3 August 2021).

3 For 'lyric necessity', see Amiri Baraka, *Conversations with Amiri Baraka*, ed. Charlie Reilly (Jackson, MS: University Press of Mississippi, 1994); for 'class struggle in music', Amiri Baraka (with David Murray and Steve McCall), *New Music, New Poetry* (LP, India Navigation, 1981).

4 Baraka, quoted in Werner Sollors, *Amiri Baraka/LeRoi Jones: The Quest for a 'Populist Modernism'* (New York: Columbia University Press, 1978), 250.

5 Amiri Baraka, *The Autobiography of LeRoi Jones/Amiri Baraka* (New York: Freundlich Books, 1984), 14–15 [afterwards cited as Baraka, *Autobiography*]; Claudia Moreno Pisano (ed.), *Amiri Baraka and Edward Dorn: The Collected Letters* (Albuquerque, NM: University of New Mexico Press, 2013), 60.
6 Amiri Baraka, *Selected Poetry* (New York: William Morrow, 1979), 103.
7 Baraka, *Autobiography*, 165, 173.
8 *Ibid.*, 116.
9 For more on these activities, see David Grundy, *A Black Arts Poetry Machine: Amiri Baraka and the Umbra Poets* (London: Bloomsbury, 2019), 35–45, 65–66.
10 Baraka, *Autobiography*, 267.
11 '"Unity and Struggle" – History of the Revolutionary Communist League (M-L-M)', *Forward*, 3 (January 1980), 12–139 and online, www.marxists.org/history/erol/ncm-3/rcl-history/chapter-1.htm (accessed 3 August 2021).
12 Komozi Woodard, *A Nation within a Nation: Amiri Baraka and Black Power Politics* (Chapel Hill, NC: University of North Carolina Press, 1999), 1–3; Michael Simanga, *Amiri Baraka and the Congress of African People: History and Memory* (New York: Palgrave Macmillan, 2015), 123–124.
13 Woodard, *A Nation within a Nation*, 119–120.
14 Baraka, *Autobiography*, 357, 433.
15 Amiri Baraka, *Raise Race Rays Raze: Essays since 1965* (New York: Random House, 1971), 130.
16 Amiri Baraka (ed.), *African Congress: A Documentary of the First Modern Pan-African Congress* (New York: William Morrow, 1972), 93–95, 97, 99.
17 Woodard, *A Nation within a Nation*, 116–122; Baraka, *Autobiography*, 278–280, 289–291, 305.
18 See Fanon Che Wilkins, 'Dispelling The Romance With Armed Struggle: Owusu Sadaukai and FRELIMO Guerillas in "Liberated Mozambique," 1971', unpublished paper presented at the annual meeting of the American Studies Association, Puerto Rico Convention Center and the Caribe Hilton, San Juan, Puerto Rico, 2014; Robin D.G. Kelley, *Freedom Dreams: The Black Radical Imagination* (Boston, MA: Beacon Street Press, 2002), 104; Simanga, *Amiri Baraka and the Congress of African People*, 111–113; Baraka, *Conversations*, 443–444.
19 Woodard, *A Nation within a Nation*, 254; Amiri Baraka, *Hard Facts (Excerpts)* (Newark, NJ: People's War, 1975), 18–19. Published in revised/expanded edition in Baraka, *Selected Poetry*, 235–273.
20 Amiri Baraka, 'Afrikan Revolution', *Black World*, May 1973, 44–48. Reprinted as a pamphlet by Jihad, and in Baraka, *Selected Poetry*, 230–235.
21 Baraka, *Autobiography*, 298.
22 Simanga, *Amiri Baraka and the Congress of African People*, 101–102.
23 For more on the Sixth PAC, see Fanon Che Wilkins, '"A Line of Steel": The Organisation of the Sixth Pan-African Congress and the Struggle for International Black Power, 1969–1974' in Dan Berger (ed.), *The Hidden*

*1970s: Histories of Radicalism* (New Brunswick, NJ: Rutgers University Press, 2010), 97–114.
24 Clairmont Chung (ed.), *Walter A. Rodney: A Promise of Revolution* (New York: Monthly Review Press, 2012), 71–78.
25 Baraka, *Conversations*, 309.
26 Baraka, *Hard Facts*, 34.
27 Baraka, *Conversations*, 309.
28 Baraka, *Autobiography*, 309.
29 Baraka, 'Some Questions About the Sixth Pan-African Congress', *Black Scholar* (October 1974), 42–6, at 45; Anthony James Radcliff, 'Liberation at the End of a Pen: Writing Pan-African Politics of Cultural Struggle', unpublished PhD thesis, University of Massachusetts Amherst, 2009, 244–245; Simanga, *Amiri Baraka and the Congress of African People*, 120.
30 Baraka, *Autobiography*, 312.
31 Kelley, *Freedom Dreams*, 103.
32 Simanga, *Amiri Baraka and the Congress of African People*, 138–139.
33 Amiri Baraka, 'Black Liberation: Socialist Revolution' (1975) in *Daggers and Javelins: Essays 1974–1979* (New York: William Morrow, 1984), 88–101. Published in abbreviated form as 'Why I Changed My Ideology', *Black World*, July 1975, 30–43, 133, and in further revised form in *Selected Plays and Prose* (New York: William Morrow, 1979).
34 Simanga, *Amiri Baraka and the Congress of African People*, 86.
35 Dayo F. Gore, Jeanne Theoharis and Komozi Woodard (eds), *Want to Start a Revolution?: Radical Women in the Black Freedom Struggle* (New York: New York University Press, 2009), 2, 3, 5, 9–10.
36 Ratcliff, 'Liberation at the End of a Pen', 246–248; Woodard, *A Nation within a Nation*, 122–124, 180–184; Baraka, *Autobiography*, xvi–xix, xxv, 421–426; Gore et al., *Want to Start a Revolution?*, 20n.4; Russell Rickford, *We Are an African People: Independent Education, Black Power, and the Radical Imagination* (Oxford: Oxford University Press, 2016), 138–142.
37 Baraka, *Autobiography*, 425. Amina Baraka's own neglected poetry is likewise an important contribution to the Black Marxist tradition. See Amina Baraka, 'Red Poem' (as Sylvia Jones), *Forward*, 3 (January 1980), 151–152; Gabrielle David (ed.), *Blues in All Hues: Poetry of Amina Baraka* (New York: 2Leaf Press, 2014); *Amina Baraka and the Red Microphone* (ESP-Disk, 2017).
38 See Torrie Hester, Mary E. Mendoza, Deirdre Moloney and Mae Ngai, 'Immigration's Border-Enforcement Myth', *New York Times*, January 2018, www.nytimes.com/2018/01/28/opinion/immigrations-border-enforcement-myth.html (accessed 3 August 2021) and Torrie Hester, Mary E. Mendoza, Deirdre Moloney and Mae Ngai, 'Now the Trump Administration is Trying to Punish Legal Immigrants for Being Poor', *Washington Post*, 9 August 2018.
39 Paul Saba, 'Lessons from One Left to the Next: *Revolution in the Air* Reissued', *Viewpoint*, July 2018, www.viewpointmag.com/2018/07/19/lessons-from-one-left-to-the-next-revolution-in-the-air-reissued/ (accessed 3 August 2021); Elbaum, *Revolution in the Air*, 8.

40 Baraka, *Autobiography*, 312; 'Council Weighing Newark Taxi Rise', *New York Times*, 15 June 1974, www.nytimes.com/1974/06/15/archives/council-weighing-newark-taxi-rise-30-rate-increase-possible-under.html (accessed 3 August 2021).
41 Simanga, *Amiri Baraka and the Congress of African People*, 98–99, 142–146; Mae Ngai, 'What do You Mean When You Say "Maoist"?', *Guardian Weekly*, 29 January 1986 (available from Marxists.org: www.marxists.org/history/erol/ncm-7/ngai-maoist.pdf (accessed 3 August 2021)); Saba, 'Lessons from One Left to the Next'.
42 Amiri Baraka, '*Raise!* Sectarianism, Undermining, Secret Agents and Struggle', *Unity and Struggle*, December 1974, 16.
43 Simanga, *Amiri Baraka and the Congress of African People*, 136, 142.
44 Amiri Baraka, 'Towards Ideological Clarity', *Black World* (November 1974), 24–33, at 26–27. Originally delivered as a CAP position paper, ALSC Conference, Howard University, 24 May 1974.
45 Mae Ngai, 'What do You Mean When You Say "Maoist"?'
46 Peter Shapiro, 'The Necessity of Organisation: The League of Revolutionary Struggle and the Watsonville Canning Strike', *Viewpoint*, August 2018, https://viewpointmag.com/2018/08/30/the-necessity-of-organization-the-league-of-revolutionary-struggle-and-the-watsonville-canning-strike/ (accessed 3 August 2021); Elbaum, *Revolution in the Air*, 272.
47 Simanga, *Amiri Baraka and the Congress of African People*, 158; Kelley, *Freedom Dreams*, 106.
48 Baraka, *Autobiography*, 433; Amiri Baraka (with others), *Stop Killer Cops* (Newark, NJ: NJL Congress of Afrikan People, 1976).
49 David Hungerford, 'Reflections on Amiri Baraka', FightBack!News website, 12 January 2014, www.fightbacknews.org/2014/1/12/reflections-amiri-baraka; 'Statement on the Dissolution of the League of Revolutionary Struggle' (1990), https://marxists.architexturez.net/history/erol/ncm-7/lrs-dissolve.pdf (both accessed 3 August 2021).
50 Angel L. Martinez, 'Amiri Baraka and the Meaning of a Revolutionary Cultural Worker' in Haki Madhubuti, Michael Simanga, Sonia Sanchez, Woodie King. Jr with Gwendolyn Mitchell (eds), *Brilliant Flame! Amiri Baraka: Poetry, Plays & Politics for the People* (Chicago, IL: Third World Press, 2018), 325–327, at 325.
51 Harold Cruse, *The Essential Harold Cruse*, ed. William Jelani Cobb (New York: St Martin's Griffin, 2002); Cedric Johnson, *Revolutionaries to Race Leaders: Black Power and the Making of African American Politics* (Minneapolis, MN: University of Minnesota Press, 2007), 184–187, 192; Robert C. Smith, *We Have No Leaders: African Americans in the Post-Civil Rights Era* (Albany, NY: State University of New York Press, 1996), 57–70.
52 Simanga, *Amiri Baraka and the Congress of African People*, 105; Baraka, *Revolutionary Party, Revolutionary Ideology*; Baraka, 'Haki Madhubuti and Jitu Weusi ... Individualism Brings Two CAP Resignations' (serialised in eleven parts), *Unity and Struggle*, June 1974–February 1975; 'State Rep. Hannah Atkins Quits Post', *Jet*, February 1975, 6; 'The National Black Political

Assembly' (statements by Ron Daniels, Hannah Atkins and Amiri Baraka), *Black World*, October 1975, 28–46, 61.
53 Baraka, *Autobiography*, 306; Baraka, *Hard Facts*, 26–27; Baraka, *Revolutionary Party, Revolutionary Ideology*; Haki Madhubuti, 'The Latest Purge: The Attack on Nationalism and Pan-Afrikanism by the New Left, the Sons and Daughters of the Old Left', *Black Scholar*, September 1974, 43–56; 'Enemy: From the White Left, White Right and In Between', *Black World*, October 1974, 36–47; Ronald Waters, S.E. Anderson and Alonzo 4X, 'A *Black Scholar* Debate: Responses to Haki R. Madhubuti (Don L. Lee)', *Black Scholar*, October 1974, 47–53; Kalamu ya Salaam and Mark Smith, 'A *Black Scholar* Debate: Responses To Haki R. Madhubuti (Don L. Lee)', *Black Scholar*, January–February 1975, 40–53; Simanga, *Amiri Baraka and the Congress of African People*, 109–112; Hoyt W. Fuller, 'Another Fork in The Road', *Black World*, October 1974 [written July 1974], 49–50, 97; Manning Marable, *Race, Reform, and Rebellion: The Second Reconstruction in Black America, 1945–2006*, 3rd edn (Jackson, MS: University Press of Mississippi, 2007), 133.
54 Smith, *We Have No Leaders*, 65–71; Simanga, *Amiri Baraka and the Congress of African People*.
55 Baraka, *Revolutionary Party, Revolutionary Ideology*, 106–107.
56 Baraka, 'Towards Ideological Clarity', 26–27.
57 Ngai, 'Democracy, Self-Determination, and Revolution', 428–438.
58 Baraka, 'Haki Madhubuti and Jitu Weusi'.
59 Simanga, *Amiri Baraka and the Congress of African People*, 110.
60 *Ibid.*, 111.
61 Baraka, *Autobiography*, 306.
62 Jamala Rogers, 'Appreciating What's Been Said: Reflections on Amiri Baraka', http://jamalarogers.com/appreciating-whats-been-said-reflections-on-amiri-baraka/ (accessed 3 August 2021).
63 Baraka, 'Plenary Address to Conference on Reparations' [2002], *Socialism and Democracy*, 16:1 (2007), 124–129, at 129.
64 Baraka, *Selected Poetry*, 291.
65 'State Rep. Hannah Atkins Quits Post', *Jet*, February 1975, 6; 'The National Black Political Assembly' (statements by Ron Daniels, Hannah Atkins, and Amiri Baraka), *Black World*, October 1975, 28–46, 61.
66 Sollors, *Amiri Baraka/LeRoi Jones*, 249–250; Baraka, *Conversations*, 157–158, 162–164.
67 Baraka, *Daggers and Javelins*; Baraka, 'In the Tradition', *Greenfield Review*, 8:3–4 (1980): 38–46 (reprinted in revised form as a pamphlet (Newark, NJ: Rising Tide, 1982)); Amiri Baraka with David Murray and Steve McCall, 'Wailers', *Poetry in Motion* (dir. Ron McCall, 1982), printed in *Callaloo*, 8: Larry Neal Tribute Issue (Winter, 1985), 248–256.
68 In Madhubuti et al. (eds), *Brilliant Flame*, 322, 252.
69 '"Unity and Struggle" – History of the Revolutionary Communist League (M-L-M)', *Forward*, 3, January 1980: 12–139 and online www.marxists.org/history/erol/ncm-3/rcl-history/chapter-1.htm (accessed 3 August 2021).

70 Baraka, *Autobiography*, xi, xxv.
71 Baraka, *Autobiography*, 426–427; Sollors, *Amiri Baraka/LeRoi Jones*, 248.
72 Baraka, *Autobiography*, 427.
73 Loren Glass, *Counterculture Colophon: Grove Press, the Evergreen Review, and the Incorporation of the Avant-Garde* (Stanford, CA: Stanford University Press, 2013).
74 Anthony Monteiro, 'Amiri Baraka: Class Struggle and Cultural Revolution', *Black Agenda Report* website, 2014, www.blackagendareport.com/content/amiri-baraka-class-struggle-and-cultural-revolution (accessed 3 August 2021).
75 Baraka, *Hard Facts*, n.p. 'Rocky' is Baraka's nickname for the then vice president Nelson Rockefeller.
76 *Ibid*.
77 Kelley, *Freedom Dreams*, 107.
78 Baraka, *Hard Facts*, 9.
79 Baraka, *Autobiography*, 312.
80 Baraka, *Autobiography*, 293–294; Baraka, *Hard Facts*, 23.
81 Baraka, *Conversations*, 111.
82 Werner Sollors, *Amiri Baraka/LeRoi* Jones, 246.
83 Sollors, *Amiri Baraka/LeRoi Jones*, 249; James A. Miller, '"I Investigate the Sun": Amiri Baraka in the 1980s', *Callaloo*, 26 (Winter 1986), 184–192, at 187.
84 Baraka, *Conversations*, 111.
85 Leo Ou-fan Lee, 'Tradition and Modernity in the Writings of Lu Xun' in Leo Ou-fan Lee (ed.), *Lu Xun and his Legacy* (Berkeley, CA: University of California Press, 1985), 3–31, at 25; David E. Pollard, 'Lu Xun's *Zawen*' in Leo Ou-fan Lee (ed.), *Lu Xun and his Legacy* (Berkeley, CA: University of California Press, 1985), 54–89, at 54–55.
86 Xudong Zhang, '"The Becoming Self-Conscious of Zawen": Literary Modernity and Politics of Language in Lu Xun's Essay Production during his Transitional Period', *Frontiers of Literary Studies in China*, 8:3 (2014), 374–409, at 380–381.
87 Baraka, *Conversations*, 111–112.
88 Gloria Davies, *Lu Xun's Revolution: Writing in a Time of Violence* (Cambridge, MA: Harvard University Press, 2013), 235–236.
89 While Baraka, under Amina's influence, publicly emphasised women's oppression, his Marxist poetry still lapses into misogyny and homophobia, and patriarchal attitudes inflect even endorsements of feminism. Baraka, *Hard Facts*, 4, 10–11, 26–27.
90 Baraka, *Hard Facts*, 24–25.
91 *Ibid*.
92 Baraka, *Conversations*, 95.
93 Chris Stroffolino, 'Amiri Baraka: A Legacy Beyond the Racist Obituaries', http://chrisstroffolino.blogspot.com/2014/06/amiri-baraka-legacy-beyond-racist.html (accessed 3 August 2021).
94 Baraka, Poetry Reading, Buffalo, 1978, http://writing.upenn.edu/pennsound/x/Baraka.php (accessed 3 August 2021); Baraka, Poetry Reading, Jack Kerouac

School of Disembodied Poetics at Naropa University, Boulder, CO, 1978 (footage available in the film *Fried Shoes, Cooked Diamonds* (dir. Costanzo Allione, 1979); full audio recording online, https://archive.org/details/Amiri_Baraka__Diane_diPrima_and_Robert_D_78P108 (accessed 3 August 2021); Baraka, *New Music, New Poetry*.

95 Baraka (with The Advanced Workers and the Anti-Imperialist Singers), 'You Was Dancin' Need To Be Marchin' So You Can Dance Some More Later On/ Better Red Let Others Be Dead' (Newark, NJ: People's War, 1976, 45RPM).

96 A 1977 live recording gives a sense of the group's repertoire and live performance: Baraka (with the Advanced Workers), *Live at the Berliner Jazztage, Philharmonie, Berlin, Germany, November 3, 1977*, www.youtube.com/watch?v=4DqLDnp1AFo (accessed 3 August 2021).

97 This said, Cold War positioning saw NCM organisations support repressive regimes, from Enver Hoxha to Kim Il-Sung. During the Angolan civil war, NCM organisations endorsed the China-supported UNITA over the Soviet-supported MPLA. Yet UNITA received support from apartheid South Africa, and later Reagan's America, and inadvertently fostered the rise of Chinese neo-colonialism in Africa. Ratcliff, 'Liberation at the End of a Pen', 251–253; Simanga, *Amiri Baraka and the Congress of African People*, 121–123; Elbaum, *Revolution in the Air*, 217–219.

98 Amiri Baraka, 'Poet Amiri Baraka on the Freedom Movement and Black Art' (Excerpts from address to the Black Graduate Students Association, University of Florida, January 2007, transcribed by Chris Zurheide), Gainesville Iguana, January 2007, www.afn.org/~iguana/archives/2007_01/20070108.html (accessed 3 August 2021).

99 Baraka, *Daggers and Javelins*, 14–15.

100 Amiri Baraka, 'Nana: 1888–1963', *Red Clay Reader*, 1 (1964), 51; Amiri Baraka, 'Churches', n.d., typescript, box 1, folder 3, Amiri Baraka Collection of Unpublished Poetry, Manuscripts, Archives and Rare Books Division, Schomburg Center for Research in Black Culture, The New York Public Library; Baraka, *Selected Poetry*, 175; Amiri Baraka, *The Fiction of LeRoi Jones/Amiri Baraka* (Chicago, IL: Lawrence Hill, 2000), 1–4; Pisano, *Amiri Baraka and Edward Dorn*, 60.

101 Baraka, *Selected Poetry*, 277.

102 Amiri Baraka, *Digging: The Afro-American Soul of American Classical Music* (Berkeley, CA: University of California Press, 2009), 19–28; Amiri Baraka, *SOS: Poems 1961–2013*, ed. Paul Vangelisti (New York: Grove Press, 2014), 358.

103 Karl Marx, *Early Writings*, trans. Rodney Livingstone and Gregor Benton (London: Penguin, 1992), 244.

104 Baraka, *Selected Poetry*, 182.

105 Baraka, *Hard Facts*, 6.

106 Baraka, *Selected Poetry*, 329.

107 Baraka, *Hard Facts*, n.p.

108 Baraka, *Selected Poetry*, 294.

109 Amiri Baraka, *Home: Social Essays* (New York: Akashic Books, 2009 [1966]), 170.
110 Baraka, *Hard Facts*. Baraka refers here to Mao Zedong (Tse-Tung), *Talks at the Yenan Forum on Literature and Art* (1942), trans. Foreign Languages Press, Peking, 1960, www.marxists.org/reference/archive/mao/selected-works/volume-3/mswv3_08.htm (accessed 3 August 2021).
111 Baraka, *New Music, New Poetry*.
112 Baraka, *Home*, 197–203.
113 *Countries Want Independence, Nations Want Liberation, and the People, the People Want Revolution!* A Poem for the Unity of RCP (M-L-M) and LRS (M-L)' [October 1979], *Forward*, 3 (January 1980), 8–9.

# Afterword

*Hakim Adi*

The important essays in this volume contribute to a growing literature relating to the influence of Marxism on Africans and those in the African diaspora, during the twentieth century. The focus of this volume, the presentation of biographical accounts of key figures, permits the reader to reflect on the profound impact of the revolutionary events in Russia in 1917, especially the 'Great October Socialist Revolution'. Wilfred Domingo made clear the immediate significance of both the revolution and the creation of the new Soviet Union in the following manner:

> Will Bolshevism accomplish the full freedom of Africa, colonies in which Negroes are the majority, and promote human tolerance and happiness in the United States by the eradication of the causes of such disgraceful occurrences as the Washington and Chicago race riots? The answer is deducible from the analogy of Soviet Russia, a country in which dozens of racial and lingual types have settled their many differences and found a common meeting ground, a country that no longer oppresses colonies, a country from which the lynch rope is banished and in which racial tolerance and peace now exist.[1]

As is clear from Brian Kwoba's chapter above, Hubert Harrison was reported to have considered 'Bolshevism the salvation of America', while Cyril Briggs later explained that his initial interest in Communism was sparked by 'the national policy of the Russian Bolsheviks and the anti-imperialist orientation of the Soviet state birthed by the October Revolution'.[2] Over half a century later, and in very different circumstances as other chapters here show, Walter Rodney and Amiri Baraka were still being inspired by the revolutionary events of 1917.

The creation of the Communist International (Comintern) in 1919, was no less momentous and influential, not least for its concern with the 'Negro Question', as the liberation of those in Africa and the diaspora was referred to at that time. The Comintern was important for the criticisms which it made of the lack of attention paid to the 'Negro Question' by the Communist parties in South Africa and the United States, as well as those in

Britain and France during the interwar period. Its policies clearly impacted on the lives of Cyril Briggs, Grace Campbell, Lamine Senghor and Paul Robeson for example, as well as many others in Africa and throughout the diaspora, in the years between the two world wars.

The Communist International was particularly important because of its impact on the policies of the Communist parties in the United States and South Africa. In the former it encouraged the controversial 'Black Belt thesis', the right of African Americans to empower themselves and become the decision-makers in the Southern states of the United States, where they constituted a clear majority. This policy drew inspiration not only from the writings of Lenin but also from traditions to which Cyril Briggs also contributed, as Jak Peake's chapter above outlines. The ramifications of this policy endured for far longer than the existence of the Comintern, as the chapter on Amiri Baraka demonstrates. In South Africa, the Comintern was pivotal in encouraging the 'Black Republic thesis', changing the orientation and leadership of the Communist Party to reflect the fact that those of European heritage were only a minority of the population and that the country was essentially a special kind of colony. The changes in leadership and orientation were, in part, measures to address the criticisms that had been levelled at the Communist Party by Kadalie and others, as well as by some black Communists, that it was mainly an organisation of 'white revolutionaries', only concerned with a narrow view of class struggle and not the liberation of the majority population. It also sought to address the racist views of some Communist Party members, who proclaimed that black workers 'could not possibly appreciate the noble ideals of Communism'.[3] The demand for majority rule also outlived the Comintern period and undoubtedly inspired the political activities of later South African Communists, such as Walter Sisulu and Nelson Mandela. As a result of the intervention of the Comintern, the Communist Party was more able to open its ranks to members such as Josie Mpama, who is reported to have told workers in 1932:

> What the workers of Russia had done was a lesson to every worker irrespective of colour. She said she knew that it was hard for the black workers of South Africa to realise that they could win freedom in the same way as the Russian people had done but I can tell you that it is just as easy for you as it was for the Russian people. You might say they were not oppressed in the same way you are, but they were, and what they have done, if you do [it, it] will make you free people.[4]

The chapters above also highlight the fact that those who engage in revolutionary politics do so in opposition to the status quo and the powers that be. They are normally under surveillance, their phones monitored, and mail intercepted by the security agencies. The state authorities do everything possible to curtail the activities of these activists, including infiltrating political organisations with spies and informers and, sometimes, taking measures to physically eliminate those they consider particularly dangerous to their interests. This is most obviously the case with Walter Rodney, who is widely believed to have lost his life as a consequence of an assassination perpetrated by the government of Guyana, possibly with external foreign assistance. However, many others lost their lives in the struggle in South Africa as well as many other countries. Figures such as Paul Robeson paid for their political commitment in other ways too, since the government of the United States did its utmost to silence him and prevent Robeson from working and travelling abroad. It may have taken other measures in an attempt to silence him.[5]

Sometimes surveillance activities can often seem to be a boon to researchers because the police and security services collect information which is then sometimes placed in archives at the disposal of historians. The archives at Aix-en-Provence in France are a particularly rich source for researchers, as David Murphy explains, but many others, including those in Britain and the United States, draw on similar material gathered by espionage and other forms of surveillance. As Britain goes through its 'Spycop' enquiry it's perhaps a good moment to reflect both on the nature of such material, how much is made public but also how reliable it is. I recall looking at documents in the Aix-en-Provence archives in France, which reported on a meeting during the 1930s in which two of the three people present were police agents and both submitted different reports, neither of which could be relied upon. There is also the problem of disclosure, or lack of disclosure. The National Archives, or rather the state, in Britain is notorious for withholding information, or claiming that it has been destroyed, only for some of it to emerge years later. It is also always useful for historians to reflect on how they portray those who risked life, limb and the loss of liberty for what they considered to be the advancement of humanity.[6]

The biographical accounts presented above offer fascinating insights into the lives of key activists during the twentieth century and highlight the need for much more work to establish the influence of Marxism and Communism on Africans and those in the African diaspora from the nineteenth century onwards. Especially in the twenty-first century it is often forgotten, both by historians and more generally, that such Marxist-orientated approaches to the liberation of Africa and all those of African descent have been among the most significant influences on the lives of many black activists throughout the twentieth century. Those influenced include W.E.B. Du Bois, George Padmore, Elma Francois, Claudia Jones, Jacques Roumain, Audley Moore, Josie Mpama, Aimé Césaire, Frantz Fanon, Kwame Nkrumah, Angela

Davis, Carlos Marighella, Amílcar Cabral, Thomas Sankara and Nelson Mandela, as well as organisations as varied as the Black Panther Party and the Tigray People's Liberation Front, which since the latter part of 2020 came under such a fierce attack by the government of Ethiopia.[7] Even in regard to organisations such as the Black Panther Party, it is intriguing that even though several cinematic presentation of the history have been presented, there is only one book devoted to Fred Hampton and nothing detailing the activism of Raymond 'Masai' Hewitt, recognised as one of the main Marxists within the organisation.[8]

Moreover, too often key figures are somehow separated from the ideologies and even organisations that guided them. The most well-known examples are Nelson Mandela and Claudia Jones, the former perhaps for understandable reasons. Claudia Jones, who had the distinction of being the first Communist to be honoured with a postage stamp in Britain, was then misleadingly presented on it as merely a civil rights activist.

Claudia Jones is also exceptional in other respects. She is one of the few black women activists who has been the subject of extensive biographical research, although there has also been some interest in other women activists including Lucy Parsons, Elma Francois and Hermina Huiswoud and, more recently, Louise Thompson Patterson and Esther Cooper Jackson.[9] Lydia Lindsey's chapter on Grace Campbell demonstrates what new research can contribute, since it provides a much more nuanced appreciation of Campbell's life and activism. It also highlights the importance of other black women in and around the African Blood Brotherhood and the Communist Party, about whom more needs to be written, such as Audley Moore and Williana Burroughs. As Lydia Lindsey comments, it is often more difficult for historians to capture the life histories of women, especially those who did not leave a large body of writings or have the ability to produce autobiographical material. Nevertheless, Lindsey's chapter is a fine example of what can be achieved in regard to Campbell and demonstrates what could also be achieved in relation to other revolutionary black women in the United States. In recent years the work of McDuffie and Harris has greatly extended our knowledge of the role of these women but there is still room for much more research, not least because the role of black women has often been underrepresented in studies concerned with the history of Marxism and Communism in the United States.[10]

However, it is not accidental that much of the above focuses on women in the United States. Scholarly studies of the 'Black and the Red' have tended to focus on those activities and individuals associated with the Communist parties in the United States and South Africa, rather than those in other countries. However, in the case of the latter there appears not to have been very much research on black women activists other than Josie Mpama.[11] If history is not to be left with the impression that the Communist Party in South Africa was largely the preserve of men, or women such as Ruth First and Ray Alexander Simons, much new research needs to be undertaken. Elsewhere in Africa, whether during the period of the Comintern, or after, researching the history of Marxist-oriented movements and organisations is still in its infancy and there is much room for further research. In the struggle for independence many political organisations adopted elements of a Marxist orientation, in such countries as Mozambique, Angola and Guinea-Bissau, for example. However, the histories of these movements, as well as more recent ones, have resulted in few studies focusing on the twin concerns of this volume and there is much opportunity for new research. In Africa, the focus has often been on key male figures – Cabral, Sankara, Mandela – although often without sufficient attention being paid to the Marxist underpinnings of their work, nor the collectives in which they developed their world view. Not surprisingly the role of female Marxists and women activists in general is all too often neglected. It is to be noted that in Henry Dee's chapter he makes an interesting passing reference to Doris Pierce, which will perhaps inspire further biographical research not only about her but also on other women activists during this period of South Africa's history.

In regard to the Caribbean there is the notable recent research of Margaret Stevens, who introduces her work with the assertion that between the two world wars 'black workers in the West Indies were critical to the development of Communism', a pronouncement that clearly suggests the need for much more research, not least on the political activities of Jacques Roumain, the founder of the Communist Party of Haiti, as well as other key figures.[12] We are now starting to see some biographical accounts of the early activists of the Communist Party in Cuba, such as Sandalio Junco; however, since before 1959 this party was known as having a mainly Afro-Cuban membership, there is ample opportunity for further research on key figures such as Jesús Menéndez Larrondo and Lázaro Peña, as well as their female comrades such as Esperanza Sánchez Mastrapa, Rosario Guillaume Pérez and Inocencia Valdés Fraga.[13]

Indeed, in the Caribbean, especially in countries such as Cuba, Haiti, Guadeloupe, Martinique, Suriname and the Dominican Republic, as well as Puerto Rico, where there are, or have been, Communist parties and strong Marxist traditions, there appear to be great opportunities for further research. This is especially the case because figures such as Jacques Roumain, the founder of the Communist Party of Haiti, and André Aliker, a revolutionary editor assassinated in Martinique in 1934, as well as many others, remain little known in the anglophone world. Research on women is also sparse and it is vital to build on Rhoda Reddock's important work on Elma Francois.[14] More recently key figures in the Grenadian Revolution and New Jewel Movement, especially Maurice Bishop, have also received some attention, while Bernard and Phyllis Coard have written their own autobiographical account of their activities and the subsequent invasion of the island by the United States government.[15] In regard to the modern Communist Party in Cuba there is also room for much research, as the lives of Víctor Dreke Cruz and others have only become widely known relatively recently, largely as a result of his own memoirs but also through the efforts of historians.[16]

In other geographical areas, such as South America and Europe, there is still much scope for further research. David Murphy's article highlights the fact that there has now been some considerable work on radical black organisations connected to the Communist Party in France, such as the Comité de Défense de la Race Nègre, and its successors the Ligue de Défense de la Race Nègre and the Union de Travailleurs Nègre. However, we still know very little about the key individuals involved, other than Tiemoko Garan Kouyaté, and little about key women activists of the period, other than those associated with the Negritude movement. Here too, there is much room for further research on key figures from both the nineteenth and twentieth centuries. In other European countries, such as Germany and Holland, research is still in its early stages. The most well-known figures connected with the Communist movement in Germany are probably Joseph Bilé and Hilarius Gilges, and in Holland Otto Huiswoud, one of the founders of the Communist Party of America.[17] However, there is also a strong tradition of revolutionary politics among the Surinamese community in Holland that remains underresearched, especially connections with the short-lived Communist Party of Suriname and the assassinated revolutionary journalist Abraham 'Bram' Behr in the 1970s and 1980s.

The same might be said of research in relation to Britain. There has been some work on those organisations and individuals associated with the Communist Party from the 1930s onwards, such as Chris Jones, Desmond Buckle and Harry O'Connell, but this is really the tip of the iceberg.[18] There has been a great focus on the life and work of C.L.R. James, but it would be helpful to have much more information on activists from the interwar period such as Charlie Hutchinson, who fought in Spain, Rowland Sawyer, a sometime playwright, as well as those active in the post-war period.[19] Key women activists connected with the Communist movement, including Dorothy Kuya, Jessica Huntley and Pansy Jeffrey in the post-war period, are largely unresearched, although the same might be said of male activists from the same era, such as Billy Strachan and those connected with the London branch of the Caribbean Labour Congress, as well as their West African counterparts.

In South America, most notably Brazil, there is both a large population of Afro-descendants and a long tradition of Communist and Marxist organisations, but very little research has been published. Carlos Marighella, 'the father of urban guerrilla warfare' is, in the anglophone world, perhaps the most well-known of those to emerge from these movements, largely because of his *Minimanual of the Urban Guerilla*, but there are many other key figures.[20] However, there is a rich history of Afro-Brazilian activists including Communists like Claudino José da Silva who, like their counterparts in other countries during the 1930s, built organisations to oppose the fascist invasion of Ethiopia.

The chapters on Clements Kadalie, C.L.R James, Walter Rodney and Amiri Baraka highlight the necessity to conduct research on a broad range of activists, not only those connected with Communist parties. What might be broadly defined as the Black Power movement of the 1960s and 1970s saw the emergence of many organisations like the Black Panthers in North America, Britain and the Caribbean, as well as those originating from the Black Consciousness movement in Africa, that adopted elements of a Marxist political orientation. However, as yet there is little biographical material on the key figures involved and so there are great opportunities for future research.

## Notes

1 Hakim Adi, *Pan-Africanism and Communism: The Communist International, Africa and the Diaspora, 1919–1939* (Trenton, NJ: Africa World Press, 2013), 13.
2 Brian Kwoba's and Jak Peake's chapters in this volume; Adi, *Pan-Africanism and Communism*, 15.
3 Henry Dee's chapter in this volume (chapter 5).
4 Robert R. Edgar, *Josie Mpama/Palmer: Get Up and Get Moving* (Athens, OH: Ohio University Press, 2020), 82.
5 Martin Duberman, *Paul Robeson* (London: Pan Books, 1989), 498–499; Jeffrey St Clair and Alexander Cockburn, 'Did the CIA Poison Paul Robeson?', *Counterpunch*, 1 April 1999, www.counterpunch.org/1999/04/01/did-the-cia-poison-paul-robeson/ (accessed 12 February 2021).
6 David M. Anderson, 'Guilty Secrets: Deceit, Denial and the Discovery of Kenya's "Migrated Archive"', *History Workshop Journal*, 80:1 (2015), 142–160.
7 Joshua Bloom and Waldo E. Martin, Jr (eds), *Black Against Empire: The History and Politics of the Black Panther Party* (Oakland, CA: University of California Press, 2016), 310–312; John Young, *Peasant Revolution in Ethiopia: The Tigray People's Liberation Front, 1975–1991* (Cambridge: Cambridge University Press, 1997).

8 Jeffrey Haas, *The Assassination of Fred Hampton: How the FBI and the Chicago Police Murdered a Black Panther* (Chicago, IL: Lawrence Hill, 2010).
9 See e.g. Marika Sherwood, *Claudia Jones: A Life in Exile* (London: Lawrence and Wishart, 2000); Carole Boyce Davies, *Left of Karl Marx: The Political Life of Black Communist Claudia Jones* (Durham, NC: Duke University Press, 2008); Carolyn Ashbaugh, *Lucy Parsons: American Revolutionary* (Chicago, IL: Charles H. Kerr, 1976); Joyce Moore Turner, *Caribbean Crusaders and the Harlem Renaissance* (Chicago, IL: University of Illinois Press, 2005); Keith Gilyard, *Louise Thompson Patterson: A Life of Struggle for Justice* (Durham, NC: Duke University Press, 2017).
10 LaShawn Harris, 'Running with the Reds: African American Women and the Communist Party During the Great Depression', *Journal of African American History*, 94:1 (2009), 21–43; Erik S. McDuffie, *Sojourning for Freedom: Black Women, American Communism and the Making of Black Left Communism* (London: Duke University Press, 2011); also Minkah Makalani, 'An Apparatus for Negro Women: Williana Burroughs, Black Communism and the Institutional Space of Diasporic Black Radical Feminism', *Women, Gender and Families of Color*, 4:2 (2016), 250–273.
11 Edgar, *Josie Mpama/Palmer*.
12 Margaret Stevens, *Red International and Black Caribbean: Communists in New York City, Mexico and the West Indies, 1919–1939* (London: Pluto Press, 2017).
13 Anne Garland Mahler, 'The Red and the Black in Latin America: Sandalio Junco and the "Negro Question" from an Afro-Latin Perspective', *American Communist History*, 17:1 (2018), 16–32.
14 Rhoda Reddock, *Elma Francois – The NWCSA and the Workers' Struggle for Change in the Caribbean in the 1930s* (London: New Beacon, 1988).
15 Godfrey Smith, *The Assassination of Maurice Bishop* (Kingston: Ian Randle, 2020).
16 Lisa Brock, 'El Comandante Victor Dreke: The Making of a Cuban Revolutionary', *Souls – A Critical Journal of Black Culture, Politics and Society*, 21:4 (2019), 261–287.
17 Robbie Aitken, 'To Cameroon to Germany and Back via Moscow and Paris: The Political Career of Joseph Bilé (1892–1959), Performer, "Negerarbeiter" and Comintern Activist', *Journal of Contemporary History*, 43:4 (October 2008), 597–616; Maria Gertrudis van Enckevort, 'The Life and Work of Otto Huiswoud: Professional Revolutionary and Internationalist (1893–1961)', PhD thesis, University of the West Indies (Mona), 2000; 'Hilarius Gilges – Black German Communist who Fought Nazis', *Socialist Worker*, 20 October 2020, https://socialistworker.co.uk/art/50805/Hilarius+Gilges+black+German+comm unist+who+fought+Nazis (accessed 10 February 2020).
18 Hakim Adi, 'Forgotten Comrade? Desmond Buckle: An African Communist in Britain', *Science and Society*, 70:1 (January 2006), 22–45: David Featherstone, 'Harry O'Connell, Maritime Labour and the Racialised Politics of Place', *Race & Class*, 57:3 (2016), 71–87; Christian Høgsbjerg, 'Mariner, Renegade and

Castaway: Chris Braithwaite, Seamen's Organiser and Pan-Africanist', *Race & Class*, 53:2 (2011), 36–57.
19 Richard Baxell, 'Charlie Hutchison: The Only Black Briton in the International Brigades', 19 October 2018, https://richardbaxell.info/hutchinson/ (accessed 10 February 2020).
20 John W. Williams, 'Carlos Marighella: The Father of Urban Guerrilla Warfare', *Terrorism*, 12:1 (1989), 1–20.

# Index

Africa 1, 5, 9, 20, 40–41, 45, 72, 75–79, 82–84, 119, 124, 145–151, 154–155, 164, 172, 175, 177–179, 184–186, 188, 196, 217, 220, 224, 228–230, 237–239, 241–243, 246, 255–256, 262, 267–269, 279, 286, 291, 304–306, 308, 310
African Blood Brotherhood (ABB) 5, 12, 45–46, 62, 64, 72–73, 75, 77–79, 81, 83–87, 94, 97, 107, 116–124, 127, 280, 307
African National Congress (ANC) 145–146, 152, 160–164
Aldridge, Ira 5, 193–202, 204–205, 207–209
American Negro Labor Congress (ANLC) 87, 116, 123–124, 127, 156, 219
anti-Semitism 202, 205–207, 213, 219
Arab Spring 235
archives 15, 173–174, 177, 218, 231, 306
art and activism 172, 195, 290
Austria-Hungary 195, 207

Baraka, Amiri 6, 275–293, 295, 304–305, 310
Belgium 158, 194
Berenberg, David P. 60–61
*Black and White* (film) 64, 202
Black Belt thesis 14, 94, 111, 124–125, 305
Black Lives Matter 20, 235, 237, 250

black masses as vanguard 122, 226, 231
Black Panther Party 278, 282, 307, 310
Black Power 86, 239, 243, 246, 265, 278, 282, 285–286, 310
Bolshevism 42, 62, 76, 81, 94, 152, 304
Boulin, Herbert S. 84–85
Bowen, Robert 77, 79, 81
Braithwaite, Chris 8, 309
Brazil 19, 310
Briggs, Cyril V. 5, 12, 17, 40, 45–46, 48, 56, 64, 72–79, 81–88, 109, 117–119, 121, 280, 283, 304–305
British Empire 7
British Guiana *see* Guyana
Burroughs, Nannie 97, 107, 117
Burroughs, Williana 'Liana' 17, 126, 307

Campbell, Grace P. 5–6, 12–14, 17, 45, 78, 94–127, 305, 307
Caribbean 5, 7–9, 12, 32–33, 49, 55, 72–75, 77–78, 84, 188, 235–236, 238, 240–243, 248, 255–257, 259–260, 262, 265–269, 286, 308–310
Carter, Martin 257, 269
Central America *see* Latin America
Central Asia 11
Césaire, Aimé 17–18, 188, 267, 285, 306
*Chicago Defender* 40, 150
Cold War 4, 15, 282, 295

Committee for the Defence of the Negro Race 181–186, 191
Communist International (Comintern) 19, 76, 146, 159–161, 176, 180, 184, 245, 280, 304–305, 308
Communist Party of Great Britain (CPGB) 8, 19, 162
Communist Party of South Africa (CPSA) 145–146, 152–164
Communist Party of the United States of America (CPUSA) 5, 17–18, 87, 120–121, 125, 280–281, 285
*Crisis* 48, 77, 79, 119, 186
*Crusader* 40, 62, 72–73, 75–87, 107–108, 113, 117–120
Cruse, Harold 64, 239
Cuba 18–19, 55, 82, 265–266, 268, 308–309

*Daily Worker* (USA) 95–96, 123, 204
Diagne, Blaise 175–178, 186
District of Columbia 96–99
Domingo, Wilfred A. 5, 12, 15, 17, 40–41, 44–45, 55–56, 58–66, 73, 78, 81, 83–84, 87, 304
Du Bois, W.E.B. 11, 17, 63, 74, 94, 117, 119, 121, 186, 238, 260, 283, 306
Dunayevskaya, Raya 5–6, 13, 217–231
Dyson, Zita E. 97, 99, 130

Egypt 46
Eisenstein, Sergei 202–203
elegies 16–17, 255–256, 258–259
*Emancipator* 40, 44, 64, 81, 83
Ethiopia 12, 83, 123, 196, 238, 307, 310

Fanon, Frantz 17, 256, 265, 267, 277, 288, 306
fascism 19–20, 265, 292, 310
Federal Bureau of Investigation (FBI) 64, 122, 278
First World War 1, 19, 31, 40–41, 47, 73–74, 85, 104–105, 109, 172–173, 175–177, 180, 185
Ford, James W. 18, 87, 121

François, Elma 17, 306–309
French Empire 22, 173

Garvey, Amy Ashwood 43, 73
Garvey, Amy Jacques 73
Garvey, Marcus 1–2, 10, 32, 39–48, 55–56, 61–62, 64, 66, 72–74, 78, 80, 83–87, 122, 124–125, 147, 157, 160, 164, 183, 238, 242–243
Garveyism 4, 43–44, 46, 49, 147, 151, 155, 219, 238
gender 6, 13–15, 39, 94–96, 98–99, 101–103, 105–107, 110–112, 115–116, 122–126, 243, 256
gendered politics 6, 14, 96
Germany 19, 41, 57, 153, 200, 207, 260, 309
Ghana 13, 20, 229–230, 262, 281
Gilmore, Reuben 19
Guyana 8, 20, 245, 248, 256, 259–265, 267–269, 306

Haiti 4, 8–9, 19, 164, 202, 239, 241, 243, 267, 308
Harlem (New York) 20, 32–33, 36, 39–40, 43–49, 55, 64, 66, 78, 94, 104–107, 109–110, 113–118, 120–127, 203, 277, 281
Harlem Renaissance 49, 126
Harrison, Hubert Henry 5, 12, 17, 31–49, 55–56, 58, 62–63, 66, 73–74, 76, 78, 84, 105, 117, 304
Haywood, Harry 5, 17, 78, 280–281, 283–284
Hegel, Georg Wilhelm Friedrich 217–218, 221–224, 235, 238, 244, 260, 266
Horne, Gerald 4, 9, 17, 204, 208
Hughes, Langston 9–11, 17, 202, 283, 285, 288, 293
Huiswoud, Hermina 73, 110, 127, 307
Huiswoud, Otto 9, 45, 73, 78, 105, 109–110, 117, 121, 309
Hungary 195, 229, 235

Imperial Russia 193, 196, 199–200, 204
India 7, 40, 46, 60, 82, 149, 185, 242, 244
Industrial and Commercial (Amalgamated) Workers' Union (ICWU) 151–152
Industrial and Commercial Workers' Union of Africa (ICU) 14, 145–164
Industrial Workers of the World (IWW) 37–38, 59, 155
International Federation of Trade Unions (IFTU) 158
International of Seamen and Harbour Workers 8–9
intersectionality 95, 110, 112–113, 125–126
Ireland 40, 82

Jamaica 1, 5–6, 9, 12, 19, 43–44, 55, 64, 66, 84, 96, 107, 172, 202, 257, 260–263, 265, 268
James, C.L.R. 6, 8, 13, 16–18, 64, 94, 146, 164, 218, 220–221, 223, 235, 237–238, 247–248, 256–257, 261, 283, 309
James, Winston 12, 60, 65, 90
Jim Crow 5, 12, 34, 40, 100, 109, 118, 204
Johannesburg 148–151, 154, 156–157, 160–162
Johnson-Forest Tendency (JFT) 220–222
Johnson, Linton Kwesi 6, 16, 255–259, 261, 266–267, 269–270, 285
Jones, Claudia 13, 17, 64, 124–125, 267, 283, 296, 306–307
Jones, James Wormley 85–86

Kadalie, Clements 6, 13–14, 145–159, 161–164, 305, 310
Kenya 269
Khaile, Eddie 145, 154–155, 160
Kingston 55–56, 66
Kouyaté, Tiemoko Garan 9, 184, 186, 188, 309

La Guma, James 145, 147, 152, 154–162, 164
Latin America 20, 43, 124, 217, 286
League Against Imperialism (LAI) 158, 179, 184–188, 191
Lenin, Vladimir 11, 27, 41–42, 60–62, 66, 76, 78, 155, 219, 221, 235–236, 238, 241, 246–248, 250, 263, 266, 278, 280, 286–287, 293, 305
*Liberator* 45, 86–87, 126
Liberty League 39–44, 46, 56, 66, 78
life writing 7–8, 10–11, 14, 17–18, 26
Locke, Alain 49, 67
London 10, 13, 19, 34, 43, 63, 86, 196, 200, 208, 210, 257, 262, 291
Lusk Committee 15, 55, 57–58, 60–61, 63, 81
Luxemburg, Rosa 223, 241

Maclean, John 19, 27
Malcolm X 84, 256–257, 279–281, 285
Mandela, Nelson 305, 307–308
Maoism 275, 281, 287, 291
maritime spaces 4, 6
Marx, Karl 36, 112–113, 208, 218, 221, 223–228, 230–231, 238, 240–244, 247, 233–264 *passim*, 278, 293
McKay, Claude 9–11, 17, 19, 45, 55, 62, 73, 78–79, 84, 87, 111, 117, 121–123, 127, 172, 202, 267
*Messenger* 40, 44, 48, 56, 58, 61–62, 64, 79, 81, 108
Mexico 75, 220, 240
Minh, Ho Chi 176, 179, 189, 280
Moore, Audley 10, 124, 140–141, 306–307
Moore, Richard B. 12, 45, 56, 64–65, 78, 87, 105, 109, 118, 121
Morocco 46, 179–181
Moscow 62, 76, 118, 158, 162, 178, 184, 199–200, 202, 204–207, 209, 263, 267, 280
Moten, Lucy E. 99

Mulzac, Hugh 1–5, 8–9, 18, 20
Mulzac, Una 20
Münzenberg, Willi 184, 186–188

National Association for the Advancement of Colored People (NAACP) 2, 40, 81, 110, 116, 126
National Maritime Union (NMU) 2, 4, 8–10
*Negro Champion* 87, 95, 123, 156, 219
*Negro World* 40, 44–46, 56, 61–62, 77, 85, 157
*Negro Worker* 56
*News & Letters* 223, 229
New York 2, 4, 13, 15, 20, 32–33, 35–36, 38, 43–44, 55–57, 63–64, 72–74, 77–78, 81, 94, 96, 99, 101–102, 105–106, 119, 125, 127, 208, 219, 276–277, 279, 281, 283
*New York Age* 104
*New York Call* 35, 38
*New York Herald* 118
*New York Sun* 34
*New York Times* 58, 60, 83–84, 119,
*New York World-Telegram* 202
Nigeria 229, 246
Nkrumah, Kwame 9, 230, 262, 279, 306

Occupy Movement 235, 250
O'Connell, Harry 8, 309
*Opportunity* 48, 64
*Othello* 194, 199–201, 207–208
Owen, Chandler 40, 42, 44, 55–56, 58, 64, 75, 78, 81, 104–105

pacifism 180
Padmore, George 9–10, 17, 19, 123, 146, 164, 188, 236–237, 245–248, 267, 306
Palmer's report 79–81
Pan-Africanism 172, 188, 235–238, 243, 245, 248–250, 257, 259, 262, 279, 284
Paris 63, 99, 172, 175, 180–181, 184, 186

Patterson, Louise Thompson 17, 125, 307
Patterson, William L. 17, 203
Petrograd 62, 155
poetry 6, 19–20, 45, 147–148, 197–198, 200, 255–261, 264, 266, 268, 275–276, 283, 285–295
Pushkin, Alexander 196–198, 205–206

racial uplift 95–98, 101–102, 104, 109–110, 117–118, 125–126
racism 1, 2, 4, 5, 9, 12, 35, 37, 98, 100, 102, 110, 123, 148, 153, 183, 188, 193, 196–198, 200, 202–204, 209, 225, 231, 243, 246–247, 250, 275–276, 279, 285, 305
Randolph, A. Philip 32, 40, 42, 44, 55–56, 58, 64, 75, 78, 81, 104–105, 109, 149–150
Rand School of Social Sciences 15, 55–57, 60–61, 63, 81
Rastafarianism 257
Reagan, Ronald 283, 291–292, 302
Red Summer (1919 race riots) 12, 56, 72, 77
Robeson, Eslanda 13, 106, 193, 202–204, 208–209,
Robeson, Paul 5–6, 11, 13, 15, 17, 19, 27, 106, 193–194, 198, 201–209, 283, 305–306
Rodney, Walter 6, 14, 16–17, 236–237, 245–248, 255–270, 273, 279, 285, 295–296, 304, 306, 310
Roumain, Jacques 285, 306, 308
Russian Empire 196, 199, 201, 205, 207, 219
Russian Revolution 4–6, 8–9, 11–13, 20, 41–42, 55–56, 118, 121, 157, 164, 202, 219, 236, 240, 247, 257, 263, 265–266, 287
Russian Social Democratic Workers' Party *see* Bolshevism

Scottsboro Boys 124, 280
Second World War 2–4, 205, 217, 220

Senghor, Lamine 6, 9, 13, 17, 172–189, 305
slavery 9, 35, 97, 100, 115, 151, 155, 178–179, 183, 185, 187, 193, 195, 199–200, 224–227, 238, 240–242
Smith, Ferdinand 9, 17
Socialist Party of America (SPA) 31–32, 34–39, 42, 44–46, 56, 58–61, 63–64, 78, 81, 85, 96, 105, 107–109, 117–118, 126–127, 162
South Africa 6, 13–14, 46, 145–151, 153–157, 159–161, 235, 250, 278, 304–308
Southern Africa 145–147, 150–151, 164, 268, 279
Soviet Union 5, 6, 11, 19, 64, 193, 202–205, 207–209, 217, 220–221, 235, 246, 248, 257, 291, 304
Spanish Civil War 19–20, 220
SS *Booker T. Washington* 2–4
Stalin, Joseph 163, 205, 217–218, 220–221, 237, 246, 257, 278, 282, 287
state surveillance 15, 42, 85, 121, 173, 182, 195, 305–306
subaltern histories 8, 15, 174

Tanzania 262, 266, 277, 279–280, 284
Terrell, Mary C. 101, 117, 142
theatre history 194–196, 198–201, 205, 207, 209, 277
Trinidad and Tobago 17, 19, 249
Trotsky, Leon 62, 218, 220–221, 236, 240–241, 266–267
Tulsa riots 83–84, 87, 118
Tyamzashe, Henry Daniel 150, 157–158, 161–162

*Union Intercoloniale* (UIC) 176–182
Universal Negro Improvement Association (UNIA) 1, 43–47, 56, 72, 78, 85–87, 124–125, 147, 156, 164
   see also *Negro World*

Warsaw Ghetto song 205–207
Washington, Booker T. 34, 43, 79
white labourism 146–149, 153–154, 164

EU authorised representative for GPSR:
Easy Access System Europe, Mustamäe tee 50,
10621 Tallinn, Estonia
gpsr.requests@easproject.com

www.ingramcontent.com/pod-product-compliance
Lightning Source LLC
Chambersburg PA
CBHW050202240426
43671CB00013B/2219